The Slaves' War

Date: 9/1/11

973.711 WAR
Ward, Andrew,
The slaves' war :

The Slaves' War

The Civil War in the Words of Former Slaves

Andrew Ward

Houghton Mifflin Company
Boston • New York
2008

For information about permission to reproduce selections
from this book, write to Permissions, Houghton Mifflin Company,
215 Park Avenue South, New York, New York 10003.

www.houghtonmifflinbooks.com

Library of Congress Cataloging-in-Publication Data
Ward, Andrew, date.
The slaves' war : the Civil War in the words of former slaves /
Andrew Ward.
p. cm.
Includes index.
ISBN 978-0-618-63400-2
1. United States — History — Civil War, 1861–1865 — Personal nar-
ratives. 2. United States — History — Civil War, 1861–1865 — Ameri-
cans. 3. Slaves — Southern States — Biography. 4. Freedmen — United
States — Biography. 5. African Americans — Biography. 6. United
States — History — Civil War, 1861–1865 — Social aspects. I. Title.
E464.W29 2008
973.7'11—dc22   2008001532

Book design by Melissa Lotfy

Printed in the United States of America

MP 10 9 8 7 6 5 4 3 2 1

For my four children

We may look upon [the Civil War] as God's controversy with the nation, his arising to plead by fire and blood the cause of his poor and needy people.

—FRANCES ELLEN WATKINS HARPER

The old flag never did wave quite right. There was something wrong about it. There wasn't any star in it for the black man. Perhaps there was in those you made in the North; but, when they got down here, the sun was so hot, we couldn't see it. But, since the war, it's all right; the black man has his star.

—"TOM"

For twenty-five years after slave times, there ain't no race of people ever traveled as fast as the Negro did.

—MINNIE HOLLOMON OF ARKANSAS

I sure believes in always telling the truth and nothing but the truth. We better tell the truth here, for some of these days we all gwine where nothing but the truth will be accepted.

—CAROLINE SMITH OF ARKANSAS

CONTENTS

PREFACE

—◆—

ANYONE BROWSING THROUGH the history section of a secondhand bookstore or a university library might reasonably conclude that the American Civil War need never be recounted. Their shelves groan with not only the great comprehensive histories but a multitude of books detailing a particular theater, army, commander, regiment, battle, skirmish, even a single day of combat. And that does not include the thousands of collections of soldiers' diaries and letters; the memoirs and biographies of generals and statesmen; the encyclopedias, gazetteers, chronologies, pictorial histories, and atlases; nor the thousands of web pages devoted to some aspect of the Second American Revolution. Perhaps this is why, despite all the slave testimony I kept encountering while researching other books, it took me almost a decade to realize that there was a story of the war that remained to be told: in the voices of the very people it so imperfectly freed.

So imagine we are entering an aftertime in which the life spans of some three thousand African Americans have been brought into temporary alignment. We are met in a vast tent or meetinghouse with a range of grandparents, parents, children, and grandchildren who have gathered here magically as elderly contemporaries. Some were born free, but the majority were born slaves, and they have come to tell us about the Civil War.

Most of them are poor, many can't read or write, but they have all upheld the oral traditions of the slave society into which they were born.

The youngest can remember the war only from their childhoods, or pass on the stories their forebears told. But the oldest can remember when, as adults, they bore the full burden of servitude and the brunt of war. They talk vividly of the conflict's great battles and vaunted personages, but also of skirmishes, ambushes, and raids; of horrors, shame, and pride; of sorrows, losses, betrayals, and hope.

Folding their arms and jutting their chins, some refuse, at first, to speak. Some launch into stories they have embellished beyond recognition. But others recount memories that were seared into their consciousness during a period in American history that was so perverse, so cruel and outlandish, that no sooner had the war brought it to its formal end, than it became almost unimaginable. Constrained by the selective amnesia of their former masters and their white descendants, and weary of their own progenies' scorn for a slave-born culture of obedience and lying low, some had long ago concluded that to survive the fires of Jim Crow they must not stir the embers of slavery.

But now they find in their posterity a ghostly refuge where it is safe to speak of such things. At first they talk in turns, but none of them is short of opinions. Soon their monologues become a chorus, and the chorus a cacophony, as each tries to get a word in edgewise. Some orate, some speak shyly, others read aloud from their memoirs and biographies. Some can remember the war only in flashes, like a nightscape lit by lightning.

From these voices, sifted from literally thousands of interviews, obituaries, squibs, diaries, letters, memoirs, and depositions, I have tried to assemble a slaves' history of the Civil War. The result, I hope, is an account of the war as it was remembered and construed and imagined by slave civilians: a retrospective view from the fields, the kitchens, the slave quarters, the roadsides, the swamps, the camps, the battlefields — a back-door, ground-level slant on the savagery that changed their posterity, and their country, forever.

How I have gone about assembling and employing the material that comprises this history I shall save for the Author's Note at the end of this book. But I should explain some of my choices at the outset. Though it is remarkable how many battles and personages are covered by slave testimony, some readers may look in vain for accounts of battles of particular interest to them. Though in a few cases this is a consequence of my failure to locate such accounts, in most cases it was because what testimony

I could find was too generic or too similar to accounts of more decisive engagements.

I have worked these accounts into a chronological narrative, swinging back and forth between the Eastern and Western Theaters of the war, and interspersed them with thematic chapters on certain aspects of the slaves' general experience: first encounters with Yankees, slaves guarding their masters' property, "refugeeing," Emancipation, Contrabands, and so on. Since I intend this to be a civilian history, I have for the most part excluded the testimony of the blacks who served as soldiers in the Union Army except as it pertained to their experience as slaves and freedmen. Over the past thirty years there have been a number of fine books on the vital contribution black soldiers made to the Union cause, and I decided not to run the risk of allowing their story to crowd out the people for whom they fought. I have included some of their civilian recollections, but subordinated them to the reminiscences of the men and women who served both armies as bodyguards, valets, grooms, teamsters, scouts, spies, foragers, and woodcutters; laundresses, nurses, and cooks.

The result is an aggregate chronicle of the American Civil War as it has never before been recounted. It is a history infused with irony, humor, horror, and bitterness. The former slaves who speak in these pages demonstrate a keen ear for white hypocrisy and provide shrewd assessments of the disposition of power. Their appraisals of the great men who led America into war are canny and often deflating. But many of them also express an astonishing empathy for the plight of former masters ruined by defeat. Slaves knew what white people were capable of inflicting on black people, but in their recollections they grieve with a kind of pitying sorrow over the scandalous, escalating brutality whites seemed so determined to inflict on one another: a wondering perplexity at the seeming inability of whites to settle their differences peacefully.

Though you will find in these pages the occasional Victorian flourish, most of the witnesses gathered here speak in a luminous vernacular. I don't mean the Uncle Remus dialect by which their speech was usually misrepresented, but a vital, stripped-down, cut-to-the-chase rhetoric rooted in Africa, camp meetings, folk songs, and the Bible: a language as bald and vivid as the tragedies and triumphs they recount. For theirs was a war not of glory or grand strategies, but of terror, suffering, and hope. For many slaves, the conflagration that consumed their world seemed at first as random and unaccountable as a tornado or a flood. But in the end they came to see the catastrophe of war as not only the cost of their own freedom, but the price the nation was fated to pay for subjecting an entire race to more than two and a half centuries of slavery.

Part I

The Union

1850 to 1860

"We Done Now"

Fort Sumter • Gladness and Lamentation

W ELL BEFORE SUNRISE on Friday, April 12, 1861, George Gregory joined a group of his fellow slaves on the Charleston waterfront and gazed across the harbor at Fort Sumter's dismal, hulking silhouette. Sumter's commander, Major Robert Anderson, had been holding out since the previous December, refusing demand after demand that he turn the fort over to Secessionist South Carolina. Now his time was up. "Abe Lincoln had sent the word that he going to send provisions to the fort," recalled a local slave named Josh Miles, and "the whole town of Charleston" went down to see "the first shot fired."

White Charlestonians darted around crying, "Everybody get back! The fort will fire on the town and kill every person," Gregory remembered. "But nobody care, cause they figure if one going to be killed, they all going to be, and it don't make a difference no-how. And just as the light commence making the sky red, and it's light enough to see who that is standing by you — BOOM! — the first gun went off!" from the Secessionist batteries. "The light from it shone in the sky, and made it redder! The war done commence," and all around Gregory "the folks shout, and some cry, and some sing."

That morning William H. Robinson was driving his master and a companion to Wilmington, North Carolina, when they heard the booming of cannons "echoing down the Cape Fear river" and across "the broad bosom of the Atlantic." Slapping his hands together with a curse, his master looked "deathly pale" as he turned to his friend and said simply, "It's come."

He hastily jotted a note and handed it to Robinson to take back to his mistress. But as was his habit with all his master's mail, Robinson stopped first at the cabin of a literate slave named Tom to hear it read aloud. "We have fired on Fort Sumter," it said. "I may possibly be called away to help whip the Yankees; may be gone three days, but not longer than that." Robinson's master went on to instruct his wife to tell their overseer "to keep a very close watch on the Negroes, and see that there's no private talk among them," and to give two local whites suspected of abolitionist tendencies "no opportunity to talk with the Negroes."

Soon after the firing on Fort Sumter, Louis Hughes was waiting with his team outside a store in Pontotoc, Mississippi, when his owner emerged. "What do you think?" blustered master Ed McGee, climbing into his carriage. "Old Abraham Lincoln has called for 75,000 men to come to Washington immediately. Well, let them come," he snarled, "we will make a breakfast of them. I can whip a half dozen Yankees with my pocket knife."

Arriving home, McGee instituted daily pistol practice that required Hughes to run over and check the target after each of his master's rounds. "He would sometimes miss the fence entirely, the ball going out into the woods beyond," but when he managed to shoot within the bull's-eye's vicinity, he would exclaim, "Ah! I would have got him that time," by which he meant a Yankee soldier. It seemed to Hughes that "there was something very ludicrous in this pistol practice of a man who boasted that he could whip half a dozen Yankees with a jackknife."

WHEN SUMTER FELL, recalled Sam Aleckson of South Carolina, "in the big house there was gladness and rejoicing, while at the quarters there was groaning and lamentation." His fellow slaves "believed that as long as Major Anderson held Fort Sumter, their prospects were at least hopeful; but when Sumter fell, they felt that their hopes were all in vain." "We done now," they kept repeating. But then an old slave named Ben stepped forward to declare that though the white folks could "laugh now," slaves should "wait till by and by." When a young slave eyewitness to Anderson's surrender "drew himself up" and imitated the major declaring to the Rebels that "if I had food for my men, and ammunition, I be damned if I would let you come in those gates!" Ben's wife, Lucy, took heart. "Amen! Bless the Lord!" she cried, and admonished her fellows to "hope and pray."

Their master took Aleckson and Uncle Ben to Charleston, where they found whites "going about the streets wearing blue cockades on the lapels of their coats. These were the 'minute men,' and the refrain was frequently heard, 'Blue cockade and rusty gun / We'll make those Yankees run like fun.'" One day young Aleckson overheard recruits saying "they were on their way to the 'Front.'" "Uncle Ben," Aleckson asked, "where's the 'front'?" The old man "made no immediate reply," but eventually looked up at young Aleckson with a scowl. "The front is the Devil," he said, and returned to his chores.

1

"Before Their Time"

Harbingers of War • *John Brown* • *Masters' Panic*
Abraham Lincoln

N OW EVERYTHING was stirred up for a long spell before the war to free us come on," said Temple Wilson. For well over a decade, the nation had been roiling over the slavery issue. Though the Compromise of 1850 had reinforced the Fugitive Slave Act, which required Northerners to assist in returning escaped slaves to their masters, and despite various Northern states' efforts to exclude them, thousands of escaped slaves continued to seek refuge above the Mason-Dixon Line. In 1854, the Republican Party was founded to campaign against the extension of slavery into free territories. Congress passed the Kansas-Nebraska Act, which held that the settlers living in the two territories could determine for themselves whether they would join the Union as free or slave states. The result was a savage war between pro-slavery and abolitionist émigrés that would result in hundreds of deaths. A year later, several Northern states enacted laws forbidding state officials to enforce the Fugitive Slave Act. In 1856, as slaves in seven Southern states revolted against their masters, abolitionist Charles Sumner of Massachusetts was almost caned to death for denouncing slavery on the floor of the Senate. The following year, the Supreme Court ruled that an escaped slave named Dred Scott remained his master's property and therefore could not sue for citizenship in the North. And all the while there had been the rising, accelerating drumbeat of Northern abolitionists on the one side and Southern apostles of disunion on the other.

As their masters waxed hysterical about Yankee agitation, many of their slaves sought prophecy in signs and omens. "It was talked and threatened and all kinds of bad signs pointed to war," said Temple Wilson, "till at last they just knowed it was bound to come on." "I saw the elements all red as blood," recalled Frank Patterson, "and I saw after that a great comet; and they said there was gonna be a war." Harriet Gresham of Florida recalled that "there were hordes of ants, and everyone said this was an omen of war." "One night before the war come," Dora Jackson's mother "and some other women was washing clothes down at a creek, when all at once they look up at the sky, and they see guns and swords" streak across the firmament and stack themselves together. "They was so scared they run to the house and call old Master and tell him about it. He laughed at them and told them they was just imagining things, but it was just a few days before the war come, and they saw them guns just like they did in the sky."

In the winter of 1860 to 1861, Mississippi experienced the worst freeze "that us had ever had," recalled Liza Strickland. "The limbs of the trees got so heavy with ice till they broke off. It sounded like guns firing." Strickland knew "right then and there that was a bad sign, and a war was sure coming, and when it did break out us weren't surprised at all, and us had to stay scared to death for four long years."

Before the war "I seen troubles in this land," declared Lu Perkins of Texas. "I seen a big black wave of hating going on over the land and the folks getting poorer and poorer and starving for the childrens and the old." Perkins had a vision of "new kinds of soldiers and folks fighting till blood run over the land," starting in the "far corner of the world and spread over the country" — the judgment, she said, "for folks being mean and greedy." One night she awoke and saw a "blazing star dragging its long tail along the ground," whereupon a white man ran out into the night crying, "Judgment! Judgment is on us!"

IN THE EAST the first concrete sign that something momentous was at hand came in the fall of 1859 when a shard from the war for Kansas arced eastward. After leading murderous raids on proslavery encampments along the Missouri border, the abolitionist John Brown and a party of whites and freed blacks set out to spark a servile insurrection by attacking the Federal arsenal at Harpers Ferry, Virginia.

Jared Maurice Arter's master had departed for work as the arsenal's inspector of arms when Arter heard that Brown and a party of freedmen had galloped "through the county on the previous night, taken into custody a number of the leading citizens, captured Harpers Ferry and the arsenal, and barricaded himself and his men in the engine-house," where they were "holding the captured citizens as prisoners." Arter recalled that "all the day long, groups of men on horseback, armed with revolvers, shot guns, and rifles, could be seen going towards Harpers Ferry, the scene of excitement."

But these vigilantes "accomplished nothing," and it would take Colonel Robert E. Lee and a squadron of marines to dislodge Brown and his comrades. Lee's young slave Jim Parke recalled sitting on his master's broad veranda at Arlington when a soldier rode up. "Been driving his horse hard," Parke recalled. "The Colonel come to the door, and took some papers, and read them. He look right solemn-like." Parke's sister overheard Lee telling his wife to "spread the word among the servants" that he "had to go catch John Brown and all his men."

"The soldiers marched right in front of our house," recalled Frank Smith of Virginia, "right by the front gate, when they was going to Harpers Ferry to kill Old John Brown." Two days after his raid commenced, Brown was captured and eventually condemned to death. According to Hillary Watson, Brown declared that though "you Southern people can hang me," the cause he was dying for was "going to win, and there'll soon be a man here for every strand I've got on my head, fighting to free the slaves." "The excitement ran so high and fear was so great" that Brown's Northern supporters "might attempt to rescue him, that few persons except strong men were permitted to witness the execution." But nine-year-old Arter "stood beside my mother, holding to her apron, and saw hanged four of Brown's men" in a scene Arter remembered as "very war-like."

John Brown's failure fortified many slaves' belief that only God, not man, could free them, and in His own good time. Pharaoh Chesney concluded that Brown's "fanaticism" made him "a victim to an ill-timed movement," and that abolition "suffered more from such abortive steps than from the combined arguments of the pro-slavery men." Frank Smith believed simply that Brown "was killing white folks" and freeing slaves "before their time." "What God says has got to come, comes," said Jerry Eubanks of Mississippi. "This is written in the Bible." White people might regard Emancipation as the work of man, "but colored people looks cross years at everything. God did it all." "According to what was issued out in the Bible," Charlie Aarons testified, "there was a time for slavery, people had to be punished for their sin, and then there was a time for it not to be."

"IT WAS IMPOSSIBLE to keep the news of John Brown's attack on Harpers Ferry from spreading," recalled George Albright of Mississippi. A literate slave named Sam Hall remembered the thrill of fear that passed through his master's community in North Carolina. "It was suspicioned by the whites" that their slaves "planned to organize an uprising" and had chosen Hall to command them; and Hall did not know "at what moment I might be led out by the whites and hanged." The attack on Harpers Ferry "threw a scare into the slave owners," Albright remembered. "One day not long after the arrest of Brown, a boy in a nearby orchard shot off a pop gun, and my mistress ran in terror to the house, screaming that the insurrectionists were coming."

As their fathers had done after Nat Turner's abortive slave rebellion thirty years before, masters cracked down on their slaves in John Brown's wake. Suddenly they enforced to the letter longstanding but hitherto loosely observed laws against black assemblies, literacy, gun ownership, and alcohol consumption. "Some of the slaveholders would double the proportion of work," recalled William Henry Towns. "They just whipped the slaves so much to keep them cowed down, and cause they might have fought for freedom much sooner." A slave from Paris, Tennessee, said that as a young boy he did not realize he was a slave until just before the war, when local whites "cut Darkies' heads off in a riot" and "put their faces up like a sign board."

BROWN'S RAID MAY have failed to spark a slave uprising, but in the fall of 1860 many Southern whites regarded the election of "Black Republican" Abraham Lincoln as an even graver threat to slavery. "I think it has come to a pretty pass, that old Lincoln," Mattie Jackson's mistress harrumphed, "with his long legs, an old rail splitter" intended to put black people "on an equality with the whites." Before she would see her children on such a footing, she said, "she had rather see them dead."

In their recollections, a number of former slaves would claim to have laid eyes on Lincoln before the war. Some may well have encountered not *the* Abraham Lincoln but his cousin and contemporary of the same name, or perhaps an English immigrant named William Ellaby Lincoln, a somewhat unbalanced Oberlin College theological student who roamed the South before the Civil War, preaching against the sins of slavery.

But it was not the flesh-and-blood Lincoln former slaves conjured so much as a furtive abolitionist phantom swirling through Dixie, stirring up slaves and masters. Not long before the war began, Margret Hulm answered her master's door, and "there stood a big man with a gray blanket around him for a cape. He had a string tied around his neck to hold it on. A part of it was turned down over the string like a ghost cape. He had on jeans pants and big mud boots and a big black hat: kind of like men wear now. He stayed all night. We treated him nice like we did everybody when they come to our house. We heard after he was gone that he was Abraham Lincoln, and he was a spy."

"Lincoln came to North Carolina and ate breakfast with my master," recalled Frank Patterson. As he pitched into his "ham with cream gravy made out of sweet milk," biscuits, poached eggs on toast, "coffee and tea, and grits," a presumably sated Lincoln nevertheless warned his host that if whites descended to "conceiving children by slaves" and then buying and selling their "own blood," it would "have to be stopped."

"I knowed the time when Abraham Lincoln come to the plantation," Alice Douglass insisted. "He come through there on the train and stopped overnight once." Some slaves "shined his shoes, some cooked for him, and I waited on the table; I can't forget that. We had chicken hash and batter cakes and dried venison that day. You be sure we knowed he was our friend, and we catched what he had to say." She would "never forget so long as I live" his parting words to her master: "If you free the people, I'll bring you back into the Union." But if "you don't free your slaves," he said, "I'll whip you back into the Union."

Another story had it that Lincoln had turned against slavery after his wife witnessed the flogging of a pregnant slave in Richmond. "Mrs. Lincoln was horrified at the situation and expressed herself as being so," Irene Coates contended, "saying that she was going to tell the President" as soon as she returned to Washington. Richmond slaves claimed it was this incident that marked "the beginning of the President's activities to end slavery."

Sarah Walker depicted Lincoln passing through Saline County, Missouri, "investigating conditions of the slaves." Lincoln's "height and dignity frightened the children, and they fled in hiding" until Walker's father "assured them that Master Lincoln wouldn't harm them," and "they left their places of refuge." Lincoln stood "in all dignity and charm," she recollected, "and yet you had the feeling he was saying all the time, 'I am no better than you are.'"

"My mother used to say that Lincoln went through the South as a beggar and found out everything. When he got back, he told the North how slavery was ruining the nation." "I believe I see'd that man once," said Henry Gibbs of Mississippi. Lincoln "come to Marse David's house, pretending to be crippled. Marse David had me show him the way off the place. When we was out of sight, that man put them crutches across his shoulder. I always have believed that man was Lincoln." J. T. Tims of Arkansas was told that "Abe Lincoln come down in this part of the country" with "his little grip" in his hand and asked a farmer for work. "Wait till I go to dinner," the farmer replied. "Didn't say, 'Come to dinner,'" said Tims, "and didn't say nothing about, 'Have dinner.' Just said, 'Wait till I go eat my dinner,'" as he might any poor white who came knocking at his door. For this discourtesy, Tims concluded, Lincoln would plunge the South into war.

2

"A Grand Man"

Class • Poor Whites • Miscegenation • African Royalty
Jefferson Davis • Elizabeth Keckley • A Clash of Titans
Davis's Inauguration • Alexander Stephens • Robert Toombs
Thomas Hill Watts

T HE SOUTH THAT WAS about to wrest itself from the Union was a
slave oligarchy. Like their masters, slaves tended to see the world
through the fractured lenses of race and class. "There were three
classes of white people in the South," recalled William A. Yancey,
a former slave from North Carolina. "First was the aristocratic class, the
big slave holders, who gave shape to the government and tone to the society. They had the right of way in business and in politics.

"The second and third classes were servants to the first class," whose
success "depended on their obedience. The second class included the
small slave holder, the overseers, managers and clerks" whom slaves
called "the half strainers." (Any poor white who "was aiming to get up
and was making some headway," explained James Thomas, "the blacks
spoke of him as 'a strainer.'") "They tried to be rich and class themselves
with the rich white folks," recalled Lucindy Hall Shaw. "The first class,"
wrote Yancey, "did very little whipping themselves, but they required
their overseers to do it for them." It was at their hands that "most of the
cruelty was practiced."

The third class "was composed of the poor, ignorant dirty whites" who
lived "from hand to mouth. No one cared for them; even the slaves were

warned not to have anything to do with them. The first and second classes looked down upon the poor white trash," Yancey wrote long after the war, "just as all of the Southern white people look down upon the Negroes today. They did not invite the poor whites to their homes anymore than they invite the Negroes to visit them now. The Negroes were taught to hate the poor whites, and that caused the poor whites to hate the Negroes." The result, according to a Tennessee slave, was that "the poor white folks has been the terror of the colored all their days."

Just as slaves would divide white people into "big bugs," "college bred," "strainers," and "poor white trash," they made sharp class distinctions among themselves. "Our people, both slave and free, were not all a common lot on one level," wrote Levi Jenkins Coppin. "There were divisions, classes and distinctions among them." Some were classed as "industrious or lazy, 'smart' or ignorant, of good or bad character." Though the experience of house slaves — butlers, valets, houseboys, hack drivers; cooks, maids, seamstresses, and wet nurses; many of them their own masters' offspring — ranged from the kindest to the most brutal treatment, they generally looked down on field hands.

"I was born and raised right among the white aristocrats of 'Old Kentuck,'" recalled Nancy Bell after she and her husband immigrated to Africa. "When I looked out my window in Liberia," she saw "nothing but blacks: blacks everywhere. And so me and my old man just got up and come back." Mary Anderson recalled that as a house slave she used to follow her master's daughter around on visits to other plantations. "She taught me how to talk low and how to act in company," she proudly recalled. "My association with white folks and my training while I was a slave" were why she talked "like white folks" now. But Louis Hughes was unimpressed by his mistress's pretensions to gentility. It was her habit to reach out during meals and slap her slaves on the head. "Such an exhibition of table manners by a would-be fine lady!" he exclaimed. "Such vulgar spite and cruelty!"

"The field hands, and such of them as have generally been excluded from the dwelling of their owners," wrote former slave Austin Steward, "look to the house servant as a pattern of politeness and gentility." The house slaves were the field hands' only conduit for "knowledge of the manners of what is called 'genteel society'" and were therefore "regarded as a privileged class." Some were "greatly envied," others "bitterly hated." Ed McCree recalled that some field hands so resented house slaves that they "slipped around and cut their feather beds and pillows open just to see the feathers fly." The "most despised" house slave was "the deceitful 'white man's'" Negro who spied on his fellow slaves.

Among the general slave population, social standing largely depended on a master's wealth. "A servant owned by a man of moderate circumstances was hooted at by rich men's slaves," recalled Louis Hughes. "It was common for them to say, 'Oh don't mind that Darkie. He belongs to poor white trash.'" A white "gentleman" could lose his status in a twinkling, and masters and slaves did what they could to keep up appearances. "When the team was in good order, and the driver looked well, you could bet on his belonging to a first-class gentleman," recalled James Thomas. "If the driver and horses looked poor and shabby, somebody would ask, 'Who is your master, boy? Why don't he give you shoes? I expect he is an ousted Yankee.'" It was a mark of prosperity if a master's slaves ate meat, and Millie Simpkins recalled how a slave owner in Nashville used to smear the mouths of his slaves with grease every Sunday and instruct them that "if anybody asked if they had meat," they were to reply, "Yes, lots of it." An elderly Georgia slave owner told a visitor that "if a man could sit on his porch and see fifty Negroes ride his mules in from work — that was aristocracy. But if he went broke" and had to sell a slave, "his reputation was gone, and he could not borrow a dollar."

Though a visiting Irishman reported that Virginia slaves of both classes "display great contempt" for poor freedmen "who are generally dirty and ragged," aristocratic masters put freedmen on a par or somewhat above poor whites. "The free Negro was tolerated around the gentleman's home as his barber, and frequently served to wait the table in case of need if regarded worthy." James Thomas, himself a barber, never saw "a poor white man make his appearance anywhere about or around the rear of the premises, nor the front either." Poor whites were merely "the hangers-on who were ready to chase a runaway Negro or go on the patrol force to watch slaves and free Negroes." They used to "stand on the corner a whole day simply to get a nod from a gentleman when he passed," but the richest slaveholders "wanted nothing to do with a white man that could not rise above that." "When I was a boy," recalled Waters McIntosh, "we used to sing, 'Rather be a Negro than a poor white man.'" "I think I'm better than a certain class of white folks," declared a Tennessee slave who had known "white folks from the cradle up," and he didn't "mind telling them so, neither."

Masters "didn't never allow us to mix with what they called the poor white trash," a Tennessee slave recalled, for fear "they would learn us how to steal and drink; and it was the truth, too." "I believe that those poor white folk are to blame for the Negroes stealing," agreed Octavia George, "because they would get the Negroes to steal their master's corn, hogs, chickens and many other things and sell it to them for practically nothing."

Miscegenation vastly complicated the intricacies of the South's class structure, for though people might escape their class, they could never entirely escape their race, and in the South race was paramount. "Slavery was a curse to this nation," declared Amy Elizabeth Patterson of Kentucky, "a curse which still shows itself in hundreds of homes where mulatto faces are evidence of a heinous sin, and proof that there has been a time when American fathers sold their children at the slave marts of America."

"There was two classes of white folks," as far as one former slave from Tennessee was concerned: "some who wouldn't bother" with black women "and others who would. But the ones who wouldn't would not mix with those who would." Jacob Manson, however, maintained that "it was a hard job to find a master that didn't have women among his slaves. That was a general thing among the slave owners." During slavery "the women had to do what their masters told them to do. If they didn't, they pick on them and whip them." Jacob Aldrich's Texas master "was bad about that, and his sons too. Master would come round to the cabins in the quarters" and sometimes tell a slave's husband "to go outside and wait till he do what he want to do. Her husband has to do it, and he couldn't do nothing about it." Aldrich's master even had children "by his own children," and kept them all in slavery.

BY 1860 A HIGHER percentage of blacks than whites had been born in America. In fact, only one percent were African-born. No group except Native Americans had deeper North American roots. Nevertheless ancestral Africa was a living presence in the slave community. Though the descendants of some tribes acquired reputations as troublesome, many slaves subscribed to the common wisdom among masters and speculators that certain tribal pedigrees were preferable. At the beginning of the nineteenth century, slaves had been prominently advertised as "very prime Congo Negroes," "very prime healthy Mandingo Africans," and "choice Gold Coast Africans." And some slaves would claim descent from kings and chiefs. "I ain't had no daddy," said Ann Parker of North

Carolina, "cause queens don't marry, and my mammy, Junny, was a queen in Africa" to whom her fellow slaves bowed down. "I don't know much about my grandparents," said Octavia George, "other than my mother told me my grandfather's name was Fransuai, and was one time a king in Africa." "Old Ben," Charles Ball's grandfather, "claimed kindred with some royal family in Africa," and always "expressed contempt for his fellow slaves, they being, as he said, a mean and vulgar race, quite beneath his rank, and the dignity of his former station." And James Thomas remembered a "tall, dignified," and bewigged slave from Virginia "who claimed to be a prince from Madagascar," and whose fellow slaves seemed to believe "he was all he claimed to be."

Robert J. Cheatham, in turn, was proud that his family was "all black," deeming it "proof of the honor of his and his forefathers' masters that their blood was never mingled together to produce a mixed race." Many slaves of mixed parentage chose to deny any white lineage by ascribing their sharp features and lighter skin to Indian blood. Native American ancestry was also said to account for a slave's ferocious temper. L. R. Ferebee recalled that because her mother was part Indian she was "a spirited woman and would not suffer to be imposed upon by her master nor mistress." Solomon Northrup admired the bold defiance of a slave woman named Lethe he encountered at an auction house. "She had long, straight hair, and bore more the appearance of an Indian than a Negro woman. She had sharp and spiteful eyes, and continually gave utterance to the language of hatred and revenge." She had been so badly treated by her master that she didn't care any longer who bought her. "Pointing to the scars upon her face, the desperate creature wished that she might see the day when she could wipe them off in some man's blood!" "With all my Negro blood and all that I have passed through," wrote Isaac Johnson of Kentucky, "I would rather be in my black skin" than in the white skin of his slave-trading master or his white father. "Think of being obliged to associate with men of their stamp, say nothing about being their slaves!"

VIEWED THROUGH SO highly polished a prism of class, Abraham Lincoln appeared to many blacks to be merely a "strainer": a rough-hewn, sparsely educated, only moderately prosperous Kentucky emigrant who owned no slaves. "Mr. Lincoln was a good man," a house slave named Isaac Stier conceded, "but they tells me he was poor white and never cut

much figure in his clothes. That's why he never understood how us felt,"
he said. "It takes the quality to understand such things."

There was no doubting the quality of Lincoln's Confederate counterpart, however. An erudite slaveholding patrician, a hero of the war with
Mexico, a senator from what was then the richest if most oligarchic state
in the Union, Jefferson Davis of Mississippi cut a far more familiar and
impressive figure. Slaves might guess that Lincoln was "a black man, and
the son of a queen," but they told "no such stories on Jefferson Davis,"
recalled Edward Jones of Mississippi. "Both the white and black knowed
he was a grand man." "Every Negro in Mississippi knows me," Davis himself would declare after the war as he fled from his Yankee pursuers.

Davis was the second of James Lucas's three masters. "Only he
weren't no president then. He was just a tall, quiet gentleman with a
pretty young wife what he married in Natchez. Her name was Miss
Varina Howell, and he sure let her have her way." Davis "was always
calm-like and saving on his words," but "his wife was just the other way.
She talked more than plenty." One of those whose ears she bent was
a freed slave named Elizabeth Keckley, who would have the singular
distinction of serving the wives of both Jefferson Davis and Abraham
Lincoln as modiste. Keckley recalled a December day in 1860 when
Varina Davis engaged her to sew a silk dressing gown for her husband. As
South Carolina prepared to secede from the Union, "almost every night,
as I learned from the servants and other members of the family, secret
meetings were held at the house," some of them "protracted to a very
late hour." Though Davis had sadly concluded that war was "certain,"
Keckley overheard Mrs. Davis remark to a visitor, "I would rather re-
main in Washington and be kicked about, than go South and be Mrs.
President."

As she prepared to follow her husband south, Mrs. Davis offered
to take Keckley with her. "When the war breaks out," she warned her,
"the colored people will suffer in the North. The Northern people will
look upon them as the cause of the war, and I fear, in their exasperation,
will be inclined to treat you harshly." If the Rebels prevailed, however,
Mrs. Davis foresaw that she would "come back to Washington in a few
months" and lay claim to the White House. But Keckley declined Mrs.
Davis's invitation. She had determined that "the show of war from the
South" would lead "to actual war in the North"; and with "the two sec-

tions bitterly arrayed against each other, I preferred to cast my lot among the people of the North."

The Davis family returned to Brierfield plantation in Mississippi, "the most beautifulest place" Fanny Johnson ever saw: "All the cabins was whitewashed good. The trees was big and the whole place was just lovely." Brierfield had been bestowed on Davis by his patriarchal older brother Joseph. In a lifelong struggle to reconcile slaveholding with his utopian ideals, Joe Davis had granted favored slaves an unusual degree of responsibility and autonomy, even to the extent of having them try one another for their transgressions and carry out their punishments.

On February 10, 1861, Florida Hewitt watched as a rider on a lathered horse galloped through Brierfield's gates and up to the Davises' front yard. Throwing his reins over the garden palings, the rider rushed up onto the veranda shouting, "Glorious news, Mr. Davis! Great news from Montgomery! You have been elected President of the Confederate States!"

Davis rose from his chair and bowed. "Thank you, sir," he said, and turned to Varina. "My dear, will you please look after this gentleman?" Then he "stumbled into the house with his head bent" down.

The next day, in a scene that would be replayed on farms and plantations throughout the South, Davis called his slaves together for a farewell address. "In case of trouble to the plantation," he told them, "I depend upon you all to take care of the family, and if it becomes necessary, to fight for them." "We all cheered him," Frank Loper recalled, "and promised that we would," because Mr. Davis had been kind to them. "Whenever we were sick, he would come and see about us himself," and he "never would allow us to be whipped."

Davis's liberality extended little further than his house slaves, however. He sold James Lucas, and he would later try to trade Frank Loper, Loper's mother, and four of his brothers "for some mules." Though a Davis field hand named Rhoda Bones conceded "that the Davises were fine to their house-servants," they "cared little for those that worked in the fields." Chided once for lifting his hat to one of his slaves, Davis replied, "Do you think I would allow a Negro to be more polite than I am?"

Davis's attitude toward slavery was typical of a certain breed of upper-crust planter. Two weeks after the commencement of the war, he would declare that American slavery had turned "brutal savages into docile, intelligent, and civilized agricultural laborers," supplying them "not only with bodily comforts, but with careful religious instruction, under the supervision of a superior race. Their labor has been so directed as not only to allow a gradual and marked amelioration of their own condition, but to convert hundreds of thousands of square miles of the wilderness into cultivated lands covered with a prosperous people. Towns and cities have sprung into existence," and America had "rapidly increased in wealth and population under the social system of the South."

Early in the war, slaves compared Lincoln unfavorably to Davis in a song their masters taught them: "Jefferson Davis rode the milk-white steed / Lincoln rode the mule. / Jeff Davis was a mighty fine man / and Lincoln was a fool." But as the meaning of the Confederate cause sank in, their estimation of Davis would decline, until it was Lincoln mounted on the milk-white steed and Davis on the mule. "Mr. President Davis wanted us to stay bound down," said Will Sheets of Georgia. "I didn't like that Mr. Davis after I knowed what he stood for." "I never did hitch my mind on Jeff Davis," declared Mary Colbert. "He had his time to rule." William McWhorter believed that Davis "ought to be ashamed of hisself" for trying to keep Negroes in bondage. Though some said "he was a mighty good man," nobody could expect black people "to believe he was so awful good." "Don't tell me about old Jeff Davis," snapped Fannie Parker. "He ought to been killed." Apparently a fellow slave agreed with her, for after the Davises moved to Richmond, he would set fire to the president's mansion.

AT FIRST, HOWEVER, many slaves identified more with their masters than with the alien Northerners who now threatened to invade what slaves had come to regard as their homeland. "Now look," a slave owner once expounded, leaning back in James Thomas's barber chair, "them blue-bellied scoundrels went to Africa, rounded up Negroes, brought them here, sold them to us, then stole them from us, starved them and otherwise mistreated them. And now they want to tell us what to do with the balance of them?" In the face of such Yankee meddling, a slave named Charlie Davenport concluded that Davis "done the only thing a gentleman could have done. He told Marse Abe Lincoln to attend to his own business, and he'd attend to his. But Marse Lincoln was a fighting man, and he come down here and tried to run other folks' plantations. That made Marse Davis so all fired mad that he spit hard 'twixt his teeth and say, 'I'll whip the socks off them damn Yankees.' That's how it all come about."

Davenport was not alone in conceiving of the war as a clash of titans:

an impression that may have derived from glimpses of the political cartoons of the day. "My freedom was brought about by a fight that was fit
twixt two men," said Elisha Doc Garey of Georgia. Phil Towns of Georgia believed that "Lincoln had sent several messages to Davis requesting
that he free the slaves." When "no favorable response was received,"
Lincoln "had a conference with Mr. Davis, and to this meeting he carried
a Bible and a gun." Failing to convince Davis with the Gospel, Lincoln
finally set both the Bible and the gun on the table and told Davis to
choose. When "Davis picked up the gun," said Towns, "Lincoln grasped
the Bible and run home." And that's why "Davis began the war."

"When the trouble first came up about the slaves," contended Dempsey Pitts of Mississippi, "Mr. Lincoln made this offer to the South: he
said, 'Every slave should be turned loose with a horse and bridle, when
he was twenty-five years old.' The South won't accept that. So then he
said, if they won't do that, they just have to get together and fight it
out. That suits Mr. Davis, so that what they done." "Father Abraham was
a ox driver," William Edward Black contended. "But after he was president, he became a charitable gentleman toward the Caucasian race as
well as with the Ethiopian race. His proposition to the slave owners was
to free the slaves as they got to be twenty-one years old and to pay them
pensions. The United States Government was to pay half the pension
money." And indeed, upon his election Lincoln did propose something
of the kind.

If Davis "hadn't have been mulish," Isaac Stier contended, "he'd have
accepted the proposition Mr. Abe Lincoln made him," and then slavery
"would have lasted always. But he flew into a huff and swore that afore
he'd let his wife and daughter dabble they pretty white hands in dish water and wash tubs, he'd fight till every gun and sword in the country was
gone. After that he say he'd whip the Yankees with corn stalks. That
made Mr. Lincoln mad, so he set about to free the slaves."

ON FEBRUARY 18, 1861, John Wright accompanied his master to the
temporary Confederate capital in Montgomery, Alabama, to attend Jefferson Davis's inauguration. "Soldiers and officers come up to attention.
All the people shouted and clapped they hands. Master Davis come out
on the portico, and stood between two of the columns." He was "a fairly
tall man, slender and pale face, with a little Van Dyke beard. He smiled a
little, then looked solemn-like," Wright recalled. "A man stepped out
with a book and swore him in. Then he made his speech," and "when he

got through, everybody went to hollering and carrying on. You'd thought the Confederates going win the war, sure enough! Everybody knowed the war was coming on and seemed right glad of it." Everybody, it seemed, but Wright's master, who looked "right solemn when we go back home," for though he was "glad Davis was president," he was never "sure the South going to win."

FORMER SLAVES WOULD vividly recall other movers and shakers in the Confederate government, especially its diminutive and erudite vice president, Alexander Stephens. Claiborne Moss described Stephens as a "deformed, big-headed rascal." "He was a little fellow," agreed Marshal Butler, "slim, dark hair, and blue eyes." "But he had sense!" Moss declared. Stephens's slave Georgia Baker remembered that Alexander and his brother Norwood owned "a heap" of slaves, "and all of us was kin to one another." Stephens used to come down to the cabins to "laugh and talk" to his slaves and, in his high, piping voice, sing a "cakewalk" song for the children: "Walk light ladies, / The cake's all dough. / You needn't mind the weather / If the wind don't blow."

Neither Stephens nor his brother "ever married." Norwood "didn't have no use for womans. He was a sissy," Baker explained. Alexander himself "never stayed home enough to tend to things hisself much, cause he was all the time too busy on the outside." In the late 1850s, Stephens had been "all the time having big mens visit him up at the big house." Decidedly proslavery, he would declare that the Confederate cause rested on the "great physical, philosophical, and moral truth" that "the Negro is not equal to the white man; that slavery, subordination to the superior race, is his natural and moral condition." Stephens had nonetheless labored hard to talk his fellow Southerners out of seceding. "One time, out in the yard, him and one of them important mens got in a argument about something." Baker overheard Stephens say, "I got more sense in my big toe than you has got in your whole body." "And he was right," said Baker. "He did have more sense than most folkses." In fact, Stephens "had so awful much sense in his head that folks said it stunted his growing," and as "long as he lived, he weren't no bigger than a boy." "On Sundays, whenever Marse Alec was home, he done lots of reading out of a great big old book. I didn't know what it was, but he was powerful busy with it. He never had no parties or dancing that I knows about, but he was all time having them big important mens at his house," including his political ally Robert Toombs.

"A big, fine looking man," Toombs had also opposed Secession. But once the Confederacy was established, he nevertheless believed he should have been its president. He almost certainly would have made a better one than Davis. But he had to settle for secretary of state instead, only to be ignored by his highhanded superior. His slave Alonza Fantroy Toombs claimed that he was "the best stump speaker in the State" and could boast "more friends than a graveyard has ghosts. He was sure a king man." Marshal Butler recalled that Robert Toombs always kept an "unlighted cigar in his mouth. He was the first man I saw who smoked ten cent cigars," whose stubs his slaves used to scramble after. Toombs "never wore expensive clothes and always carried a crooked-handled walking stick. He never cussed," and sometimes "gave us nickels and dimes," and always referred to his slaves as "colored people," the most respectful term a slave could hope to be called in that time and place.

Slaves did not recall the Confederacy's ineffectual and unpopular attorney general so fondly. By 1860 Thomas Hill Watts owned 179 slaves on his Alabama plantation. "They says he had his servants whipped till the blood run. They had a white man for over-looker" who was "big and strong. He didn't show no mercy to the black people," and Watts "didn't care if he didn't." Watts posted one of his slaves at the train station, "where they shipped off all the things for the soldiers: corn, and meat, and such-like that the white folks give out of their own cellars, and barns, and smoke-houses, for the soldiers." Watts wouldn't allow his slave to wear shoes, "and the hot cinders and all burnt his feet." But when the slave tried to bind them up, "his master burned the rags off."

3

<hr/>

"The Union, Gentlemen, the Union"

Lincoln's Inauguration • Bracing for War • The Grapevine
Slave Children • Dangerous Talk • Politics • Praying for Freedom
A Breakfast Job

ON MARCH 4, 1861, two weeks after Davis's inauguration, young Louis Meadows stood on a street in Washington and watched "Mr. Lincoln riding by with Mr. Buchanan" in a rockaway carriage "with the seat high up." A Negro coachman, "all dressed up, was sitting up in front, and a little black boy was sitting on the seat behind," with his feet "resting on the low steps." Meadows was too young to follow the new President's speech, with its "mystic chords of memory" that Lincoln hoped might yet bind North and South together, and the "better angels of our nature" that might yet avert a civil war. But many of the capital's slaves — and they would officially remain slaves until the end of the war — could sense the import of Lincoln's accession to the presidency.

In Washington, "no President and his family," wrote the freed modiste Elizabeth Keckley, "ever excited so much curiosity." Lincoln had "grown up in the wilds of the West, and evil report had said much of him and his wife." Keckley's skill as a seamstress would soon provide her with a unique opportunity to determine the truth of such rumors for herself. After her stint with Varina Davis, Keckley's fame had spread among the ladies of Washington, including the wives of Senator Stephen Douglas and Navy Secretary Gideon Wells, who recommended her to the First Lady. Shortly before the inauguration, Mary Lincoln summoned Keckley to the White House to repair and alter a "bright rose-colored moire-antique" inaugural gown on which the First Lady had spilled coffee.

As she helped Mrs. Lincoln into her gown, the President "came in, threw himself on the sofa," laughed with his young sons "Willie and little Tad, and then commenced pulling on his gloves, quoting poetry all the while." "You seem to be in a poetical mood tonight," said Mrs. Lincoln. "Yes, Mother," Lincoln replied, "these are poetical times."

"Mrs. Lincoln took the President's arm, and with smiling face led the train below." Keckley was "surprised at her grace and composure. I had heard so much, in current and malicious report, of her low life, of her ignorance and vulgarity, that I expected to see her embarrassed on this occasion." The country's curiosity about the Lincolns "was insatiable," and during the next four years, as Keckley grew ever more intimate with the First Lady, she had to keep reporters, spies, and the President's political opponents at bay, refusing the bribes they offered her in exchange for betraying the family's secrets.

James Thomas of Nashville was no admirer of Northern whites, but he recognized Lincoln's virtues. "Different men's opinions were given daily," but Lincoln "was steadfast for the preservation of the Union. No compromising with Lincoln. The Union, gentlemen, the Union. The people laughed at 'Uncle Abe's' grammar, and the way he said things, and used to compare his language with Mr. Jeff Davis, who was a finished scholar." But, concluded Thomas after the war, "now we only hear what 'Abe' said: never hear of Jeff."

AFTER LINCOLN TOOK office, a chill settled over many of the plantations of the South. "The white folks begin to treat us different," recalled Robert Murray of Beaufort, North Carolina. "They seemed to be strange toward us. Been treat us like we's one of the family till they got talking about Lincoln and the abolition. Mistress used to instruct us in letters," and "we sleep anywhere and eat all we please" so long as "we treat the white folks respectable and work hard." But with Lincoln's accession, "it all different. Children go to the big house, and Missus meet us at the door. 'We busy this evening,' she say. That happen time or two," until Murray's mother finally told her offspring, "Don't go in the Big House no more, children. I know what the trouble. They suppose we all wants to be free." Reverend Green of Tennessee came to believe that his master became especially cruel in the early days of 1861 "because he felt that the war was coming and that we slaves would be freed," so "he got harder and harder."

"Do you want to keep your homes where you get all to eat, and raise your children?" William M. Davis heard a white preacher ask a congregation of slaves in San Jacinto County, Texas, "or do you want to be free to roam around without a home, like the wild animals? If you want to keep your homes, you'd better pray for the South to win. All that want to pray for the South to win," he commanded, "raise your hands." "We all raised our hands because we were scared not to," John Adams recalled, "but we sure didn't want the South to win."

Davis and his fellow slaves met in a hollow that night to decide what to do about the coming war. Finally an elderly slave they called Uncle Mack stood and told a story about two old slaves named Tom and Bob back in Virginia. "They were mad at one another," he said, "and one day they decided to have a dinner and bury the hatchet. So they sat down, and when Uncle Bob wasn't looking, Uncle Tom put some poison in Uncle Bob's food. But he saw it, and when Uncle Tom wasn't looking, Uncle Bob turned the tray around on Uncle Tom, and *he* got the poison food. That," he said, was "what we slaves are going to do: just turn the tray around and pray for the North to win."

WHETHER HOUSE SERVANTS or field hands, slaves would astonish Yankees and Rebels alike with the speed with which they learned the news — an alacrity that was all the more amazing considering the pains their masters took to keep them in the dark. Slaves weren't "allowed to know or hear" any more "than could be helped," recalled Sylvia Floyd of Mississippi. "The slaves couldn't read nor write, and what few of them that could wasn't allowed to read a thing that was writ on a piece of paper." Though Vice President Stephens would claim he deplored the South's prohibitions against teaching slaves to read, his slaves were "more scared of newspapers than they is of snakes now, and us never knowed what a Bible was them days." Whenever Stephens wanted to send a message, he "just put George or Mack on a horse and sent them on. But one thing sure, there weren't no slave knowed what was in them letters." "When the white folks wrote notes to each other," recalled Squire Irvin of Tennessee, "whosoever carried the note" would try to "pick up all the news he could gather both going and coming," but "it was powerful little we heared even that way."

Such benightedness was the exception, however, even among the most illiterate slaves. "While there was not a single slave on our plantation that could read a line," recalled the black educator Booker T. Washington, "in some way we were kept informed of the progress of the war almost as accurately as the most intelligent person. The 'grapevine' telegraph was in constant use."

"When seemingly absorbed in work," wrote the missionary Elizabeth Hyde Botume, "they saw and heard all that was going on around them. They memorized with wonderful ease and correctness." She once overheard escaped slave women talking about how they had gotten the news. "My father and the other boys," said one, "used to crawl under the house and lie on the ground to hear Master read the newspaper to Missus when they first began to talk about the war." "See that big oak-tree there?" another said. "Our boys used to climb into that tree and hide under the long moss while Master was at supper, so as to hear him and his company talk about the war when they come out on the piazza to smoke."

"I couldn't read, but my uncle could," an escaped slave confided to Botume. "I was waiting-maid, and used to help missus to dress in the morning. If master wanted to tell her something he didn't want me to know, he used to spell it out." But she would memorize the letters, "and as soon as I got away, I ran to uncle and spelled them over to him, and he told me what they meant." When Botume doubted her story, she said, "Try me, Missus! Try me, and see!" So Botume spelled out "a long sentence as rapidly as possible, without stopping between the words," whereupon the girl "immediately repeated it after me, without missing a letter."

No one was more revered by his or her fellows than the rare slave who could read. "Slaves who could read and could buy newspapers thereby obtained the latest news and kept their friends posted," recalled Henry Bruce, "and from mouth to ear the news was carried from farm to farm, without the knowledge of masters." Victoria McMullen's grandmother used to steal newspapers from her Louisiana master "and take them down to the quarters and leave them there where there were one or two slaves that could read and tell how the war was going on."

Trusted, ignored, or underestimated by their owners, on many plantations and farms slave children were the first to receive and relay the news. When young John Adams heard a white person reading aloud, "I would always go and stand around and listen. They often asked me what I wanted. I would always say, 'Nothing,'" but then proceed to "go and tell my father and mother. And they would say, 'Try to hear all you can, but don't let them know it.'" Slave children thereby learned "pretty much what was going on," though most of them "didn't give it much thought, one way or the other," but "kept right up with our little games of ball and marbles."

Though the tide of battle never reached his master's plantation, George Brown would know when "there was a war going on. I'd be waiting on the table, and I'd hear the white folks talking. I couldn't *keep* all I heard." As a young table servant, Thomas Rutling often overheard his owners conversing about the war. "Now, Tom," his mistress would admonish him, "you mustn't repeat a word of this." Rutling "would look mighty obedient," he remembered, "but — well — in less than half an hour, *some* way, every slave on the plantation would know what had been said up at Master's house."

However much they might urge their children to spy on their owners, adult slaves rarely took their own offspring into their confidence. As a matter of self-protection, "the olden people never did allow they children to set and hear them talk no time." Slave hunters used to bribe slave children with candy to tell them where runaways were hiding. Annie Huff recalled that her mistress used to trick slave children into informing on their elders. "Often, when their childish prattle had caused some adult to be punished, Mrs. Huff would keep them in the big house for a night to escape the wrath of the offender."

"Mothers were necessarily compelled to be severe on their children," explained Elijah Marrs, "to keep them from talking too much," because "many a poor mother has been whipped nearly to death on account of their children telling the white children things, who would then go and tell their mothers and fathers." One ex-slave recalled that when slave catchers captured him during the war, they offered not to whip him if he told them what they wanted to hear. "You ought to heard me telling!" he exclaimed. They asked him if he had heard slaves shooting guns, and he told them yes. But "I couldn't go to none of the parties after that," for his fellow slaves "would kick me out if they saw me."

Charity Morris recalled how a small boy's song got his mother killed. After submitting to another in a series of sexual assaults, Charity's pregnant aunt Sallie had beaten her abusive owner to death with a poker, and then, with the help of her son, Little Joe, burned his body in her fireplace. "That day in the field Little Joe made a song: 'If you don't believe Aunt Sallie killed Marse Jim / The blood is on her under-dress.'" Her owner's family overheard him and, finding bloodstains on her clothes, jailed Aunt Sallie until her child (and probably her master's) was born, whereupon she was tried and hanged.

Children were by no means a slave's sole source of news. "Some of the lower classes of whites" used to steal into the slave quarters, "and with a person watching to see if Master was coming, would read about the coming war." They did so at great risk. According to Harry Smith of Kentucky, "If any were caught reading to the slaves, or giving them any information, they were tied and received fifty lashes."

Pierce Cody's people got the news from Yankee peddlers "who came to the plantation to sell bed-ticking, etc." If Harry Smith's master saw his slaves talking to a passing white man, he would demand to know what he had told them: "Did he want you to leave here and go to the war? Did he ask any questions about the war?" "The slaves did not tell many things that were said by these men," recalled Cody, "as Master would pursue, overtake and kill them. And many a Northern man was never heard from after reaching the South, but was killed in this way."

Tines Kendricks of Arkansas remembered a Reverend Dickey who "preached freedom" for slaves, declaring "that they all should be set free and given a home and a mule." Dickey's sermon outraged "the biggest of the slaveowners," and "they fired him from the church, and abused him, and some of them say they gonna hang him to a limb" or "ride him on a rail out of the country. Sure enough, they made it so hot on that man he have to leave clean out of the state."

Ruben Fox dismissed a lot of what he heard from his fellow slaves. "You never could put no dependence in what they told. Every time the news changed hands, it was told a little different. By the time it got to the end of the line, you wouldn't know it was the same story." "We was told all kinds of things," Simon Durr recalled, "but didn't never know just what to believe."

But such skepticism wasn't typical. "The slaves managed to get hold of a good deal of news," recalled Allen Parker, "and the idea was fast gaining ground that in some way they were soon to be free." According to her biographer, "We is gwine to be free" was constantly repeated among "Aunt Dice's" fellow slaves. As a senior slave, Aunt Dice responded "with a sharp reprimand and a sidelong look which invited no further argument. But even her strong will could not quell the rising spirit of freedom among the slaves. The meaning of the war, so often spoken of in subdued accents throughout the quarters, dawned slowly upon her," but only meant, "to her at least," her master's ruin.

Slaves like Aunt Dice did their best to discourage "dangerous talk." "They didn't want the slaves talking about things," recalled Lee Guidon. "One time I got roughed up, and I say I was going to freedom." But his mother "put her hand over my mouth," and told him, "You don't know anything about what you saying, boy." "The colored boys," James Thomas remembered, "would be frequently advised not to get too smart, go slow, be careful."

"When an election was going on," recalled John Adams of Virginia, "they did not want the Negro to know anything," but Adams tried "to learn all I could so that I might tell father and mother." In 1856, when Republican John C. Frémont ran for the presidency against James Buchanan, whites "commenced having great meetings, and they would make speeches, saying the streets would run with blood before the North should rule." "Many things were said" that slaveholders "thought the Negroes could get along without hearing," said James Thomas, so whites hired watchmen "to drive them off, but they would slip around and mix with the crowd somewhere else." "That was the first the colored people knew about another nation wishing for the slaves to be free," recalled William Webb, "and the scales of ignorance fell from their eyes." When Frémont was defeated, "a great anger arose among the colored people," and they "began to study how they would get free." Some talked of "attacking their owners, but others urged them to "wait for the next four years," in hopes that "the next president would set the colored people free."

"OH, HOW THOSE PEOPLE prayed for freedom!" recalled Susie King Taylor of Georgia. "I remember, one night, my grandmother went out into the suburbs of the city to a church meeting, and they were fervently singing this old hymn: 'Yes, we all shall be free / When the Lord shall appear.'" Sam Clement recalled that the "strong Christian" slaves he knew "earnestly prayed each day that the dark clouds of slavery would pass away, and they would be as free as their mistresses and masters."

"Some believed they'd get freedom and others didn't," Laura Abromson recalled. "They had places they met and prayed for freedom.

They stole out in some of their houses and turned a wash-pot down at the door." According to Edie Dennis, the pot was intended "to keep the sound of their voices from 'escaping' or being heard from the outside. Then the slaves would sing, pray, and relate experiences all night long. Their great, soul-hungering desire was freedom — not that they loved the Yankees or hated their masters, but merely longed to be free and hated the institution of slavery. Everyone felt the spirit of the Lord," and just before daybreak, after chanting for "fifteen or twenty minutes, all would shake hands again and go home: confident in their hearts that freedom was in the offing."

But what was this freedom that beckoned to them? "We people on the plantation didn't know much about the war," wrote Robert Anderson. "It was impressed on us indirectly by everyone, that there was little chance of the slaves being set free. Some didn't care whether they were free or not, as there was little to look forward to either way." If freedom came, "what will we do?" they wondered. "We have no home, no money, no clothes, no nothing." On the other hand, "for some of the people, there could be no existence worse than the one they were in. It was a problem either way."

Such divergent hopes and fears were to be expected of people who came from a wide range of backgrounds. To the white observation that blacks seemed "divided in sentiment," James Thomas pointed out that "Negros were not all alike. Some were brought from Guinea, some from other sections of the Dark Continent. They differed as much as our Indian tribes." Some slaves, like Thomas himself, were "the children of the most exclusive set: men in high places in government. Some are the children of Irish, German, Jew and Negro. So it is not to be wondered that they should have different ideas," even about freedom and war and slavery itself.

"Sometimes I thinks freedom is better," declared Smith Simmons, "and sometimes I don't." "Us slaves never understood much of what it was all gonna come to," recalled Simon Durr of Mississippi, "or what it was gonna mean to us. We wanted to be free at times," but then "we would get scared and want to stay slaves." According to Ike McCoy, some slaves "didn't know what war nor freedom was, excepting the Yankees come tell them something, and then they couldn't understand how it all be."

Elderly former slaves were no more immune to nostomania than any other senior citizen. After decades of oppression and hardship in the

Jim Crow South, some would come to equate freedom with hardship, rootlessness, bigotry, and toil; and slavery with prosperity and the security and idleness of childhood. "Everybody wants to be free, and they should be," Mark Oliver conceded. "I don't believe it's right to live in bondage. But I do say it bold and above-board" that, compared to the 1930s, "the slaves with good masters like mine was a heap better off." Oliver remembered "having everything I wanted, and it takes a long time to get used to not having nothing." According to Henry Bland's interviewer, "the outcome of the war did not interest him at all" because he had "such a good master he didn't care whether he was freed or not."

Other slaves were not so impressed by their masters' kindness. "There was no such thing as being good to slaves," declared Thomas Lewis. "Many people were better than others; but a slave belonged to his master, and there was no way to get out of it." Melvin Smith of Georgia allowed that his "old Master was good and kind," but "back then we couldn't go nowhere unless we had a pass. We don't have no overseer to bother us now. It ain't that I didn't love my master," he said, "but I just likes to be free."

"Liberty and freedom" was all Wylie Nealy "ever heard any colored folks say they expected to get," and they were "mighty proud of that." Rachel Adams agreed: "It's mighty good to do just as you please, and bread and water is heaps better than that someone treat us bad to slave for." "When you is in bondage," explained Virginia Harris, "you ain't got no more chance than a bull frog." "I sure had rather be free," declared Alec Bostwick. "Who wants a gun over them like a prisoner? A person is better off dead." "Oh, *sure* I'd rather be free," exclaimed Jefferson Franklin Davis. "And I believes the Negroes is got as much right to freedom as any other race; indeed I does believe that." "Liberty," declared an anonymous runaway, "is as good for us as the birds of the air."

Slaves were "tired of getting beat up," and wanted freedom "so they could come and go just like white folks, and not have the patroller getting them." "The Lord said, 'The World was made sufficient for all to have a living.' He never intended bondage for nobody," declared Lizzie Norfleet. "That's why he made the world big enough for everybody to have a home." "If you had your hands tied and some one come and cut them loose," asked Mary Barnes of Maryland, "wouldn't *you* be glad?"

"I CAN REMEMBER how my master tell about how they decides it won't be much of a war if they has any at all," recalled John Majors of Texas.

"Just take two or three months to whip the damn Yankees and teach them to tend to they own business and let the folks down South alone with they slaves." In Mississippi, as Jennie Webb's master's sons rode away, "they told us to be good to our old Missus, that they was gwine to whip them Yankees" faster than "hell can scorch a feather." When John G. Hawkens's master's son asked his mother if she would not rather free her Negroes than send him to war, she assured him, "It won't be nothing but a breakfast spell" and sent him on his way.

"When the war what freed the Negroes started," the kinfolk of Lucy Pulliam McBee's master joined the Rebel army. On their last night home, "they all ate dinner together, marched around the dinner table, and went off to war." Tom McAlpin of Alabama "seen our Confederates go off laughing and gay; full of life and health. They was big and strong, singing Dixie, and they just knowed they was going to win."

Rachel Harris of Arkansas "went with the white children and watched the soldiers marching. The drums was playing, and the next thing I heared, the war was going on." Rebel recruits "went by just in droves from soon of a morning till sundown. They said they was gonna head off the Yankees." The clatter and blare of military drills and bands terrified some slave children. "I never had heard such noises in my life," recalled Easter Reed. "I hadn't never heard a fife or a drum; so, when the band started playing, I got under Old Miss's skirt and stayed there." Mandy Johnson of Arkansas remembered hearing "the big bell go bong, bong," and "the old drums go boom, boom," and everybody shouting, "There's gonna be a war! There's gonna be a war!"

When his master's son promised to "bring back a Yankee scalp," a young Alabama slave named General Lee Ballard took him literally. One day "I saw him coming from fishing, dragging an eel behind him, so I flew in the house hollering that Mr. Joe was bringing that Yankee skin with him." But the gulf of incomprehension worked both ways. When a recruit spied a boardinghouse slave in Pontotoc, Mississippi, wiping tears from her eyes as he rode off, he called out, "Don't cry Emmeline! I'll bring you a Yankee skin!" But Emmeline was crying because he and his comrades had been "our best paying boarders."

Many servants shared their masters' conviction that a Confederate victory would be swift. "All the time I felt we was born to win that war," recalled Doc Quinn of Arkansas. When Henry Smith of Texas accompanied his master to a Rebel camp near Houston, "I never see'd so many men together, and us say for sure the North ain't gwine be no trouble at all to whip." "Them campfires, with ten thousand men around!" exclaimed Isaac Pringle. "You never saw anything like it. It looked like the whole world was lighted up." Smith's master and his comrades "sign a paper that they gwine to fight three years. But Marse Jim he say that just foolishment: that us ain't gwine be gone from home no time."

Other slaves, however, heard in all their masters' bluster a note of desperation. "A great company of men met at our house," recalled Louis Hughes. "They were wild with excitement." But he wondered if all their volubility weren't "an admission that their confidence in their ability to whip the Yankees, five or six to one, was not so strong as they pretended." When push came to shove, Hughes's own pistol-shooting master's "courage oozed out," and he bought a substitute to serve in his stead.

"In answer to the call of the Southern Confederacy at the beginning of the Civil War," explained the former slave William Yancey, the "aristocratic and middle-class whites volunteered to start the fight. But as soon as the battle got hot, they looked to the young men of the third class" — poor whites — "and hired them to go to war as substitute for them." Willie Blackwell was contemptuous of the poor white his owner lured into the Confederate Army with a promise of slaves. He remembered seeing his master light up a cigar for the man and promise that if he would "get in that fight, and fight to win," he would give him twenty-five slaves. The poor white fell for it, "and he goes off to the war, thinking when he comes back he'll have plenty for the rest of his life."

Slaves were careful to disguise their opposition to the Confederate cause, for a single slip could have fatal results. As his master's son rode off in his new uniform to fight for the Confederacy, an enormous slave named Leonard exclaimed within his master's hearing, "Look at that goddamn soldier. He fighting to keep us from being free." An anonymous slave recalled that his master leveled a gun at his breast and demanded that Leonard open his shirt. The slave "opened his shirt and stood there, big as a black giant, sneering at Old Marse." Over his mistress's tearful protestations, his master shot him down, and Leonard died where he lay with "that sneer on his black mouth."

"They said the South couldn't be beaten," Barney Alford remembered, "and then one day old Marse rode away on one of the fine horses, and old Missus cried and cried, and said he was gone and maybe get killed." Lu Perkins watched the white men of her county ride off singing, "'Goodbye mother; goodbye sister. / Farewell, farewell.' Lots of people weeped." Virginia Sims of Arkansas recalled that when her master was about to set off to join his regiment, her mistress said, "Virginia, if you think he ain't going come back, you ought to kiss him goodbye." But as her mistress's daughter "went up the ladder and sat right on the roof and watched the soldiers going by," Sims refused. "I ain't gonna kiss no white man," she replied.

Decades later, many former slaves would recollect their masters' braggadocio with mordant satisfaction. "Young master say he gwine to war to kill a Yankee and bring he head back," recalled John Moore. "He didn't bring no Yankee head back," but he did return with his own "shot-up arm." One master bragged that he "could eat breakfast at home, go and whup the North, and be back for dinner. He went away," Hannah Crasson of North Carolina mordantly remembered, but "it was four long years before he come back to dinner. The table was sure set a long time for *him.*"

Part II

The East

1861

4

"Worser for Us Than Ever"

Robert E. Lee • Divided Loyalty • Slavery's Cradle • Big Bethel
First Bull Run • A Son's Death • Libby Prison • Rebel Victories

F ROM THE REPUBLIC'S FOUNDING, slaveholders had been among the wealthiest and most influential men in the country. Planters like George Washington had struggled to shake themselves free of the moral burden of slaveholding, but most either embraced an institution that had secured their prosperity or, like Thomas Jefferson, affected a kind of lofty fatalism. For his part, the preeminently pedigreed Robert E. Lee approached what he conceded to be "a moral and political evil" with pious complacency.

His father-in-law, George Parke Custis, had been an active member of the American Colonization Society, whose object was to rid the country of slaves by converting, educating, and emancipating them, all on condition that they return to Africa. The society subscribed to an inherent contradiction: that literate, Christianized freedmen would be a civilizing influence on Africa, whereas their exportation would spare American whites their corrupting influence. The slaves Custis emancipated during his lifetime were sent to Liberia, the exception being the family of his table servant Charles Syphax, to whom the old man gave seventeen acres of his own farmland because, according to family tradition, Charles's wife, the daughter of George Washington's maid, was Custis's own daughter.

Lee himself deemed slavery "a greater evil to the white man than to the black race, & while my feelings are strongly enlisted in behalf of the latter, my sympathies are more strong for the former." His father-in-law left his slaves — "in number about seventy" — to Lee and his wife, but stipulated that they be emancipated no later than 1863, five years after his death. Lee tried to soften the economic blow by contriving to emancipate them no *earlier* than five years after Custis's death. In the meantime he scrambled to make the most of their labor.

According to a Custis slave named Wesley Norris, "it was the general impression among the slaves of Mr. Custis that on his death they should be forever free; in fact this statement had been made to them by Mr. C. years before." So after Lee announced "that by the conditions of the will we must remain slaves for five years," Custis's slaves began to doubt they would ever be free. Norris remained at Arlington "for about seventeen months, when my sister Mary, a cousin of ours, and I determined to run away, which we did in the year 1859." But they were caught in Westminster, Maryland, thrown into prison for fifteen days, and hauled back to Arlington. When Lee "demanded the reason why we ran away, we frankly told him that we considered ourselves free. He then told us he would teach us a lesson we never would forget." According to Norris, Lee took them to a barn and arranged for a constable to "lay it on well." After stripping them to the waist and whipping them, the constable took Norris and his cousin to jail, and his sister to Lee's Richmond shipping agent. Norris and his cousin would remain in jail for a week before Lee's agent hired them out to work on railroads in Virginia and Alabama.

The Lee family's favored slaves were raised to be cultivated servants steeped in the etiquette, protocols, and fashions of the day. During the war a missionary named Lucy Chase would present a strip of gingham to one of them in a fugitives' camp on Caney Island, Virginia. Chase assumed that "she would make from it an apron with a waist," but Lee's former house slave emerged "with a short, fancy apron," informing her benefactress that "aprons with waists are out of fashion now." She explained that she couldn't help caring so much about her clothes, for "it was born in me." "We never went to a party in our lives," another of Lee's slaves told Chase. "Mother would not let any of her children go to parties with bad company. We were as genteelly brought up as white people."

In 1856, Lee wrote a letter in which he warned that if Northern agitators continued with their abolitionist machinations, the nation would face "a civil and servile war." He argued that since black people were "immeasurably better off here than in Africa, morally, physically, and socially," what he called "the painful discipline they are undergoing is necessary for their further instruction as a race, and will prepare them, I hope, for better things." How long this preparation would take he was content to leave "in the hands of Him who chooses to work by slow influences, and with whom a thousand years are but as a single day."

DURING THE WEEK that followed Fort Sumter's fall, Lee was still struggling to decide whether to serve in the U.S. Army or join his fellow Virginians under the Confederate flag. His eighteen-year-old servant Jim Parke could see how "worried and sad" he looked. "War coming on, and he's got to take sides. North going to fight against the South," and Lee "couldn't sleep much of nights" with his mind so "full of troubles."

Lee rode to Washington "right frequent. Lincoln wants him to command all the armies of the North to whip the South. If he won't do that, he's bound to lose" his plantation at Arlington, across the Potomac from Washington, "cause the Yankees going come over and take it." Parke recalled how Lee would go out onto his veranda and "walk back and forth, back and forth, hands behind his back, trying to decide what to do. Virginia's a slave state. Wouldn't do to fight his own people, yet he's freed all his slaves, excusing us Arlington servants that's heired to him" by his father-in-law's will.

When Lee finally made up his mind that he was "going to fight with Virginny! Quit the United States army!" his wife "put her arms about his neck, and kiss him goodbye, and cry right smart. He look solemn-like at the big mansion, and wave us goodbye. Said he'll be back in a few months," Parke recalled, but a "mighty long few months it was."

Hearing of Lee's decision, a retainer named William Mack Lee rushed to the Confederate capital and volunteered to serve his master. "And he was right glad to see me!" exclaimed William. "Indeed he was." "William, I'm going make you my body servant and cook," Lee told him. "You can take care of me!"

A month after Lee resigned his commission, the United States Army occupied his plantation at Arlington. Obtaining a military pass through Alexandria to join her husband, Mary Custis Lee entrusted the house, including its many Washington-family heirlooms, to her maid, Selina Norris Gray. Gray and her husband took this trust seriously, protesting to General Irvin McDowell when officers began to abscond with the mansion's treasures, whereupon McDowell ordered everything removed to Washington and placed in safekeeping at the patent office.

VIRGINIA WAS THE birthplace of North American slavery. Though slaves had accompanied Spanish explorers to the New World, the first Africans to have been brought to North America for sale were a small boatload of men and women deposited at Jamestown in 1619 by a Dutch trader. Their descendants' status quickly declined from indentured servitude to outright slavery defined entirely by race, and yet by the 1850s masters throughout the South had come to regard a slave with a Virginia pedigree as "choice" — a kind of servile aristocrat. Virginia itself became the flagship of the rebellion, so important to the Confederate cause that its congress voted to move its capital from Montgomery, Alabama, to Richmond. "Slavery's cradle" was about to become the scene of some of the most decisive battles of the Civil War.

A Union officer recalled that he never encountered Virginia slaves "who did not perfectly understand the issue of the war and hang with terrible anxiety upon its success or failure." As early as June 10, 1861, during the Battle of Big Bethel, they "crowded together in little squads about the streets" of Hampton, "listening to the reports of the cannon in the distance, or the accounts of those who came in from the field. Many of them were almost insane with anxiety, and expressed themselves extravagantly." "If the 'Unioners' get the fight," the officer asked one such squad, "what will it do for you?" "Then we'll be free!" they answered. And if they lose? "Oh, then it be worser for us than ever," they said, "shaking their heads mournfully," for they seemed to believe "that all the issue of the war hung upon the result of that day." Fortunately for them it did not, for the Rebels won this first of Virginia's land battles, inflicting eighty-seven casualties at a cost of only eight, and sending the Yankees reeling back to Hampton.

BY THE MIDDLE OF July 1861, Rebel troops had massed just a few miles south of the United States' capital. "The Confederates had been kicking up around here for some time," recalled a slave blacksmith named Andrew J. Redmon of Groveton, Virginia. "We were looking for a battle but didn't know which way it would be coming in." It finally came in from the north when Union General-in-Chief Winfield Scott ordered General Irvin McDowell to advance on the Confederate force at Manassas Junction. "The Union troops come down through a little village called Centerville," Redmon recalled, "six miles east of here. A long-range cannonade was begun," and with it the first major land battle of the Civil War.

At first "there was no musketry, just a little artillery skirmish with guns stationed on both sides of the Run firing back and forth." Redmon's Secessionist owners "took a big lot of us slaves down in the Bull Run bottom to blockade the road" by chopping "great big oaks" just to the point where "it wouldn't take much" to topple them. If the Northern army "got too strong, we was expected to bounce up, throw the trees, and escape," but the Yankees "fell back to their camp, and we slaves went home."

Two days later, "everything was calm, and the sun was shining bright and hot," Redmon recalled. "I'd had my breakfast and was standing in the yard before my shop door, looking to see what I could see, when I heard the boom of a cannon. I looked down the Fairfax Road and seen a smoke rising above the trees. Then I heard the pop of a return shot from the Southern side. The cannon kept on firing, and the people around here were all looking on from their houses."

From his hilltop vantage point, Redmon saw Yankee infantry cross Bull Run at Sudley Ford, "and then I could see them going helter-skelter crossways and every way hardly a mile distant." He heard the guns booming and saw the smoke rising, and "a constant flicker of firing" that sounded like "a hailstorm on a roof." He recollected that the barrage "continued until about two," when "the whole Northern army retreated," falling back on Washington. "We couldn't see the men, but we could see a mountainous cloud of dust rising up through the tops of the trees from the roads they were on. The Southern troops followed them across the Run and kept up their cannonading until about four o'clock."

The next day, "lots of people come from all directions and went perusing on the battlefield, and I went over that way myself. But I soon turned back after I began to come across dead men. I'd seen enough. I heard the Southern soldiers say that some of their men were killed with poisoned bullets," though later in the war Northern soldiers would assure him that their bullets had been lubricated merely to keep from fouling their barrels.

"WHEN WE COLORED people knew the Northern army had been beaten," Redmon recalled, "we felt just like we were worse off than we ever was." Their masters were elated, however, and regretted only that the victorious Confederates under Joseph E. Johnston had not finished off the Federals for good. "When I came back with the papers from the city," Louis Hughes recalled, "the house was soon ringing with cries of 'Victory!'" "Why, that was a great battle at Bull Run!" his master exclaimed. "If our men had only known, at first, what they afterwards found out, they would have wiped all the Yankees out, and succeeded in taking Washington!"

Robert E. Lee had restlessly monitored the battle from the Confederate capital. He stood "straight and dignified and didn't talk much, but he'd walk up and down on the front gallery, and the orderlies brung him telegraphs from Bull Run, where us and the Yankees was fighting," recalled Frank Smith, who "lived closest to the big hotel where General Lee and a whole passel of soldiers stayed." When Smith overheard them talking about "Bull Run," "I allowed somebody's bull had got out, and us and the Yankees was trying to catch him and get him back in the pasture!"

But for Tines Kendricks's owners, getting the "bull back in the pasture" came at a tragic cost. Kendricks used to listen as his mistress read aloud from her Rebel son's letters. He'd written most recently that he wished they would "hurry and start the battle so as he can get through killing the Yankees and get the War over and come home." But after Bull Run she received a letter from a Rebel army surgeon informing her that her boy had fought "a hard fight" at Bull Run, where a minié ball had torn "a big hole right through the side of his neck." The doctor said he "done sew the wound up" and assured her "he not hurt so bad" and would soon return to his company. "But it wasn't long before they writ some more letters to Old Mistress," reporting that her son's wound was not "healing to do no good. Every time that they sew the gash up in his neck, it broke loose again."

A few nights later, just after dark, screech owls alighted "in the big trees in the front of the house. A mist of dust come up," Kendricks recalled, "and the owls, they holler and carry on so that Old Marse get his gun and shot it off to scare them away." For Kendricks and his fellow slaves, the swarm of owls portended a death in the family, and "sure enough, the next day they got the message that Marse Sam dead. They brung him home all the way from Virginny and buried him in the graveyard on the other side of the garden with his gray clothes on him and the flag on the coffin." Kendricks's mistress summoned all her slaves "and allowed them to look at Marse Sam," and "he sure looked like he peaceful in his coffin with his soldier clothes on." But Kendricks later heard from his young master's body servant that the young soldier had "bucked and reared just before he died, and tried to get out of the bed," cursing "to the last."

After Bull Run, the Rebels hustled about a thousand prisoners off to Richmond, where they had to improvise a prison for them in a warehouse. The lone survivor of a commercial complex that slaves had burned down when their owner reneged on a promise to free them in his will, the facility was named after its most recent occupant, a chandler named Libby, and would eventually house an aggregate 50,000 Union captives over the course of the war. When Henry Smith of Texas rode into Richmond with his master, "one of the first things that our boys see'd" were some of the Yankees who "had been took prisoners" at Bull Run. Among them was "a Mister Congressman," Republican Alfred Ely of New York, who had "come out from the town of Washington in his buggy just on purpose to see the Rebels whipped."

"At first the Northern people were chagrined and disheartened" by the Union defeat at Bull Run, William Robinson remembered, "but then came a renewed determination." Now they understood "the real character of the war, and no longer dreamed that the South could be subdued by a mere display of military force. They were to fight a brave people" — their fellow Americans — "who were to be conquered only by a desperate struggle." During the first year of the war the Confederates would capture "the large arsenals at Harpers Ferry, near Norfolk" and triumph "in the two great battles of the year — Bull Run and Wilson's Creek," in Missouri — and in "minor engagements at Big Bethel, Carthage, Lexington, Belmont, and Ball's Bluff." Nevertheless, wrote Robinson, the Union had saved "Fort Pickens and Fort Monroe, and captured the forts at Hatteras Inlet and Port Royal." They had gained a few small victories in the field, but more important, Lincoln was managing, with a combination of political and military pressure, to prevent the slave states of Kentucky, Missouri, Maryland, and Delaware from seceding, "thereby casting the whole South into a state of siege," with Federal armies threatening from "the north and the west by land, and the navy by sea, maintaining a vigilant blockade."

5

"They's Folks!"

Yankees and Banshees • Union Hordes • Masters' Flight
Children • Gentlemen of the North • Turning the Tables

To PREVENT THEIR human chattel from communicating with the
Yankees, masters played on their slaves' insulation, superstition,
and trust by depicting Union soldiers as demons. The very word
"Yankees" gave them a leg up, for to some slaves' ears it had a dev-
ilish sound, akin, perhaps, to "banshees" — the malign spirits that slaves
believed haunted Dixie's woods and bogs. Masters told their slaves that
"the real, genuine Yankee had only one eye, set in the middle of his forehead, and a horn on the top of his head." Another slave was told that "the
Yankees would take colored men and drive them in swampy, low marshes
and there cover them with wild geese feathers."

Slaves who had accompanied their masters on trips above the Mason-
Dixon Line were told that the people they had encountered in the North
"were only Southern people after all, that had gone north and returned,
but the real Yankees were blood-thirsty and savage. When Joe Bouy's
master "come riding up on his black horse shouting, 'Ma! Ma! War's been
declared!'" Bouy and his fellow slaves were terrified that "the Yankees
gonna get us and cut our necks off." "I used to hear them talking about
the Yankees," recalled Alice Johnson of Arkansas, "and I didn't know if
they was horses or mules or varmints or folks or what not." When the
Yankees rode by in their dark capes, a Tennessee slave mistook them at
first for buzzards.

Masters warned slaves that "if the soldiers caught us, they would hang us all," recalled the cowboy Nat Love. Other slaveholders claimed the Yankees "would send them all to Cuba and make their condition far worse than it ever had been," or might even drown them in the ocean. But as the war ground on, "the white folks didn't try to scare us about the Yankees cause they was too scared theirselves." By then most slaves had learned to rely on the evidence of their own eyes and ears. Mittie Freeman remembered her mistress begging her to flee from an approaching Yankee force. "Ain't I always told you Yankees has horns on their heads? They'll get you. Go on now, do like I tells you." But Freeman wanted to see for herself, and was hiding in the branches of a tree when a Yankee called up to her. "Come on down here," he said. "I want to see you." But Mittie refused to climb down until the Yankee agreed to "take off his hat and show me his horns." "There was a little Negro slave boy living on the farm," recalled his white mistress, "and he had heard quite a bit about the Yankees. So one day they happened to pass through where he could see them, and he rushed into the house and said, 'Miss Lulu, I saw a Yankee, and he was a man!'" "Why," a slave exclaimed after he first laid eyes on Union soldiers, "they's folks!"

But even the bravest slaves were slow to dismiss their masters' depictions of Yankees as monsters. According to missionary Laura Towne, a South Carolina slave named Susannah simply had refused as an adult to be whipped. "Whipping never does me no good, ma'am," she explained to her mistress. If she did wrong or made a mistake, "I'll explain," she said, "and I'll do better next time. I only wants to know what you want, and I'll do it." Because, she continued, if her "pride and principle won't make me do right, lashing won't." She had "never asked no wages," she said, "but my two clothes for the year," and she agreed to "do anything for them if they wouldn't lick me." But it wasn't until her master sold away the last three of her twenty-two children that she and her husband, Marcus, announced they were "going to the Yankees." "Oh, Zannah," her mistress cried, "the Yankees will kill you. If you see a Yankee, it'll drive you crazy." "Why, Miss?" Susannah asked. "Ain't they natural folks?" "Oh, no, Zannah," replied her mistress, "they don't look like us."

For a time Susannah took her mistress's warnings to heart, but when Yankee soldiers came to the plantation, her husband told her simply to step forward and see what they wanted. As the soldiers approached, they could see that Susannah's hands were trembling. "We are not going to hurt you," said one. "We only want you to get us something to eat, and we'll pay you for it." "O such pretty men!" Susannah recalled years later. "And so respectful!"

Such encounters with real Yankees would destroy much of whatever remained of their masters' credibility. A runaway who escaped his pursuers by swimming out to a Union gunboat told his rescuers that his masters had described Lincoln to him as a man-eating ogre "with tail and horns" who intended to "devour every one of the African race" and lay waste to the South. "Lord," the slave exclaimed, "I don't know nothing, but I knows too much for that there. I knows Master Lincoln wasn't that kind of a person. Them there horns and tails," he said, laughing out loud at his master's ludicrous overestimation of his slaves' credulity, "I — I couldn't swallow the horns and tails. Them was too much for this black man, sure."

SLAVES ACCUSTOMED TO the tiny populations of rural towns and farms were thunderstruck by the size of the Union horde that marched into the South. "I never see'd so many mens at one time in my life before!" exclaimed Addie Vincent. Jeff Rayford claimed that it took four days for a Union wagon train to pass by his master's plantation. "They was just as thick as you ever saw black birds on the ground." They passed in a continuous line "from six o'clock in the morning till five o'clock at night," and the dust from their march "blotted out the sun" so completely, Henry Murray contended, that "a lot of people thought the world was coming to the end, and they run in the river and drowned theirselves." After they passed, it looked to Wylie Nealy of Georgia as though a tornado had touched down. Nevertheless, recalled Richard Parrott of Kentucky, "there was considerable feeling among the slaves for the Union Cause. Every opportunity they had to befriend a Union soldier they took in rather bold fashion."

UPON SPOTTING UNION gunboats steaming toward his employer's landing, an overseer rushed up to the kitchen yelling, "The Yankees are coming! The Yankees are coming! The gunboats are down the river. You must all keep out of sight," he told the slaves. "I tell you, them Yanks are the very devil!"

"Never fear," one of them replied. "We'll run sure. We'll run so the Devil hisself couldn't catch we!" "Don't you worry, Master Jim," said the old cook. "We all hear about them Yankees. Folks tell we they has horns and a tail. I is mighty scared myself, and I has all my things pack up, and when I see them coming I shall run like all possessed."

As they watched the overseer flee, however, the slaves began to mutter under their breath, "That's right. Skedaddle as fast as you can," they said. "When you catch we again, I suspects you'll know it. We's gwine to run sure enough; but we knows the Yankees, and we runs that way."

As Yankee sailors disembarked from their gunboat at a plantation landing on the Mississippi, the mistress "got wild-like." "Yes, they are stopping!" she exclaimed to her two house slaves. "Mill and Jule, run! Tell all the Negroes in the quarters to run to the woods and hide! Quick! For they kills Negroes!" But Mill made no move to obey her. "Mill," her mistress asked, "why don't you go?" Because "I ain't feared the Yankees," she replied. "Jule," her mistress persisted, "you run and tell all the Negroes to run to the woods, quick. Here they are coming right up to the house! Now, Mill," she asked suddenly, "you won't *go* with them will you?" "I'll go if I have a chance," she calmly replied. Her mistress then turned to Jule. "Jule," she said, "*you* won't go will you?" "I shall go if Mill goes," said Jule. Her mistress "began to wring her hands and cry." "Now, remember," she admonished them, "I brought you up. You won't take your children away from me, will you, Mill?" "Mistress," replied Mill, "I shall take what children I've got left." "But if they find that trunk of money and silver plate," their mistress begged, "you'll say it's yours, won't you?" "Mistress, I can't lie over that," Mill answered. "You bought that silver plate when you sold my three children." Later, as Mill and Jule climbed aboard the gunboat with their children, their mistress "followed us crying, 'Now, Mill and Jule, I know you'll suffer when you leave me.'" Whereupon one of the sailors turned to her and said, "They won't suffer again as they have done with you." "And we all got on the boat in a hurry," Mill recalled, "and when we's fairly out in the middle of the river, we all give three times cheers for the gunboat boys, and three times cheers for big Yankee soldiers, and three times cheers for government; and I tell you every one of us, big and little, cheered loud and strong, and made the old river just ring again."

Betty Krump had belonged to a master who worked her mother as a farm hand plowing fields "when she was pregnant same as other times," until the Yankees came and broke up the plantation. "I'm so glad the Yankees come," Krump exclaimed. "They so pretty. I just love the Yankees for freeing us." When a Union force came to Dawson, Georgia, Clayborn Gantline remembered, "they acted different and was naturally better to servants than our masters had been." "They was very nice to the colored people," said Sarah Jane Patterson of Bartow County, Georgia. "Never beat them or nothing."

After a Presbyterian minister had taken to whipping his cook after service every Sunday, her outraged brother had concluded never to "have faith in white folks' religion." But after associating with Yankees he changed his mind, for it seemed to him that while religion "was a make-believe in slave-holders," Jesus had "hid his Spirit" in the white people of the North. Kluie Lomack would reach the same conclusion. "The Lord," she said, "got into their hearts."

CHILDREN WERE SOMETIMES the chief beneficiaries of Yankee raids. Oliver Jones watched as the Yankees marched into Brookhaven, Mississippi, "and smashed in store doors and windows." Jones recalled that "all us little chillen sure did have a fine time, because we got pies and candy and such like: much as we could eat. We wished the Yankees would come every day!" "A Yankee Army appeared in our village one day," Hannah Austin remembered. "They practically destroyed Mr. Hall's store by throwing all clothes and other merchandise into the streets." Catching sight of Hannah and her little sister, one of the soldiers declared, "Little Negroes, you are free. There are no more masters and mistresses. Here, help yourselves to these clothes; take them home with you." "Not knowing any better," Austin remembered, "we carried stockings, socks, dresses, underwear and many other pieces home. After this, they opened the smoke house door and told us to go in and take all of the meat we wanted."

It took some children longer to trust the Yankees. Though the soldiers called out that "they wasn't gonna harm nary a hair on us's head, and they didn't," Laura Hill and her fellow slaves "didn't know nothing but to run" from them. But when slaves "didn't run and hide," recalled Liza McGhee, the Yankees would give them plenty to eat. "The Union soldiers has a camp not so far from we-uns," recalled Van Moore, "and I slips down there when Old Missy not looking, cause the soldiers give me black coffee and sugar what I takes to my mammy. I had to walk in the sand up to the knees to get to that camp. Lots more children went, too, but I never see'd no cruelness by the soldiers."

When the Northern soldiers came, a Georgia slave known as Uncle Dave hid under his mother's bed. But "a Yankee followed me into the house, dragged me out, lifted me up on his shoulder and toted me round, just to show me he meant no harm." When the first Yankees passed their master's house in Arkansas, Elcie Brown and her brother "got scared and ran in the house, crawled in bed and thought they were hid, as they had scrutched down in the middle of the bed with the door locked. But the soldiers bursted in and moved the bed from the corner." One of the soldiers took Elcie's brother "by one arm and one leg and stood him on his feet, patted his head and told him not to be afraid, that they would not hurt them," and then stood Elcie up as well. Reaching into "a bag lined with fur," the soldier handed them each "a stick of candy."

Yankee soldiers were not above playing and toying with slave children. George Owen of Georgia recalled how Union troops "shamed" him awfully for his scanty attire: a one-piece garment, or plantation "privilege," made like a "cross between a sack and a shirt." But most of their teasing was harmless enough. Charlie McClendon used to ask Yankee pickets to "give me a pistol." "Come back tomorrow," they'd tell him, "and we'll give you one." "They had me running back there every day," McClendon said, "and I never did got one." Melvina Roberts had a fonder recollection of First Lieutenant Charles Mallet of the 51st Indiana Infantry, who "would always tease me and tell me to cook him some dinner. So I would make some mud pies and call him to eat some. He would come out in the back yard," Roberts remembered, "and make out like he was eating them."

SLAVES WERE ESPECIALLY impressed by Yankees who behaved like gentlemen. The Union soldiers who passed through the Wilson Hunter plantation in Washington County, Alabama, were commanded by "a Captain that was good and kind," Dellie Lewis testified. "I heared him say that there weren't going to be no stealing and tramping through folks' houses. They slept out in the yard for one night" and moved on. Emma Chapman recalled that one of a pair of Yankees who passed by her mistress's farm "wanted to take the last mule she had." "No," said the other, "Mrs. Montgomery is a widow, and from the appearance of her slaves, she has treated them well." The soldier even promised to return "Old Spunk," a horse that the Union Army had appropriated, "and sure enough, one night about midnight, they heard a horse whinny, and Emma's grandfather said, 'There is old Spunk,'" and there stood the mistress's missing horse, waiting outside the door.

"The Yankees didn't do nobody no harm," Louis Lucas declared. Rebel guerrillas often came to his master's farm to steal "stock and the slaves too, if they got a chance. They cleaned the old man's stock out one night," but the Yankees recovered his animals and returned them to the house. Though "they kept all the other horses and mules for their own use," they gave the stallion — "a great big fine horse" — back to Lucas's master after he refused their offer of five thousand dollars. "If they hadn't give him back the stallion," Lucas said, "the old man would have died," for "that stallion was his heart."

After demanding entrance to a slaveholder's home "in a gruff voice," a Yankee officer asked the mistress where she had acquired the ring he spied on her finger. "When told that the ring belonged to her husband, who was dead, the officer turned to his soldiers and told them that they should 'get back; she's alright!'" "One day during the War," recalled Belle Caruthers of Marshall County, Mississippi, a Yankee officer "sat on the front porch and talked to Old Miss. She told him she had six sons in the Southern Army and wished she had sixty to give. He said he admired her patriotism. Then she told him if he would have her house guarded, she would cook him the best meal he ever ate. And he did, and she had a grand dinner cooked and served him in style."

One day four Yankees "come riding up to the house," remembered Tom Morris, "and Mammy said they was soldiers. They took nearly everything we had to eat. They left us to near about starve. They drunk all the milk, and took all our meat. One man who was setting on the big fine horse, the one with big shiny buttons on his coat, rid up and made the soldiers give us back a little in the kitchen," Morris recalled. "He was a fine gentleman."

"Madam," Samuel Smith of Nashville heard a foraging Yankee officer tell his mistress, "I am sorry to do this, but we must eat too. I hope you will not think that we are not gentlemen, because we are. It is bad that we have to fight, but we fight no women, and we are not robbers. I hope you forgive us, and since you can buy what we can't, I beg to leave this for you." Bowing and doffing his cap, he gave her twenty dollars. "After they was gone, Miss called me and say, 'Sam,' she say, 'all the Yankees are not mean, cause I know that one was a real man.'"

THEY MAY NOT HAVE been mean at first, but they were different. "Yankee looks just like you is," Abram Harris told his interviewer, "only he do talk funny and fast: more so than the kind of white folks that I has always been around." They could also swear a blue streak. Hammett Dell reported to his master "what terrible language" the Yankees used. "First cussing I ever heard done was one of them soldiers. I don't know what about," said Barney Laird, but "I never heard nobody cuss so much over nothing as ever I found out."

"I suppose them Yankees was all right in their place," sniffed Hannah Irwin of Louisville, Alabama, "but they never belong in the South. Why, one of them ask me, 'What am them white flowers in the field?' You'd think that a gentleman with all them decorations on hisself would have knowed a field of cotton!" James Thomas of Nashville regarded the Yankees in general as "a little tiresome."

With abolitionist zeal, some Northern troops tried turning the tables on the slaveholders they encountered. "They run white folks out of the houses," Betty Krump recalled, "and put colored folks in them." "The Yankees come to our place and runned Master Jim away and took the house for a hospital," recalled Mary Ella Grandberry of Barton, Alabama. "They made the white folks cook for the colored and then serve them while they ate. The Yankees made them do for us like we done for them. They showed the white folks what it was to work for somebody else."

But once the Federals rode off, the tables were soon turned around again, and it seemed that some Yankees were less interested in helping slaves than humiliating their masters. In Helicon Springs, Georgia, Alice Green's mother, Milly, was working in the kitchen when her mistress cried, "Look out of that window, Milly! The Yankees is coming for sure!" Swarming into the yard, the soldiers broke into "the smokehouse, chicken yard, corncrib, and everything on the place. They took what they wanted" and told the slaves that "the rest was ours to do what us pleased with. They said us was free and that what was on the plantation belonged to us." But then, as quickly as they had appeared, they departed, "and us never see'd them no more."

Yankee cavalry forced Shang Harris's master "to haul corn all day Sunday to feed they horses." Ike McCoy recounted the day the Yankees "come and made the white women" help their slaves "cook up a big dinner." His mother was so frightened "she couldn't see nothing she wanted. She said there was no talking. They was too scared to say a word." In Athens, Georgia, people claimed that the Yankees stopped "a white woman on the street," snatched away her earrings," and "put them on a Negro woman." The Yankees who trotted up to a plantation in Cloverport, Kentucky, tried to get the slaves "to rise up." The soldiers "told them to take anything they wanted to take: take Master's silver spoons and Miss's silk dress." "If they don't like it," they said, "we'll shoot their brains out."

Whether or not such booty was offered with the best of intentions, accepting it placed the better-treated slaves in a peculiar bind. Robert Shepherd of Georgia recalled how Yankee raiders assembled all of Joseph Echols's slaves "and told them they was free and didn't belong to nobody no more. The slaves could take all they wanted from the smokehouses and barns and the big house, and could go when and where they wanted to go." But when they "tried to hand us out all the meat and hams, us told them us weren't hungry, cause Master had always done give us all us wanted. When they couldn't make none of us take nothing, they said it was the strangest thing they had done ever see'd, and that that man Echols must have sure been good" to his slaves. "When them Yankees had done gone off, Master come out to our place" and blew on a bugle "to call us all up to the house." Echols was so moved by his slaves' refusal to loot his stores that "he couldn't hardly talk." "Master said he never knowed before how good us loved him. He told us he had done tried to be good to us and had done the best he could for us, and that he was mighty proud of the way every one of us had done behaved ourselfs."

As a Georgia master named William Neal "hid hisself in a den with some more money and other things," Callie Elder remembered, Yankees "took what they wanted of what they found and give the rest to the slaves." But after the soldiers departed, Neal's slaves "give it all back to Master cause he had always been so good to them."

Part III

The West

1861 and 1862

6

———— ❖ ————

"Grant Shelling the Rebels!"

*Missouri • Camp Jackson • Wilson's Creek • George Knox
Mill Springs • The Mississippi River • Fort Henry
Fort Donelson • Panic in Nashville • Yankee Occupation*

I F VIRGINIA WAS slavery's venerable stronghold, Missouri was its raw frontier. By 1861 its slaves had watched whites savage each other for six years over whether slavery should be contained or extended. They did not need to be told that a war was coming, nor that it would be fought over them.

SLAVES SAW HOW even a small Yankee success could strike fear into the hearts of their owners. In early May 1861, Rebel soldiers commanded by General Daniel Marsh Frost camped for a week near the St. Louis residence of Mattie Jackson's master. On May 10, Union General Nathaniel Lyon moved out from his St. Louis arsenal and demanded the Rebels' surrender. "I told my mistress that the Union soldiers were coming to take the camp," Jackson recalled. "She replied that it was false," that Confederate General John Herbert Kelly "had come to re-enforce General Frost." In a few moments "the alarm was heard." But when Mattie reported that the Unionists had fired on the Rebels, her mistress replied that "it was only the salute of General Kelly. Late that night her husband came home with the news that Camp Jackson was taken" and that Lyon had paraded his captives through the city "and then confined them in prison." Mattie's mistress asked her husband how the Union soldiers could take seven hundred men "when they only numbered the same." He replied that they had actually numbered seven thousand.

Mattie's mistress was "much astonished, and cast her eye around to us for fear we might hear her." A few days later, she "came down to the kitchen again with another bitter complaint that it was a sad affair that the Unionists had taken their delicate citizens who had enlisted and made prisoners of them: that they were babes." But Mattie's mother reminded her mistress that at Fort Sumter the Rebels had served Major Anderson "the same, and that turnabout was fair play." At this her mistress "hastened to her room with the speed of a deer, nearly unhinging every door in her flight, replying as she went" that the slaves and the Yankees "were seeking to take the country."

BY AUGUST 1861, however, it began to look as if the Secessionists would take the country. Nathaniel Lyon and his Army of the West left their camp at Springfield, Missouri, determined to get the drop on an approaching Rebel force under Brigadier General Ben McCulloch. On the afternoon of August 10, they collided southwest of Springfield at Wilson's Creek. The Yankees drove back McCulloch's cavalry and withstood three attempts to break their line. But Lyon was killed, and though the Confederates withdrew, Lyon's replacement, Samuel D. Sturgis, decided that his men were too beat-up to pursue the Rebels and retreated to Springfield, leaving his foe in control of southwestern Missouri. A slave from Springfield named Ellaine Wright recalled seeing the exhausted Northern soldiers return from Wilson's Creek. But her master, Thomas Evanson, was apparently unimpressed by McCulloch's victory, for soon afterward Wright, "with all the other Evanson slaves, was hurriedly shipped as far south as possible to hide them from the Unionists."

Of all the ex-slave witnesses to the war in the West, none was more confiding than George L. Knox. Soon after Tennessee seceded from the Union, his master, W. C. Knox of Wilson County, had enlisted in the Confederate cavalry. Unwilling to leave his wife alone and unprotected, he decided to send her to her parents' home in neighboring Rutherford County. So his seventeen-year-old slave George drove his master's family to Murfreesboro, where W.C. climbed aboard the train to Nashville. Over the years, W.C. had grown so fond of George that his wife sometimes accused him of putting George's interests above hers. Now, as they bade each other goodbye, "we both shed tears. I felt that my only friend was gone" and that if W.C. were killed, his mistress would sell him "away to the South."

After bidding his master farewell, George proceeded with his mistress into a region of Tennessee so renowned for its slaveholders' brutality and vast plantations that it was known as "Young Mississippi." George drove past enough "slave-holders living in splendor" that by the time "we got fifty miles away from home, I felt that the North never could whip the South." Laboring as a farm hand for his mistress's father, George was confirmed in this belief by a string of Confederate victories and by the sermons of a local preacher who declared that the Southern cause was divine and every Rebel triumph ordained by God.

But then in January 1862, Union Brigadier General George H. Thomas defeated Major General George B. Crittenden's Confederates at Mill Springs, Kentucky, and chased them down to Murfreesboro. "Some of the boys who went out so brave," George Knox mordantly recalled, "got so badly scared that they ran away and never stopped until they got home." Knox took great pleasure in breaking the news to the preacher, and "the look that settled upon his face was a study."

FROM THE BEGINNING of his term, Abraham Lincoln understood that controlling the Mississippi River and its tributaries was the key to winning the war in the West and crippling the Rebels in the East. In February 1862, Brigadier General Ulysses S. Grant set his sights on two proximate river bastions: Fort Henry on the Tennessee and, twenty miles to the east, Fort Donelson on the Cumberland.

Answering Grant's summons, Yankee units came streaming down from the North. On her farm in Webster County, Kentucky, Samuel Watson's mistress, "accompanied by a number of slaves, was walking out one morning" when they were "startled by the sound of hurrying horses. Soon many mounted soldiers could be seen coming over a hill in the distance." Warned that the Yankees were appropriating horses and "enlisting Negroes into service whenever possible," she sent her slaves into hiding and chased her husband's "splendid horses" into the woods, so that "when the soldiers stopped at the Watson plantation," they were disappointed to find "only a few old work horses standing under a tree."

An escaped slave named William Webb was working as Union General Lew Wallace's servant in Cairo, Illinois, when orders came to board boats and proceed to Fort Henry. Landing a few miles north of the

Rebel stronghold, General Wallace marched with General John Alexander McClernand "up on the right of the river" to Fort Henry while General Charles Ferguson Smith "marched up on the left." Slowed down by rain and mud, they would not arrive before Flag Officer Andrew Foote's fleet had pummeled the Rebels into submission. Webb could see the Rebel shells "strike the gunboats and dash over them." One shell even whistled through the porthole of the Union ironclad *Essex*. Striking the boiler, it sent steam roiling "up through the pilot house," killing the pilot and scalding his men. But after a few hours' siege, "General Grant came dashing back to the boat I was on, and told the officers that the victory was theirs, that the camp was on fire, and a great many of the Rebel batteries were disabled, and could not stand much longer." After the Confederate garrison surrendered, Webb "went over the ground, and the first thing I saw was one of the Rebel cannon bursted and four men lying dead beside it. I went on farther, and saw all the cabins they had were burning and some of them knocked to pieces, and a great many dead people scattered around in the fort." But Webb just "stood, looking on and enjoying our victory."

FOOTE'S GUNBOATS GIDDILY ventured all the way down to Alabama, destroying a railroad bridge and sinking Rebel gunboats, then came back up the Tennessee, turned eastward onto the Ohio, and steamed down the Cumberland to join Grant's attack on the more formidable Fort Donelson. Twelve miles farther east, at Smith's Landing, George Fordman could hear the guns firing, as could Charles Graham of Clarksville, Tennessee. "I remember hearing the cannons roar: 'long toms' they used to call them." "That's General Grant opening fire," an elderly uncle told Graham, who would never forget exulting with his family at the roar of "General Grant shelling the Rebels!" At the sound of Union artillery, the husband of a local slave named Betty Guwn "said he would free himself, and he did," running away from his master to help "Grant take Fort Donelson."

"In about eight days," William Webb recalled, "General Wallace commanded me to pack up" for the march on Fort Donelson. "At that place we had a very hard fight," he remembered, in weather that had turned bitterly cold. "I went up close to the place where they were fighting, and I saw one regiment cut all to pieces. I wept with sorrow to see that Union regiment cut up so." Though forbidden to fight, men like Betty Guwn's husband were nevertheless observed picking up weapons from dead

Yankee soldiers and joining the fray. But when shells and minié balls "kept whistling around me," Webb dropped back and climbed a hill to observe the Rebel cannons firing.

On Saturday, February 15, Webb overheard Grant command Wallace "to take the left wing immediately" and charge the fort. "A great many men fell," Webb recalled, "and the troops fell back and rested Saturday evening." Though the Confederate left had succeeded in pushing back the Yankees, at the unaccountable command of Fort Donelson's dithering, buck-passing commanders, their men fell back to their trenches, only to find them occupied by Yankees. Although outnumbered two to one, the Rebels might have escaped to Nashville, as Nathan Bedford Forrest and his men defiantly managed to do, but their generals decided instead that they had no choice but to surrender.

"The colored people came to General Wallace's tent that night and said that the Fort had surrendered and a great many of the people were leaving. The next morning a gunboat sent two shells into the Fort, and it did not receive any answer," so one of General Wallace's officers, "with a detachment of soldiers, went into the Fort" and returned with "the news that the Fort had surrendered, and we rejoiced" over its fall.

Webb also rejoiced at the news that the Yankees intended to take their thousands of Rebel prisoners to Indiana. "I listened very carefully, for I had heard General Wallace talking about it being a free country." So he passed himself off as a Rebel servant and climbed aboard a prison boat.

As he steamed up to Cairo, Illinois, Webb encountered one of his former masters among the prisoners huddled in the steamboat's hull. "He was pleased to see me, and wanted to know how I came to be a prisoner. I told him my other master was going to take me off to some other place, and I got away from him and went to the Union Army, and now I was going North." His former master confirmed that Indiana was "a free country," Webb recalled, and advised him "to be industrious and not to claim more than my labor came to."

THE FALL OF Fort Donelson threw Tennessee's Secessionist capital at Nashville into a panic. The night before, Governor Isham Harris had addressed a torchlight rally to celebrate the Rebels' impending victory. But the next morning, just as church was letting out, Harris rode through the city sounding the alarm. Convinced that Foote's gunboats would steam down the Cumberland and raze the town, Nashville's whites raided warehouses, blew up a powder magazine, set riverboats ablaze, destroyed the railroad bridge across the Cumberland, and fled the city.

Seeing their masters in such a panic frightened some slaves. But others were delighted, and sang mocking songs about their owners' unmasterful panic: "He look up the river, / And he see that smoke / Where the Lincoln gunboats lay. / He big enough, and he old enough, / And he ought to know better, / But he gone and run away."

Apparently Governor Harris was among the first to run away, for he was the first refugee to pass through Rutherford County, where George Knox spotted him riding in a four-horse omnibus, "making his way south." Then, "a little later on in the evening, here come a man with a lot of horses and slaves making his way south. One of the white men asked the colored men what the news was. They said the Yankees were coming."

The women of Wilson County "had been told that the Union people had no respect for sex and that all kinds of depredations would be committed." But for the time being the Union Army was content to occupy and fortify Nashville, its first captive Rebel capital. When W. C. Knox's one-year enlistment ran out, he deemed it safe to return with his family to his farm in Wilson County. There, after the Confederate Congress passed a law exempting schoolteachers, he took a sudden interest in education, while his slave George prospered making boots for the Confederate soldiers encamped around Murfreesboro.

Nashville's whites had to accustom themselves to the new Yankee order. "The morning the Yankees came to town," recalled a local slave, his master struck him. The master "didn't know the Yankees were in town, and when he found out, he come back begging me to stay with him, and said he was sorry."

7

"The Blood Run Deep"

*Shiloh · Rebel Wounded · Memphis I · Helena · Gallatin
Corinth · Perryville · Texas · Corpus Christi · Galveston
Sabine Pass · Fayetteville I*

B Y NOW THE YANKEES had pushed Confederate General Albert
Sidney Johnston and his forces southward out of neutral Kentucky
and much of western and central Tennessee. Johnston consoli-
dated his troops along the vital railway that connected Memphis
to Richmond and, ultimately, Charleston, South Carolina. In early April
1862, he led his army out of Corinth, Mississippi, to strike at Ulysses S.
Grant's forces near Pittsburg Landing.

ADELINE ROSE LENNOX remembered hearing the distant rumble of
guns "when they were fighting up near Shiloh, Tennessee." "They had a
big battle seven or eight miles from our home," recalled William Geat of
Bedford County, Tennessee. "It started at daylight Sunday morning,"
April 6, "and lasted till Monday evening." As the Rebels brought an unprecedented sixty-two guns to bear on the Yankee line at what they
called the Hornet's Nest, there "was a roar and shake, and we could hear
the big guns plain. It was times to be scared."

Holt Collier would survive slavery and become a famous hunter, capturing the black bear for Teddy Roosevelt that would give rise to the
teddy bear craze. But in April 1861, Collier was serving as a fourteen-
year-old bodyguard for the Rebel sons of his master, Colonel Howell
Hinds. "I did not see my old colonel again until we met on the battle-

field of Shiloh," he remembered. "Holt," said the colonel, "I have worried a heap about you." "Yes sir," Collier replied, "but I got as good a chance as you." And he was right. Though "the soldiers were falling thick and fast," in what was the bloodiest battle of the war to date, Collier "was never hit once." He was "only a few yards away," however, when Albert Sidney Johnston, seated on his "big white horse," was struck in the thigh by a Yankee minié ball that severed his femoral artery. "Six soldiers carried him to the shade of a tree," Collier remembered, "where he died in a short while." Upon Johnston's death, General Pierre Gustave Toutant Beauregard became "the leader of the Southern army" and withdrew what was left of it back to Corinth. Though the Yankees had lost 13,000 men, some 2,500 more than the Confederates, William Geat declared "the North whupped."

For young Oliver Jones of Brookhaven, Mississippi, the plight of the retreating Rebels was his first intimation of the horrors of the unfolding war. "After Shiloh was fought, some of the soldiers was brought here to a kind of hospital white folks made out of a two-story store," he recalled. "Once I remember when me and my brother come in to town to sell eggs, we saw through the window a doctor putting a plaster or bandage on a soldier's back, and before he was done with it, the soldier fell over dead."

Unaware that the Rebels had retreated, Louis Hughes's master "came hurrying in one morning right after breakfast." "Lou, Lou, come!" he called out. "We have a great victory! I want to go up and carry the boys something to eat." So Louis and his wife "pitched in" to cook a batch of "biscuit, bread, hoe-cake, ham, tongue" for his master's friends. "He had a son, a nephew and a brother of his wife" in a unit known as the Como Avengers. The day after his master rode off to deliver the victuals, Hughes went to the post office and picked up the mail for his mistress, who snatched it from his hands and said, "in great excitement," "Louis, we want to have you drive us into town, to see the Yankee prisoners, who are coming through, at noon, from Shiloh."

They reached Oxford in time to see the train come in, "but the prisoners that were reported to be on board were missing." The train was filled not with Yankee prisoners but Rebel wounded. Among them Hughes's mistress caught sight of her brother Edward's servant Jack and beckoned him to her carriage. "Where is your master?" she asked. "He's in the car, Missus," said Jack. "He's shot in the ankle." Hughes's mistress burst into tears, and "Jack and I went to the car," Hughes recalled, "and helped him out, and after some effort, got him into our carriage" and drove home. There they were met by Fanny, Edward's slave and "wife in all but name," who would tend to him for the duration of the war.

AFTER SERIALLY CAPTURING an archipelago of Confederate forts along the Mississippi, the Union Army's Mississippi fleet laid siege to Fort Pillow, a vast bastion on a bluff some forty miles upriver from Memphis. The Rebels held out for months, but the constant muffled throb of mortars and cannons set the citizens of Memphis on edge. Louis Hughes recalled how the owners of the Memphis & Ohio Railroad began to lay tracks down the city's Main Street to connect their stock to Jackson, "where they imagined their property would be safe from the now terrible Yankees." At this, the locals panicked. "Some fled at once, for they imagined that this act of the railroad officials indicated that the Yankees must be coming pretty near." Hughes's master, Ed McGee, "became so excited, at this time, that he almost felt like going away, too. The family grew more and more uneasy; and it was the continual talk: 'We must get away from Memphis.'"

After the roar ceased echoing down the Mississippi from Fort Pillow, the first sign that the stronghold had fallen to the Yankees was "a transient boat" that turned up at the riverfront, having lost part of its wheelhouse to Union gunfire. "This increased the excitement among the people; and our folks became alarmed right away, and commenced talking of moving and running the servants away from the Yankees to a place of safety." His own master's "vaunted courage," sniffed Hughes, "seems to have early disappeared. His thought was chiefly devoted to getting his family and his slaves into some obscure place, as far away as possible" from the same Yankees he had once dismissed as "easily whipped."

THE JULY 12, 1862, Union occupation of Helena, Arkansas, made less of a difference to the course of the war than it did to the life of a slave blacksmith named Thomas P. Johnson. "Uncle Tom was the best reader, white or black, for miles," recalled Cora Gillam. "That was what got him in trouble. Slaves was not allowed to read. They didn't want them to know that freedom was coming; any time a crowd of slaves gathered, overseers and bushwhackers came and chased them." Gillam ascribed Johnson's ferocity to his Indian blood. He was "not scared of anybody. He had a newspaper with the latest war news and gathered a crowd of slaves to read them when peace was coming." Convinced he was trying to stir up an insurrection, a white mob hauled him off to jail. "Twenty of them say they would beat him, each man, till they so tired they can't lay on one more lick. If he still alive, then they hang him. Wasn't that awful?" asked Cora. "Hang a man just because he could read?" But "big extra strength seemed to come to him. First man what opened that door, he leaped on him and laid him out. No white man could stand against him in that Indian fighting spirit. They was scared of him. He almost tore that jailhouse down" before his master took him home, "but next day the white mob was after him" again and threw him back in jail. "Then listen what happened," said Gillam. "The Yankees took Helena, and opened up the jails. Everybody so scared, they forgot all about hangings and things like that." Eventually Tom enlisted in the 54th U.S. Colored Infantry and followed his regiment to Little Rock.

"I could walk when I first see'd the Yankees," recalled Molly Horn, whose master's farm lay near Helena. "I run out to see them good. Then I run back and told Miss Becky. I said, 'What is they?' She told Ma to put all us under the bed to hide us from the soldiers. One big Yankee" stepped inside and asked Horn's mistress if she owned any slaves. "No," she replied, but just then Molly came toddling out from under the bed, asking for a piece of bread. The officer cursed her mistress and "made the other four come out from under the bed. They all commenced to crying, and I commenced to cry. We never see'd nobody like him before. We was scared to death of him. He talked so loud and bad."

The Yankees loaded all four children into a wagon, in which they were soon joined by Horn's mother and transported to Helena. "He put us in a camp and kept us. Mama cooked for the Yankees six or seven months," and it was from them that she first heard that freedom might be in the offing. Then "you ain't going to keep me *here* no longer," she declared, and returned home.

JOSEPH WILLIAM CARTER was kept hidden from the Yankees when they moved on Gallatin, Tennessee, firing chains that "cut down trees as the balls rolled through the forest." The corn crop "was ready to bring into the barn," Carter recalled, "and the soldiers told Mr. Mooney to let the slaves gather it and put it into the barns. Some of the soldiers helped gather and crib the corn," then let their horses "eat what had fallen to the ground." Carter wanted to help out, but his mistress hid him in her cellar for fear the Yankees might, by persuasion or force, take the boy away with them. "There was a big keg of apple cider in the cellar, and every day Miss Puss handed down a big plate of fresh ginger snaps right out of the oven, so I was well fixed."

CORINTH LAY IN Mississippi's northeast corner, just south of the Tennessee line. It had been nothing more than a dusty crossroads until the 1850s, when it became the intersection of the Memphis & Charleston and the Mobile & Ohio railways. By 1861, 1,200 people had settled around a business district consisting of three hotels, five churches, and a depot. After the catastrophe at Shiloh, Holt Collier and his master had joined the Confederate retreat to Corinth, from which they were "detailed for scout duty along the Mississippi River and up near Old Greenville." The region was "a wilderness, and if our boys got lost I could always find the way out. I had been raised in this part of the country and had hunted in the woods all my life." He and his master "did a heap of good too" by Collier's lights: "saved our folks' property and ran the Unions out."

At the outbreak of the war, Pet Franks had also accompanied his master to Corinth, and though he "never seen much of the real fighting," he tended to "the soldiers what got wounded." Then, at the end of May 1862, the approach of an enormous Union force under Henry Halleck forced Beauregard to evacuate the town, which the Rebels managed with such ingenuity and stealth that Halleck's victory was widely denounced as so barren as to amount to a defeat.

James Spikes had joined the Union troops as a servant, and "was with them when the Yankees taken Corinth and whupped" the Rebels, and still later, when "the Rebels tried to take it back and the Yankees whupped them again." "Lots of the Confederate soldiers begins to pass," recalled James West of Ripley, Mississippi. "There was men on foot, and men on horses. Some men pulling cannons, and some pulling wagons. Near our place was a creek, and in there some of the wagons gets mired while crossing it, and they was left there."

"A couple of days after the soldiers begin to pass," young West and his fellow slaves "was just sat to the table for to eat breakfast, when all of a sudden, we hear, TAT, TAT, TAT, TAT, TAT, BOOOM, just like the drum corps." West ran from the table and "starts for some place to hide." He ran "to one place, then I hear, BOOOM! Then I runs to another place." West finally "crawls under the shed and there's where I stays. The Master and my mammy tries to coax me out. They threatened to whup me, and they offered me candy. But it weren't no use. I was saving my head. They was too big to crawl in after me, so they had to let me stay."

A lot of his master's kith and kin "was fighting in that battle, and some was killed. Buck and I goes to the battleground after they's quits fighting. There was dead horses: lots of them. Lots of trees and brush was cut down from the bullets and cannon balls. I pick up a number of bullets and balls and takes them home. They was laying on the ground everywhere." But they did not see "any dead soldiers," for the Rebels "had dug the trench and buried them."

Late in the summer, Confederate General Sterling Price's Army of the West forced the Yankees to abandon Iuka, twenty miles east of Corinth, and rendezvoused with General Earl Van Dorn's Army of West Tennessee. In early October, 22,000 Rebels marched on Pocahontas and then turned southeast to wrest Corinth from the slightly larger Yankee force that General William Rosecrans had positioned in two entrenched lines. Two days later, the battle commenced, and as Van Dorn's troops hacked their way through a gap between two Union divisions, forcing the Yankees to retreat to their innermost line, a Rebel victory seemed inevitable.

Watching from Corinth's refugee camp, Mary Gaines's elders witnessed the ensuing carnage. Her grandfather told her that "the blood run sure enough deep in places. He didn't see how he ever got out alive. Grandma and Mama said they was glad to get away from the camps. They looked to be shot several times." Convinced he could wait until morning to finish off the Yankees, Van Dorn let his troops rest in their lines for the night. By the time the Rebels resumed their attack the next day, however, Rosecrans had regrouped, and now Union artillery ripped through their lines. Though Van Dorn's men made some headway, the Yankees turned them back. "The regiment I was with," James Spikes recalled, "whupped them away from several places and kept them running" all the way to the Hatchie River, from which they were driven in turn to Holly Springs, Mississippi, by a Yankee force that could have but failed to capture and destroy both of Van Dorn's armies. At Corinth, the battlefield "was so thickly covered with the dead and wounded," Doc Quinn recalled, "that you couldn't touch the ground in walking across it. And the onliest way to bury them was to cut a deep furrow with a plow, lay the soldiers head to head, and plow the dirt back on them." Gaines's grandfather always told her that "war was awful." "Colored folks is peace loving by nature," she said. "They don't love war."

ALLEN ALLENSWORTH TOOK a job as a nurse with the 44th Illinois Infantry as it joined Major General Don Carlos Buell's campaign to run Confederate General Braxton Bragg out of Kentucky. Hoping to force the Bluegrass State to abandon its ambiguous arrangement with the Union and take up arms against the North, Bragg had made an end run around Buell and transported his men by rail to the state capital at Frankfort, where he waited in vain for his ranks to fill with Kentucky Rebels. The Unionist governor had fled to Louisville, and Bragg was installing a provisional Secessionist governor with all due pomp when the festivities were cut short by a report that the Yankees were approaching in force. Bragg and his governor designate evacuated the city in the nick of time.

On October 7, as Buell's Federals overtook Bragg's rear guard near the crossroads town of Perryville, word traveled "down the line that they would have a big fight." Soon the "cannons were booming," Allen Allensworth remembered, "and the troops were forming into line," and it was "not long before wounded men were being brought in for treatment." The next day, the Confederates broke through the Federals' left flank, but an infusion of Yankee artillery brought the battle to a standstill.

"I was tied up all day in that battle," recalled Isaac Pringle, a slave bodyguard in the 24th Mississippi Infantry. A colonel was "riding up and down in front the lines, and, when the first shells come over, it scared his horse so bad he run away straight through the Yankee army, and we never did see him no more." As the Confederate assault disintegrated, the Yankees pursued the Rebels through Perryville's streets. After Rebel defeats at Iuka and Corinth prevented him from receiving reinforcements, Bragg abandoned his hopes for a Secessionist Kentucky and turned south.

FELIX HAYWOOD PROBABLY spoke for many of the slaves who spent the war in the farthest reaches of the Lone Star State. "It's a funny thing how folks always want to know about the war," he remarked. "The war wasn't so great as folks suppose. Sometimes you didn't know it was going on. It was the ending of it that made the difference. That when we all woke up that something had happened. Oh, we knew what was going on in it all the time, because old man Gudlow went to the post office every day, and we knew. We had papers in them days just like now. But the war didn't change anything. We saw guns, and we saw soldiers, and one member of master's family, Colmin Gudlow, was gone fighting somewhere. But he didn't get shot no place but one," and "that was in the big toe. Then there were neighbors who went off to fight," though he contended that "lots of them pretended to want to go as soon as they *had* to go." His master's ranch ran "just like it always had before the war." The local preacher, "saw to it church went on. The kids didn't know what was happening. They played marbles, seesaw, and rode. I had old buster, an ox, and he took me about plenty good as a horse. Nothing was different."

BUT TEXAS WAS NOT entirely spared the ravages of war. In the summer of 1862, a Union naval lieutenant named J. W. Kittredge went charging up and down the Texas coast in his gunboat *Arthur*, intercepting Southern blockade runners as they tried to smuggle goods in and out of Mexico. By August he had captured and acquired enough shallow-draft boats to cross the bar at Corpus Christi and steam into the bay.

Walter Rimm and his fellow slaves "hadn't even known there was a war on" until August 13, when Kittredge gave the Confederate commandant forty-eight hours to evacuate the town. "The first we knows about it am when some Union Ships comes into the Bay and bombards Corpus Christi. When the shooting starts, all the older folks tooks to the woods, and several am still gone. I's hears several joins the Union Army and makes good soldiers." But the refugees in the woods were "powerful scared and shaking all over."

After an extended siege, Rimm spotted "some small boats coming our way from the big boats, and when they gets closer, we sees some soldiers." To his master's horror, Rimm's father, Robert, sauntered down to the shore to meet them. "When the soldiers beaches the boats, they climbs out and shakes hands with Father" and asked where they might find drinking water. Watching from above, Rimm's mistress cried, "Old Robert going to run away with the damn Yankees already!" But it was "no use for Master and Mistress to worry about father," because Robert Rimm would not leave without his family. The Federal occupation of Corpus Christi forced slaveholders to flee west with their slaves. The Parks family of Arkansas had run with their slaves along the Texas coast, "but when they got to Corpus Christi," Minerva Lofton remembered, "they found the Yankee soldiers there just the same, so they came back to Arkansas."

Though only a year old when the Union Navy blockaded Galveston, Allen Price could relate stories handed down to him by his grandfather, a slave of a family named Price. "The Price family done fight for the Confederacy all the way down the line of the family, to my own pappy, who went with he master when they calls for volunteers to stop the blockade of Galveston." Master Price had hoped he would "escape the worst of the war when he come to Texas," and indeed, for a time they lived more or less peaceably, raising and ginning cotton. But "when the Yankees has the Texas ports blockade so the ships can't get in," John Price "done take my pappy for bodyguard and volunteers to help." Finally, on New Year's Day, 1863, General John B. Magruder broke up the Union blockade with troops and "two old cotton steamers what have cotton bales on the decks for breastworks," thus opening up this small Texas port to Rebel trade. ("Just before they had the War in Galveston," explained Maria Mintie Miller, "they took the steamships in Buffalo Bayou and took the cabins off and made ships out of them. They put cotton bales all around them and build them up high," because "bales is good to catch the cannon balls in.")

But then on January 10, Federal gunboats commenced an intense bombardment. Jacob Branch and his brother had just risen to milk their master's cows when "all at once came a shock that shook the earth. The big fish jumped clean out of the bay, and turtles and alligators ran out of their banks. They plumb ruined Galveston! We ran into the house, and all the dishes and things jumped out of the shelf."

Shake Stevenson, Branch's master's son, had "volunteered and got killed somewhere in Virginia." But his brother Tucker "didn't believe in war, and he said he was never going to fight. He hid in the woods so the conscript men couldn't find him. Old man LaCour came around and said he had orders to find Tucker and bring him in dead or alive. But because he was Old Master's friend, he said, 'Why don't you buy the boy's services off?' So Old Master took the boat — cat rig, we called it — and loaded it with corn and such, and we poled it down to Galveston. The people needed food so much, that load of supplies bought off Master Tucker from fighting."

Many of Galveston's slaves ran away to Mexico during the war. "The

Mexicans rigged up flatboats out in the middle of the Rio Grande, tied to stakes with rope," Branch recalled. "When the colored people got to the rope, they could pull themselves across the rest of the way. The white folks rode the Mexican side of that river all the time," searching for runaways, "but plenty of slaves got through." Branch used to nurse the Rebel pickets assigned to wade through the Rio Grande. "I had to get smartweed and boil salt water to bathe them in," he remembered, for they had "rheumatism so bad from standing day and night in the water."

ALLEN PRICE'S FATHER would see his last combat in Texas on September 8, 1863, at the Second Battle of Sabine Pass. "The Yankee general, Banks, done send about five thousand troops on transports, with gunboats to force a landing" and march upriver to Port Arthur. The impediment was Fort Griffin, which lay on an expanse of salt grass a few miles up from where the Sabine River, separating Texas and Louisiana, emptied into the Gulf. Yankee success seemed guaranteed, for the Rebel garrison was manned by only forty-four recruits: Irish dockworkers banished to Fort Griffin for disorderly conduct. But unbeknownst to the Yankees, Lieutenant Dick Dowling of the Texas Heavy Artillery had kept them occupied firing cannons at targets in the river.

Now, as the Yankee flotilla veered out of the Gulf and up the Sabine, they opened a blistering and unusually accurate fire. "My pappy helped build breastworks when them Yankees firing." He told his son that some of Dowling's men "didn't have real guns; they have wood guns, what they call camouflage nowadays." But they had enough real guns to do the job. In perhaps the most lopsided victory of the Civil War, "Dowling done run them Yankees off," capturing two Union vessels, including the gunboat *Clinton,* and some two hundred men.

IN FAYETTEVILLE, ARKANSAS, in the late fall of 1862, Yankee enlistees camped "in tents and some of the officers were in houses." They constructed "barracks for the men of upright logs" and turned a college building into a hospital. A slave named Adeline Blakeley recalled "lots of times seeing the feet of dead men sticking out of the windows."

"Both sides were firing buildings: the Confederates to keep the Yankees from getting them, and the other way about. But the Southerners did most of the burning. Mrs. Blakeley's little boy was sick with fever." Mrs. Blakeley, Adeline's mistress, was a Secessionist, and her neighbor was a Unionist, but each stood up for the other. "It was like that in Fayetteville," Adeline recalled. "There were so many folks on both sides, and they lived so close together that they got to know one another and were friends." So Mrs. Blakeley would sit "in one doorway and the other in the building next," and when arsonists of either army approached, each would plead for the other, and "between them they kept the buildings from being burned," thus saving the life of Mrs. Blakeley's "little sick boy."

Fayetteville's civility began to affect the Yankees as well. An officer once announced to Mrs. Blakeley that he was going to hunt down "Old Man" John Parks of Prairie Grove, but on being told that Parks was Mrs. Blakeley's father, "he came over to apologize. Said he never would have made such a cruel remark if he had known." In any case, when the Yankees came to her father's house, "Mr. Parks went out of the back and the women surrounded him until he got away."

One day, Yankees paused at the house of Adeline Blakeley's master "and wanted us to cook for them. Paid us well, too." One man put a young slave named Nora on his lap "and almost cried. He said she reminded him of his own little girl he'd maybe never see again. He gave her a cute little ivory-handled pen knife."

IN EARLY DECEMBER, Confederate Major General Thomas C. Hindman set out to attack two Union divisions under Generals Herron and Blunt before they could join forces. Positioning his troops between them, Hindman attacked Herron first, but Yankee infantry pushed him back to a ridge northeast of Prairie Grove Church. On receiving orders to march on Prairie Grove, the fond Yankee soldier who had dandled little Nora on his knee asked Mrs. Blakeley if he could leave his pistols with her until he came back through Fayetteville. She told him this was asking too much, for what would happen to her and her family if the Rebels found a Union soldier's weapons in her possession? But he persuaded her that it would be for only a few days, and so she "hid them under a tub in the basement" as the Yankee set off on horseback.

After an exchange of cannon fire, Hindman's Rebels flung back two Union charges and then counterattacked, but by then Blunt had turned up and attacked Hindman's left flank. The result was a stalemate with about equal casualties on both sides. A year would pass with no word from the officer who had left his side arms with Mrs. Blakeley. Con-

cluding that the fond Yankee had been killed at Prairie Grove, she gave
the pistols to her brother.

GEORGE KNOX'S boot buyers had multiplied as Bragg holed up for the
winter by the west fork of Stones River, near Murfreesboro, Tennessee. By late December, Major General William S. Rosecrans had determined that Bragg's army was on the brink of dissolution. "Word ran
through the camp," Union nurse Allen Allensworth recalled, "that General Rosecrans was going to give Bragg's army as prisoners to the United
States for a Christmas gift." But the gift would have to wait until New
Year's, for not until Boxing Day, 1862, did Rosecrans lead his Army of
the Cumberland out of Union-occupied Nashville and march on
Murfreesboro.

It was "not long before the entire army was closed in on Bragg,"
Allensworth recollected. But then on New Year's Eve, Bragg got the
drop on Rosecrans by attacking his right flank. The two forces fought all
that afternoon and early evening, "and the wounded commenced coming
in," keeping Allensworth and his fellow nurses busy all night. At about
daylight on December 31, the entire Union corps was being driven from
its position. As George W. Arnold's mother tried to flee with her children,
"a large cannon was fired above us, and we watched the huge ball sail
through the air and saw the smoke of the cannon pass over our heads. We
poor children were almost scared to death," Arnold recalled, "but our
mother held us close to her and tried to comfort us."

During the battle, George Knox remembered, "the slave-holders would
go down to the battlefield, and, when their side seemed to be successful,
you could hear them yell and order the slaves around." But the next day,
"as it seemed the Union troops were winning, they would come back and
say, 'Will you do so and so?' and were kind as could be to their slaves."
But the Federals' fortunes waxed and waned at Murfreesboro. In the
Union rear, Allensworth emerged from his hospital tent to find "riderless
horses running past," as Union soldiers "with and without guns were running into the hospital, many of them severely wounded." He reported
what he'd seen to the surgeon. "Let's get out," the surgeon replied, and
they both fled, leaving the wounded behind. Allensworth jumped atop a
stray cavalry horse, "turned his head toward Nashville," and kept riding
"until he reached that city."

In fact, the battle was beginning to look like a Union victory, for
though the Yankees had been driven back, General Philip H. Sheridan

arrived, deployed his men across the pike, and held the line against Bragg's assault, inflicting heavy casualties.

As the Rebels gave up hurling themselves against the Yankee line, Knox spotted a man "coming down the road on a horse, just as hard as he could ride. Someone asked him what the news was." He replied that Bragg's army was "moving on to Murfreesboro, and we have been defeated." "This news just suiting me," Knox went "from house to house to deliver it," slyly adding what a shame it was "that the Yankees had whipped us again."

On January 4, 1863, Bragg evacuated Murfreesboro and withdrew his forces to Shelbyville and Tullahoma. To George Arnold, however, watching the Yankees stagger into the abandoned Rebel encampment, all this did not look like much of a victory for either side. "Long lines of tired men passed through Guy's Gap on their way to pick up the dead from the battlefield." But Arnold and his family "were proud we had seen that much of the great battle" in the war that "was to give us freedom."

8

———◆———

"I Couldn't Leave"

Standing by Mistress • Rescuing Master • Valuables
Sabotage • Protectors

T HE FEATURE OF the slave South that most puzzled and disappointed the more idealistic Yankees was the diligence with which so many of the slaves they encountered protected and sustained their Rebel masters' plantations. Educated on the subject of slavery by abolitionist tracts and Harriet Beecher Stowe's *Uncle Tom's Cabin,* New Englanders especially expected slaves, if given half a chance, to turn on their masters and abandon their plantations. "One time the Yankees come and drunk the sweet milk," a slave recalled. "I'm gonna tell Marse Joe you drink all this milk," she scolded them. The soldiers began to berate her until one of them growled, "Let the damn fool alone. Here we are trying to free her, and she ain't got no sense."

BUT SOME SLAVES, especially house slaves, adhered to a deeply instilled servile code of honor. They had concluded from hard experience that they were less likely to be sold away from one another if their masters flourished. Pragmatic, and shrewd judges of the disposition of power, they calculated that if they abided by their masters and labored safely on their farms and plantations, they might ride out the war, whatever its outcome. "What I see'd of slavery," Oliver Bell said, "was a bad idea, I reckon. But everybody thought they master was the best in the land. Us didn't know no better. A man was growed plum green before he knew the whole world didn't belong to his old master."

Some had come to believe that if all that was theirs was their masters', then all that was their masters' was in some way theirs. "I remember when the Yankees come and took things," recalled Lee Randall of South Carolina. "I just fussed at them. I thought what was my white folks' things was mine too." When the Yankees took away "my old master's horse, my daddy went amongst them and got it back."

"I never can forget the day that Marse had to go," recalled Dave Walker. "When he told us goodbye, every slave on the place collected around him and cried, afraid he would never get back. We loved him, and the slaves stuck by him while he was away. The farming was carried on the best it could be with the cavalrymen taking and destroying." "Us had a hard time keeping things going," Walker's brother Edwin confirmed. "A heap of things give out that us couldn't replace and had to make-shift around." On farms where male slaves accompanied their masters into Confederate service, "us women folks and children had a hard time," said Emma Randolph, because even female house slaves "had to look after the stock and work in the fields."

"With but few exceptions," wrote Pharaoh Chesney, the slaves around Mecklenburg County, Virginia, "went about their work with greater diligence, and were more careful and industrious owing to the greater responsibilities placed upon them in their masters' absence." A mistress might "assume the duty of overseer and direct the farming affairs," but her slave's judgment "in executing the work was the secret of success," for he could cultivate and gather the crops unmolested, "when the owner would have run a great risk of his life even to be seen in the community."

If no slaves remained to look after things, explained John Love, "the plantations all grown up in weeds," and the "horses may be running wild again." In his portion of Alabama, most of the young slaves ran away to the Yankees. "The ones that stay are the oldest ones that was faithful, and these are the ones that kept the homes from being broken up, and the land all gone to waste. They is the ones that folks knows stood true to the trust the master put in them."

MANY FIELD HANDS were rooted in the earth they and their forebears had cleared and cultivated, investing their masters' crops with their own sweat and blood, if for no more reward than their masters' favor. Country people who had sustained themselves on so little and scrimped so much, slaves were horrified by the Yankees' sheer profligacy. Wylie Nealy "sure did hate to see the Yankees waste everything." "They went down to the milk room — it was built near a spring so as to keep the milk cool — and they filled up they canteens with fresh milk, drinked all they could hold and then poured the rest on the floor," Mary Ann Kitchens recalled. Nathan Best watched them "pull the plug out of a barrel of molasses and pour it out in the road." "They took two legs of the chickens and tore them apart and threw them down on the ground," Betty Curlett recalled, "leaving piles of them to waste."

"They sure was destructive," Minerva Evans agreed. "They come back and caught all Old Miss's geese and cut off their heads and throw them down. That sure did scandalize all of us to see them geese killed." "They ate up and wasted the rations," said Henry Nelson, "then humor up the black folks like they was in their favor when they was setting out wasting" whatever the slaves had "made to live on." "They tramped the wheat and oats and cotton down and turned the horses in on the corn," Wylie Nealy remembered. For many slaves, the Union Army left such devastation that they had little choice but to follow its line of march. After the Yankees "took all they could find and wasted a lot of it," recalled Ida Rigley, "the slaves put their beds and clothes up on the wagons and went off behind them."

SOME SLAVES DISPLAYED almost pathological loyalty. The Yankees entrusted a slave named Ben with some loot they had captured after a battle, including "five horses, five sacks of silverware, and five saddles." But Ben turned around and brought them to his master, whose farm had been plundered by Yankee raiders. "Uncle Ben didn't know what to do with it," Claiborne Moss recalled. Figuring that since the Yankees had taken all of his master's valuables, "Ben give it to him," and his master "took it." In December 1861, the *Charleston Mercury* ran this news item: "A Negro woman aged about 35 — a cook belonging to Mr. Wm. Stevenson — was burned to death in his residence, whither she had rashly returned to save some articles belonging to her mistress."

"Old Master, he went off to the war with a whole passel of soldiers, and he been gone a long time," recalled an Alabama slave named Jane. Nobody was left "to look after the plantation, except Mistress and Uncle Jude, what was Old Master's first slave he ever had. Old Master and Uncle Jude was borned the same day, and Old Master's pappy give Uncle Jude to him, whenst they was little bitsy ones." Uncle Jude worked his fellow slaves "harder than Old Marse did, to make corn, and oats, and fodder, and meat for the soldiers" of the Confederate Army.

THOUGH FORMER SLAVEHOLDERS would comfort themselves with fond memories of the loyalty of their "Old-Time Negroes," many slaves had no choice but to abide. In large parts of the South, turning on one's owner and running away was at least as risky as it had been before the war. The chances of capture lessened somewhat, and potential havens proliferated in the occupied South, but the punishments runaways risked became ever more dire: severe whippings and even wholesale executions, meted out by Home Guards, guerrillas, soldiers, patrollers, and masters who — convinced slavery was doomed, and outraged by what they considered their slaves' growing arrogance, disloyalty, and ingratitude — no longer valued or protected them.

In some parts of the South slave catching ceased because "all men who were fitted for such mean work found a better place for it on the field of battle among their comrades." But slaves were regarded as so vital to the Confederacy's success that not only masters but the Rebel army itself assigned patrols "to watch the slaves to prevent their escaping."

To weed out disloyal slaves, Confederates tried to trick them into betraying their Northern sympathies by dressing in captured Union uniforms. One such squad threatened a senior slave named Aunt Dice "with fire, steel, and ugly army pistols if she did not disclose to them the hiding place of some 'rebels' in the vicinity," wrote her interviewer. But she steadfastly refused, and when the disguised Rebels rode away with "a rousing cheer for Aunt Dice," she realized "that she had been under trial." She had indeed, for in some Confederate units it was considered sport to trick slaves into confiding that they wanted freedom and then shoot them down. "I remember when Wheeler's Cavalry come through," recalled Sarah Debro. "They was Confederates, but they was mean as the Yankees. They stole everything they could find" and killed "a pile of" slaves. "They come around checking," asking slaves "if we wanted to be free. If they say yes, then they shot them down, but if they say no, they let them alone. They took three of my uncles out in the woods and shot they faces off."

FEAR ALONE COULD not account for every slave's act of fidelity, however. A kind of chivalrous sympathy for their stranded mistresses also

played a part, as well as a determination to protect not only their masters'
families but their own. "During all the years of the war," recalled Jim
Polk Hightower of Sardis, Mississippi, "the farm was managed by the old
mistress and the head man among the slaves. Not a white man on the
plantation and but few in the settlement." But there were many slaves,
"and I must say to the credit of them that there was not an assault committed, to my knowledge, during the four years of the war."

"I couldn't leave," explained Prince Johnson of Mississippi, "because
the men folks all went to the war, and I had to stay and protect the
women folks." Lizzie Gibbs was her mistress Pat Henry's bodyguard all
during the war. When master Calvin Newsome rode away with his regiment, he ordered Jefferson's father "to look after the mistress, and Pappy
did," because "every one of the slaves loved my mistress, and they would
fight for her." After Newsome was killed, "my mistress never got over it"
and kept Lewis Jefferson in the house for her protection. "I slept right on
the floor in the corner of her room," he remembered, "and she had a big
bull dog that stayed in there with us, and nobody better not come about
us to hurt us."

A Yankee straggler in Troup County, Georgia, demanded a glass of
buttermilk from a Mistress Pullen and drank it dry. Then, drawing his revolver, he threatened to shoot her if she did not tell him where she had
hidden her valuables. But her slave Beverly stepped between them. "If
you have to shoot," he said, "shoot me, not my mistress." Shamed, the
soldier lowered his pistol and departed, but not until he had shattered
his glass on the ground. This "made Beverly so mad that if it had not
been for the restraining hand and kind words of his mistress, he would
have gone after the soldier."

"When the war come," Abraham Jones's master "left me to run the
grist-mill." One day a starving white woman turned up and asked Jones if
he would grind some oats for her children. "I ground the oats, and told
her, 'Old Mistress, I knows just how it is, and I'll be glad to give you a
peck of meal if you will use it.'" She said, "Of course I will!" Jones recalled with pride. "Just put it in with the oat meal, and I sure will appre-
ciate it."

Mistresses turned to their slaves to intercede with the Yankees on
their behalf. "Before the Yankees come, the white folks took all they
clothes and hung them in the cabins. They told the colored folks to tell
the Yankees that the clothes was theirs. They told us to tell them how
good they been to us, and that we liked to live with them." Rivana

Boynton's mistress instructed her in what to say to the Yankees. "Now you beg for us," she said. "If they ask you whether I've been good to you, you tell them, 'Yes.' If they ask you if we give you meat, you say, 'Yes,'" though in fact she never did give her field hands meat. But she did give some to Boynton and her other house slaves, so in obeying her mistress's instructions she didn't have to "tell a lie." "Our missus is good," she told the first batch of Yankee raiders to come through. "Don't you kill her! Don't you take our meat away from us! Don't you hurt her! Don't you burn her house down!" They backed off, but then a second wave of Yankees swept in who "never stopped for nothing. Their horses would jump the worn rail fences, and they come across fields and everything. They bound our missus upstairs so she couldn't go away." But as they began to pillage the farm's smoldering outbuildings, "we begged and begged for her" until they too let her go. "They took all the things that were buried: all the hams and everything they wanted. But they did not burn the house," Boynton proudly recalled, "and our missus was saved."

"Juno, this place is horrid," a Unionist North Carolinian mistress told her slave. "If you can make your way to the Yankees, do it. You see how poor we are, and how my children are compelled to suffer. Take this basket of eggs as a present to General Burnside from me, and tell him, If he can rescue a Union woman, for God's sake do it!" So Juno set off in a canoe down the Neuse River with her own children, determined to "come to the Yankees" encamped at New Bern. "A breeze came up, which rocked the canoe badly, and they rowed for the shallow water, where, however, the waves were higher." So Juno jumped out and, wading for twelve miles, kept the boat steady all the way to New Bern. Juno pleaded her mistress's case with the Yankees, insisting that she was not only a Unionist but kindly too. Years before, she told them, after one of Juno's children died, her Secessionist master "refused to assist in its burial," whereupon her mistress, "with her own fair, white hands, sawed out some boards, made a coffin, dug a grave and buried the little corpse." At last, "a boat's crew, going ashore for provisions, at the place where her mistress lived, rescued the woman and so relieved the heart of her faithful servant."

At the very beginning of the war, when the Confederate Army began to muster troops, "my master came right on the back porch and called my mother out and told her she was free, that he wasn't going in no war," recalled Julia Haney. "And he didn't go neither. She stayed with him till after Emancipation. She was as free as she could be, and he treated her

as nice as anybody could be treated. She had the keys to everything."
Mrs. Hardy Sellers of South Carolina "was awful good and the men just
looked after her and took care of her. Me or Maw stayed at the house
with her all the time, day and night. When anybody got sick, she sent
somebody to wait on them and went to see what they needed, and sometimes she had them brought up to the house and give them the medicine
herself."

WHERE MASTERS REMAINED at home, some slaves interceded to save
them from themselves. As Yankee troops approached his gate, an elderly
Texas slave owner ran for his gun. "When he come hustling down off the
gallery," recalled Liza Jones, "my daddy come running. He see'd Old
Master too mad to know what he doing. So, quicker than a chicken could
fly, he grab that gun and rassle it out of Old Master's hands. Then he push
Old Master in the smokehouse and lock the door" to keep "Old Master
out of trouble."

  "I remember one time the Yankees come by," Olin Williams remembered. "They just tore up things as fast as they could find them," and Williams "had to hide out Master so they couldn't find him, cause they sure
would have killed him." Charlie Tye Smith remembered that Union
troops "caught Old Marse Jim and made him pull off his boots and run
bare-footed through a cane brake" with half a bushel of potatoes tied
around his neck. "Then they made him put his boots back on, and carried
him down to the mill, and tied him to the water post. They were getting
ready to break his neck" when a slave named Peter Smith begged them
to "let me die with Old Marse!" Shamed, the Yankees "let Old Marse
loose and left."

  Evelina Morgan of North Carolina remembered that "they took one
old boss man and hung him up in a tree across a drain of water — just
let his foot touch — and somebody cut him down after while. Those
white folks had to run away." "Old Master was at home," recalled Elizabeth Finley of North Carolina, when the Yankees "got off of their horses
and come in the house. They asked him where was his money, and he
wouldn't tell them; he say he didn't have no money. They took him upstairs and hang him up till he tell them where some of his money
was hid."

  When Sam Word's master refused to tell the Yankees where his money
was, "they tied his hands behind him and had a rope around his neck."
Word was "just a boy, and I was crying, cause I didn't want them to

hang Old Master." But then "a Yankee lieutenant come up and made them quit."

Yankee recruiters in Tennessee "picked a white fellow up and had him tied with a rope and carried him down to a creek and were tying him up by his thumbs," when he spied a slave named Bill Street approaching. "There's a colored man I know!" he shouted to his captors. Street confirmed that he knew the man, and assured the Yankees that he had never harbored bushwhackers. The Yankees released him, and long afterward, whenever he saw Street, he would say, "Bill, you sure did save my life."

As a small boy, Chaney Mack "heared a racket down the road that went: 'Shacky — shacky — shacky,'" and saw something coming. "The world has turn blue," Mack reported to his mother, "and is shining." His mother had been nursing her baby and her mistress's infant, but hurried to the door "and hung up a white strip of cloth that meant 'peace.'" Meanwhile her master "run up that ladder to the loft and dropped that door down quick. My mother grabbed the ladder and broke it up before them Yankees could get there and throwed it in the corner for fire wood."

The Yankees "asked my mama who she belong to. She told them she don't belong to nobody but herself." Then "what you doing with that white baby and that black baby?" they wanted to know. "This white child is my old Mistress's baby," she told them. "My old Mistress die when this baby was born. This black baby is mine and Tom's." Convincing them that she "didn't have no money," she cooked them "some hams and hoecakes," and they departed.

A squad of Union soldiers stopped at a plantation in Louisiana and "just laughed and talked" with its owner, John Williams. "But he didn't take the jokes any too good. Then they asked him could he dance, and he said, 'No,' and they told him to dance or make us dance. There he stood inside a big ring of them mens in blue clothes, with they brass buttons shining in the light," recalled Charlie Williams of Louisiana, "and he just stood and said nothing, and it look like he wasn't wanting to tell us to dance. So some of us young bucks just step up and say *we* was good dancers, and we start shuffling" while the rest of the slaves stood "pat."

SLAVES "WELL KNEW how little sympathy and respect" the Yankees had "for all things belonging to the Rebels, that they secreted everything capable of being hidden from the Yankees, and thus saved it for the family," said Pharaoh Chesney. "The corn and bacon were carried to caves, or cellars were dug in the side of the hill, the produce put in, and covered over with dirt and leaves until all danger had passed. The horses and cattle were haltered and driven off into some far-off thicket, and allowed to remain until the soldiers had passed on. Pens were built off in the woods and the hogs coaxed into them, to remain until the Yankees were gone."

Neal Upton's father hid his master's horses in the smokehouse and the hen house. When the Yankees turned up, a slow-witted slave named Jake tried to tell them where the horses were, "but he was trembling so, he couldn't talk plain. Old Master heared the fuss they made, and he come down to the kitchen to see what was the matter." When the Yankees ordered him to hand over his horses, "Master called Daddy and told him to get the horses." But Upton's father, imitating Jake, "played foolish-like and stalled around like he didn't have good sense. Them soldiers raved and fussed all night long about them horses," Upton remembered, "but they never thought about looking in the smokehouse and hen house for them, and about daybreak they left without taking nothing."

Levi Ashley of Atchafalaya, Louisiana, failed to save one of his master's prize mules. "Some of the soldiers got behind the mule to drive him through the gate, and as he came, a soldier standing on the side stuck his bayonet in him. I couldn't stand this no longer," recalled Ashley, "and I picked up a stick and whacked the man that struck Marse Dan's mule." Ashley was so angry, "I didn't know what I was doing." "Get away from here, you little black devil," cried the Yankee, "or I'll get you." But Ashley "whacked him again," whereupon "he slapped me right side of my head and knocked me down." Ashley ran into the house, yelling, "Miss Elvira, they done killed Marse Dan's big mule!" "Hush child," she told him. "They'll come in here and kill all of us." "In less than ten minutes they had the hide off that mule and had a fire made from the rail fence and was cooking that mule. We watched through the kitchen window" in horror, but Ashley had to confess that "that mule meat did smell good." After they left with the rest of his master's mules, "I went out there and got some of that meat, and it was so good that to this day, when I see a fat red mule, it makes my mouth water."

Della Briscoe's young master had a favorite horse he had trained to perform tricks. When the Yankees tried to take it from him, the boy refused to dismount. "As they were about to shoot the horse out from under him," Briscoe recalled, "the slaves began to plead. They explained that the boy was kind to everyone and devoted to animals, after which explanation he was allowed to keep his horse." Reverend Henry Clay

Moorman described how masters "would hide all their silverware and other articles of worth under the mattresses that were in the Negro cabins for safe keeping."

Even when Yankees caught on to such ploys, slaves were still able to fool them. Soon after Union troops invaded Pontotoc, Mississippi, they stormed into the cabin of a slave named Emmeline, who had just given birth. When they commanded her to get out of bed so they could look under her mattress, she saw an officer peering at her through a window. With an imploring look, she held up her baby, and the officer ordered his men to leave her be. "I sure was glad too," she said, for she "was lying on rolls and rolls of silver, gold, guns, and other things Miss Adeline Bell had hid under me."

Melissa Munson's fellow slaves saved their master's plantation house by flourishing his Masonic apron, at the sight of which the Yankee colonel, presumably a fellow Freemason, called off his arsonists. According to Johanna Isom, Jacob Thompson's slaves participated in a deception that saved the fortunes of not only their master but his neighbors. Thompson "sent word to the white folks for miles around to bring they silver to his house and put it in a big two-room house" he had built for his slaves, which "was big enough to hold four double beds." By the time the Yankees approached, one room "was full from floor to ceiling" with boxes of silver, and Thompson had posted elderly slave women to keen and wail "with a whole mess of childrens in the other room, with a curtain over the doorway and a sign reading, 'Small Pox in Here.'" When "the Yankees saw that sign, they cleared out."

William Brown's slaves picked up his "big box of treasures and carried it out in the forest and hid it under the trunk of a tree that had been marked. None of the Negroes ever told the Yankees where it was," and though "the war left him without some of the things which he used to have," because the slaves protected his valuables Brown "never suffered." Lewis Favor had to not only keep his mistress's $2,000 worth of gold and silver hidden, but dig it up periodically and spirit it off to her "so that she might count it."

In an almost slapstick act of sabotage, Pharaoh Chesney's fellow slaves confounded a pair of Yankee soldiers who came to his master's farm to steal his chickens. "One of them took a light and climbed up into the hen house," Chesney recalled, "and would hand down the chickens to the other man at the door, who would wring off their heads, and pitch them out into the yard. They would flutter out into the darkness," where one of his master's daughters "and several small Negro children were standing. One of these would pick up the chicken, hand it to another, this one would pass it to another, and so on, until one of them would carry it off and hide it. This continued until every chicken had been taken from the roost and killed." Then the Yankees emerged "to gather up their chickens and leave, but — Lo and behold! — not a chicken could be found." The Yankees "cursed and swore and ripped and tore, and threatened all kinds of vengeance against the children unless the chickens were produced. But old 'Aunt Lucy,'" who was the "mother of some of the children, put on a bold and defiant front and told them that she would break their heads if they dared to molest the children." After the soldiers departed, "there was a general cleaning of chickens, which were dressed and packed away for home use."

Some masters mistook their slaves' self-protective behavior for loyalty. When the Yankees reached David Ross's plantation in Putnam County, Georgia, they slapped a little slave girl named Della for shrieking an alarm that gave her master an opportunity to hide. Binding her father's hands behind him, they forced him to reveal the whereabouts of Ross's mules. After they had raided the smokehouse and departed, Ross emerged from his hiding place in a "cool well" and began to chide his slaves for giving away "my meat and mules." "Master, we were afraid," they replied. "We didn't want to do it, but we were afraid not to." "Yes, I understand that you could not help yourselves," Ross relented, and then he turned to the children. "Bless all of you," he said, "but to little Della, I owe my life" for warning him of the Yankees' approach. "From now on she shall never be whipped, and she shall have a home of her own for life." Sure enough, after the war was over, Ross gave her three acres of land, a house, and livestock. "Master thought I screamed to warn him," Della said, but "I was only frightened."

Yankee soldiers tricked slave children into betraying their masters' hiding places. "One of them put me up on his knee and asked me if I'd ever seen Master with any little bright, round shiny things," Anna Baker recalled. When the Yankee made a circle with his fingers the size of a silver dollar, Baker said, "Sure! Master drops them behind the mantelpiece." And they tore "that mantel down and get his money."

Some slaves, of course, cooperated fully with the Yankees. Mary Reynolds's fellow slaves led Yankee foragers to "a big pit in the ground, bigger than a big house. It has got wooden doors that lifts up, but the top am sodded and grass growing on it, so you couldn't tell it. In that pit is stock, horses, and cows and mules and money and chinaware and silver and a mess of stuff them soldiers takes." Celestia Avery remembered that her brother Percy took the Yankees "straight to the swamps" where his master had buried his treasure "and showed them where the money was hidden." "Old Master had his horses and mules hid down in the swamp," Wadley Clemons recollected, "but my uncle Tom went and got them and brung them to the Yankees at the big gate. He didn't had to do it," Clemons maintained. "He was just mean." Ever since the war began, he had hidden himself "off in the swamps most of the time." After handing over his master's livestock, Tom "went with them into Master's bedroom, and they just throwed Master's and Mistress's clothes all out of the closet and wardrobe, and he give them Mistress's gold earrings and bracelets, and they took the earrings and put them on the horses' ears and put the bracelets on the horses' ankles."

"NO VIOLENCE WAS DONE" by slaves, declared the barber James Thomas, even though the owners they protected "had shown them no mercy and had given the Negroes good reasons for retaliating." It was not as though "they knew no better. The Negroes knew as well what was going on as other people did." "We knew how we were treated," wrote Henry Adams, "but father told us that we must be good to them, work for them in the daytime and take care of them at night. Should you ask them today, they will tell you the same," and yet it still troubled Adams that "all this was done" when their masters' sons "were in the Rebel army." Nevertheless, said Ellen Brass, "the white folks ain't got no reason to mistreat the colored people. They need us all the time. They don't want no food unless we cooks it. They want us to do all their washing and ironing" and their "sweeping and cleaning and everything around their houses. We handle everything they wears and hands them everything they eat and drink. Ain't nobody can get closer to a white person than a colored person. If we'd have wanted to kill them," she said, "they'd have all done been dead."

The "coarse and profane" class of whites might call him names, James Thomas continued, and grant him "no right to standing room on God's blessed foot stool." But "while the Negro's superiors were trying to break up the best government on Earth, the Negro was caring for the defenseless."

Part IV

The East

1862

9

"This Child Just Pray"

Fort Pulaski • Susie King Taylor • The Peninsula Campaign
The Monitor and the Merrimac • Yorktown • Seven Days' Battle
Gaines' Mill • Fighting for Master

FORT PULASKI LAY on an island off the Georgia coast, guarding the mouth of the Savannah River. On April 10, 1862, Union artillery opened fire from the mainland with rifled cannons that made short work of what had been heretofore considered an impregnable bastion. "I remember what a roar and din the guns made," recalled Susie King Taylor, for whom the bombardment of Fort Pulaski was the beginning of a passage from slave to teacher and nurse.

Furtively taught how to read by a freedwoman, Taylor had heard and read "so much about the 'Yankees,' I was very anxious to see them. The whites would tell their colored people not to go to the Yankees, for they would harness them to carts and make them pull the carts around, in place of horses. I asked grandmother, one day, if this was true. She replied, 'Certainly not!' that the white people did not want slaves to go over to the Yankees, and told them these things to frighten them." "Don't you see those signs pasted about the streets?" she asked her granddaughter. "One reading, 'I am a rattlesnake; if you touch me I will strike!' Another reads, 'I am a wild-cat! Beware,' etc. These are warnings to the North; so don't mind what the white people say." Taylor was therefore eager "to see these wonderful 'Yankees'" who were "going to set all the slaves free."

The firing on Fort Pulaski "jarred the earth for miles," and when Yankee shells began to explode near the garrison's powder magazine, the Rebels ran up a white flag lest they be blown to smithereens. Union Major General David Hunter issued an order declaring that all the slaves in the vicinity were now free. Lincoln overruled Hunter's decree as beyond the power of a military commander, but not before hundreds of slaves had already escaped their masters.

Among these were Susie Taylor and her family. On April 24, she and about thirty other slaves climbed aboard the Union steamboat *Putumoka,* bound for nearby St. Simons Island. "Captain Whitmore, commanding the boat, asked me where I was from." She told him that she hailed from Savannah and could read and write. To test her, Whitmore "handed me a book and a pencil and told me to write my name and where I was from." When she had done so, he asked if she could sew as well. "And on hearing I could, he asked me to hem some napkins for him. He was surprised at my accomplishments," Taylor remembered, "for he said he did not know there were any Negroes in the South able to read or write."

That afternoon, "the captain spied a boat in the distance, and as it drew nearer, he noticed it had a white flag hoisted." But before the boat had reached the *Putumoka,* Whitmore ordered all of his passengers below decks, "so we could not be seen, for he thought they might be spies. The boat finally drew alongside," and a man whom Taylor recognized as Edward Donegall demanded that the captain turn over his two slaves, Nick and Judith. ("He wanted these," Taylor explained, "as they were his own children.") But the captain said "he knew nothing of them, which was true," for they had already been transported to St. Simons Island.

Taylor was asked to establish schools for the fugitive slaves' children, but Rebels still roamed the island, harassing and even kidnapping fugitive slaves, until about ninety armed runaways hunted them down and killed them.

IN THE SPRING of 1862, capturing Jefferson Davis's capital and defending his own remained Lincoln's chief objectives in the East. After the disaster at Bull Run, the President put his Federal Division of the Potomac into the hands of George Brinton McClellan, a dashing young officer who had slightly brightened the North's horizons a few days after Bull Run with a minor triumph in West Virginia. As the war sputtered and flared in the West, McClellan spent the fall and winter turning his battered and demoralized force into an enormous, formidable fighting machine.

ON MARCH 8, the Confederate ironclad *Virginia*, better known to posterity as the *Merrimac*, sailed out of Norfolk to Newport News, sank two Federal warships, and a day later fought the Union ironclad *Monitor* to a draw. Afraid the *Merrimac* would steam up the Potomac and reduce Washington to rubble, Lincoln and his secretary of war, Edwin M. Stanton, urged McClellan to give up his elaborate plan to advance on Richmond and proceed instead by boat to the peninsula that lay between the York and James rivers. But McClellan refused, and by April 4 had landed his forces and commenced his march on Richmond.

From the beginning he seemed loath to risk his splendid army. At his first encounter with Rebel troops, he laid siege where an attack by his overwhelming force would have promptly swept the Confederates from their lines. This gave Davis's chief military adviser, Robert E. Lee, time to reinforce the Rebels on the peninsula with most of the rest of his troops. They still didn't add up to more than 60,000, as against McClellan's 112,000. But McClellan fretfully overestimated the size of the Rebel force, and proceeded so cautiously that by the time he finally attacked, on May 3, the Confederates had formed a front in positions around Richmond that McClellan's delays had given them ample time to fortify.

Union gunboats steamed up the James only to be repulsed, and Confederate General Thomas "Stonewall" Jackson's sly maneuvering through the Shenandoah Valley prevented McClellan from receiving reinforcements from that quarter, which he insisted he required. Due in part to faulty maps of the area, and the need simultaneously to support a Federal advance from Fredericksburg and attack Richmond, the Union expedition found itself straddling the Chickahominy River. But poor coordination prevented the Rebels from taking advantage of McClellan's vulnerability, allowing him to move south of the Chickahominy, leaving only one corps across the river, under Fitz-John Porter.

ON MARCH 9, Henry Smith marched to Yorktown, Virginia, with his master's Texas cavalry brigade. "Old General McClellan was there," Smith recalled, "and he boasted that he gwine coop the Rebel Army up in what they call the Peninsula and mop them off the face of the Earth.

The river that they call the Chickahominy, it just bends around Richmond, but it about seven miles from the town. Well, us didn't get much done, and on the 5th of May the Texas Brigade was put in what the white gentlemens call the Post of Honor, but they weren't no post there; they just marched behind the real Army and took all the danger. They march that way all day, and the next day another command took their place at Williamsburg. After when the Southern soldiers had got quite a piece from Williamsburg, some of the Northern soldiers run into them, and a powerful fight was going on. But the Texas Brigade wasn't in that cause they was still in what they call the Peninsula," and on May 7 "they hurried to a place name Eltham's Landing" where "a lot of the Northern soldiers had got off their gunboats" to attack a Confederate supply line, "and there was a little shooting. But the Southern soldiers kept on retreating" from their line at Williamsburg, "and the Yanks couldn't stop them."

ON JUNE 1, Robert E. Lee took command of the newly dubbed Army of Northern Virginia from a badly wounded Joseph E. Johnston. Lee summoned Jackson from the Shenandoah and aimed him at Porter's isolated force. But Confederate General J.E.B. Stuart tipped McClellan off by recklessly circling the Union camp, and the Union commander deftly changed his army's position, setting the stage for what came to be known as the Seven Days' Battle. On June 26, Henry Smith and his master "could hear the cannon what the Southern boys was shooting at the Yanks on the other side of the Chickahominy from where us was. Marse Jim, he say that they was fighting at a place call Mechanicsville," in the second of the seven collisions that would end McClellan's Peninsula campaign. Listening to the roar, "this child just pray, 'Is I going to ever see my old Miss and my Mammy?' But they done told me to go along with Marse Jim and take care of him, and I's got to stay."

On June 27, Smith and his master were marching through the woods when they reached Gaines' Mill on Powhite Creek, and "a cannon ball come crashing through the trees, and hit the ground a few steps in front of our company. Our boys just marched on with their chins up," but Smith's "knees trembled so I almost fall." His master laughed and said, "Come on, big boy. Don't fall, now, or the damn Yanks'll cut you in two." "And us just waded right through the pond up above that mill, and us get up on high ground where us officers am waiting for us." By now Porter's corps had driven off several Confederate attacks, inflicting heavy casualties. But "about seven o'clock that night," the Rebels "all lined up to fight." His officers told Smith to stay behind, but if he obeyed their command, he asked himself, "how I going to look after Marse Jim?" So Smith armed himself with a straight razor and a club and joined the fray. "My God!" he exclaimed to his interviewer, "the blood sure run like a flood." But the Texans "just ran them Yanks across a little branch and chased them till they call us back," to celebrate a victory that for the time being had saved Richmond from the Yankees.

SMITH WAS NOT the only Rebel body servant to take up arms against the Union. Wherever a slave's ultimate loyalties might lie, Yankee shells menaced slave and master alike. At Brandy Station two of them would pick up discarded weapons and join in the Rebel charge, capturing a "Yankee Negro" and taking him back to the Confederate camp to be their servant. An armed slave belonging to Captain Thomas Buchanan of the 15th Tennessee Cavalry reportedly fought alongside his master. Ninety-one black Tennesseans and their families would apply for pensions for service in the Confederate cavalry.

"I fit, too," bragged Wiley Brewer of Mississippi. "I killed a thousand Yankees." His interviewer looked dubious, but he insisted "it's the truth. Some of them Yankees I shot, and some of them I drowned. Master always told me Yankees was the worst friends I had." "When the big war broke out," Isaac Stier recalled, "I sure stuck by my master. I fit the Yankees same as he did. I went in the battles along side of him and we both fit under Marse Robert E. Lee. I reckon everybody has heard about *him.*"

After the war, a slave named Luke would ask for a parole when his master, a Confederate colonel, surrendered to a Yankee officer in Columbia, Mississippi. "Luke, you don't need one," said his master. "You never been a soldier." "Yes, I has been a soldier — for four years," Luke replied. "Now you and that man don't want to do me that way." The Yankee officer declared that Luke "made more sense" than the colonel did, and gave him his parole.

10

"A Squally Time"

*Second Bull Run • Antietam • Hillary Watson in Sharpsburg
Toombs for Dinner • Potshots*

O N AUGUST 28, 1862, Stonewall Jackson lured John F. Pope's
Federal Army of Virginia into open battle by attacking a Union
column on a farm on the Warrenton Turnpike. The two sides fought
to a standstill. Apparently convinced that he had cornered Jackson,
Pope launched attacks on Jackson's line the next day that were costing both
sides dearly when James Longstreet arrived with Rebel reinforcements.

Two days later, Confederate artillery decimated Fitz-John Porter's
command, after which Longstreet sent 28,000 men charging the Union
line, crushing Pope's left flank in the largest simultaneous assault of the
war. Christopher Heard's Secessionist master was killed at what Northerners called the Second Battle of Bull Run. "My uncle Chris went to the
war with Marse Tom," Robert Heard recalled, "and he come back with
only one arm. He say the blood on some of them battle fields come up to
the top of his boots."

The Yankees managed to defend their line of retreat, thus preventing
a rout as pell-mell as the first Union flight from Bull Run the previous
summer. The Confederate victory was otherwise complete, and brought
the Army of Northern Virginia ever closer to the outskirts of Washington
itself.

REINSTATED AFTER POPE'S disaster at Second Bull Run, in September 1862, McClellan led his Army of the Potomac in pursuit of Lee's

Army of Northern Virginia. Buoyed by Stonewall Jackson's recent capture of the Federal arsenal at Harpers Ferry, and betting on McClellan's
cautiousness, Lee confronted the Yankees at Antietam Creek, not far
from the little crossroads town of Sharpsburg.

Early on September 15, David F. Otto's slave foreman watched from
his master's farm as "the Rebels come in here" until "the hill at our place
was covered with them," Hillary Watson remembered. "They'd walk
right into the house and say, 'Have you got anything to eat?' like they was
half starved. We'd hardly fix up for a couple when a lot more would come
in." Watson's mother, Nancy Lee, "was in the kitchen giving them bread
and bacon. They was great fellows for milk, too. Some sat down at table,
and some would just take a chunk of food in their hands. They ate us out
directly."

In Sharpsburg itself, the Rebels had also emptied the larder at
Delaney's Tavern. "The two armies was just feeling for one another," the
tavern's slave cook recalled. "The Rebels was keeping the Yankees back
while more of their men was crossing the Potomac." That evening, "a
young fellow come in and asked for something to eat." "We ain't got
nothing for our own selves," said the tavern keeper. "You soldiers have et
us all out." The soldier sulkily departed, but "it wasn't ten minutes before
the barn was afire. The men just had to get up on top of the house and
spread wet blankets all over the roof to keep the tavern from burning.
We couldn't save the barn. That burnt down to the ground, and the
chickens and everything in it was burnt up. Oh! It was an awful time."

That night, Hillary Watson returned from visiting his wife in
Sharpsburg to find "the Rebels was sleeping along the edge of the road
same as a lot of hogs might. I stumbled over some of them, but they
didn't say anything. Their guns was laid aside, and they didn't know they
had them, I reckon." The next morning, David Otto fled with his family,
leaving his slave Watson to look after the farm. Watson locked "the house
tight and walked up in the field." But he got the feeling he had better go
back, and found that "someone had broke a pane of glass in a window."
Watson searched the house and finally found a young Rebel looting upstairs. "You dirty hound, you!" Watson shouted. "I have a notion to take
you and throw you down those steps!" But the soldier saved Watson the
trouble, and the next day the Confederates posted a guard at the house
to prevent further pilfering.

Watson's master returned that evening to report that Robert Toombs,
who had by now resigned as Confederate secretary of state to become a

brigadier general in Lee's army, was coming to supper. "We fried some meat and made some biscuit," Watson recalled, "and the old general got his supper. But he didn't get no breakfast there. The firing commenced so strong on Wednesday morning that he had to hurry to his post." His brigade vastly outnumbered by Ambrose Burnside's Federals, Toombs would be severely wounded commanding his beleaguered men while trying to prevent Union reinforcements from crossing a vital stone bridge.

That same morning the tavern cook was serving breakfast to General Lee's staff when "a shell come right through the wall and busted and scattered brick and daubing all over everything. There was so much dirt you couldn't tell what was on the table. I was bringing in coffee from the kitchen and had a cup and saucer in my hand. I don't know where I put that coffee, but I throwed it away, and we all got out of there in a hurry."

Out on the street the cook encountered an elderly fellow slave carrying an iron pot on his head. "He said the Yankees had got the Rebels on the run, and there'd be fighting right in the town streets. He was going to get away, and he was carrying that pot so he'd have something to cook in." Rather than flee, the cook and her mistress set up housekeeping in the cellar. "We carried boards down there and spread carpets on them and took chairs down to set on. There was seven or eight of us, white and black, and we was all so scared we didn't know what we was doing half the time." They remained down cellar all day "while they was fighting backwards and forwards. My goodness alive! There was cannon and everything shooting." From the cellar she "could hear them plain enough. The cannon sounded just like thunder, and the small arms the same as pop-guns. Sometimes we'd run up and look out of a window to see what was happening, but we didn't do that often: not the way them guns was firing. Lord have mercy, man!"

Hillary Watson recalled that his master's family fled to a hiding place on a nearby hill, leaving their slave behind again. "The shells soon begun flying over the house and around here, and while I was out in the yard there was one that appeared like it went between our house and the next, and busted. I could see the blue blaze flying, and I jumped as high as your head, I reckon. I didn't like those shells flying, and I got on one of the horses and led some of the others and went off across the Potomac to the place of a man who was a friend of my boss." There Watson "stayed all day, listening to the cannon."

In the middle of the morning, the people of Sharpsburg were ordered out of town. The tavern keeper's household emerged from his cellar into bedlam. "There lay a horse with his whole backbone split wide open," recalled his cook. "The ambulances was coming into town, and the wounded men in them was hollering, 'O Lord! O Lord! O Lord!' Poor souls! And the blood was running down through the bottom of the wagons. Some of the houses was hospitals, and the doctors was cutting off people's legs and arms and throwing them out the door just like throwing out old sticks." The tavern keeper's party hadn't gone more than two doors down from the tavern "when a shell busted right over our heads. So we took back to the cellar in a hurry. The way they was shooting and going on we might have been killed before we was out of town. After they'd fit all day, and it got to be night, they ceased fighting and wasn't doing much shooting," so she and her owners "come up and got a little mouthful of food." Outside the house the Rebels were retreating, "and we heard them hollering." She asked one of them whether they had had a hard fight. "Yes, Aunty," he said as he rushed down the street, "the Yankees give us the devil, and they'll give us hell next."

"I went in the house and laid down, but I couldn't sleep none because I didn't know when they'd break in on me. O Lord, that was a squally time!" As the Rebels retreated early Thursday morning, "they run in every direction. You couldn't hardly tell what direction they wasn't running to get across the Potomac into Virginia." Having claimed more than 26,000 Union and Confederate casualties, the bloodiest battle in American history was over. But "we was afraid there would be more fighting, and we went out of the town directly and stayed with a farmer till the next day." The cook returned with her mistress on Friday, "and then we had everything to clean up. But we thanked the Lord we wasn't killed, and we didn't mind the dirt."

After listening all day to the two armies' artillery, Hillary Watson was riding back to his master's farm when he "began to see the Johnnies laying along the road, some wounded and some dead. Men was going over the fields gathering up the wounded, and they carried a good many to our barn, and they'd pulled unthreshed wheat from the mow and covered the floor for the wounded to lay on." Watson tried to get them to move on by warning them that the Yankees would catch them if they lingered. "But they said that was what they wanted; then they'd get a rest."

Climbing a nearby stone wall, Watson came upon a wounded Yankee. "I asked him when the Rebs left him." "Last night about twelve o'clock," he groaned. "They found me wounded, and I reckon they did the best they could, but that wasn't much. They didn't have much to do *with.*" "A week later," recalled Watson, "the wounded was moved off our place to a camp hospital, and the family come home. The house, as well as the barn, had been used as a hospital, and whatever had been left in it was gone. Besides, every bit of our hay and stuff had been taken to feed the army horses." Over the years, Watson would plow up "many a shell in our fields since the battle. You'd find them most anywheres. Often, I've broke them in two. There was balls inside, and brimstone and stuff," and "it's a wonder I wasn't killed."

JARED MAURICE ARTER, whose master had served as inspector of arms at Harpers Ferry, lived at a Virginia crossroads over which both armies swept in a tidal ebb and flow. After the Battle of Winchester in May, Jackson's raid on Harpers Ferry, and the battles of Antietam and Shepherdstown in September, he saw "the great Federal and Confederate armies marching along the highway, moving sometimes westward, sometimes eastward, sometimes deliberately, sometimes in hasty retreat." Twice in the course of the war his master's farm was caught "between the firing lines of the two armies," and for four years Arter "could scarcely venture to go to the spring, wood-pile or garden without being shot at."

11

◆━◆

"Ain't God the Captain?"

Joseph Lawson · *Fredericksburg* · *"Stonewall"*
Fannie Dawson · *Ghosts*

FTER ANTIETAM, Lincoln gave up all hope of the grandiose and fastidious George McClellan taking any decisive action against Lee, and replaced him as commander of the Army of the Potomac with a reluctant Ambrose Burnside. Lincoln expected the handsome, whiskered general to prove his mettle by crossing the Rappahannock and marching on Lee's Army of Northern Virginia while it was still divided. But delay compounded delay, giving Lee time to unite his forces near the town of Fredericksburg, Virginia, and destroy the bridges across the Rappahannock.

TO PROTECT HIS barrel-making business, a local freedman named Joseph Lawson decided to remain in town with his wife and four children. "There wasn't many who did that," he recalled. "As soon as the Yankees got here, the slaves begun to run away from their mistresses and masters by hundreds. You'd see them getting out of here same as a rabbit chased by a dog. Some carried little bundles tied up, but they couldn't tote much. Often one of the women would walk along carrying a child wrapped up in a blanket. Fifteen miles from here they got to the Potomac, and the Yankee gunboats would take them right to Washington. Then they'd pile in wherever they could get. They never come back this way."

Down the lane from Lawson's workshop, Lieutenant Colonel David

Lang's 8th Florida Regiment was picketed. When a local house slave named Fannie Dawson refused to allow any of Lang's soldiers to enter her master's house, her mistress scolded her. "Fannie," she said, "you ought not to be so hardhearted." "Well," Dawson replied, "I ain't gwine let them come in. I have a whole passel of children here, and those men are lousy. They'd be dropping their lice all around. Besides, the first thing they'd do, they'd pick up my two little children that are twins and want to take them out to camp." One day a Rebel asked her for a drink of water, but Fannie noticed that he had lesions on his neck. "You've got diphtheria," she told him. "I can't let you drink out of any of my cups." So the soldier "went along to the next house, and drank out of a cup there. Some of the family used it afterward," she recalled, "and two of the children died of diphtheria."

As Burnside's massive army approached the Rappahannock, an elderly Virginia slave who had lived through the War of 1812 exclaimed, "Well, I declare before God, there's the damn Britishers again!" Not only townspeople but "a good many of the Rebel soldiers stole off, too, so they could get into the Yankee lines," observed Joseph Lawson, "and not have to fight." But they might have fared better with Lee.

On the morning of December 13, 1862, Lawson was awakened by a distant rumble. "I thought it must be near about daybreak, so I got up and went to the barn and fed my horse. But what I'd heard was the Yankees fixing to come over here from the other side of the Rappahannock on pontoon bridges." Lieutenant Colonel Lang's Floridians joined a contingent of Mississippi snipers in firing on the Yankees as they tried to arch the river with a pontoon bridge. Taking positions in Fredericksburg itself, Lang's snipers "killed about seventy-five men who were making the pontoon bridges: swept them off clean as a whistle," at which point the Yankees began to shell the town. "I didn't get no warning and didn't know a thing of it till I saw people running. Some ran with their nightclothes on. They didn't have any time to play, I tell you. All that could, got out into the country and the woods was full of them: white and colored."

Judging by the continuous explosion of shells, Lawson figured there must have been "two hundred Yankee cannon over the river on the hills." The artillerists seemed able "to shoot the bombs and balls just where they wanted to. I know two people was killed dead in bed that morning: an old man and an old woman." A white innkeeper named Thomas F. Knox "got up when the signal gun fired and put on his clothes as quick as he could and got out of town on foot," and he was "hardly out of the house when a shell come in and split his pillow open."

Lawson's neighbors crowded into his house "when the shells begun to fly. We had the greatest quantity of women and children there," all of them seeking "plenty of company so if any of them got hurt, the others could help them." Suddenly a twelve-pound shot "come right through my house" and "cut one of the big house timbers plumb in two, and I never saw so much dirt flying around in my life. It took the end off the bureau just as clean as you could with a circular saw, and it left dust and everything else all over the room as if someone had been sowing seed."

The children "was not so scared as the grown folks because they didn't know the danger." But the adults were "just scared to death, all hands of them, and some was more uneasy about the children than they was about themselves. That was an awful day: *awful* day. But the firing stopped up some by noon, and we all come up and took a peep. I went out in the back yard where I could look and see the Yankees like bees on them heights across the river."

Burnside's notion of sound strategy was not to attack Lee's flanks but to charge where Lee least expected it: his center. Whether or not Lee expected this, he greatly appreciated it, for the center was where his line was strongest, well entrenched along a ridge called Marye's Heights. "*That* was a hot place," Lawson remembered. "The Yankees never had no chance to win there. They kept charging a stone wall at the foot of the Heights. But, Lord have mercy, they was all cut to pieces every time. Some got up to the wall so they could put their hands on it, but they couldn't get no further. That wall still stands, and when there comes a rain, they say the bloodstains show on it even yet."

When the fight "got cool," Lawson went out to the battlefield "and took a look around." The ground "appeared like somebody been *doing* something. It appeared awful bad. The dead was scattered around, and some looked like they was fast asleep. When a man had been hit by a shell that exploded, it bust him up in such little pieces you wouldn't have known he was ever the shape of a man. Out in front of the stone wall was the Yankees where they'd fallen one up on top of the other. A good many bodies was all laid in a row side of the stone wall with blankets over their faces." Lawson came upon the corpses of elderly "gray fellows" who had "had no business to be in the war at their age." The Federals suffered a total of 12,653 casualties, including 1,284 dead, as against 595 Rebels killed out of 5,309 casualties — the costliest battle in proportion to the forces engaged of any single battle of the war.

After the valiant survivors of Burnside's catastrophic assault fell back to their lines, the Floridians returned to retrieve their gear from their encampment. "Some of them was so smoked up" from gunpowder that Lawson couldn't tell "whether they was white men or black men. They was nasty and dirty, and their clothes was dreadful. If a Rebel wanted a good pair of pants or shoes, he had to shoot a Yankee to get them. Every Union man that was killed was stripped, and you often couldn't tell the Rebels in their borrowed clothing from the Northern soldiers."

STONEWALL JACKSON HAD tried to address this problem by ordering his men "to take off their pants and just have on drawers" so they could distinguish themselves from their foe. But "they wouldn't do it, and I don't blame them. They didn't have much to take off no-how, I reckon, and it was winter weather. Jackson's men didn't wear no shoes. Instead, they had on each foot a piece of leather tied up behind and before with leather strings." According to Lawson, "Old Stonewall was a terrible man. He didn't think anything" of marching his troops thirty miles in a night. "Do you know what kind of food he gave them? Three times a day each man got one raw ear of corn." He didn't even allow them "to stop marching to eat it, but gnawed and chewed it as they tramped along." Jackson may have been "a honey" of a general, concluded Lawson, but as a man he was "a plague."

INFORMED BY HER owners that the Union Army had been defeated, Fannie Dawson refused to believe it. "Ain't God the captain?" she cried. "He started this war, and He's right in front. He may stop in his career and let you rest up a little bit now," she warned her mistress, "but our Captain ain't never been beaten. Soon He'll start out again, and you'll hear the bugle blow, and He'll march on to victory."

Her master and mistress called her a fool to think so, but Fanny angrily pressed on. "You-all will be getting your pay sure for the way you've done treated us poor black folks," she told them. "We been killed up like dogs, and the stripes you've laid on us hurt just as bad as if our skin was white as snow. But I ain't gwine to run away or throw my children in the river as some slaves have," she declared, "for I'm as certain this war will set us free as that I stand here." Then she turned and glared at her master. "When I was a young girl," she said, "you sold ninety-six people at one time to pay a debt . . ."

But here Dawson faltered, collapsed onto a kitchen chair, and, as "the white people stood" and laughed at her, she began to sob. "Lord," she moaned, "I'd rather be dead than have my children sold away from me." By now her master had "sold my brother and three sisters down in Alabama," leaving Dawson entirely alone. Their new master had whipped her brother to death for preaching the gospel, and had not only abused her sister but used her oldest daughter "so bad it made her crazy." To console herself, Dawson turned to a passage from Scripture she had learned by rote. "Be not afraid" was how she remembered it, "you shall set under your own vine and fig tree."

"That means us slaves," she told her mistress, "and I tell you, we're going to be a free people."

FOR DECADES AFTER the Battle of Fredericksburg, local people would swear that the town was haunted by soldiers' ghosts. "About midnight," Fannie Dawson claimed, "a man in soldier's clothes was in the habit of riding a horse through the street back of the depot. People said they could see his buttons and everything, and that they could hear the horse's hoofs — ker-flop-up, ker-flop-up — just as plain as could be." Once during a revival meeting a young man "couldn't seem to get religion. So the old folks told him he sure would get religion if he'd go and pray in the woods away from the wickedness of the town." So he walked "way out toward the wilderness onto an old battlefield. Then he got down on his knees" and had just "started praying when something told him to look behind him. He looked, and there was a skull, and he got up and flew. He didn't try to get religion no more," Dawson said, "and he ain't got it yet!"

Part V

The West

1863

12

"I Rejoiced All I Could"

Tubman's Dream · Emancipation Proclamation
Spreading the News · Jubilee I · Contrabands · Joining Up
Buttons · Yankee Promises · Human Shields · Looting
Matrimony · Hardships · Retaliation · Pride

N OT LONG BEFORE the war, while the guest of a black New
York preacher named Henry Highland Garnet, the indomitable
Underground Railroad heroine Harriet Tubman awoke from a
dream crying, "My people are free! My people are free!" Singing
the words "in a sort of ecstasy," she joined her host for breakfast. "Oh,
Harriet, Harriet," groaned Garnet. "You've come to torment us before
the time. Do cease this noise! My grandchildren may see the day of the
emancipation of our people, but you and I will never see it." "I tell you,
sir," Tubman replied, "you'll see it, and you'll see it soon. My people are
free! My people are free."

ON JANUARY 1, 1863, Lincoln signed the Emancipation Proclamation,
"which made me and all the rest of my race free," wrote William Henry
Singleton. "We could not be bought and sold any more or whipped or
made to work without pay. We were not to be treated as things without
souls any more, but as human beings. Of course, I do not remember that
I thought it all out in this way when I learned what President Lincoln had
done. I am sure I did not." Lincoln did not believe he had the right or the
power as President to appropriate property the Supreme Court deemed
constitutionally protected, and as a political strategist he was loath to risk

alienating the precariously neutral slave states of Maryland, Delaware, Kentucky, and Missouri. So he applied his Proclamation only to the Confederacy's slaves. "Abraham Lincoln, that wily wretch," went a Rebel doggerel, "freed the slaves he couldn't ketch."

LINCOLN COULDN'T CATCH them yet, perhaps, but he could at least try to reach them with the news. "When the Emancipation Proclamation was signed, the plantation owners tried to keep the news from us," recalled George Washington Albright of Mississippi. "The Washington government, however, organized an underground information service to inform the slaves of their freedom. The slaves themselves had to carry the news to one another." This became Albright's "first job in the fight for the rights of my people: to tell the slaves that they were free, to keep them informed and in readiness to assist the Union armies whenever the opportunity came." At fifteen years of age, he "became a runner for what we called the 4-L's — Lincoln's Legal Loyal League. I traveled about the plantations within a certain range, and got together small meetings in the cabins to tell the slaves the great news. Some of these slaves in turn would find their way to still other plantations — and so the story spread. We had to work in dead secrecy," with "knocks and signs and passwords."

The more prescient masters who lived in neutral states where there was a significant Union Army presence recognized that by signing his Emancipation Proclamation, with its provision that slaves "of suitable condition will be received into the armed service of the United States," Lincoln had spelled the Confederacy's doom. Though the Proclamation did not apply to neutral Kentucky, a Nelson County planter named George M. Hays prepared to announce to his forty-two slaves that they were free. "One morning as the slaves were eating," Harry Smith recalled, "Master Hays came in and walked around the table very uneasy, and, bracing himself up in the best manner possible," spoke to his slaves as follows: "Men and women, hear me," he said. "I am about to tell you something I never expected to be obliged to tell you in my life. It is this: it becomes my duty to inform you, one and all — women, men and children, belonging to me — you are free to go where you please." But he could not refrain from adding that, if Lincoln were standing by him, "I would kill him for taking all you Negroes away from me." After Smith's master "had cooled off from this painful duty," he doled out whiskey to everybody, and "commenced a great jubilee among not only the slaves but Old Master, and all on the plantation seemed to join in the festivities." The slaves were "cheering Abraham Lincoln, while Old Master was too drunk to notice much." Hays "repaired to his room," and "his daughter, a fine young lady never known to drink, was much the worse for drinking. Old Aunt Bess, an old colored woman, and very religious," sang a number of "old time songs, which added very much to the celebration." They sang and danced all night, and Smith would apologize to his interviewer that he could not adequately describe "the rejoicing on this plantation and other places in the vicinity, on the announcement of the freedom of the slaves." "Bless the Lord," Aunt Bess exclaimed. "I'm glad the Lord has spared me to see this great day. My children are all free!"

"After the Proclamation was issued," recalled Elijah Henry Hopkins of Union-occupied Arkansas, "the government had agents who went all through the country" to see "how the Proclamation was being carried out." "You are free," they'd tell the blacks they encountered. "How are you working? What are you getting?" If someone replied, "I ain't getting nothing now," the agents "would take that up, and they would have that owner up before the government." "A Provost Judge followed the advance of the army," Anna Scott recalled, "and he obtained a list of all of the slaves held by each master. Mrs. Dove gave her list to the official, who called each slave by name and asked what that slave had done on the plantation." "You are free now and must be paid for all of the work you have done since the Proclamation was signed," the judge told them, as well as "all that you will do in the future. Don't you work for anybody without pay." Dellie Lewis said Lincoln had signed his Proclamation because "the Yankees just thought the South too rich and getting richer by having the slaves work for them, which of course, was wrong. As Mr. Lincoln said, 'All men should be equal.'"

AFTER LINCOLN ISSUED his Emancipation Proclamation, "and there was a great jubilee among the friends of the slaves," people kept asking Harriet Tubman why she didn't join in. "Oh," she answered, "I had my jubilee three years ago. I rejoiced all I could then; I can't rejoice no more."

Others could. In March 1863, a Union gunboat was slowly bumping along a Mississippi canal. The crew had brought a number of slaves on board along the way, and when a slave driver tried to lay claim to some of them, the captain facetiously instructed him "to get a written order from the admiral for them." At one plantation they were almost mobbed by jubilant slaves. One of the fugitive slaves on board "called to one of them," recalled an officer, "asking her if she would fight for freedom." "Yes," she answered, "bless the Lord, I's ready. Just take me along. See if I don't fight." "Not now," he replied, "but we'll all soon be free." "Glory to the good Lord," another called out. "Do take me along now," cried out the first woman, running along the bank. "I does hate to see you go without me. I's afraid never to see you again."

"Glory to the good Lord," shouted a heavyset woman as she tried to keep up. "Hold your tongue," scolded another slave. "How you know?" The woman answered, "Hasn't I done told you long ago that the Lord told me so?" "How you know was the Lord?" "Cause I see'd him," she said. "He's the same Lord that led the children of Israel through the fiery furnace and the Red Sea, and kept Daniel sure in the lion's den," she declaimed. "I told you long ago the Lord and the Abolitions done set the Darkies free. Glory to the good Lord." "And thus," concluded the officer, "we left her shouting." Even the most dour Yankee could be swept up in such joy.

A few days after being captured by the Yankees and pledging allegiance to the Union, William Robinson had the honor of liberating his own mother in Greenville, Tennessee, albeit with the support of a squad of Union troops. Her master had locked her in the house, and threatened to shoot William for beating on her door with an ax. But before her master could raise his gun, "dozens of muskets were aimed at *him.* By this time I had the door open, and there stood my mother" with her things all packed.

Loading her into a carriage, Robinson moved on to the next plantation to liberate his uncle Isaac. "The veranda was filled with men, women and children, singing, shouting, and praising God in the highest," Robinson recalled. His uncle "was soon by my side, picking me up and carrying me around, shouting at the top of his voice, while I was struggling to get down, and trying to drown his voice so I could tell him that he was free, and to pack up at once and go with us."

After the slaves had stripped their cabins of their few belongings, the Yankees beat down the door to the big house and invited them to carry off any of their master's possessions they pleased, and "'twas but a few minutes until the great place was gutted." Robinson would never forget the sight of slave children crowding around the wagons. "They were of all sizes and colors; they were black, dark brown, pumpkin colored, yellow and half white. And they were all crying with a different voice, giving different tunes to the song they were singing." A Contraband entertained the Yankees by singing: "Old Master drilled so hard, they called him captain, / But he got so dreadful tanned, / He's going down yonder amongst the Yankees / To pass for a Contraband."

"CONTRABAND" WAS a name applied to slaves who flocked to the Union lines, and derived from the notion that, like confiscated cotton or livestock, runaways with Rebel masters were contraband of war. It was said that Union General Ben Butler had invented the term by applying it to three runaways who turned up at Fortress Monroe in the spring of 1861. At first, however, Butler had refused to provide them with a haven. In May 1862, he returned a number of fugitives to their masters, some of them "in irons," while excluding others from his lines. But after Brigadier General John W. Phelps protested this policy on humanitarian grounds, Lincoln forbade Butler to return them to their owners or refuse them food and shelter. In any case, the term "Contraband" stuck, and it would remain in wide use over the course of the war — a kind of ironic indication of the confused status of runaway slaves.

"WHEN PRESIDENT LINCOLN issued his Proclamation freeing the Negroes," said Mary Crane, "I remember that my father and most all of the other younger slave men left the farm to join the Union army." There had already been a few black units formed beyond the notice of the federal government, and the navy had gotten the drop on the army by enlisting black sailors. But from August 1862, when the first African Americans were mustered into the Louisiana Native Guards, through the Emancipation Proclamation's call for Negro troops, to the Rebel surrender at Appomattox in April 1865, approximately 300,000 black men would serve in the Union Army. Of these, some 180,000 saw combat. More than 38,000 lost their lives, 2,870 of them in combat. Without them, the war might have been fatally prolonged, for they not only fought bravely in 449 engagements — some sixteen black soldiers and four black sailors won the Congressional Medal of Honor — but guarded prisoners and held down occupied towns. In 1864, they would thus enable General William Tecumseh Sherman to leave the Union's western strongholds in their keeping and embark with his veterans on his decisive campaigns in the East.

SLAVES WERE DAZZLED by their first encounters with black troops. "You ought to seen them big black bucks!" exclaimed Pinkey Howard of

Arkansas. "Their suits was so fine trimmed with them eagle buttons, and they was gold too. And their shoes shined so they hurt your eyes." "Was I afraid of the soldiers?" said Anna Woods of Mississippi. "No ma'am. I wasn't. I remember that they wore long-tailed coats." In Georgia, three or four black infantrymen approached George Lewis's mother and asked if she would cook them breakfast. "I never shall forget the look that came across my mother's face," Lewis recalled. When they were done, "they took money out of their pockets and paid my mother for her food for the trouble. These were *Negro* troops!"

"There was 450 colored and five white Yankee soldiers come and ask my father if old mistress treated us right. We told them we had good owners," Jane Osbrock recalled. "Them colored soldiers was so tall and so black and had red eyes. Oh yes, they had on the blue uniforms. Oh, we sure was afraid of them. You know them eyes." "Now uncle," they told a senior slave, "we want you to tell the truth. Does she feed you well?"

BUT SOME SLAVES took a more doubtful view of soldiering for the North. "Mamma said the Yankees told the Negroes that when they got them freed they'd give them a mule and a farm" just to "make them dissatisfied and to get more of them to join up with them, and they were dressed in pretty blue clothes and had nice horses and that made lots of the Negro men go with them." But none of them "ever got anything but what their white folks give them." William Sherman believed that slaves were fools to join the Union Army. "Those slaves who joined were trained about two days," he said, "and then sent to the front. Due to lack of training," he claimed, "they were soon killed."

Squires Jackson agreed. In a horse stable in Wellborn, Florida, he encountered "wounded colored soldiers stretched out on the filthy ground." A white soldier asked one of them to what regiment he belonged. He replied that he served in the now legendary 54th Massachusetts, which had been decimated in a courageous assault on Fort Wagner. "The sight of these wounded men and the feeble medical attention given them by the Federals was so repulsive" to Jackson, he decided not to join the Union Army. "In the silent hours of the evening, he stole away to Tallahassee, thoroughly convinced that war wasn't the place for him."

Susie King Taylor recalled the case of a black soldier who was unjustly treated. Robert DeFoe was among several soldiers of the 33rd U.S. Colored Infantry who had been captured by the Rebels while tapping some telegraph wires for the Union Army. "Confined in the jail at

Walterborough, South Carolina for about twenty months," he escaped as Sherman's troops were approaching and returned to his regiment. "He had not been paid, as he had refused the reduced pay offered by the government," but before the regiment reached camp, "where the pay-rolls could be made out, he sickened and died of small-pox, and was buried at Savannah, never having been paid one cent for nearly three years of service. He left no heirs," Taylor said, "and his account was never settled."

WILLIAM BALL WILLIAMS III "was away to Louisville to join the Yankees one day. I was scared to death all the time." Union soldiers "said they was fighting for us: for our freedom." But they "put us in front to shield themselves. Piles of us was killed. I wanted to quit, but they would catch us and shoot us if we left." Nor could Solomon Lambert recommend serving in the Union Army. He heard that when the Yankee line "begin to get slim" at Helena, Arkansas, "then they made the Darkies fill up and put them in front." "They put any colored man in the front where he would get killed first," recalled Liney Chambers of Memphis, while the Yankees "stayed sort of behind in the back lines. When they come along they try to get the colored men to go with them, and that's the way they got treated." But then that was also the way some servants got treated by their masters. "Young Master John went off to war and took my Uncle Robert with him," recalled Simon Hare. "Told him he was taking him to hold his horse. But, bless God!, when they got there, he put Uncle Robert out in front at the breastworks where he supposed to be his self."

WHEN IT CAME to looting, some slaves saw little difference between the Union Army's black and white troops. "While the war was going on, I remember one day, my mother was working in the field. Who should come riding up on beautiful horses but two black soldiers. Everybody said they was Yankees. They stop right where Ma was working and said they had come to get all our horses." Smith Simmons's mother had hid the horses, "but that didn't do no good. They got them just the same." As they rode off, his master's "flock of geese was crossing, and them soldiers shot every goose and left them there in the big road." Charlie Davenport heard stories about black troops "plundering some houses." At Pine Ridge, Mississippi, "they killed a white man named Rogillio. But the head Yankee soldiers in Natchez tried them for something or another and hanged them on a tree out near the Charity Hospital. They also strung up the ones what went to Mr. Sargent's door one night and shot him. All that hanging seemed to squelch a heap of lousy goings-on."

Having a husband or brother in the army often meant harsh treatment for his womenfolk. A slave who joined the Yankees worried that if he was unable to get home to control his sister, her defiant nature would get her killed. A Private Glover received word from his wife that her overseer had "most cruelly" whipped her with a buggy harness, while a soldier's widow reported that when her master discovered that her husband had enlisted, he whipped her, and then beat her again when he learned that he had been killed fighting for the North. Some masters simply refused to provide for the families of slaves who joined the Union Army.

THE NORTHERN MISSIONARIES who descended on the South tried to deal with what they saw as promiscuity and "unchastity" by arranging mass weddings of as many as seventy-five Contraband couples at a time. Many of them were already living together and regarded themselves, under the custom of slavery, as man and wife. But it was a law of the camp that men and women could not live together unless united in marriage. The chaplain made them promise to avoid "improper intimacy with any other till God shall separate you by death." They were each presented with wedding certificates "bearing a picture of the 'old flag,'" a visiting Englishman named James William Massie reported. Afterward the brides and grooms who were learning to read "begged the chaplain and others who went around to see their tablets to take some of the wedding cake for themselves and friends." "I done lived to waltz on the Citadel Green," exulted Harriet Gresham, "and march down the aisle of soldiers in blue, in the arms of my husband, and over my head the bayonets shined."

SOME BLACK SOLDIERS managed to bring their families into Union lines only to have them ejected by Yankee officers. Many Union soldiers believed that the presence of women was a source of pestilence and corruption, or expected their masters to provide for them, or took bribes from masters bent on retrieving their runaway slaves. "A mounted guard came to my tent and ordered my wife and children out of camp," Joseph Miller of the 124th U.S. Colored Infantry wrote from Camp Nelson in neutral but slaveholding Kentucky. "I told the man in charge of the guard that it would be the death of my boy," and that his "wife and children had no place to go." But the guard told his family that if they didn't climb into his wagon to be transported out of camp, "he would shoot the last one of them," whereupon his wife and children climbed into the wagon and were driven away. "The wind was blowing hard and cold, and, having had to leave much of our clothing when we left our master, my wife with her little one was poorly clad." They were taken to "an old meeting house belonging to the colored people" that had only one fire. "My wife and children could not get near the fire, because of the number of colored people huddled together by the soldiers." After acquiring a pass and walking six miles from camp, Miller found his wife and family "shivering with cold and famished," with the exception of his sickly son, who had expired "directly after getting down from the wagon, killed by exposure to the inclement weather." The next day, Miller went back to the meetinghouse and "dug a grave myself and buried my own child" before returning to his regiment.

Slaves witnessed the humiliations as well as the hardships to which black troops were subjected. Mistresses insulted them with impunity. "We kept a bucket of water on the front porch for drinking purposes, with a gourd in it as a substitute for a dipper," recalled a slaveholder named T. B. Swearingen. When a company of black troops "gathered about the bucket of water — some drinking, others waiting for their turn at the gourd — my sister Fannie stepped to the bucket, seized the gourd," and struck it against the wall, "breaking it to pieces to prevent the Negroes using it." Nashvillians openly cursed black troops in the streets. "I will die on the pavement," vowed one lady, before she would ask a black man "to let me pass." Not until black troops shot a white man for crossing a picket line did the citizens of Nashville begin to treat black troops with respect.

BUT SLAVES ALSO witnessed acts of retaliation by black troops that did their hearts good. A white officer of the 1st Kansas Colored Regiment asked a captive bushwhacker what he thought of black troops. "He said they were too damn stinking," the officer recalled. "In a moment he was dismounted and placed in the rear guard, between a file of 'stinking' soldiers, and marched about twenty miles, with one of the soldiers mounted upon his horse." That night, after a "drumhead" court-martial, "the butternut was given ten lashes and hooted out of camp." In September 1861, a former slave of Colonel William O. Brown was apparently "tickled to death" to have killed his master in the Battle of Boonville. "Master," a black soldier was overheard telling his former owner as he hustled him off to jail in Clarksville, Tennessee, "you put me in there two or three years ago. Now I put *you* in there, Master. Yah, yah, yah!"

FOR MOST SLAVES the sight and sound of black troops marching and cantering in formation was a source of inexpressible pride. "Put a United States uniform on his back," wrote an officer, "and the chattel is a man." "Where the Negro had been kicked around before," wrote James Thomas, "he was now lifted to the highest gift or elevation: his government's protector. Should a foot be lifted to give him a kick, he would reply, 'Dont touch these clothes,'" and "'Show the Eagles on his coat.'" To George Pretty's delight and astonishment, companies of black and white troops marched past him, all of them "manly and walking proudly." "My old mistress slapped me till my eye was red," recalled Anna Williamson, "cause one day I says, 'Ain't them men pretty?'"

Claude Augusta Wilson found Jacksonville, Florida, "full of colored soldiers, all armed with muskets. Horns and drums could be heard beating and blowing every morning and evening. The colored soldiers appeared to rule the town!" A Georgia slave named Eugene remembered black troops singing a song as they paraded by: "Don't you see the lightning? / Don't you hear the thunder? / It isn't the lightning, / It isn't the thunder, / It's the buttons on the Negro uniforms!" A Tennessee slave remembered hearing them sing, "Look up the road / And see the cloud arising. / Look like we're gonna have a storm. / Oh, no, you're mistaken / It's just the Darkies' bayonets / And the buttons on their uniforms." "O Slavery chain is broke at last," black troops in Virginia used to chant on their marches. "Praise God until I die."

13

"Ungodly Times"

*Murfreesboro · Knox Escapes · Fayetteville II · Vicksburg
Siege · Starvation · Port Hudson*

I
N EARLY 1863, the Confederates passed a new conscription act that removed the exemption for teachers, thus compelling the pedagogic W. C. Knox to abandon his schoolhouse and return to the 8th Tennessee Cavalry. But this time he brought his slave George along with him. W.C. was just a private, and Richmond had recently decreed that only officers could bring servants into camp. So W.C. had George wait on his wounded captain, James Madison Phillips. "I cooked and waited upon my master," George Knox remembered, "and Captain Phillips also."

After his chores were done, Knox used to "take a walk around camp to see what was going on. The Rebels at this time were very rough, swearing and cursing at every Negro they thought would be glad to leave them to go to the Yankees." One day they captured two slaves in the company of Union soldiers. "The Rebels were very rough to these fellows" until their captives convinced them that the Yankees had kidnapped them. But they later confided to Knox that they had indeed run away to a Yankee camp, where "they had a very good time, and that the Yankees were in favor of giving us our freedom. I asked them if they liked it well enough to go back again. They said the first chance they got," and soon thereafter they vanished. "Angry and abusive to those who did not go," the Rebels declared that they would never again spare a captured slave who "had once been with the Yankees."

By now George Knox was fed up with his master and the entire Confederate Army. The abuse of officers' slaves continued, but it was the small humiliations that wore him down. "If a Rebel soldier saw a colored man have on a good hat, and he had an old one, he would drive up and take it off his head, throw his old hat at him, and gallop away."

One night, after Yankee skirmishers raided his master's camp, Knox "saddled up my little filly" and made his way home through a driving rain. "Everybody had gone from the country except the women and children," and Knox remembered feeling "almost that the day of jubilee had come." He labored on W.C.'s farm for a month or so, but on observing a crowd of runaway slaves following in the wake of a Union column, he resolved to run to the Yankees. He hesitated at first because "a young lady for whom I had the greatest regard" begged him "not to go, and began to cry." Then his master turned up. Relieved to find his slave at home, but angry that he had gone off without permission, W.C. announced that he intended to take George back with him into Rebel service. Though George "insisted I did not want to go," W.C. declared he must, otherwise "the Union army would come and take me."

By now George had decided, however, that the time had come for him to break free of W.C. Pretending to prepare for their journey together, George slipped off into the countryside, and after a lonely week in a dank hillside declivity crawling with snakes, he was joined by three other slaves, including his brother, Charlie. Braving John Hunt Morgan's Rebel cavalry, they made their way together through the Union lines at Murfreesboro, where Brigadier General George D. Wagner gave them odd jobs about the camp. W.C. had filled George's ears with tales of the Yankees' sending runaway slaves to Cuba, and now a couple of Hoosiers seemed determined to confirm his worst fears. "*There's* a big fellow up there," one soldier said, pointing to one of Knox's comrades and guessing aloud that he "could get $2,000 for him in Cuba." Nearby, another soldier kept striking the ground with a bullwhip, "as though he would strike at some one." Passing Charlie, Knox whispered, "It seems that our master's words are about to come true." Though he soon realized that it was "all for mischief," nevertheless he and his friends found themselves "in the midst of strangers, all new faces to us." "This is hell isn't it?" he asked Charlie. "It is," agreed his brother. But Knox tried to convince himself that now that they had "made our bed hard, we would lay on it, and never go back until we were taken or times were better."

Times did not improve that summer. Knox got a job as a teamster, but the oldest of his fellow runaways died, and his brother sickened and had to be carried to the hospital. Knox "waited on him the best I could," for "the nurses there did not take very good care of him." At one point he encountered an elderly black man lying beside a young runaway. The old man told Knox that it had taken them two weeks to realize that they were father and son, for they had not laid eyes on each other since the day twenty years before when their master had separated them. The encounter only added to Knox's sense of foreboding, and the next day his gloom deepened immeasurably when Charlie died. "My heart was filled with grief," Knox remembered. "The only brother I had, dead and gone from me."

THE LITTLE OZARKS hamlet of Fayetteville, Arkansas, "suffered all through the war," Adeline Blakeley recalled. "You see we were not very far from the dividing line, and both armies were about here a lot. The Federals were in charge most of the time. They had a Post here, set up breast works and fortified the square." It seemed to her strange "that there wasn't more real fighting about here. There were several battles, but they were more like skirmishes: just a few men killed each time. They were terrible just the same."

Even the local children had been "taught to listen for bugle calls and know what they meant and how to act when we heard them." On April 18, 1863, Blakeley was looking forward to "peas for dinner, with ham hock and corn bread. I was hungry that day, and everything smelled so good. But just as the peas were out of the pot and in a dish on the table, the signal came, 'To Arms.'" Confederate Brigadier General William Lewis Cabell had led his 1st Arkansas Cavalry against its Union counterpart, scattering the Yankees and opening up with two cannons from a position east of town.

As shells burst over Fayetteville's rooftops, Blakeley and her household "all ran for the cellar, leaving the food as it was. The cellar was dug out only a little way down," and rainwater had seeped in and "filled a pool in the middle," so the adults "placed a tub in the water" that "floated like a little boat" and put Blakeley and two white girls into it as "the grown folks clung to the damp sides of the cellar floor and wall."

After the worst of the bombing was over, the wife of a Northern officer turned up to search for the pistols her husband had left behind in his rush to the front. "She had tried to follow him, but the shots had frightened her. We called to her to come to the basement. She came, but in trying to climb up the slick sides she slid down and almost into our tub. She looked so funny with her big fat legs that I giggled. Mrs. Blakeley slapped me: one of the few times she struck me. I was glad she did," because "it didn't do to laugh at Northerners."

The Federals succeeded in chasing off the Rebels, costing Cabell seventy casualties. "It was night before the fighting was over. An old man who was in the basement with us went upstairs because he heard someone groan. Sure enough, a wounded man had dragged himself to our door. He laid the man, almost fainting, down before the fireplace. It was all he could do. The man died. When we finally came up, there wasn't a pea, nor a bit of ham, not a crumb of cornbread," for stragglers had "cleaned the pot until it shone."

IN THE SPRING OF 1863, Ulysses S. Grant set his sights on the Rebel river bastion at Vicksburg, Mississippi, one of the last and certainly the most formidable obstacles to Yankee dominion over the Father of Waters.

Brandon Johnson had been sold downriver at the early age of five, but ascribed his defiant temperament to his Kentucky birth. He fought any man who tried to whip him, and spent so much of his bondage hiding out in the wilderness around Vicksburg that when the war began, his master "let me go down to Vicksburg Sundays" to work as a roustabout, hauling "cotton and the sugar on and off the boats." He was paid "forty cents an hour in Secesh money," plus an occasional bonus: "Any time a hogshead broke," he remembered, "you could eat all the sugar you wanted." He also took as much as he could carry back to his wife and four children.

As the Confederates strengthened Vicksburg's defenses against a Yankee attack, "every planter had to send so many hands to dig trenches. The officers would come and press you," Johnson remembered. "I was one of those that had to go. We camped a little outside of the town. They kept us working pretty hard digging pits and making forts. But I was a man then, and they couldn't hurt me with no work." By the time Grant began to move on Vicksburg, Johnson and his fellow slaves had dug trenches that stretched in a miles-long arc on the town's eastern, landward side.

According to a local slave named Litt Young, there may have been an invisible chink in Vicksburg's defenses. Young's cruel Secessionist mistress had "married a Dr. Gibbs," who was "a powerful man in Vicksburg." But not in his own home. "Before the war he'd tell Missy, 'Darling, you oughtn't whip them poor black folks so hard. They is going to be free like us someday.'" "Shut up," his wife would snap back. "Sometimes I believe you is a Yankee, anyway." A rumor circulated that Dr. Gibbs "was working for the North all the time of the war," and had secretly informed Grant how "the Confederates have a big camp there at Vicksburg and cut a big ditch on the edge of town." Though "Mistress didn't know it till after the War," Litt Young believed that Gibbs "was a Yankee," and "the occasion of Yanks taking advantage of Vicksburg like they done."

"Taking advantage" would prove a tall order, however. The previous winter had seen the failure of three massive Union Army efforts to cut and dredge its way to Vicksburg through Louisiana's treacherous and pestilential bayous, tangles, and swamps. Despite these setbacks, heavy losses from disease, disruptions in his supply lines, criticism in the Northern press, and opposition from his own generals, Grant devised a plan to send three of his corps on a drive south and east of Vicksburg and then attack with support from an armada of gunboats and transports under Rear Admiral David Dixon Porter.

The plan was fraught. Moving his corps below Vicksburg involved building a military road west of the Mississippi and getting Porter's fleet past Vicksburg's batteries in order to ferry Grant's troops across the river in transports — all while large detachments created far-flung diversions in an attempt to thin the town's garrison; harass its commander, Lieutenant General John C. Pemberton; and ultimately prevent a relief force under Joseph E. Johnston from coming to Vicksburg's aid.

Mose Evans "was just a little thing when the war was going on," but he did recollect standing in his mother's doorway and watching Grant's Yankees marching to Vicksburg. "I wasn't afraid of them; didn't have sense enough to be, I guess. Looked sort of pretty to me, dressed all in blue that way. And they was riding fine horses. Made a big noise, they did. They was riding by in a sort of sweeping gallop." Frank Fikes recalled that it took them "a whole day" to pass.

As Porter sneaked his fleet past Vicksburg's battlements in two stages, Litt Young joined the throng of slaves who went down to the river to see "the Yankee gunboats when they come to Vicksburg. They told us to get plumb away, because they didn't know which way they was going to shoot." As Pemberton tried to contend with the Union's feints, Porter began to ferry Grant's infantry from Hard Times, Louisiana, to Bruinsburg, Mississippi, a landing place Grant had chosen on the advice of a local slave. The Yankees seemed to proceed from strength to strength, defeating Pemberton's detachments at Port Gibson and Champion's Hill, and cutting off Johnston at Jackson. Champion's Hill was especially bloody. Ephraim Robinson of Hinds County, Mississippi, recalled seeing "soldiers in blue piled up, killed in enemy position, and so the same was true of the soldiers in gray." He helped load carts with the "arms and legs that army surgeons had removed at the hospitals in order to save lives," limbs that were "later buried by colored helpers."

On May 18, Grant approached Vicksburg's defenses with three corps. As Sherman positioned his men on the heights overlooking the Yazoo River, Grant's remaining corps attacked Vicksburg. "My Lord, that was some fight," recalled Virginia Harris, whose father "was right in the thick of it. He said when the two armies got close up, they stopped shooting and went to jabbing each other with their swords and sharp things on their guns." Despite Grant's past successes against Pemberton, the garrison repelled two assaults, inflicting many Union casualties. "The first battle lasts two days and nights, and they was about 800 men killed," as near as John Ogee could recall. "Some of them you could find the head and not the body." "Heaps of them was all tore to pieces," Isaac Stier remembered, "and crying to God to let them die." The Yankees, Virginia Harris declared, "sure paid for taking that town with many a soul."

Forced to conclude that Vicksburg could be taken only by siege, from May 22 to July 4 Grant subjected the town to a more or less continuous bombardment. Grant "blowed a horn," recalled Litt Young, "and them cannons began to shoot and just kept shooting." Brandon Johnson had remained in the slaves' camp at Fort Hill, digging entrenchments. "The Rebels kept us in that camp until they was ready to let us go, and it looked like they wanted to have us get killed. We couldn't leave the camp at night without striking a picket line, and them pickets would shoot the heart out of you." Yankee artillery threw "balls over this-a-way from the river through the courthouse steeple, and they'd throw them right into camp and get us running worse than dogs." Finally "the Yankees come and run us away" to a spot five miles from where Porter's mortar boats were anchored, belching shells into the town. Hiding out of sight along the riverbank, "we thought we was out of their reach, but we wasn't. They throwed those grape and canister just for a pastime. You could see the shells coming in the night red as blood, and we'd hide behind trees. If a shell bust where some people was, it would kill everybody around. Sometimes a solid shot would hit and cut off a tree, or it might cut off a big branch which would fall and kill the people down below. They fired solid balls bigger than your head."

The Rebels reciprocated with their guns, the most effective of which was an 18-pounder "up here on Fort Hill that the soldiers called 'Whistling Dick.' She growled when she fired, like she was going to eat you up." Whistling Dick "set up there keeping the Yankees back, and I didn't think they'd ever get her, but they did. They throwed a ball right plumb in her mouth," a steel-pointed projectile whose "front end was finished like an auger. When it struck anything," even "mighty thick iron, it would bore its way through."

Before the attack on Vicksburg, a diminutive escaped slave named Rose Russell had heeded the North's call for nurses. Behind the Union lines at Vicksburg she now "waded through blood and slime to carry wounded soldiers to a comfortable place to rest and die" as bullets fell around her feet like hailstones. One of them grazed her neck, leaving a scar she would carry for the rest of her life. Half a century later she could still "hear the faint and piteous cry of badly wounded soldiers." The only refuge Russell could find was a chicken house that was devoid of chickens, but not lice. "It took her a long time to grow up," wrote her biographer, "as she was bitten so by chicken mites."

The magnitude of the bombardment was unprecedented, and the boom and smoke of the guns at Vicksburg rolled up and down the Mississippi. Jack Island and his Arkansas master's son "was out in the yard making frog nesties with our bare feet in the sand" while a hundred miles away in Vicksburg "they was doing a whole lot of shooting. You could hear it one right after the other, and it got so smoky I thought it was thundering." He told his mistress it was going to rain. "But Old Missus say: 'O Lordy, that ain't thunder. I wish it was. That's guns and that what you sees is smoke and not clouds." Jack's daughter Talitha "heard my mother say it got so smoky the chickens didn't get off the roost while they was busting all them big cannons." Rina Brown of Monroe, Mississippi, some eighty miles from Vicksburg, recalled how "the glass in the windows would shake and rattle like a earthquake was coming." Some hundred miles away, in Marion, Louisiana, Tom Douglas's people "could not keep our dishes upon the table whenever they shot a bomb. Those bombs would jar the house so hard, and we could see the smoke that far."

Lewis Jefferson's Pike County mistress "would cover up her face and hide every time she heard that noise, and pray for the soldiers." The bombardment's effect on their owners terrified young slaves. Rebecca Phillips came upon her mistress "setting in her chair crying. I ain't never see'd Old Miss cry before. Them tears was worse to me than all that battle what was going on. My throat just started choking up. I didn't say nothing to her, but I went over and put my hand on hers. She look at me with her eyes still full of tears, and says, 'Child, you run now and play.'" But "there weren't no play left in my heart, and there weren't no power could make me leave her. So I says, 'Yes, ma'am!' But I didn't go nowhere."

For Glasgow Norwood of Simpson County, the siege "sounded all the time like the world was coming to an end." Added to the incessant barrage from Union batteries were the occasional explosions from the mines Grant's men tunneled under the Confederate lines. "Old Master and my father was both killed in the Vicksburg siege," recalled Peter Blewitt. "They was fighting down close to the river just before the battle was over." Robert Young's father told him that "blood run down the streets like water after a rain." One dark morning, some "Negro boys were sent to a run nearby to dip up water to make coffee for the soldiers," Tom Bones remembered, but when they returned to camp they discovered "that this water was blood from the battlefield." "In that town," recalled John Ogee, "was a well about 75 or 80 feet deep"; by the end of the siege it was filled with dead bodies.

Vicksburg's shopkeepers charged astronomical amounts for food, and those residents who sought shelter from the bombardment in the caves that perforated the bluffs above the city paid enormous rents. "Before the war," Isaac Stier remembered, "I never knowed what it was to go empty," but "the hungriest I ever been was at the Siege of Vicksburg. That was a time I'd like to forget. The folks ate up all the cats and dogs and then went to devouring the mules and horses." When they ate mule, "they give it the French name, 'Mule tongue cold, à la bray.'" George Brown of Marengo County was told that during this period "General Grant went up in a balloon and counted all the horses and mules they had in Vicksburg," to calculate how long its residents could hold out.

"Even the women and little children was starving," recalled Brown. "They stomachs was sticking to they backbones." Slaves were reduced to soaking "sweaty horse blankets" in the "mud holes where the horses tromped. Then us wrung them out in buckets and drunk that dirty water for pot-liquor. It tasted kind of salty," Stier remembered, but it was "strengthening," like a broth. "Folks wouldn't believe the truth," Stier contended, "if I was to tell all I knows about them ungodly times."

"That battle," said Harriet Walker, "it just didn't look like it would ever end." Though reduced to printing their editions on patches of wallpaper, Vicksburg's newspapers "would not give up hope. They say, 'The great General Grant intends to celebrate the Fourth of July'" by suppertime, "but he has to catch his rabbit before he cooks it." As it happened, Grant did catch his rabbit. According to Virginia Harris's recollection, Pemberton himself "walked out one day, and he say, 'Mr. Grant, do you reckon you is ever gonna see inside of Vicksburg?' Mr. Grant say, 'I don't know, but I sure is gonna try.' And that very night they took the city." "I tell you," Stier protested, "them Yankees took us by starvation. 'Twasn't a fair fight. They called it a victory and bragged about Vicksburg falling, but hungry folks ain't got no fight left in them. Us folks was starved into surrendering."

"When they said Vicksburg was captured," recalled Frank Larkin of Arkansas, "Old Master come out hollering and crying, and said they taken Vicksburg, and we was free." But after some six weeks of unremitting horror, many white Mississippians were relieved "when the capture of the city took place," insisted Henry Warfield of Copiah County, "as mothers who had sons still in the army knew that if the war continued, their sons would either be wounded or slaughtered. So they were glad to get over the worst day of all," just as the slaves "were glad to have the guns cease firing, as they didn't know yet what it meant to their freedom."

"After the fight," Young claimed, "the Yanks cut the buttons off the coats of them that was killed." For Edwin Walker the carnage at Vicksburg was "the worst sight I's ever see'd afore or since: everything tore up and dead folks all over creation. And it was the worst smell I's ever heard of: so much blood had been shed, and so many soldiers and horses killed." "It took three days to bury them" in the entrenchments that Brandon Johnson and his fellow slaves had excavated.

After Vicksburg's fall, the Yankees arrested the Unionist Dr. Gibbs's Secessionist wife "and brought her out to the farm and locked her up in the black folks' church. She had a guard day and night," Litt Young was pleased to recall. "They fed her hard-tack and water for three days before they turned her loose," and then only on condition that she free her slaves. In the meantime, however, her husband had taken his most able-bodied slaves away to buy feed corn, and then continued westward through Louisiana and into Texas, where they would remain for the rest of the war.

"As soon as Vicksburg went up," Brandon Johnson fetched his wife and four children and brought them into the city. "We wanted to be where we'd have the Union soldiers for protection. I put my family in the old Prentiss House, which was a big hotel with twenty or thirty rooms. More than three hundred black people was in there." But a smallpox epidemic ensued, and "they died like sheep, and we lost all our children but one." Johnson joined the Union Army and sent his wife money for the remainder of the war. But upon his return to Vicksburg, he found "the Prentiss House, where I'd left my wife, was gone. It was torn down in a hundred pieces. Some said my wife and child had gone up the river on an island. But I couldn't never find them or hear anything more of them."

When Cora Gillam's master had one of his frequent spells, it fell to her "to stand by his bed and scratch his head for him," for it "pacified him. It always made him sick to hear that freedom was coming closer. He just couldn't stand to hear about that." Gillam would always remember the day he died. "It was the fall of Vicksburg."

The slave name of Omelia Thomas's father had been George LeGrande. But after running to the Yankees in late 1862, he had dubbed himself George Grant, after the general. "He was shot in the hip" at Vicksburg. For the rest of his life "he still was having trouble with that wound." But he bore it as a badge of honor, and "many a day" he would remind Omelia that as a soldier in his namesake's army, he'd been "part of the cause that you are free."

WITH THE FALL of Vicksburg, Port Hudson became the last remaining impediment to Yankee hegemony over the Mississippi River. It sat on a bluff on the great stream's eastern bank, about twenty-five miles north of Baton Rouge. Admiral Farragut had fired on Port Hudson's batteries in March 1863 as he passed on his way to the siege of Vicksburg. And Union gunboats attacked again in May, silencing the port's guns. From late May to early July, the Army of the Gulf, under General Nathaniel Prentiss Banks, laid siege.

"The Yankees make it unpleasant," Louis Love recalled; so unpleasant that by the time the Rebels surrendered Port Hudson on July 9, its garrison had been reduced to eating rats. "The master come down" to St. Mary Parish on the Gulf "and order everybody to be ready to travel the next morning. They was about 300 peoples in the travel wagon. They camp that night at Camp Battery Fusilier, where the Confederates have a camp. They make only five miles that day and stopped the next night near Vermillionville," where Love's half-starved brother died. "Master bury him hisself," and "after the funeral they kept on travel. Before sundown they find a place side of a wood near town and make they camp," and "kept on that way till they come to Trinity River," where Love would remain as slave and freedman for the next five years.

14

⸺◆⸺

"Ain't Over Yet"

Adelia Wicker · Thomas Coles Escapes · Chickamauga
Chattanooga I · Knox Alone · Union Retreat

N 1862, CHATTANOOGA, TENNESSEE, "was only a steamboat landing," recalled a slave named Mathis: "full of ponds, bullfrogs, water moccasins, and everything else. It was just a village; and, if you got on top of a hill, you could count every house around in ten minutes." Only three or four houses "was of brick," Adelia Wicker remembered, "and a good many were little log cabins with whitewashed walls" arrayed around what she described as "a mud hole."

But this unlikely little town was the junction of railroad lines that ran from Memphis to Charleston, Nashville to Atlanta, and Knoxville to Virginia. It lay on a bend in the Tennessee River, some seventeen miles above where the northeast corner of Alabama and the northwest corner of Georgia met the Tennessee border. Surrounded by hills and ridges verging on mountains, the "Gateway to the Deep South," as its boosters dubbed it, had begun to loom as large in Lincoln's calculations as Richmond itself.

One summer night, Adelia Wicker's freedman uncle Amos returned home in the company of a short white man "with jet-black hair." Adelia and her sister stood and gaped as her mother served the white man supper, but he was so "anxious about his safety" that her staring unnerved him. "Who's that little girl?" he wanted to know. "I'm afraid of her. She watches me so tight." But her uncle assured their visitor that Adelia could be trusted, and after dinner he "took him out and put him in the corncrib and covered him up in the shucks. Uncle got him a gray suit," Wicker recalled, and in the wee hours of the following morning the stranger darted off to the depot and caught a train out of town.

The Yankees had apparently sent the little man to assess Chattanooga's defenses in preparation for Rosecrans's campaign to wrest this vital link from Rebel control. Despite repeated urgings from Washington to attack Chattanooga immediately, George Knox was told that Rosecrans delayed his departure from Murfreesboro in order to wait until the local "roasting ears and peaches" were ripe enough to feed his men during their arduous march into southeastern Tennessee.

ON SATURDAY, AUGUST 21, a Hoosier artillery battalion reached the opposite bank of the Tennessee and opened fire on the town. "The Yankees throwed in bombshells, log chains, and everything." Wicker "could see the chains twisting through the air like snakes. A piece of a bomb struck a white woman right above our house just after dark that evening and killed her." Uncle Amos told his wife to flee to a bluff "right in town on the edge of the river, and the women and children, black and white, all went there together and got under the rocks. A lot of them carried bedclothes, but no one did much sleeping. We had fires all along in front and kept them burning till morning."

Wicker moved with her uncle and aunt to a thirty-acre farm on nearby Missionary Ridge. On Friday, September 8, "the old folks took the wagon and the two horses and went into town" while Wicker and her two sisters remained behind. Convinced that Rosecrans was advancing on Chattanooga with overwhelming force, Bragg had ordered his troops to abandon the town and withdraw into Georgia. But some simply deserted. Soon after her family's departure, Wicker saw "four or five Rebels come running through the yard and smashed their guns against the trees and stumps."

GEORGE KNOX FOLLOWED Rosecrans's army with the wagon train. He had just driven his mules into the Sequatchie Valley, twenty miles west of Chattanooga, when the last of his fellow runaways announced that he was going home. "What's the matter with you?" Knox snapped. "You've lost your reason, haven't you?" But his friend refused to listen, and Knox angrily "told him to go, and, when he got back, to say he left me in

Sequatchie Valley, and that I am never coming back until the times are better, and I can be a freeman."

As his companion slipped off into the wilderness, Knox drove his wagon to the top of a hill. "No one ever knew how my heart was filled with sadness and loneliness," he wrote. "As I would think that I was the only one left out of four, I would look down the valley again while the tears began to roll down my cheeks." Things "can't always be thus," he tried to tell himself. "There is something better awaits me."

The wagon train continued on its perilous way, along the edge of precipices no more than a couple of feet wider than the length of their axles. "Just above us was about three or four hundred feet of rock or stone, and had we fallen we would have gone down amidst the panthers and wild cats." At last Knox reached the Tennessee River and was the first Union teamster to ferry his wagon into town.

Driving his mules down the main street, he entered what "seemed to be a deserted hotel," where he found "a lot of Rebel clothes. I selected a white coat with a blue collar, blue cuffs and brass buttons," and this became "my uniform." Foraging what food he could find, Knox could not figure out why the Rebels abandoned the town and began to suspect that Bragg had "moved out for the purpose of drawing us into a trap." In a matter of hours he heard "the roaring of cannon," and told his fellow wagoneers "that we were going to have a hard time, because the Rebels knew what they were doing when they vacated the place."

THE YANKEES IMMEDIATELY laid claim to Chattanooga, "and the first thing I knew," Adelia Wicker recalled, "their wagons was out in front, and the men tore down the fence and drove in our cornfield. They began to break off the ears and throw them into the wagons. Oh, they like to have scared me to death! The road was full of soldiers. They were all dressed in blue and covered with dust, and they had canteens and guns and bayonets. They did look scary!"

When a party of soldiers asked, "Where's your father?" Wicker "felt like I was having a chill. My tongue cleaved to the roof of my mouth. They were swearing at me and had me most dead, when a captain rode up to the gate." "What are you-all doing here scaring children?" he asked, and ordered his men "out of the yard and told them to go about their business." "Where are the Rebels?" he asked Wicker. "They're gone across the mountain," she replied, and informed him that her "old folks were in Chattanooga." "We've put out our picket lines," he told her, "and your people can't come back through them. It won't be safe for you to stay here. I'll take you to town." So Wicker and her two sisters "just left everything standing as it was," and the officer "carried my little baby sister on the horse in front of him" while Wicker and her other sister "walked right by the captain's stirrup," ahead of a line of wagons "loaded with corn." Wicker directed him to her uncle's place, where the captain "delivered us to the old folks." "Here's your children," he said, and her people "thanked him and thanked him."

THOMAS COLES WAS the slave of one Robert T. Coles, whose property lay just below the Tennessee line in Jackson County, Alabama. By 1863, his master was serving as adjutant in the 4th Alabama Infantry, while his overseer, Sanderson, held the fort back home. Cautioning Coles "not to go off the plantation too far," Sanderson allowed him to join a hunting party, thus giving Coles the opportunity he had long been waiting for: "to go to the free country where they ain't no slaves."

When the hunting party spread out, he and a friend "crosses the river and goes north." Sometimes he thought he heard bloodhounds trailing him, "and I gets in the big hurry. I's so tired I couldn't hardly move, but I gets in a trot. I's hoping and praying all the time I meets up with that Harriet Tubman woman," who "travels at night and hides out in the day." But she did not materialize. "I eats all the nuts and kills a few swamp rabbits and catches a few fish." He built a cooking fire at night, but to avoid detection, he hid half a mile away until it was "down to the coals." Nearly starved, Coles trembled "all the time, afraid I'd get catched." The North Star eventually led him to a thicket where he began to make out the sound of guns in the distance.

"I sure am scared this time: scared to come in and scared to go out, and while I's standing there, I hears two men say, 'Stick you hands up, boy. What you doing?'" "Uhhh," said Coles, "I don't know. You ain't gonna take me back to the plantation, is you?" The soldiers asked if he wanted to fight for the Union, and Coles "says I will, cause they talks like Northern men. Us walk night and day and gets in General Rosecrans's camp," where the general himself accused Coles of spying for the South. "They asks me all sorts of questions and says they'll whip me if I didn't tell them what I's spying about." But he insisted that he had come to fight the Rebels, and at last they decided to trust him, "and puts me to work helping with the cannons." Coles felt "important then," he remembered, though had he known "what was in front of me," he might have "run off again."

WITH ROSECRANS IN lumbering pursuit, Bragg made a U-turn in Georgia and veered northward, intending to defeat at least a portion of the Army of the Cumberland and thus force his adversary to abandon Chattanooga. When the two foes blindly converged along Chickamauga Creek, about sixteen meandering miles south of Chattanooga, Thomas Coles had just begun to help Rosecrans's artillerists place their cannons in strategic positions among the hills when "the first thing I knows — bang, bang, boom — things has started, and guns am shooting faster than you can think, and I looks round for the way to run. But them guns am shooting down the hill in front of me and shooting at me, and over me and on both sides of me."

Coles tried to dig himself a foxhole, but a cannoneer began "kicking me and wanting me to help him keep that cannon loaded. Man, I didn't want no cannon," Coles remembered, "but I has to help anyway. We fit till dark and the Rebels got more men than us, so General Rosecrans sends the message to General Woods to come help us out." When the messenger departed, "I sure wish it am me slipping off, but I didn't want to see no General Woods." Coles just wanted to go home. "I done told General Rosecrans I wants to fight the Rebels," but now "he wasn't just letting me do it, he was *making* me do it. I done got in there, and he wouldn't let me *out*."

The hill had become a hellish landscape across which men lay "wanting help, wanting water, with blood running out them and the top or sides of their heads gone." That night, as the firing eased off, Coles promised "the good Lord, if He just let me get out of that mess, I wouldn't run off no more. But I didn't know then He wasn't gwine let me out with just that battle. He gwine give me plenty more."

For the Battle of Chickamauga "ain't over yet." The next morning "the Rebels begins shooting and killing lots of our men, and General Woods ain't come. So General Rosecrans orders us to retreat," and as the Yankees withdrew, "the Rebels comes after us, shooting, and we runs off and leaves that cannon what I was with setting on the hill, and I didn't want that thing no-how." As General George Thomas earned his nickname, "the Rock of Chickamauga," by holding his embattled line, Coles and his comrades "kept hotfooting till we gets to Chattanooga."

LISTENING FROM HER uncle's house in town, Adelia Wicker and her people had heard the guns at Chickamauga eight miles off. The second day of the battle it had been "boom, boom, boom, boom from morning till night." Union ambulances rattled into Chattanooga "all the time, bringing the wounded, some with their arms broken, some with their legs shot off. Officers and soldiers was just piled in on top of each other. Some of them were moaning, and some were hollering, 'Lord, have mercy!' All the churches was full of the wounded," as well as many of the houses.

"One wounded man come to our house. A bullet had gone in one cheek and out the other, and it shot some of his teeth out, too. His tongue wasn't hit, but he couldn't talk very well: only just mumble a little bit. He told us he was starved to death almost, and I made some mush right quick. My little sister cried because she was sorry for him. He had to hold a handkerchief on each side of his face so the food wouldn't run out when he swallowed."

As Rosecrans's battered army swarmed into Chattanooga, Adelia saw a small black-haired man come "from the battlefield and lean up against our fence. He didn't have any gun, and he was dusty and wore out and all broke down. He asked for water," so she fetched him a drink, and only then did she realize he was "that spy!"

"GENERAL ROSECRANS RETURNED to Chattanooga claiming he had been wounded," but soon word circulated that the only wounds he had suffered had been to his confidence, pride, and will. Knox himself "did not understand what he had come back for. I said that I believed they were whipping us, and so it was. Not long before 12 o'clock I had orders to take my team and go down near the foot of Lookout Mountain" where the Yankees were bringing in their dead and wounded.

Soon General Thomas returned with his shattered force to report that the Rebels were right behind him. "The excitement was running very high," Knox recalled. "The soldiers were trying to get away" and "the bridges were crowded." "Our army there was completely defeated and demoralized," he remembered. "If the Rebels had known, they had but to move upon us." But the ever-cautious Bragg suspected a trap and called off the pursuit, thus failing to turn his costly victory at Chickamauga into the destruction of Rosecrans's entire command.

The Yankees scrambled to fortify their perilous position. "Houses were torn down to build breastworks," and Knox would always remember "a sad sight": a white woman who had rescued a rocking chair from the ruins of her house and was carrying it down the street "as though she had resolved if she never had anything else in the world she would have that rocking chair. She seemed to be so very sad: her house torn down over her head, and she turned out a wanderer."

Sadder still was the field hospital Knox would pass on his lumber-hauling rounds. "There we saw the limbs of the wounded soldiers being amputated and thrown to one side, as though they had been cut off so many cattle." To try to boost his men's morale, a discredited Rosecrans distributed diluted whiskey and rode around urging his men to hold out for twenty-four hours, to which they contemptuously replied that they would "hold out twice twenty-four hours," or as long as it took.

15

"Running from the War"

Refugeeing · Hiding Out · Fleeing South · Floods · For Texas
The Writing on the Wall · Selling Off Slaves · Kill Them First
Rescuing Kin · Fatal Journeys

IN PERHAPS THE MOST hapless and futile migration in American history, thousands of masters set off for the Deep South or the Far West to keep their slaves out of the liberating reach of the Union Army. The phenomenon became known as refugeeing, but at first slaveholders simply tried to hide their slaves from passing patrols in nearby forests and swamps.

"TIMES WERE SO HARD" for the slaves during the war, Elizabeth Hines remembered, because her "white master took them into the bottoms and hid them, so they wouldn't run off with the Yankee soldiers." Hattie Sugg of Calhoun County, Mississippi, remembered how "colored people come by in droves a quarter mile long and said they was going to the Mississippi bottom running from the Yankees. Old boss man and his family would be riding in the wagon" and let the slave children "ride with them, but the big ones had to walk." Jordan Lambert hid his slaves in the bottoms on the Arkansas side of the Mississippi River. "We carried provisions," Solomon Lambert remembered, "and they sent more along. We stay two or three days or a week when they hear a regiment or a scouting gang coming through. They would come one road and go back another road." Solomon was content to remain hidden. "We hear the guns," he said. "We didn't want to go down there. That was white man's war."

Komma Morris's master went so far as to "put up some cabins to live in and shelter the stock" in the bottoms, where "the cane was big as ma's wrist."

Other masters fled to the hills. "Folks around our settlement," recalled John F. Van Hook of Georgia, "put their Darkies on all their good mules and horses, and loaded them down with food and valuables, then sent them to the nearby mountains and caves to hide until the soldiers were gone." Jerry Eubanks's master and his neighbors gathered about three hundred slaves and took them up to a hiding place between Sand and Johns mountains.

SLAVES HAD A PARTICULAR horror of travel. In their experience, it had meant sale or flight: separation, death, oblivion. But as Yankees swarmed across the South, masters ventured farther and farther from home to find a safe haven for their slaves. George Thomas's master led the Yankees a merry chase. "Us refugeed from Mississippi to Mobile, then to Selma, then to Montgomery and from there to Uchie, near Columbus, Georgia." "After being sold, I first lived about three miles from Rome, Georgia," Jim Gillard recalled. "Then, when the Yankees come into Georgia, us refugeed first to Atlanta, then to Columbus and later to Salem."

Masters fled not only the Yankees but the Rebel press gangs that went from farm to farm, rounding up slaves to labor on Confederate works. Vincent Colyer, superintendent of refugees at New Bern, North Carolina, recalled two freedmen who had hidden in the woods rather than build Rebel fortifications. Tines Kendricks would have joined them if he could. Confederates had required all slave owners to provide slaves "to work digging the trenches and throwing up the breastworks and repairing the railroads what the Yankees done destroyed." Each master was to send one slave "for every ten he had." Kendricks "was one of them that Marse was required to send. That was the worst times" he ever saw, "and the way them white men drove the slaves, it was something awful. The strap, it was going from before day till way after night. Heaps of slaves just fall in they tracks — give out — and them white men laying the strap on their backs without ceasing."

In addition to conscription and Emancipation and war, floodwaters would chase slaveholders from their farms. The great deluge of 1862 washed away the lower Mississippi's badly neglected levees, forcing John Majors's master to flee the Tennessee bottoms for Oxford, Mississippi. The flood inundated the Baton Rouge sugar plantation of Filmore Ramsey's mistress, "and she took us all and everything she had and brought us back to Mississippi." But the flood carried Sally Dixon and her family out of northwestern Mississippi and up to freedom. "We went back to Mister Frank's place to get away from the overflow," she recalled. "We hadn't been there so very long when the Yankee soldiers came marching by, put us all in wagons, and carried us up" to Union-occupied Memphis. "They had a place for us to stay, and we was fed out of the commissary." Dixon's father joined the Union Army and served in the city "till the war was over."

Rather than risk encountering a stray Yankee patrol, some masters followed the Rebel army with their slaves. "Many slave owners left the county taking with them their slaves and followed the army," recalled a former slave named Adeline. "During the Civil War, Mr. Parks took all his slaves and all of his fine stock, horses and cattle and went South to Louisiana, following the Southern army for protection." The Confederates encouraged planters to move their slaves beyond the reach of the Union Army. "Every sound male black left for the enemy," wrote one Southern officer, "becomes a soldier whom we have afterward to fight." Seabe Tuttle's master was an officer whose family, slaves, and livestock followed the Confederate Army wherever it led.

"Ma's first owner what I heard her tell about was Master Ed McGehee in Virginia," recalled Mag Johnson. One day slave traders drove up in front of McGehee's yard and "hung around till he got ready and took off a gang of his own slaves with him. They knowed he was after selling them off when he left with them." But Yankee cavalry chased after them "and they got separated." Johnson's mother "hid in a cave two weeks and not much to eat," only to be reclaimed by the slave traders and sold to Ben Trotter of Somerville, Tennessee.

"We was running from the war," Charity Morris was told. She and her fellow slaves were refugeed during a cold winter, "and at night we would gather round a large campfire" and play such games as "Jack-in-the-bush" and "Ole gray mule." On their way from North Carolina to Arkansas, "we drove ox teams, jennie teams, donkey teams, mule teams and horse teams. We sure had a good time." They traveled on until they encountered what was apparently a Union outpost: a red house that to Morris and the others "represented freedom. The white folks wouldn't go that way because they hated to give us up. They turned and went the other way, but it was too late. The news come that Mr. Lincoln had signed the papers that made us all free, and there was some rejoicing, I tells you." Rosa Simons could "recollect when they took us and started to Texas and got as far as El Dorado," Arkansas, only to be told that Lincoln had freed the slaves.

TEXAS WAS THE likeliest destination, at least for masters from the Confederacy's western states. Conceived as a slaveholding nation independent of the United States, the Lone Star State was becoming the Confederacy's last hope of sustaining the Peculiar Institution. Some believed that if the South held out long enough, Lincoln might be persuaded to permit Texas alone to secede. Some entertained a "purple dream" of conquering Mexico and establishing a vast slaveholding empire stretching who-knew-how-far into Central America. But less visionary masters simply saw this vast region as a refuge, however temporary, from the Yankees.

"That was sure some trip when us come to Texas," recalled Jake Wilson. "Old Master had done been to Texas and traveled round through the state looking for a place to locate," and purchased "three hundred and twenty acres of land at what they call Whitehall," southwest of Waco. "There weren't no roads much, nor no bridges in Texas, and none to brag about back in the old states, cause the men folks, they gwine away to the war." On their way to Texas, "there was a big crowd of us along of the white folkses, the children and the slaves," bumping along in "covered wagons, loaded with bedding, clothes and some furniture, and they was pulled with oxes." Masters or slaves sat "on top and in the front seat. Then there was the Mistress's big carriage with the butler man and the driver." Some whites "had carriages and phaetons, or some such, too. The young white boys, they rode horses. Some of the oldest men slaves rode horses too and helped the overseer, Master White, to keep track of the cattle and such. There was boxes of chickens, geese, and pigs too. Us brung some plows and such too. Us children and young shavers made a picnic of the trip, but the older folkses always told me that it was sure a lot of worry all the way. Us would stop and hunt and fish during the hot part of the day, and the oxes and the cattle, they didn't travel none too fast no-how. It took us about three months to get to the place in McLennan County where us gwine locate."

Some of Wilson's master's neighbors "decided to come along because it was safer for a crowd to travel together in them unsettled times, when bushwhackers and runaway slaves and infamous scalawags" roamed the countryside. But no bushwhackers "come nigh enough to us on this trip to get no damage done" because his master had hired some of his former comrades to act as "scouts what ride ahead and watch. One of them had one leg, and the other had lost a arm. They'd been sent home on a furlough too, same as Master. Old Marse Ben J. said they wasn't no whole men in that bunch, but that they made up in grit for a few arms and legs." But such escorts served as guards as well as scouts. On her flight to Texas, Litt Young's mistress "had Irishmen guards, with rifles, to keep us from running away."

SLAVEHOLDERS ARGUED OVER what to do with their human chattel. The least resolute masters simply gave up. "We had started to Texas," recalled Parrish Washington of Arkansas, "but the Yankees got in ahead of us in the Saline bottoms, and we couldn't go no further. My boss had so much faith in his own folks, he wouldn't leave here till it was too late." So they all "come back to Jefferson County" to find that "the Yankees had done took Little Rock and come down to Pine Bluff." Sarah Gray's master heard that the Yankees were coming and "started to send us to Texas," only to learn it was a false alarm, "so we went back home." Hannah Allen's Sabula Hollow, Missouri, masters "started to take the slaves to Texas, but gave up in Rockport, Missouri."

Wiser masters read the writing on the wall. Anne Page's mistress "wanted to send us away to Texas, but Old Master say it weren't no use. Cause if the Yankees won," they would just "have to bring us back. So we didn't go." "When the Yankees were coming," Annette Milledge's Georgia master intended to send his slaves away to Edgefield. "He was a Yankee hisself, but he wanted to run us from the Yankees. Then he said he would wait till tomorrow, and send them next day," but by then "the whole place was covered with Yankees." Ultimately, however, such procrastination would make little difference.

"The war was getting hot then, and Old Master was in debt," recalled Mandy Johnson of Alabama. "Old Mistress had a brother named Big Marse Lewis. He wanted to take all us folks and sell us in New Orleans" to get them "out of debt. But old master wouldn't do it." Lewis took his brother-in-law's slaves to the "jail house in Bastrop." When Johnson's master got wind of this, he rushed into town to rescue them, but "Marse Lewis shot him down. I went to my master's burial," recalled Johnson, af-

ter which his widowed mistress wouldn't allow the traders to take her
slaves "to New Orleans either."

OTHER SLAVES WERE not so fortunate. "After old Mr. Jones left for
the war," Adeline Hodge recalled, the overseer and his black slave drivers "began to drive us round like droves of cattle. Every time they would
hear the Yankees were coming they would take us out in the woods
and hide us." When that wasn't enough, the Jones family decided to sell
their slaves. "They grabbed up all the little children that was too little to
walk and put us in wagons, and then the older folks had to walk. They
marched all day long, then at night they would strike camp." Hodge saw
young slaves "with their legs chained to a tree or the wagon wheels. They
would rake up straw and throw a quilt over it and lie that way all night,
while us children slept in the wagons." When they reached Demopolis,
Alabama, Rebels were withdrawing from the riverfront in steamboats.
"It was in Demopolis us were sold, and a man named Ned Collins of
Shubuta, Mississippi, bought me." But others "were sold to people in
Demopolis, Alabama; and Atlanta, Georgia; and some to folks in Meridian." The result was that even in old age Hodge "don't any more know
where my own folks went to then you does."

Dedonia Black's master brought her, her father and mother, and
two sisters, Martha and Ida, from Brownsville, Tennessee, to Memphis,
and from there by steamboat to De Valls Bluff, Arkansas, where they
were auctioned off on the riverfront. "They was all sold," recalled
Dedonia's daughter-in-law Beatrice. "Her father was sold and had to go
to Texas. Her mother was sold and had to go back to Tennessee, and the
girls all sold in Arkansas." "Old Man Menefee" refugeed fifteen-year-old
Henry Banner into Tennessee, near Knoxville, and "sold me down there
to a man named Jim Maddison. He carried me down in Virginia near
Lynchburg, and sold me to Jim Alec Wright. The last time I was sold, I
sold for $2,300" in Confederate money, Banner remembered, or about
$450 U.S. — which was "more than I'm worth now," he would remark in
1937. Before Henry Smith's master took him away to war, "he sold all the
slaves he could. But he get paid in Confederate money," Smith pointed
out, "and in the long run he lose most everything anyway."

When John Wells's master drove his slaves to Texas, "Uncle Tom and
his wife and Uncle Granville went too." But Granville had to leave his
wife behind because "she lived on another white man's farm. I never
see'd my father after the closing of the war. He had been refugeed to

Texas." "Our white folks took some of us clear out in Texas to keep the Yankees from getting them," recalled Henrietta Ralls. "Miss Liza was Miss Netta's daughter, and she was mean as her old daddy. She said, 'Oh, yes, you little devils? You thought you was gonna be free?'" Her brother tried "to swap a girl for me so I could be back here with my mammy, but Miss Liza wouldn't turn me loose. No sir, she wouldn't."

Matt Fields of Georgia owned Mary Crosby's mother and sent her "father and all the other men folks to Arkansas the second year of the war." "My mother's sister was refugeed back to Charlottesville, North Carolina, before the end of the war so that she wouldn't get free," Rachel Fairley remembered. "After the war they were set free out there," but they "never came back." A few masters spirited their slaves all the way to California, where they would find themselves stranded after the war. To earn her passage back home to Arkansas, Clara Walker would turn to prospecting. "Many's a day I've stood in water up to my waist panning gold. In them days they worked women just like men. I worked hard." And when Clara was "ready to come home, I bought my stage fare, and I carried $300 on me back to my old mother."

SOME SLAVES TOOK the opportunity refugeeing presented to escape. Samuel Hall, a foreman and slave, headed southeast from North Carolina with his master, William Wallace, searching for sanctuary in the Deep South. "But after he had traveled a day Hall came to himself and, getting up the next morning, hitched up his team of mules. When the man in charge of the refugees asked him what he was doing, he said, 'I ain't going another damned step south,'" and drove his team home. "All the colored folks of the community were invited in to make merry at the celebration in honor of Mr. Wallace's returned foreman," and "no one would have thought, to see him, that he had a single other thought than thoughts of gratitude toward his dear master." But along the way Hall had heard that "the Emancipation Proclamation had been issued just two days before," and soon afterward he ran away to the Union lines.

Myra Jones remembered how her master "come out in a big hurry and told us all to get some things together in no time: that he was gonna refugee us a way off somewheres. The first thing we knowed, we was off on that journey," but though "Marse managed to keep most of us," Jones's father, "along with some others, run away." "Marse put us all in boats and moved us up to Sabine Pass, Texas," recalled Henry Lewis McGaffey. "We settled on a farm and got four cattle, and all of us went to work." But after McGaffey's mother ran away, "Marse tried to find her but couldn't," and McGaffey "never knowed where she went."

A FEW SLAVEHOLDERS vowed that before they saw their slaves go free they would kill them. A pair of drunken slave owners named Gum and Alex Jordan "was all on the way to the woods where they had planned to do the killing," but according to Jim Threat, "Alex Jordan's gun went off and blowed the top of Gum's head off," and that "broke up the killing game." When a slave owner learned that one of his sons had been killed in the war, he "jumps up and starts cussing the war, and him picks up the hot poker," crying, "Free the slaves will they? I'll free the slaves!" He hit Annie Row's mother on the neck, "and she starts moaning and crying and drops to the floor." Then he "takes the gun off the rack and starts for the field." Row and her sister "sees that, and we starts running and scream- ing, cause we has brothers and sisters in the field. But the good Lord took a hand in that mess, and the master ain't gone far in the field when him drops all of a sudden," and died the next day.

Katie Rowe of Arkansas recalled how her master, a remote man who left his slaves entirely in the care of his overseer, galloped up to them in the fields one day late in the war. "You been seeing the Confederate sol- diers coming by here looking pretty raggedy and hurt and wore out," he said, "but that no sign they licked! Them Yankees ain't gwine get this far, but if they do, you all ain't gwine to get free by them, because I gwine free you before that. When they get here they gwine find you already free, because I gwine line you up on the bank of the Bois d'Arc Creek and free you with my shotgun!"

FREEDMEN DID WHAT they could to keep masters from refugeeing their enslaved kin. "In the fall of 1863, the slave-holders were running their slaves to Texas, either to sell them or prevent them from enlisting in the Federal army." William O'Neal had a brother who was included in this general exodus, and William wished to buy him in order to keep him from going. He thought he would have to pay about $5,000 for him, but to his surprise he was able to purchase him for $3,000 in Confederate money, or about $600 U.S.

Not that freedmen were safe from the vicissitudes of war. Bush- whackers took advantage of the anarchy that ensued to kidnap freedmen and try to sell them farther south. "The Fisher boys and the Vinson boys had been given their freedom," recalled Robert J. Cheatham. "They had worked in Indiana and several other states and had accumulated money enough to lease a farm" in Henderson County, Kentucky.

"My brother and I were reading and talking to Joe Fisher," recalled one of the Vinson brothers, "when somebody knocked at our door. When we opened the door, the storm was so bad we could only see a few feet outside the cabin. We told the stranger to come in out of the storm. He walked in, and we saw he was a white man. Soon there was another knock. We was scared to open the door again, and in a few minutes the door was battered against by a big piece of log, and the wooden bolt gave way. There was three of us, all without gun or any other weapons while the four white men were armed, so all we could do was to go with them. They took us to the trader's yard in Tennessee, where we were put up in a sort of barracks or slaves pen to be sold also." "Who will buy this young man?" the auctioneer called out. "He's as strong as an ox, healthy and smart. He is a left handed fiddler!" "Soon a purchaser came and bought me, then bought one of my brothers but sold him within a few hours. I never met either my brother nor my friend again."

Vinson's buyer "started out with a wagon train toward the South. We had only struck camp one night when my new master met a number of Union Soldiers." When the commander "of the Union encampment ordered his men into action," Vinson's purchaser "was scared almost to death and ran away as fast as his horse could run, leaving wagons, provisions and slaves to the Union Soldiers. We slaves joined the Union forces, and I fought until I received my honorable discharge and was a free man again," said Vinson.

THE HARDSHIPS OF refugeeing cost many slaves their lives. Milton Richie's sister "was down in the bottoms with all the slaves and cattle when she took sick and died suddenly." John Wells's mother "died on the way to Texas, close to the Arkansas line. She was confined," Wells remembered, "and the child died too." Senia Rassberry's mother would die in Texas "with a congestive chill." Emma Barr's mother "was run from the Yankees and had twins on the road. They died or was born dead, and she nearly died." "Mama died in Texas," recalled Jane Oliver, who had been conceived out of wedlock by a fellow slave. "They buried her the day they read the free papers." When Oliver crept in to see her mother and asked, "Mama, is you dying?" her mother replied, "No, I ain't. I died when you was a baby." "She was a Christian," explained Oliver. "She meant she had died in sin."

Masters also died on their desperate flights. Jeff Burgess's master fell dead en route to Texas trying to refugee his slaves. Millie Evans's North Carolina master packed up his wife, his daughter, and all his slaves and set off for Arkansas. But "while we was on our way," Evans recalled, "Old Master died, and three of the slaves died too. We buried the slaves there, but we camped while Old Master was carried back to North Carolina."

16

"A Drizzly Day"

Fleeing Georgia • Mathis • Chattanooga Cut Off • Foragers
Pine Bluff • Grant • Chattanooga II • Lookout Mountain
Missionary Ridge • Hospital Duty • Knoxville
Knox Flees to Indiana

AFTER THE LAST Yankee survivors of the Battle of Chickamauga limped back into Chattanooga, a slave named Mathis from neighboring Walker County, Georgia, resolved to run away. He worried about his wife, however, who was living on a neighboring farm in Pond Springs but had already been refugeed once. Her master had "nearly worked her to death, for she wasn't fiery or anything of that kind, and did what she was told to do without complaining. She fared so rough I didn't want her to refugee again. So before I left, I posted her to run away" if her master began to take his slaves farther south.

Mathis, his friend Moses, and two other slaves slipped off one night, taking nothing with them but the clothes on their backs and a couple of bowie knives some Rebels had left behind. The four young men "kept to the road until after sunup," when they came upon a white man named "Jack Spears out at the woodpile in front of his house. He knowed some of us, and he hollered, 'Hello! Boys! Where are you-all going?'" "To Chattanooga," Moses replied. "But the Yankees have got Chattanooga," said Spears. "Yes," Mose piped back, "that's why we're going there."

"Mose ought not to have said that," Mathis thought, and sure enough they soon made out "the sound of horses on the road coming in our direction: plockity, plockity; plockity, plockity." In the distance rode Jack

Spears in the company of five Rebel troopers. "We were on a hill at the edge of the woods, half a mile from the road, and the men never saw us but galloped on out of sight." But Mathis knew they'd turn around "before they reached the Yankee pickets" and scour the countryside, so the four runaways made a detour and burst out of the woods, only to find themselves standing on a portion of the battlefield at Chickamauga Creek.

"We didn't see a living soul there, but I declare it was something to look at. The dead bodies lay so thick we could have walked on them for half a mile. Big trees grew on the battlefield, and some that would measure three and a half feet through had been cut up into frazzles, and the bushes had all been mowed down by the bullets and shells. A *cyclone* never did do any worse harm than that."

When they finally reached Chattanooga, "Yankee officers told us we could join the army or go to work as laborers for the government." So Mathis took a job driving wagonloads of supplies from the depot to the Union camp. But all the while he studied "on going back to get my wife." One day about two weeks after reaching Chattanooga, Mathis buckled on "some pistols and a bowie knife," and spent the afternoon sitting in front of his tent with his fellow runaways, waiting for nightfall and working up the courage to sneak past the Yankee pickets and return to Georgia.

"I'm going back to where my wife is," he declared to his companions. "If they catch me, they'll kill me, but I'll never be taken alive," he vowed. "They can leave me a greasy spot on the ground before I'll let them capture me. Long as I can stand up, I intend to fight, and if I fall, I'll keep on fighting until I can't move!" But it never came to that, for no sooner had he ceased his blustering than his wife appeared before him with a bundle on her head.

His mild-mannered wife had done just as Mathis had directed. When her master decided to refugee everybody farther south, she had slipped off "to the house of an old granny lady that was crippled, and stayed overnight. An uncle by marriage and another neighbor man was getting ready to run away to Chattanooga," so she "bundled up and come with them." "I wouldn't have taken a thousand dollars for her coming," he said, "and saving me the trouble of making that trip." Rejoicing in their reunion, Mathis "drew a tent from the government, and then I went to work and made it equal to a house." He built a chimney "out of brickbats and mud, and I made a good fireplace, and we got pots and skillets so we could do the cooking." He used the tent as a roof, and "planked up the sides as high as my head" with wood from the empty crates that had accumulated from the stream of Union shipments into Chattanooga.

BRAGG'S CAVALRY SOON cut off that stream, however, as his army all but encircled Chattanooga. Mathis drove back and forth along the one remaining road, "hauling for the commissary." George Knox recalled that on their foraging rounds, "sometimes the mules would get so hungry they would cry like children." Even when the night was "so dark that we could not see our hands before us," they had to drive their teams across pontoon bridges and trails where one wrong step would cast them into the Tennessee. "When we reached camp we would give up all of the corn we had except enough to feed our mules." But food was "so scarce I have seen soldiers come up where the mules were feeding and ask for an ear of corn. I have seen horses and mules starve at the stake in Chattanooga." For six grueling weeks, Knox "was detailed to go hauling dead animals, mules, horses and cows that had starved to death" — as many as thirty-six a day. "They were dumped in the river, but the soldiers drank the water just the same."

For nine days, Mathis remembered, "we was cut off entirely from our food supplies. The soldiers got mighty mad about there being so little to eat. They were so near starved that they would pick up any little piece of hardtack they found in the mud of the streets." And yet, Mathis maintained, "it would have taken a pretty good twist to get those Yankees out of Chattanooga. They'd have died fighting before they'd have given the town up." "Let us have our way," Mathis heard them say, "and we'll whip the Rebels and get some food. We'd soon have sowbelly and hardtack."

Many Union soldiers were reduced to a diet of parched corn and water, but to Mathis "such food goes mighty well" when there's nothing else. "What I was aiming to say," he told his interviewer, "was that we fared pretty hard in Chattanooga for a while, but we didn't starve to death. That was where the Rebels was fooled again. We had to do some heavy fighting, but it was they who did the running afterward, and not us."

"FOOD GOT SCARCE," Adelia Wicker agreed. "Aunt would cook things and swap them to the Yankees for coffee. We didn't have no meal or corn, but we had rice, and we sent it to a little mill up the river and had it ground." Sometimes the soldiers traded hardtack for rice cakes. "I had good teeth," Wicker said, "and I could eat them, and they were nice if you put them in coffee or milk." The milk came from the family's "two big mooly cows." Among the Yankees with whom they bartered was the bruised and battered General James Blair Steedman, who had lost half of his division at Chickamauga. "General Steedman had a quart of milk a day from us, and we supplied him with fresh butter when we churned."

One night, some soldiers carried off the cow-pen fence for firewood and "broke into the shed and milked the cows." When Steedman "didn't get any milk the next morning," he "made the soldiers take an army wagon, haul lumber from a sawmill over on the river," and construct "a better fence than we had before." The looting continued, however, until all Adelia Wicker's family had left was a supply of meat her aunt had hidden. "The old woman had prepared for war in time of peace," and the family "had taken up some boards of the kitchen floor, dug down in the earth," and hid the meat under piles of ashes. "One day my aunt had me under the floor scratching for a ham" when General Steedman himself "pushed the door open and walked right in." "What have you got down there?" he asked. "Meat," Wicker's aunt answered. "I buried it to feed my children." "Well," said Steedman, "that's a nice Yankee trick. Let me have a ham, and you send your wagon up to my headquarters. You needn't be afraid of your children starving." So Uncle Amos drove his wagon up the street to Steedman's quarters, "and he gave us pickled beef and pork, cheese, crackers, sugar, and beans." When a Yankee soldier kicked Wicker's aunt for refusing him entry, Steedman "heard the screams, and come hisself. He told some soldiers to catch the fellow, and they carried him to camp and tied him up by his thumbs."

The harassment continued, however. "One time the soldiers got some skulls out on the battleground," Wicker recalled, "and they come to our house in the night with those skulls and set three or four of them on sticks and leaned them just against our door. Early in the morning, I opened the door, and the skulls fell into the house. I hollered and run, and Uncle Amos throwed the skulls outside. That tickled the soldiers. We could hear them laughing up in the camp. They didn't care for *anything*."

ON OCTOBER 25, 1863, Colonel Powell Clayton, commander of the Federal garrison at Pine Bluff, Arkansas, sent a cavalry company on a scout into nearby Dallas County, where his troopers promptly ran into a division of Confederates under Brigadier General John S. Marmaduke, who demanded their immediate surrender. "I remember," recalled a local slave named Dinah Perry, "when Marmaduke sent word he was gonna take breakfast with Clayton that morning." But the Yankees refused to surrender, and retreated instead into Pine Bluff, where escaped slaves quickly barricaded the courthouse square with cotton bales. "The Contrabands," Louis Lucas recalled, "were mostly slaves that they kept in camps just below Pine Bluff for their own protection." But on this day it would be the Contrabands who protected the army.

As the battle commenced, Cynthia Jones was out near Princeton, Arkansas, driving her mistress in a wagon. "When I heard them guns, I said we better go back. So I turned round and made them horses step so fast my dress tail stood out straight. I thought they was going to kill us all. And when we got home" her mistress exclaimed, "Cynthia, somebody come and broke all my windows!" But it was the roar of "them guns" that had shattered them.

Boston Blackwell was the freed manservant of a Union captain who "carried me down to the battle ground, and I stay there till the fighting was over. I was a soldier that day. I didn't shoot no gun nor cannon," he explained, but "carried water from the river for to put out the fire in the cotton bales what made the breastworks. Every time the Confederates shoot, the cotton, it come on fire." Failing to take Pine Bluff by force or fire, Marmaduke retired. During the battle, Dinah Perry's mother hid under the courthouse. As the Rebels retreated, they tried to carry Dinah off with them. "But the wagon was so full I didn't get in, and I was glad."

The following February, a correspondent for the *Waukesha Freedman* would write that having observed the Contrabands of Pine Bluff, he would never again doubt that slavery was crushed. "How can I," he said, "when right across the street is the office of the Superintendent of Freedmen, where one company a week is recruited for the war; where the accounts of two thousand freedmen and women are kept" so that their old masters can't cheat them?

"A Negro comes in, takes off his hat, and with a bow always commences, 'Master...'" But the captain tells him, "Put on that hat," "Stand up," "Don't call any man 'master,'" and asks him his name. "The Negro gives his name," and the captain informs him, "That name is to be yours hereafter." "The recorder takes it down and the Negro is enlisted as a soldier or hired out to some planter — the Negro always setting his own price on his labor."

ON OCTOBER 23, Ulysses S. Grant arrived at the besieged Yankee camp at Chattanooga via "the rough trail or wagon road around the mountain." While en route, he had replaced a badly rattled Rosecrans with the unshakable George Thomas. As commander of the newly created Division of the Mississippi, Grant set about shoring up the town's defenses and amassing a force of 72,000 men. Though hobbling along on crutches after a fall from his horse, he immediately infused the Union camp with his cut-to-the-chase determination.

Jefferson Davis had had the opposite effect on the already demoralized Army of the Tennessee by refusing to heed Bragg's senior officers' plea that he replace their morose and vacillating commander. Braggs's foremost critic was the able General James Longstreet, who commanded two divisions on loan from the Army of Northern Virginia. But Davis's idea of addressing Longstreet's complaints about Bragg's incompetence was to send Longstreet off to attack Ambrose Burnside's Army of the Ohio. With Longstreet's force more than a hundred miles away and Sherman approaching with four divisions, Grant saw his chance to attack the Rebel lines along the slopes of Missionary Ridge and Lookout Mountain.

After taking a long look at the Rebel positions east and west of Chattanooga, George Knox remarked to one of his fellow teamsters that he "did not believe that General Grant or any one else could whip the Rebels from the position they held." Soon afterward an order went out for all teamsters to "give up their teams and enter the army." Knox instead sought out the 15th Indiana Infantry and hired himself out as a servant to Captain John F. Monroe. Three days later, on November 23, "the whole army had orders to fall in, and the regimental colors were flying, and the music began to play."

IT "WAS A COLD, drizzly day," remembered Adelia Wicker, "and misty clouds hid the mountain." Thomas Coles joined the Yankees as they started their climb up Lookout Mountain, "and, when us gets three-fourths the way up, it am foggy, and you couldn't see no place. Everything wet and the rocks am slick, and they begins fighting. I expect some shoots their own men, cause you couldn't see nothing: just men running and the guns roaring. Finally them Rebels fled, and we gets on Lookout Mountain and takes it."

"As we went marching on, while the music played, and the balls whizzed around us," George Knox recalled, the Yankees "drove the Rebels out of the trenches; the shot and shell were flying thick." After sundown, "Grant had his army throw up breastworks for miles around." From her uncle's house in town, Wicker and her family "could hear the guns, but we couldn't see the soldiers. The shooting sounded like so many barrels of firecrackers, with once in a while the boom of a cannon." But when night fell, "the clouds rolled away, and we could see the campfires of both armies in two long lines that went from the valley to the mountain top, and between the campfire lines the men were still fighting." Wicker and her uncle stood and watched "the blinking lights" from their guns. "They were pretty to see."

By morning, Grant had posted his men "in every direction," which "alarmed the Rebels." And the Yankees. At noon, Knox took dinner to Captain Monroe, who "knew they had to go into battle at two o'clock," when the "whole army was to make a charge." So nervous "that he could not eat," Monroe had a premonition "that he would be killed before we could get up Missionary Ridge."

A LONG RANGE of hills led "away from Lookout Mountain, nearly to Missionary Ridge." To join in the attack, Thomas Coles and his comrades had to "come out the timber and run across a strip of opening up the hill." The Rebels "sure killed lots of our men when we runs across that opening," but "we runs for all we's worth and uses guns or anything. The Rebels turns and runs off" Missionary Ridge, "and our soldiers turns the cannons round what we's captured, and killed some of the Rebels with their own guns." Among the Rebels Coles fired on that day was his own master, Adjutant Robert T. Coles of the 4th Alabama Infantry.

George Knox watched from below as the Yankees "went over the breastworks and up the hill." General George Wagner led his brigade "up on horse back" to press the Rebel rear guard, "and of this fight we could see every movement, it was so plain." Lying in wait at the foot of the ridge, "we could hear the soldiers cheering as they were fighting," and when Joseph Hooker's men drove the Rebels back, Grant's entire army "raised a yell."

"LET US HAVE OUR WAY," the half-starved veterans of Chickamauga had grumbled to George Knox, and now it was they, and not Sherman's fresh reinforcements, who chased the Rebels up and over the ridge. "If you'd been here," said Adelia Wicker, "you'd have heard lots of old shouting in the town when the people knew that the soldiers had got through fighting on the mountain."

Knox and his Hoosier comrades "followed right on up" Missionary Ridge to join in the celebration. But as dusk approached and frost began to coat the ground, he came across Captain Monroe lying wounded in the woods. Knox and a companion carried Monroe "off on a stretcher," and returned to transport more wounded to a warming bonfire. "I heard one poor boy calling for his mother, but his voice became fainter and fainter" until "death put an end to his suffering." Flagging down an ambulance, Knox "took Captain Monroe back to the temporary hospital in Chattanooga," where the floor "was covered with wounded soldiers."

KNOX DEPLORED THE nurses who "would stop to write letters home to their friends and tell them the news. I wondered how they could write in the midst of all that suffering. The surgeon was busy removing bullets and waiting on the wounded soldiers. The house was cold," so Knox "would heat bricks" to warm the patients' feet. "The soldiers, not knowing my name, would call, 'O Darkie! O Darkie!' to designate me from the other nurses, who did not give them the attention I did." Knox learned how "to tell when one was going to die. He would begin to get deathly sick and vomit." The next morning his corpse would be "hauled out and thrown into the dead house," Knox recalled. "A man's life was not much in the army."

Not even a captain's. The doctor told Knox that he could do nothing for John F. Monroe. At his command, Knox raised him to a sitting position, "but Captain Monroe then asked me to lay him down," and "before I could do so, he died in my arms." Among those milling around the hospital was a man posing as a nurse who was "robbing the wounded and dead soldiers." When Knox collected Monroe's watch and money, the imposter offered "to help count the money. He said that there was about thirty dollars and to let him take care of it." But Knox refused, "and we came near having a fight over the Captain's dead body." In the end, Knox "gave the money to one of the men who was not wounded so bad."

AFTER HIS VICTORY at Chattanooga, Grant sent two divisions to Knoxville, where Longstreet had penned up Burnside and laid siege. But the weather was harsh, according to George Knox, "and many a soldier would march all day, only to die at night. In that part of the country, we could get nothing but buckwheat flour, which made the soldiers sick. For about three days and nights we had nothing but parched corn and not enough of that." Marching under the command of Major General John G. Parke, Knox passed "a great many dead horses, and it was a very hard matter to get water without getting it off of some dead animal." At the expedition's first camp, "I went to where I heard the water roaring and gurgling and filled my canteen for our evening coffee." But the next morning he discovered the decaying carcass of a horse lying in the current upstream. "This," he said, "was the kind of fresh water we had."

The only bright spot was the appearance of a young woman standing in a doorway as they marched past. She was "the prettiest sight our eyes had rested on for weeks," with her "white cuffs and collar and a white apron and a kind of dove-colored dress. The boys in front cheered and saluted her as an emblem of civilization. The enthusiasm and joy of the moment was contagious and was taken up by the whole moving mass of men."

By the time this "moving mass" approached Knoxville, Longstreet had abandoned his siege. The Union Army's goal now became preventing him from rejoining Lee in Virginia. After bivouacking for two sub-zero weeks by the Loudon River, General Parke's force marched to a village called Dandridge, where, Knox assumed, they could camp for the night. But Longstreet's forces were marching parallel to his pursuers, and now his men "began to throw shells at us," forcing Parke's division to withdraw.

Like Knox, Eliza Ann Taylor's husband drove his provision wagon across battlefields "no matter how those bullets and shots comed by him," and she believed "he had just as well been fighting in them battles, the way he said the shells and shots singed and hummed by his head in every direction."

WEARY OF WAR, George Knox returned to Chattanooga in February to take stock. "I was shut out from home and had no place to go. I began to talk around, and some of the boys said if they were me they would go North." So Knox accepted an offer from Captain Addison M. Dunn of the 57th Indiana Infantry to join his regiment on its veteran furlough to Indiana by way of Louisville, Kentucky.

They reached Louisville in March, but as Knox put Captain Dunn's carpetbag on his shoulder and stepped aboard the Ohio River ferry that was to transport them to Jefferson, Indiana, he "felt a crisis was upon us," for the other passengers began to snarl that they would kill the first black "they saw on Indiana soil." Before the ferry got under way, an officer "came aboard and said all the colored men would have to come off." Captain Dunn's only response was to tell Knox to hand him his carpet sack, and as the ferry shoved off, Knox and his black comrades found themselves stranded in the snows of slave Kentucky.

"There were men in the crowd old enough to be my father" who were "scared nearly to death" by the menacing whites they encountered on the streets. "I was scared as bad as any of them, but did not let on." Leading them to Union headquarters, Knox took his case to a general who heard him out and granted his party passes for the duration of the 57th's furlough. Within hours, they had boarded a boxcar on a train bound for Indianapolis.

As Knox disembarked the next morning, "everything seemed strange to me. The land seemed to be so level and most of the houses seemed to be so small." In the slave South "they always had one large house, where the white people lived, and around it were a lot of cabins where the colored people lived. So when I looked out and saw but one house, and that a small one, it seemed odd to me." Knox's master had told him how the war had broken up the North and its people, "but we found business going on the same as though there had been no war, and the women walking along the streets, wearing tall skyscraper bonnets."

Knox bought himself a suit and, in the little Hamilton County town of Boxley, rented a room from a white doctor named Isaac Collins. "His family treated me very fine," Knox recalled. "We'd been living on hard tack, and what was called sow belly, and beans, and when we went to Dr. Collins we had eggs, coffee, etc., and I was permitted to sit down to the table with the rest of the family. This was strange to me." Collins defended Knox against local whites who wanted to run him out of town, and when he came down with the measles, Mrs. Collins "treated me just as if I'd been one of the family."

But as their furlough ran out, the rest of Knox's fellow Contrabands declared "they were in a strange land, and they were going back South as they wanted to go home." Knox had no intention of returning to the army, the war, or the South, however. "I told them that I did not propose to go out of Heaven into Hell." But "Heaven" proved illusory. Over the next few years, Knox lived in constant dread as white mobs threatened to kill him, destroy his business, or at least run him out of the state. "I had gone through the army," he wrote, "passed through exciting times, had experienced the quick terror of the midnight whisper, 'The enemy is upon us.' But even on the battlefield of Missionary Ridge, that bloody spot, where men were being killed in platoons all around me, heads and legs torn off, cannon and Minié balls flying as thick as hail, at no time did I suffer in feelings" as he did contending with Northern racism. Determined to gain his neighbors' respect, he persevered, and would establish himself over the next six decades as the most successful barber in the country and as a civic booster, church leader, champion of black immigration to the North, confidant of Booker T. Washington, and editor of the influential *Indianapolis Freedman*. A canny Republican operative, three years before his death, in 1927, he would denounce the party of Lincoln for betraying black people and switch to the Democrats instead.

Part VI

The East

1863

17

——◆——

"All the Poor Soldiers"

*Chancellorsville • Death of Stonewall Jackson • Andrew Bradley
Carrying Master Home • Slave Rebellions • Defiance*

I N LATE APRIL 1863, Major General Joe Hooker set out with three
corps to cross the Rappahannock and the Rapidan and turn Lee's
left flank while two more Union corps kept the Confederates occupied at Fredericksburg. Running into ever-stiffer resistance, however,
Hooker hunkered down near Chancellorsville, where, on May 2, Stonewall Jackson attacked his left flank and destroyed one of his corps.

BUT BEFORE HIS triumphant day was over, Jackson was mortally
wounded by one of his own pickets while returning from a scout. "The
general had told them to shoot anybody going or coming across the line,"
said William Mack Lee. "And then the general hisself puts on a Federal
uniform and scouted across the lines. When he comes back, one of his
own soldiers raised his gun. 'Don't shoot. I'm your general,' Marse Jackson yelled," but William Lee was told that "the sentry was hard of hearing. Anyway, he shot his general," severely wounding him.

William Lee had never seen General Lee "sadder than that gloomy
morning when he told me about how General Stonewall Jackson had
been shot by his own men." "William," he said, "I have lost my right
arm." "How come you're to say that, Marse Robert?" William asked.
"You ain't been in no battle since yesterday, and I don't see your arm
bleeding." "I'm bleeding at the heart," Lee replied, and seeing that General Lee "wanted to be by hisself," his servant "slipped out of the tent."

After his arm was amputated, Jackson hung on for a week, but then infection set in, and pneumonia, and he died on May 10.

William Mack Lee bore scars on his hip and his head from wounds received at Chancellorsville. On May 3, while "Marse Robert was eating breakfast," William "went to get his horse — Old Traveller — for him to ride into battle." As he led Traveller toward headquarters, he "heard them jack-battery guns begin to pop and bust and roar. Just as Marse Robert came out the door, a shell hit about thirty yards away. It busted, and hit me, and I fell over. Marse Robert say he ain't never heard such hollering like I done! He had me patched up, but I hobbled round with a crutch long time." Lee would prevail that day, breaking the Federal line and ultimately chasing Hooker back across the Rappahannock. Chancellorsville was his most brilliant victory: an audacious tactical triumph over great odds that would breed in the Silver Fox a dangerous overconfidence.

BUT FOR ANDREW BRADLEY, the slave manservant of Private William Bradley of the 14th South Carolina Infantry, Chancellorsville was the beginning of a long and mournful journey. "Andy, your Master been wounded! Better go see about him!" Captain Edmund Cowan commanded, and Bradley rushed to the camp hospital, where for twelve days he remained by his master's side. On the last day, William entrusted Bradley with fifty dollars of his soldier's wages and, gripping his slave's hand, died of his wounds.

"All the poor soldiers dying," Bradley moaned, "and they bury them in Virginia: way off there." Bradley knew that his master's parents back in Abbeyville "and all the folks would be right powerful grieved to have him buried off up there. It wouldn't do," he decided. "I must get him back home." But "how do it?" When William asked a surgeon, "he just laugh. 'Carry him back? No sir.'" "Andy," another exclaimed, "you crazy! We going to bury him tomorrow. You couldn't get anywhere with him."

But Andrew was not to be dissuaded, and that night he furtively cut off a piece of William's uniform and one of his little fingers so he could later identify his corpse. "I told Lieutenant Truitt what I going to do. He say, 'You black devil, what you mean?' And he terrible upset, till I tell him, 'I just got to take my master back to South Carolina.' Couldn't bury him off like that. Lieutenant Truitt, he's a Abbeyville boy. He knows how it is. He calms down, and looks sad." "Andy," Truitt said, "maybe you can do it." So the two of them contrived to bribe a hospital guard with the fifty dollars Andrew's master had left him. "I heft Young Master on my shoulders, and Lieutenant Truitt help me, and we carry him out. Put him in the coffin-box we got waiting, and the boys help load it on the freight car what the train picks up before morning." "What he proposed to do was all but impossible," wrote his interviewer. It was 350 miles to Abbeyville, and against the law to transport bodies without military escort.

The train reached Roanoke at dawn. As the locomotive paused at the station, a "railroad boss man" discovered the coffin and threatened to arrest Andrew Bradley. But then seven drunken men intervened, and before the railway guard could make good on his threat, the train had resumed its journey. "By and by we come to Raleigh," where Bradley "had to be examined by a provost marshal. He say, 'I's gwine carry you back where the dogs can't bite you!' He swear, and he rare. He's a mean man — the meanest I ever see. The coffin-box was on the ground, by the tracks. Guard was carrying a gun close by, walking one way and then the other. Big boss of the train, what come to see about the ruckus, ask me all about what happen. I tell him how it was. He say: 'Well, tell you what do. Provost marshal mighty mad. He might shoot you. But I's the boss of the train, and you do like I say. When the train start up, the whistle gwine toot two times. When it toot, you heft the box on the car. Then jump on. If the guard don't shoot you, it's all right.'"

Bradley did as instructed and made it safely to Charlotte, where friends of his master gave him his first meal of the journey. "Next stop was in Columbia, down in good old South Carolina. Nobody gwine bother me down there. Just like home folks. I move the coffin-box over to another train." On the afternoon of the fourth day, Bradley reached Abbeyville, but he had another fourteen miles to travel on foot. He "got me a tumble cart, and put the coffin-box on," and set off for home. At last, at about ten that night, Andrew Bradley reached his master's house. "All the light out," he remembered. "They wasn't expecting us at all." "Hello!" Bradley called out, opening the gate. "Old Master hear me, and he raise the window and holler, 'Is that you, Andrew?' 'Yes sir, it is,' I say. 'Where's William?' he say, anxious-like. 'He's out here,' I tell him. 'I got him in the coffin-box!' They all come out, and start weeping about William being killed in the War. But they right glad he's back, and not had to be buried in Virginia. Servants come and fetch in the box. Lay Young

Master out in the parlor. Notified the people what I done, and by eleven
o'clock about a hundred people there, weeping with Old Master and
Old Mistress."

SUCH ACTS OF loyalty notwithstanding, throughout the South slaves
had begun to defy their masters. There had always been acts of resistance: running away, refusing punishment, stealing, slowdowns, sabotag-
ing crops, murdering overseers, burning barns. Some of the war's most
active black revolutionaries, of course, were the runaways who followed
in the wake of the Union Army, setting fire to farms and houses, and
picking over whatever Yankee foragers had left behind. But there were
acts of rebellion by slaves whose circumstances were more constrained.
In Louisiana, slave uprisings doubled in 1861. Slaves incinerated a dozen
boats along New Orleans's waterfront and openly resisted their masters.
Insurrectionists south of Baton Rouge forced whites to flee to New Orleans. In October 1862, the slaves on one Louisiana plantation drove off
their overseer and "destroyed everything they could get hold of. Pictures, Portraits and Furniture were all smashed up with Crockery and
everything else in the house. Others erected a gallows to hang their master from and marched around with drums and flags, shouting, 'Abe Lincoln and Freedom!'"

Fearful of "pernicious influences" among their slaves, Mississippi whites
hanged dozens of blacks and their white allies on suspicion of plotting insurrections. Slaves set fire to the courthouse and fourteen homes in
Yazoo City, and in Amite County a band of slaves armed themselves with
their masters' guns and rode off toward the river cheering and shouting,
only to be overtaken and killed by Confederate scouts. In Madison
County, two slaves, one disguised as a Yankee, whipped their elderly mistress. In July 1862, a group of Mississippi slaves slit their overseer's
throat.

South Carolina was rife with insurrections at the beginning of the
war, including the torching of a large section of Charleston. Confederate
authorities uncovered plots and insurrections in Florida, and reported
some five to six hundred runaway slave bandits and arsonists at large in
North Carolina. In Virginia, slaves were lashed in Charles City for plotting a revolt, a gang of runaways wiped out a Rebel scouting party, a
conspiracy was uncovered in Culpeper County, slaves rose up in Richmond's ironworks, and in the same city were suspected of setting fire to
President Davis's home. Georgia imprisoned eighteen slaves for foment-

ing rebellion, and hanged one white and two black plotters in Brooks County. Plotters were executed in Arkansas, and in Kentucky there were uprisings in Owen and Gallatin counties, there was arson in Henry County, and during a Christmas Eve parade through New Castle slaves sang Unionist anthems "and shouted for Lincoln." Finally, in December 1864, Troy, Alabama, would earn the distinction of being the site of the last documented slave rebellion of the war. How many of the plots for which slaves were hanged were real or imagined is difficult to establish, for as the war ground on, slaveholders and patrollers grew ever more vigilant and precipitous, arresting slaves at the slightest hint of defiance. Nor does the documentary evidence tell the whole story. Richmond discouraged the publication of reports of insurrection for fear it would demoralize whites, encourage desertion among Rebel soldiers afraid for their families, and spread rebellion among the slaves.

All over the South, masters executed slaves with a new ruthlessness born of their own fear and their slaves' rapidly diminishing value. During the war, according to a slave from Davidson County, Tennessee, "they used to stand slaves backwards to the river and shoot them off into the river." Masters who would have whipped or incarcerated or chained their captured runaway slaves now tended to treat them as traitors and insurrectionists. Two Memphis slaves who tried to run to the Union lines were executed, and their masters forced fellow slaves "to go and see them where they hung" at the roadside, recalled Louis Hughes, "until the blue flies literally swarmed around them, and the stench was fearful." Archy Vaughn of Memphis was captured trying to flee to the Union lines and returned to his master, who "took me down to the woods, and tied my hands, and pulled them over my knees, and put a stick through under my knees, and then took his knife and castrated me, and then cut off the lobe of my left ear." A more common practice, however, was to kidnap blacks and either put them to work on fortifications or sell them elsewhere. Working together, the city police of Nashville and the sheriff of Davidson County prospered by recapturing slaves who had strayed from the Union Army's Contraband camps and transporting them to markets in the Deep South.

OTHER SLAVES PERFORMED individual acts of defiance. After the Yankees occupied Williamson County, Tennessee, an old slaveholder attempted to beat an adolescent for laxity, but the boy pushed his owner to the ground, hefted an ax, and walked away. A slave woman in Texas killed her overseer. Swinging a two-foot length of iron, she "busted his skull" and buried him. "They never did nothing to her till after the big boss, he come back from the war," recalled John Ogee of Texas. Her master tried to make her work as well, but "she beat the boss man up and put him in bed for six months." This time she paid for her defiance, however; "she got killed." A slave named Jackson, of Lafayette County, Missouri, was sitting outside his mistress's door, waiting for his breakfast, when she "come down the steps out of the dining room" and told him he "had better go and watch for the Feds. She said they might come and get to fighting, and some one or other might get killed." "I don't care if they do," Jackson replied. "You don't?" she asked. "No, Madam," he said, "I don't." Provoked by her old slave's calm defiance, she told a gang of bushwhackers what Jackson had said. "God damn your black soul," one of them said, stepping up to him. "What do you mean talking that away?" But Jackson didn't answer. "Who is talking that talk?" another asked, and "stepped up and drew his pistol and struck me on the head." "The first thing you know," the bushwhacker snarled, "you'll be taken out and have your brains blown out."

His mistress invited the gang in for breakfast, after which one of them came out and began to beat Jackson with a hickory pole. "He just tip-toed to it and come down on me the same as if he was beating an ox." "Boys," he told the others, "you've got nothing to do, so go cut hickories and fetch them to me as fast as I can wear them out." After beating Jackson bloody, one of them ordered him "to go to the Feds now, God damn you, so that I can slip in at the dead hour of the night and shoot you." Jackson did indeed go to the Federals, and brought a charge of collusion against his mistress, on which she was convicted by a court-martial.

18

———◆———

"Fearing and Trembling"

Gettysburg • Harriet Bailey • Isaac Carter
Rounding Up Blacks • Pickett's Charge • Rebel Retreat
Aftermath

AFTER DEFEATING BURNSIDE at Fredericksburg and Hooker at Chancellorsville, a vaunting Robert E. Lee set his sights on southern Pennsylvania, if only to further demoralize an already shaken North and resupply his troops into the bargain. In early June 1863, as Lee began to move his Army of Northern Virginia up through Maryland, a beleaguered Hooker confessed to Lincoln that he could do nothing to stop him.

"The Rebels knew this country well," recalled Harriet Bailey, then a twenty-year-old domestic in the household of a family named Hartzell that lived on Chambersburg Pike, a mile or two northwest of the town of Gettysburg, Pennsylvania. "Some time before the battle they come riding all around here dressed in women's clothes spying out. We had a militia troop in the town, but the Rebel raiders drove our militia clean out of sight."

An alarmed Lincoln replaced Hooker with Major General George Gordon Meade, who, days after his promotion, closed in on Lee's army of some 75,000 troops with about 88,000 men. Scores of Pennsylvania freedmen and runaway slaves inhabited the area, including a farm hand named Isaac Carter, who lived about four miles out of town. By the time the two great armies collided, "a great many people had skedaddled, but the man I worked for stayed. We'd run off before when there'd been false alarms, and had our trouble for nothing. So the man I lived with said to me, 'Isaac, we won't run no more.'"

"On the morning the fighting begun," Bailey remembered, "there were pickets on horses all up and down" Chambersburg Pike. "We were standing at the gate watching them, when suddenly they come tearing along, shouting that there was going to be a battle, and we were ordered to go to the next house. I was baking that day, but I left my bread in the oven; and we didn't take nothing, we were so scared. Mrs. Hartzell ran along with the little girl, and I gathered up the little three-year-old boy and hurried after her."

A couple of hills flanked the pike just south of the Hartzell farm, and Bailey scrambled "up to the high ground and stopped to look back. And oh, there was the beautifulest sight: the Union Army all in line for battle. The blue coats and guns and flags stretched away a long distance as far as we could see."

BOTH ARMIES "just about ruined the country here," Isaac Carter remembered. "Harvest time had come, but we hadn't cut our wheat, and a lot of troops marched through it and laid it flat as a board. They chopped down trees to make breastworks, and they dug deep trenches and made walls of earth to get behind and shoot. The soldiers was bound to take the nearest way to where they wanted to go, and they hacked the fence posts off and tilted the fences over so they could get into the fields quick."

When the Confederates opened fire, Harriet Bailey and the Hartzells' little boy watched as a shell arced "way up in the air" and "busted." She and the family ran to the house of an elderly man named Crouse and "went down in the cellar where we'd be more safer; and how that poor old soul did pray! My Laws. You never heard such praying in your life, and I think the Lord heard his prayers and took care of us. The children and nearly everyone was crying. Once a ball come in through a window and rolled down in the middle of the floor. I was thankful it didn't hit us. I wanted to see my mother then, but I was satisfied to stay there till they were done fighting."

The roar of artillery sounded to Isaac Carter "just like continuous thunder; and the whole country was full of black smoke. I could smell that smoke way down where I was." After a first day of chaotic fighting, Lee formed his line along Seminary Ridge and Meade on a parallel along the slightly more elevated and aptly named Cemetery Ridge. Isaac's employer decided to send Carter "down an old road and into the woods" with eight of his horses and a wagonload of "provisions and grain." There he remained, "fearing and trembling, and looked after the horses. If the Rebels had happened to come through," he said, "they'd have took them and me, too."

CARTER'S FEAR WAS well founded. Ever since crossing into Pennsylvania, the Rebels had been rounding up runaways and even freedmen for transport back to the slave South. On the first day of the battle, Longstreet's adjutant found the time to advise Major General George Edward Pickett that "the captured Contrabands had better be brought along with you for further disposition." Albert Gallatin Jenkins's brigade, which formed part of Lee's advance guard, had rounded up black families at Chambersburg. According to a local paper, "quite a number of Negroes, free and slave — men, women, and children — were captured by Jenkins and started South to be sold into bondage." Some had been "bound with ropes, and the children were mounted in front behind the Rebels on their horses. Perhaps full fifty were got off to slavery." After John Singleton Mosby's boys raided Mercersburg, one of his troopers boasted that he had captured "218 head of cattle, 15 horses, and 12 Negros." Estimates of the number of African Americans Lee's troopers drove south range between 250 and 2,000.

The slave catching appalled some of Lee's own officers. "We took a lot of Negroes yesterday," wrote Colonel William Steptoe Christian of the 55th Virginia Infantry. "I was offered my choice, but, as I could not get them back home, I would not take them. In fact, my humanity revolted at taking the poor devils away from their homes. They were so scared that I turned them all loose." Others were not so merciful. A Vermont lieutenant reported finding "a Negro boy that the Rebels left in a barn, entirely naked," with his "breast and bowels" cut up and his genitals cut off, and turpentine poured over his body, because he had refused to follow the Rebel army into slavery.

Harriet Bailey was at special risk. "We were inside the Rebel lines, and the soldiers were all the time running in and out of the house. You'd hear them load their guns — clicky-click — and push them out the windows and fire. We didn't know what they was doing to us." When the clamor abated late in the afternoon, Bailey's elderly host decided to flee to the nearby farm of Frederick Hankey.

"We went up and looked out of the kitchen door, and down a little way toward the town there was a bayonet charge in a wheat field. They were just cutting and jagging; and of all the hollering and screaming and rattling of swords and bayonets I never heard the like. It was the awfulest thing to see. They had ambulances there, and as fast as the men fell they were picked up and carried off."

The little party scurried off to Hankey's farm, and it was here that the Confederates tried to add Bailey to their coffle. "His place was thronged with Rebels, and they stopped me." "Hey, what you doing with her?" they demanded of Mrs. Hartzell. "She's got to go along with us." "You don't know what you're talking about," Mrs. Hartzell replied as Bailey clung to her skirts, whereupon the Rebels moved on to bigger fish. "We got down into the cellar," she remembered, "and I crawled way back in the darkest corner and piled everything in front of me. I was the only colored person there, and I didn't know *what* might happen to me."

When an ailing Rebel officer lay down in the Hankey kitchen and summoned Bailey up to tend to him, Mrs. Hankey made him write out an order protecting her servant from his troops. "I don't know what was the matter of him," Bailey remembered, "but he just lay on the broad of his back. I had to comb his head, wash his face, and take off his shoes and stockings."

All night Bailey cooked for the wounded Rebels who sought shelter at Hankey's farm. "Good Land! They killed cows and calves and chickens and everything they come across, and brought the things to us to cook." But Bailey "couldn't have slept anyway for hearing them miserable wounded men hollering and going on out in the yard and in the barn and other buildings. They moaned and cried and went on terribly." "O," they'd cry out, "take me home to my parents."

GENERAL JOHN BELL HOOD's slave William kept as close to him in battle as the general would allow. At Gettysburg, Hood rode "back and forth hollering, 'Rally, boys! Rally!' till — Zip! — a ball tore up his right arm." In fact, it was shrapnel and struck his arm in four places. After a dazed Hood was carried off the field, William helped to "hold him while the surgeon fix that arm," of which he would never regain full use.

ABRAM HARRIS OF South Carolina was the same age as the youngest son of his master, Hodges Brown. "Us was boys together, me and Marse Hampton, and was just about the same size. Marse Hampton, he claimed me, and I going to be his property when both us grown. That is, if the war not come on." Too young to join up at the first muster, Hampton did not serve until two years later, when his older brother returned home with a minié ball in his shoulder. When his brother was "ready to go back to the company," Hampton finally persuaded his mother that he was old enough to serve. "Now that was in the spring when Marse Hampton join up with the troops, and him and me going to be eighteen that fall in October," but on the third day of the Battle of Gettysburg, Lee sent his army on a wholesale frontal assault that came to be known as Pickett's Charge. Brown's two sons were "both kilt in the charge, right there on the breastworks, with they guns in they hands — them two young masters of mine — right there in that Gettysburg battle."

By the end of the battle, the collision at Gettysburg had cost Meade over a quarter of his men, but an already outnumbered Lee had lost over a third. On July 4, under the cover of a heavy rain, a desolate Lee and his shattered army retreated south to the Potomac. "I never seen such a sight of people going with their wagons, cannons, ambulances and horses," Bailey recalled. "Nobody has an idea of the excitement and the noise. But in a little while the place was rid out," and the people of Gettysburg "were free souls then."

But not quite free of the Yankees. Bailey returned to her parents' farm a couple of miles up the pike and tended a company of Federals who had taken up residence at Kecklen's Tavern. "We used water from the tavern well," she recalled, "but it got so ugly and smelt so bad we could hardly drink it. The soldiers was sick, and we was sick. They thought there was dead frogs down in the well," so they summoned a local pump maker named McDannel to pump it out. "And by and by," Bailey recalled, "here comes up a little piece of a wrist and a thumb. They'd been cooking with that water, and so had we; and now that they knew what was the matter, there was a lot of gagging done among them. But what was down they couldn't get up."

"SOON AFTER THE battle ended, we had a rain," Isaac Carter remembered. "It just poured down; and all the streams were floating, and the roads were nothing but mud. The Rebel cavalry went through Emmitsburg with the Union cavalry pell-mell after them, and the horses' hoofs spattered the buildings up to the second story so you couldn't tell what color they were."

Harriet Bailey approved of Meade's decision not to pursue the Rebels. "The people that was in the battle needed a rest," for the Union had been badly shot up. For Isaac Carter, however, "the worst feature of the battle was the way the Rebels was allowed to escape." By the time the Confederates reached the Potomac, the rains had rendered it unfordable, and for ten days they lay on the north bank, "waiting for it to go down so they could cross." So why did Meade let them get away? "I think there was trickery," declared Carter. "You see, General Lee was a High Mason, and lots of our men was Masons, too, and they was bound to show him all the favors they could. If we'd been fighting with a foreign nation," Carter maintained, "I don't believe the war would have lasted a year."

ON JULY 6, three days after the battle, Carter ventured out onto the battlefield. "It made me sick, the bodies were so numerous and so swelled up, and some so shot to pieces: a foot here, an arm there, and a head in another place. They lay so thick" where the Rebels had made their fatal charge "that you couldn't walk on the ground. Their flesh was black as your hat — yes, black as the blackest colored person" from exposure and putrefaction, though Carter was told their color came "from drinking whiskey with gunpowder in it to make them brave."

The ground was littered with "thousands of the very prettiest kinds of muskets laying around, and any amount of blankets, and lots of other stuff. Cleaning up was a hard job, and any one who wanted to work could make big money. A man wouldn't turn around unless you gave him half a dollar." The dead were buried in long trenches, but "the work was done in a hurry, and in some places you'd see feet or arms sticking out." The smell of death lingered in the air "for quite a time after the battle," and Carter believed that he and his neighbors would have died "like flies" had it not been for the hordes of buzzards that descended on the battlefield. "There were multitudes of them, and — oh, my — they were the biggest ever seen. At night they'd go to the woods to roost, and you couldn't walk through under the trees" because "they was throwing up and everything else." Years later, local farmers would plow up stray soldiers' remains, and take their skulls home "and have them setting up on the mantelpiece for relics." But Carter "didn't want no such relics as that.

"Lots of farmers who were well-to-do before the battle were poor afterward. Their hay and feed were gone, their growing crops ruined, their cattle stolen, and on some places all the boards had been ripped off the barns for firewood. A good many who had lost their horses went to the condemned sales of army horses and mules and stocked up with those old cripples, all lame, or collar-sore, or used up in some way."

Part VII

The West

1864

19

"Still I Rebelled"

*Nathan Bedford Forrest • Fort Pillow • Rosa Hooper
Andersonville • Memphis II • Red River • Marks' Mills
Big Creek • Inducements*

IN THE SPRING OF 1864, Nathan Bedford Forrest set out to invade west Tennessee. His purposes were many: round up new recruits, supplies, and arms; chastise the black and white Unionist troops who now manned many of the Union Army's river bastions; and disrupt Sherman's supply line. On February 22, 1864, Forrest routed Brigadier General William Sooy Smith's force of 7,000 men with only 2,500 of his own. When George Ward's master sent his slaves "out to pick up the dead, we had about eighty of them that we put in trenches down there around Troy."

In late March, Forrest's men bluffed the garrison at Union City into surrendering, while Forrest himself rode into Kentucky to attack Paducah. The local Union garrison withdrew into Fort Anderson, west of Paducah, leaving Forrest free to occupy the town's business district. But Union gunboats firing from the Mississippi and a battery of black artillery firing from the fort repulsed his repeated attacks, inflicting heavy casualties.

BY APRIL, FORREST had returned to Tennessee and assembled a cavalry force of some 3,000 men. On the morning of the twelfth, they attacked Fort Pillow, a sprawling former Confederate stronghold situated on a bluff on the Tennessee bank of the Mississippi, eighty meandering river miles north of Memphis. The garrison consisted of about 650

Union soldiers, roughly evenly divided between black artillerists and white Southern Unionist cavalry. Forrest demanded the garrison's surrender, threatening that if it refused he would not be responsible for the actions of his men. But even though Forrest had kept the one Union gunboat at Fort Pillow out of range, and his men had closed in on the garrison during the truce, the Union commander refused to capitulate, and the Confederates swarmed over the parapet.

DURING HIS CIVILIAN career as a spectacularly successful slave trader, Forrest had already acted as an agency of fate in the life of Rosa Spearman Hooper. In the late 1850s, Rosa had been sold to Forrest by her Lexington, Kentucky, master and transported in one of Forrest's droves to Yalobusha County, Mississippi, where he separated her from her mother and sold her to a man named Spearman. Shortly thereafter, she moved with Spearman's three other slaves to his plantation outside Coffeeville, Tennessee, where, as Spearman's "house girl," she fell in love with Thomas Hooper, a field hand from a plantation down the road.

In early 1864, Tom and Rosa gathered up their toddling daughter, Josephine, and ran away from their masters. "One night they were missing," recalled Spearman's oldest son, "together with their child, or her child," he added, implying that Tom may not have been Josephine's natural father, "and it was learned that they had joined the Federal Army." "Josephine was a little bit of a thing," Rosa remembered, "just big enough to walk when we left home. We had to carry her. I believe it was sort of cold weather when we come off from home. We went to Corinth, Mississippi, and got there after a day and a night's travel." Hooper immediately enlisted in the 6th U.S. Colored Heavy Artillery and proved "a good, steady soldier." In early March, he was promoted to corporal and sent with his regiment to Fort Pillow. "Tom and I lived in a soldier's tent," recalled Rosa. "A good many of the soldiers had their wives with them. I lived with Tom and done his washing."

WHEN THE BATTLE began, Rosa and most of the garrison's civilians were evacuated across the Mississippi on a barge. Down on the riverbank, the fleeing garrison was caught in a deadly crossfire. Forrest's men continued to shoot well after the Federals had thrown down their weapons and begged for mercy, and many men were killed in their hospital tents. By the next morning, only about sixty-five of the garrison's nearly three hundred blacks had survived a massacre that had continued intermittently through the night. More than seventy percent of the white survivors would perish in Rebel prisons. The Rebels themselves lost only eighteen killed, all of them before the garrison had fled to the river.

Thirty-two-year-old Nick Hamer was one of a large contingent of black servants and teamsters who accompanied Forrest's cavalry throughout the war, cooking for his master, William F. Hamer, of the 5th Mississippi Cavalry. Nick served his master faithfully, and "never went home but three times during the entire time of the war." At Fort Pillow, the 5th served under Colonel Bob McCulloch of Missouri and would play a major part in the horrors that ensued. "I can only tell what I saw," Hamer testified. "The place was taken between four o'clock and sundown." Kept to the rear with the wagons, Hamer "did not see any of the prisoners killed, however there was but 109 of the people in the fort taken prisoner, and about 30 of them were women and children. I do not think there was more than a dozen colored men among the prisoners taken. The rest were white men."

Sam Hughes's male relations had run off and joined the Union Army, but Hughes himself went to war as a cook for two of Forrest's troopers, and "was along with them at the Fort Pillow fight," Sam recalled. After the battle, he walked along the corpse-strewn riverbank and came upon the body of his nephew, artillerist Charles Koon, whom he recognized by the peculiar patch of gray on his head that he had sported since boyhood.

Three of Captain William Green Middleton's slaves — Adam, Simon, and Essex — had joined the Union garrison at Fort Pillow. Adam and Simon were killed, but Captain Middleton encountered Essex hiding behind piles of driftwood by the riverbank. "Recognizing his master," recalled a comrade, "he threw down his gun" and the captain spared him. Only a few months before Middleton himself would be killed at Harrisburg, he returned Essex to slavery.

Tom Hooper was not so lucky. Shot to death atop the bluff, he was buried that night in a mass grave in which several of his comrades were interred while they were still breathing. The next day, under a flag of truce, the Yankees came to collect their wounded, and "a whole lot of us women, white and colored, were brought back to Memphis." Rosa Hooper "never saw Tom again," and thus Nathan Bedford Forrest had separated Rosa Spearman Hooper not only from her mother but from her husband as well in the massacre at Fort Pillow, the most notorious atrocity of the war.

• • •

THE WHITE SURVIVORS of the massacre were escorted to the Confederate prison at Andersonville, Georgia, where seventy-five percent of them would die. "It was about the worstest place that ever I seen," said Tines Kendricks. "That was where they keep all the Yankees that they capture, and they had so many there they couldn't nigh take care of them. They had them fenced up with a tall wire fence and never had enough house room for all them Yankees. They would just throw the grub to them. The mostest that they had for them to eat was peas." "They was a little stream run through it," Wash Dukes recalled, "and the Rebels poisoned it and killed a lot of them." But they didn't have to; the stream was employed as both a latrine and a source of drinking water, and "the filth, it was terrible," Kendricks continued. "The sickness, it broke out amongst them all the while, and they just die like rats what been poisoned." More than 45,000 prisoners were crammed into Andersonville's stockade, and over the course of only fourteen months at least 13,000 perished. "The first thing that the Yankees do when they take the state away from the Confederates," Kendricks recalled, was "to free all them what in the prison at Andersonville."

AFTER A SETBACK in July at Tupelo, Forrest would further rattle the Union cage by leading 2,000 men on a wild ride through Memphis. Patsy Moore heard them clattering through the streets as Union infantry and black artillery fired on them. Though she was too little "to be scared," she saw "black and white dead in the streets and alleys. We went to the magazine house for protection, and we played and stayed there," even as the Rebels tried and failed to break in. After inflicting 200 Federal casualties and forcing the Union commander to flee in his pajamas, Forrest and his boys withdrew under concerted fire from the surviving comrades of the fallen black artillerists at Fort Pillow.

"JUST WHAT MY feelings were about the war," sighed Martin Jackson, "I have never been able to figure out. I knew the Yanks were going to win; from the beginning, I *wanted* them to win and lick us Southerners. But I hoped they were going to do it without wiping out our company. Lots of colored boys did escape and joined the Union army, and there are plenty of them drawing a pension today." But Jackson's father was always telling his son that "every man has to serve God under his own vine and fig tree," and reminding him that "the war wasn't going to last forever, but that our 'forever' was going to be spent living among Southerners, after

Five generations of slaves on the Smith plantation,
Beaufort, South Carolina.

Field hands with a day's cotton pickings are led by a
black slave driver with a top hat and whip.

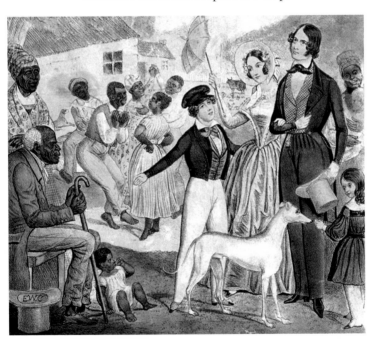

"God bless you Massa!" exclaims an elderly slave in this proslavery
broadside. "While a dollar is left me," replies his master, "nothing
shall be spared to increase their comfort and happiness."

Branded on his forehead, Wilson Chinn of Louisiana
displays the instruments of his subjugation: a
spiked collar to prevent escape through the woods,
leg irons, a paddle, and a strap.

For illiterate slaves, a glimpse of cartoons such as
this in their masters' newspapers may have confirmed
their conception of the war as a personal fight
between Lincoln and Davis.

Sixty-five-year-old Nick Biddle,
a body servant in a Pennsylvania
regiment, was said to have been
the first man wounded in the Civil
War. On April 18, 1861, he was
struck in the head by a brickbat as
his regiment marched through a
hostile mob in Baltimore.

Freed slaves pose with Union soldiers outside their master's rickety
farmhouse near Yorktown, Virginia.

Union soldiers pause for a chat with local slaves at Culpepper Courthouse, Virginia.

Contrabands cross the Rappahannock in flight from Stonewall Jackson's army.

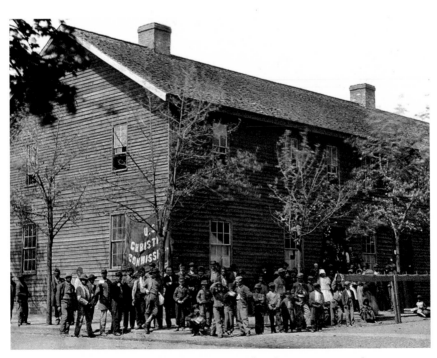

Contrabands gather to receive supplies from an outpost of
the U.S. Christian Commission in Richmond, Virginia.

A militiaman poses as a young body servant blacks a comrade's boots at Camp Cameron, District of Columbia, 1861.

George Armstrong Custer (right) with his old friend, now his prisoner, Lieutenant James Barroll Washington, CSA, George Washington's great-great-grandnephew. Before the picture was taken, Washington summoned a Contraband boy to pose with them and suggested titling their portrait "Both Sides, the Cause."

Contraband laborers for the Union army work on a railway in Virginia.

Black teamsters stand near the signal tower at Bermuda Hundred, Virginia.

Livestock killed in the Battle of Gettysburg lie in the stony
barnyard of a local farmer named Trossel.

Contrabands gather under a leaden winter sky at Aiken's Farm,
James River, Virginia.

A surgeon looks on as Contrabands collect the dead
after the Battle of Fredericksburg.

Former slaves disinter the remains of Union soldiers for formal burial
at Cold Harbor, Virginia. The picture was taken ten months after
the battle, when the war was all but over.

A lone freed slave sits amid the ruins of what was
apparently a Richmond metal shop.

A Richmond labor gang, possibly the same one that rushed to
welcome Lincoln when he visited the fallen Rebel capital.

A Union agent reads a labor contract to emancipated slaves
on the Grove plantation at Port Royal, South Carolina.

African Americans
parade through the
streets of a rebuilt
Richmond in honor
of Emancipation
Day, 1905.

During the period the WPA collected testimony from former slaves,
their descendants risked disfranchisement and lynching in their struggle
to free themselves from the sharecropping system. In January 1936, a local
judge evicted these families from the Dibble plantation near Parkin,
Arkansas, for joining the Southern Tenant Farmers' Union.

Willis Winn stands beside the horn his master
used to summon his slaves.

Elizabeth Keckley, seamstress for the Davis and Lincoln families, wears one of her creations. *Author's collection*

William Robinson, author of *From Log Cabin to Pulpit*. *Author's collection*

Henry Clay Bruce, who mocked his master's pistol practice. *Author's collection*

George L. Knox, escaped slave turned Union teamster and Hoosier businessman. *Author's collection*

Hannah Crasson's master bragged he would beat the Yankees by supper. But "it was four long years before he come back to dinner. The table was sure set a long time for *him.*"

Katie Darling's mistress used to threaten her with an eternity of servitude, but tried to change her tune when a Yankee approached. "Katie," she said, "I didn't say *anything,* did I?"

Katie Rowe's master declared that before he would let the Yankees set his slaves free, "I gwine line you up on the bank of the Bois d'Arc Creek and free you with my shotgun!"

Martin Jackson's father told him to remain loyal to the Rebels, with whom, whatever the war's outcome, he would still have to live. "I knew that-all was true," Jackson recalled, "but still I rebelled, from *inside* me."

"There ain't never been nobody fighting like our Confederates done," Tom McAlpin declared, "but they ain't never had a chance. There was just too many of them blue coats for us to lick."

"Mr. Lincoln done said we was free," recalled Gus Askew of Alabama, "but us little Negroes was too scared to listen."

"If we hadn't have had to work and slave for nothing," William Henry Towns said, "we might have something to show for what we did do, and wouldn't have to live from pillar to post now."

they got licked. He would cite examples of how whites would stand flatfooted and fight for the blacks the same as for members of their own family," and ask whether Jackson didn't owe them the same loyalty. "I knew that-all was true," Jackson said, "but still I rebelled, from *inside* me."

Jackson nevertheless continued to serve as a body servant with the 1st Texas Cavalry under Colonel Augustus C. Buchel, "a full-blooded German, and as fine a man and a soldier as you ever saw. He had had a lot of soldiering before, and fought in the Indian War."

After the fall of Vicksburg and Port Hudson gave the North dominion over the entire Mississippi River, Grant diverted Nathaniel Prentiss Banks from a proposed march on Mobile, Alabama, to join with Flag Officer David Dixon Porter in a run up the Red River. Their mission was to seize cotton and expand Union control of Louisiana, but their 35,000 troops proceeded in fits and starts. The result was that when Banks's vanguard of 5,700 troops moved from the river at Natchitoches, Louisiana, they not only left their naval support behind but, on April 8, 1864, four miles south of Mansfield, ran into a Confederate battle formation of 8,800.

The Rebels "was coming from Shreveport," a local slave named Lafayette "Fay" Price related, "to meet the Yankees from Natchitoches." "When the Confederates came to Mansfield," recalled Willis Winn, "they was carrying a red flag," but "when the Yanks come in sight they raised a white flag and wanted the Confederates to surrender." When they refused, suddenly "the whole world round there smelt like powder. Guns nowadays just goes pop-pop, but them guns sounded like thunder." From his master's farm nearby, Robert Wilson also "hears the shots, but I's not allowed to go where the fighting am taking place. I don't know but that was the best, cause I weren't anxious to go there anyway."

When the battle began, Lafayette Price was serving two of his master's Rebel brothers. "Mr. Robert was in the infantry, and Mr. Jim, they took him along to drive." Having apparently heard that the Yankee gunboats were unable to proceed upriver, Robert Carroll told Price, "Fay, you go back home and tell Ma she need not be uneasy about me, cause the Yankees is retreating to Natchitoches." Price drove the three miles back home, "but I didn't put up the team," because just as he began to reassure his mistress, "a big cannon shot overhead — Boom!" His mistress began to tremble. "O Fay," she cried, "get some corn and throw it to the hogs," and commanded him to ride to a bayou sixty miles away, to

check on her boys. "I got some corn and start to get out the crib," Price
remembered, but "they shot another cannon," and "I don't know if I ever
did get the corn to the pigs."

As they listened to the continued booming of artillery, Lafayette tried
to reassure his mistress with a piece of lore Jim Carroll had told him:
"when they was shooting the big guns, they wasn't killing men." Only
when "they hear the little guns shoot, then they could start crying cause
that mean that men was getting killed." But the next day the booming
turned to the crackle of rifle fire. "I don't know if you ever parch pop-
corn," said Price, but "that the way the little guns sound," and so it was
time "to start crying."

A Rebel captain approached and asked "if anybody here that know
the neighborhood. Here's the thing they want to know; when the soldiers
start out, they didn't want them to launch out and get mix up. So they
sent for Mr. Carroll, cause he live about a mile away. He was ordered to
stand by the tree, and the captain went by waving a sword, and pretty
soon the captain was killed. They kept on fighting, and after a while a soldier come by" and told Price "to go and help with the wounded soldiers."

When Major General Richard Taylor "come from Shreveport and
command, 'Charge!' the Yankees get in the corner of a rail fence." The
Rebels "broke right through that field of prairie, and 60 men get killed
dead before they get across." In his interview, Price deemed it "a wonderful consideration to bring up in memory" that the horses killed in battle "didn't lay on this side, nor on that side. They just squat down. They
was dead." Watching from afar, an ambivalent Martin Jackson suddenly
heard someone approaching. "It was a soldier who was half carrying Colonel Buchel in." But Jackson couldn't "do anything for the Colonel; he
was too far gone. I just held him comfortable, and that was the position
he was in when he stopped breathing. That was the worst hurt I got when
anybody died," Jackson remembered. "He was a friend of mine."

As for the Union dead, "they just dig a big hole and put them in and
threw dirt on them." Price "went back after two or three days and the
bodies does swell and crack the ground." The mass grave "was sunk in,"
Robert Wilson remembered, "like any other fill after it was rained on."
Susan Smith's master had hired his wife's nephew David McGill to serve
in his stead in the 1st Louisiana Infantry, which was now doing battle at
Mansfield. After the guns had stopped firing, a McGill slave named
Willie Weeks put his arm around Susan "and say he go to the battlefield"

seeking young David. Weeks found McGill's company, and returned after a time to report that "Little David got killed." "Oh," cried Mrs. Weeks, "don't say that!" They all rushed to the battlefield in hopes there had been a mistake, but "after a while they find him" so badly mutilated that "the only way they knowed it was him, he had two gold eyeteeth with diamonds in them." He lay amid a host of dead and wounded. "Some of the men was praying and some cussing. You could hear some of them hollering, 'Oh, God, help me.' They was laying so thick you have to step over them."

After damming the unusually low Red River to keep Porter's fleet afloat, Banks abandoned his expedition. As a result of his defeats, he was compelled to deploy 10,000 of his men to guard against Rebel raids in the West, from which the Confederates succeeded in moving 15,000 men to join Joseph E. Johnston's command for the defense of Atlanta. But Martin Jackson nevertheless claimed that this Rebel victory came at the cost of breaking "the back of the Texas Cavalry."

Katie Darling would "remember that fight at Mansfield like it was yesterday. Master's field was all torn up with cannon holes, and every time a cannon fired, Missy went off in a rage. One time when a cannon fired," her mistress called Darling a "little black wench" and warned her that the slaves "aren't going to be free" because they had been created "to work for white folks." But just then, she "looked up and saw a Yankee soldier standing in the door with a pistol. She said, 'Katie, I didn't say *anything*, did I?'" But Darling declared, "I'm not telling a lie," and repeated for the soldier everything her mistress had said.

AS NATHANIEL BANKS led his hapless expedition along the Red River, the Rebels tried to halt a Union wagon train bound for Pine Bluff to pick up supplies for Major General Fred Steele's forces. The wagon train's escort managed to fend them off until two Confederate divisions under Brigadier General James B. Fagan attacked from the rear and the front. The result was the Battle of Marks' Mills, a Union rout that prevented Steele from joining forces with Banks on the Red River. "We just lived six miles from there," Hardy Miller recalled. The Yankees "didn't have time to bury the dead. We could see the buzzards and carrion crows." When all that was left of the dead was bones, the vultures dispersed, and as they flew over her farm, Miller's mistress said, "There goes the buzzards. Done et all the meat off." Miller used to drive to and from the mill in a wagon, "and we could see the bones. Used to get out and look at their teeth."

ON JULY 25, Union General Napoleon Bonaparte Buford sent an expedition from Helena, Arkansas, to fend off a Rebel cavalry raid of Unionist plantations in surrounding Phillips County. "One night the servants' quarters was overflowing with Yankee soldiers," S. O. Mullins recalled, all of them members of black regiments. "My mother left me and my little brother, cause she didn't want to sleep in the house where the soldiers was. We slept on the floor, and they used our beds." The Yankees "left next morning" and camped all day in Mullins's master's yard "under the trees."

A day later, they rode out toward Big Creek. "When Old Mistress saw them, she said they'd get it pretty soon," and sure enough, when they crossed the creek about a "half mile from our cabins, I heard the guns turn in on them" as the Rebels attacked from three sides. After the Yankees had been routed, Mullins crossed the creek to find men lying "piled on top each other."

IN SEPTEMBER, Forrest was on another of his tears, menacing Sherman's supply lines. Swinging south, he captured the Federal garrison at Athens, Alabama, and among his captives were a number of local slaves, including James Henry Nelson. Despite his fear that he might share the fate of the black troops at Fort Pillow, Nelson, like many of the black survivors of the massacre, "was carried south. We was marching along the line," Nelson remembered, when a Confederate soldier approached. "Don't you want to go home and stay with my wife?" asked the Rebel. Nelson allowed as how he would. The Rebel took him to Millville, Alabama, where he "bound me to a friend of his, and I stayed there till the war about ended." Though Nelson had been "getting along very well" in Millville, an older slave "persuaded me to run away to Decatur, Alabama." But even in the relative safety of Decatur, he worried so much about his mother that "they let me go home."

"Jim," James Cape's Missouri master asked him one day, "how would you like to join the army?" "What do I have to do?" Cape wanted to know. "Tend horses and ride them," his master replied. "So the first thing I knew, I was in the army away off east from here, somewhere this side of St. Louis and in Tennessee and Arkansas and other places," serving in his master's stead. "After I got in the army," Cape remembered, "it wasn't so much fun, because tending horses and riding wasn't all I did. No, sir, I had to do shooting and to get shot at! One time we stopped the train, took Yankee money, and lots of other things off that train. That was way up the other side of Tennessee."

In an engagement near Independence, Missouri, on October 22, 1864, the Rebels gave Cape "a rifle and sent me up front fighting, when we weren't running." The battle was a marginal Rebel victory, but did not seem so to Cape. "We did a heap of running," which suited Cape, for he "could do that better than advance." Nevertheless, he "got shot in the shoulder in that fight, and lots of our soldiers got killed, and we lost our supplies: just left it and ran." When the order came to retreat, he said, "I was all ready."

20

"A Rugged Cross"

*Contrabands • Labor • Hard Trials • "Corrals" • Worship
Local Whites • Orphans • Infant Burial*

B Y THE SUMMER of 1863, thousands of Contrabands had found their way into the Union lines. Thirty-year-old Samuel Ballton had been hired out to the Virginia Central Railroad and transferred to a spot a day's walk from his master's plantation, where his wife, Rebecca, remained in slavery. Determined to rescue her, he abandoned his railroad crew and ran away. Posing as a kidnapped slave who longed to return to his "Old Master," Ballton made his way back to his wife. But he could not find a way to rescue her safely. Promising to return, he absconded with three other slaves, stole four mules from a neighboring plantation, and galloped off to Fredericksburg. Securing a position as cook for the 6th Wisconsin Regiment, he earned enough money to engineer another rescue attempt, and "one of the proudest moments of his life" was when he returned to her and declared, "Rebecca, I'm going to take you to freedom with me." "They stole away on a Sunday night," wrote his interviewer, "with her mother and another pair of slaves, and made the distance, more than fifty miles, to Fredericksburg, in fourteen hours, and Mr. Ballton declares they were not tired because they had something to walk *for.*"

Their destination was one of the hundreds of Contraband camps whose shacks and tents proliferated on the outskirts of almost every Union post. In November 1862, Grant had assigned John Eaton to take charge of all the fugitive slaves who entered the Union Army's western lines. They were allowed to occupy certain abandoned houses, churches, and outbuildings — or, failing that, lean-tos and castoff army tents. In Memphis, Contrabands were employed primarily as woodcutters to fuel the Mississippi steamboats that supplied the Union forces.

IN NASHVILLE "they worked in squads," wrote a Union soldier, "each gang choosing its own officers; and it was amusing to hear their captains exclaim to the wheelbarrow-men, 'Let them buggies roll, Brother Bones and Felix'; or, 'You over there, let them picks fall easy, or they'll hurt something'; &c. &c. When the attack upon the city was threatened, many of these Negroes came to the officer of the day and asked for arms to help beat off the Rebels." But he sent them "behind the works, with axes, picks, and spades, in case the enemy should come to close quarters."

Elsewhere Contrabands picked cotton, repaired railroads, unloaded steamboats, or hired themselves out to private citizens. Thomas Rutling fled his owner in Wilson County in 1865 and moved into Nashville's Contraband camp to live with his sister. "I worked at leveling breastworks for a while, then made the acquaintance of some soldiers, thinking I might get a chance to beat the drum, which had long been the height of my ambition. A surgeon wanted a boy, and I remained with him three weeks till he was mustered out." Whatever the Contrabands earned went to the army, to cover the costs of administering the camp.

A reporter visiting Fortress Monroe was impressed by the Contrabands' industry. But a local missionary reported that their diligence and piety went unrewarded. "Officers take advantage of their ignorance in every way possible, and torment them like fiends, while the government retains them on its highways and public works, and the quartermaster refuses to pay them." A Yankee chaplain observed that in the Union lines Contrabands often "met prejudice against their color" that was "more bitter than that they left behind." Over a fourth of the black laborers the Union Army impressed in 1862 and 1863 died, and yet a Union officer claimed he had yet to meet a single one who "wishes to return or does not prefer even the very imperfect freedom they enjoy with the army to slavery."

But conditions on Union labor crews were so harsh that the army resorted to sending press gangs on surprise raids on black churches, barber shops, parties, and picnics. When a Northern white accused Contrabands of lacking a work ethic, Moses Battle answered, "Don't know what for, sir, anybody think like that," for it had been "the colored

folks what been keeping up the country. When they had to work all day
for the masters, they work of nights and Sundays to make a little something for theyselves. Now when it's all day to themselves don't know what
for," they would "lie down and starve." Eaton wondered how he could be
expected to elevate black people "without the motive of reward for industry." "When paid so long after the proper time that they begin to de-
spair," explained a missionary, "they naturally become distrustful and
restless. If they did not, they would offer a living proof that they are not
of the same race as the whites but had a nature entirely different."

THEIR PAY WAS never enough. Hulda Williams recalled a Contraband
camp at Pine Bluff, Arkansas, where "there was lots of guns and soldiers.
The soldiers give each family one piece of wood every day for the camp
fire, and just enough foodstuff to keep the Negroes from starving. I remember my mammy would slip out at night and steal wood and scraps
from the soldiers' kitchen." The winters of 1863 and 1864 were especially harsh, afflicting families already lacking in shelter, blankets, and
firewood. One winter morning, a missionary found a family shivering under a tattered blanket, having burned their bedstead the day before and
eaten their last morsel of food.

Though Contrabands did what they could to keep their camps clean
— laying claim to vacant lots and digging their own privies — sanitary
conditions were abysmal. Epidemics swept away entire families of half-
starved and poorly sheltered men, women, and children. At Lexington,
Kentucky, a black soldier was appalled to find conditions so bad that
some Contrabands "gave their children away in order to get rid of them,"
and "colored ladies of Lexington stole these little children in order to
take care of them." Lice were a particular torment in the camps, and tu-
berculosis ran rampant.

In Pine Bluff, Contrabands "had to stay in a church with about twenty
other people. Two of the babies and two of my aunts died there on account of the exposure," Matilda Hatchett remembered. "The slaves that
was freed, and the country Negroes that had been run off," recalled Willis Bennefield of Georgia, "or had run away from the plantations, was
staying in Augusta in Government houses: great big old barns. They
would all get free provisions from the Freedmen's Bureau, but people
like us, Augusta citizens, didn't get free provisions; we had to work. It
spoiled some of them. When the small pox come, they died like hogs, all
over Broad Street and everywhere." A free black preacher from the

North named Thomas James served as the superintendent of a Contraband camp in Louisville, Kentucky. "Sickness broke out among the refugee women and children, and many perished by it. I sent out seven corpses in one day, and the scenes I witnessed during that visitation of disease will never fade from my recollection."

NOR WAS DISEASE the only peril. "I was forced to forbid the display of lights in any of the buildings at night," James wrote, "for fear of drawing the fire of Rebel bushwhackers. All the fugitives in the camp made their beds on the floor, to escape danger from rifle balls fired through the thin siding of the frame structures." When George L. Knox and his brother entered the Union lines in Nashville, "the Yankees were taking the Negroes out to work. There must have been about a thousand slaves, and they all had axes, going out to cut wood. One troop of cavalry went in front and another behind" to protect the slaves from snipers. "Eighty soldiers took us colored folks to the Contraband camp in Monticello," said Tim Haynes of Arkansas. "There was forty soldiers in the back and forty in front." Such escorts and restrictions felt so much like imprisonment that Contrabands took to calling their camps "corrals." "If you could get to the Yankees' camp" at Pine Bluff, "you was free right now," Boston Blackwell remembered. At least "they told me I was free when I gets to the Yankee camp. But I couldn't go outside much."

THEIR PIETY ASTONISHED Northerners. "Throughout the great circle of military camps that cover the hills as snowflakes," a reporter observed, "there is no place where God is as devoutly worshipped as by the 'Contraband' at Fortress Monroe." Unable to read, "except in a very few instances, with but little leisure to attend places of public worship, and through long and painful years of oppression, they have been blessed by the grace of God, with a simplicity and clearness of understanding of the fundamental doctrines of the truth of salvation as it is in Jesus Christ, that is most astonishing. If one would learn what precious comfort may be found in Christianity, in the midst of the severest trials, with which human nature can be afflicted, let him go among this people."

Missionaries who had expected to work in a religious vacuum discovered, to varying degrees of delight and dismay, that most slaves had already developed a Christianity of their own. "Before the war was over," Chaney Mack remembered, "we all belong to the Methodist Church with the white folks." But "soon after they was set free," emancipated slaves "started up churches of they own, and it was some sight to see and hear them on meeting days." Mattie Dilworth remembered how "the exhorters would stand on the floor and do they scuffling, and sketching, and raring. Before the surrender," she said, "I had to sit on a back seat. But there come a time sure, Lord, when I could sit right spang on the front seat!"

Not long after the war, a sympathetic Northern officer attended one such service. "A single voice, coming from a dark corner of the room, began a low, mournful chant" in a minor key "in which the whole assemblage joined by degrees." It was "not a psalm, nor a real song, as we understand these words; for there was nothing that approached the jubilant in it. It seemed more like a wail: a mournful, dirge-like expression of sorrow. At first, I was inclined to laugh, it was so far from what I had been accustomed to call music. Then I felt uncomfortable, as though I could not endure it, and half rose to leave the room." But then the "chorus rose a little above, and then fell a little below, the keynote," and he "was overcome by the real sadness and depression of soul which it seemed to symbolize." Then an old man knelt down to pray, "and pretty soon burst out with an 'O good, dear Lord! We pray for the colored people!' when the whole audience swayed back and forward in their seats, and uttered in perfect harmony a sound like that caused by prolonging the letter 'm' with the lips closed. One or two began this wild, mournful chorus; and in an instant all joined in, and the sound swelled upwards and downwards like waves of the sea."

The Union officer especially admired the black preacher as he asked "for all sorts of quaint blessings for the Union army." Speaking in "the most quiet and mellow tone," the preacher said, "I have been a slave for six and thirty years; and, though I labored faithfully for my master, I never received at any one time more than four bits; and if, as a slave, I could work for my owner six and thirty years, now that I am a freeman, surely I can work for Uncle Sam a little while — just a little while — until he can find a fitting place for me, for nothing." ("Yes, yes," people murmured. "If we're free, it's enough for now.") "Brethren," he continued, "I do not care if I am a slave; I have reached maturity, and can endure it. But," he said, his voice falling "almost to a whisper," "I have in yonder cabin a child, a boy only five years of age, whom I love as I do my life; and I thank God, *I thank God*, that I am a freeman, for his sake."

The officer found some of the preacher's phrases "epic in grandeur.

He spoke of 'the rugged wood of the cross,' whereto the Saviour was nailed," and "pictured the earthquake which rent the veil of the temple, with this extremely beautiful expression: 'And, my friends, the earth was unable to endure the tremendous sacrilege, and trembled.'" He warned his congregation that if they did not heed the Savior, "you will inevitably go to that place which is filled with the unmixed wrath of Jehovah." Like many a white before and after him, the officer assumed that such eloquent expressions must have been memorized. "But my friend assured me to the contrary. He said the man could talk as brilliantly at any time, and on any subject."

DEEMED A GREAT nuisance — a drain on resources, a corrupting and disruptive influence on soldiers, and an impediment to the army's mobility — Contrabands were often shuffled from camp to camp. In January 1864, an officer at Stevenson, Alabama, sent all of his Contrabands to Nashville, where a recruiter found them standing in the cold outside the railroad station. Grant ordered Nashville's post commander to take them in and care for them, and soon afterward General Thomas set aside a portion of suburban Nashville as a Contraband camp and central labor depot for the Department of the Cumberland, to which Northern mission societies donated cloaks, hoods, mantillas, shawls, trousers, hats, hosiery, and bolts of calico for the army to distribute among the Contrabands.

The Contrabands mixed uneasily with an almost equal number of poor white refugees "in a more hopeless and helpless condition than the Freedmen," wrote a Northern observer, "for the mass of them are just as poor and ignorant and degraded as the slaves themselves, and twice as mean, and they don't seem to have energy enough to *die* decently."

Nashville's whites were horrified by the influx of blacks. A local paper declared the city "overstocked with Negroes." Just before the war, they had numbered 3,945, but by the end of the war they totaled 10,744. Months after the war had ended, the superintendent of freedmen for the Department of the Cumberland reported that he was still overseeing 5,500 refugees in seven camps. Many Southern whites regarded the Contrabands' plight as just deserts for precipitating a war and abandoning their masters. A slaveholder named Robert H. Cartmell of Madison County, Tennessee, complained that "to one born and raised in the South, and accustomed to keeping the Sons of Ham in their proper place, the impudence of these Negroes is hard to endure. They are entirely corrupted." The general attitude seemed to be "The Yankees liberated you, now they can take care of you."

But sometimes local whites could be touched by a Contraband's plea. Too sick to work, a fugitive slave walked into the office of a nearby stockyard. "Gentlemen," he declared, "I am an ex-slave. I was loyal to my master, and as a free man I want to be a man and not a burden on my neighbors. But I am not able to work, and my wife and children are at home hungry and without food or fire. Will you help me, gentlemen?" The stockmen sent him away, but that evening "they sent me enough food and fuel to last a month."

Families received two rations a day, but "the meat was so old," recalled Nat Black, "that when thrown against a wall it would splatter like mud." Contrabands ate convulsively: one day nothing, the next great chunks of meat carved off a sickly steer they'd been permitted to slaughter. "Then we would put our meat on a long, forked pole," one of them recalled, and "such eating and smoking you never heard. It used to make me awful sick at times, and I would throw up a lot. But I was hungry, and kept trying until I made it stick in my stomach." In the camp in Jacksonville, Florida, the authorities distributed hardtack and meat they called "salt horse," something like a cross between chipped and corned beef.

DESPITE WHATEVER MEASURE of freedom the Contrabands enjoyed, they remained plagued by the fear of separation from families already fractured by sales, deaths, hirings, flights, and refugeeing. "Many a sad scene I witnessed at my camp of colored refugees in Louisville," wrote Thomas James. "There was the mother, bereaved of her children, who had been sold and sent farther south lest they should escape in the general rush for the Federal lines and freedom"; and children "orphaned in fact if not in name, for separation from parents among the colored people in those days left no hope of reunion this side of the grave."

A Union captain asked a Northern missionary named Laura Haviland to persuade a group of slaves to allow the army to transfer them from Cairo, Illinois, to an island camp in the Mississippi. But the slaves suspected her of intending to enslave them again, and no promises of food and clothing would budge them. The captain finally stepped forward and persuaded them to go by pledging "that their freedom was a fixed fact; that they would never see the day again when they would be separated by being sold apart." But before they could board their boat, one of their

children died, and his mother begged the soldiers to give her time to
bury him. The captain refused, but promised he would bury the child after they departed. "Oh, Missus," the mother sobbed to Haviland, "it appears like I can't leave him so; they'll leave him here tonight, and these
wharf-rats are awful. They ate one dead child's face all one side off, and
one of its feet was all gnawed off. I don't want to leave my child on this
bare ground." After Haviland assured her that she would see to it that
the child was buried properly, the woman bade her dead son goodbye
and steamed off to St. Simons Island.

When Haviland urged the captain to bury the child that afternoon, he
"seemed very indifferent." "What is the difference if that child should be
buried this afternoon," he wanted to know, "or whether wharf-rats eat it
or not?" He told her she shouldn't "allow such things as these to break
your heart," for he had seen his men "buried in a ditch, with no other
coffin or winding sheet than the soldier's dress. For the time being we
bury hundreds just in that way; and when from five to fifteen die in one
day, as sometimes is the case in these large camps, we cannot make
coffins for them, but we roll them up in whatever they have. If we can get
a piece of board to lay them on when we put them in their graves, we do
well." But Haviland insisted, and saw to it that the little boy was provided
with a pine coffin and carried at dusk "to the burying ground."

21

"Don't Want Any Such Again"

A Yankee Prisoner Shot • *Franklin* • *Nashville*
"Negroes Will Fight" • *Exposure and Death*

T HOUGH HALF A DOZEN forts at Nashville had been linked together by twenty miles of entrenchments and breastworks, the
Tennessee capital had remained under a remote and sputtering
Rebel siege. Forrest, Morgan, and Joe Wheeler attacked Federal
forts and supply lines throughout central Tennessee, and Secessionist
residents boldly jeered Yankee soldiers in the street in the belief that
someday the Rebels would reoccupy the city.

GUERRILLAS RAMPAGED through the surrounding counties. One evening they entered a slaveholder's house in Williamson County, leaving a
captive Union soldier tied up outside. As Thomas Rutling cautiously approached the prisoner, "his eyes changed to the softness of those of a
dove, and, with his head, he beckoned me," and said, "Untie my hands."
But just as Rutling "stooped to comply," one of the guerrillas came
around the corner of the house and kicked and slapped at Rutling.

"As the sun went down, the 'Bushwhackers' rode into the forest with
their prisoner," Rutling recalled, "and before the last rays of the sun disappeared from the sky, a sharp crack of rifles was heard, and a fine young
man fell." The guerrillas left the soldier to bleed to death, but late that
night a party of slaves found him still breathing, fashioned a litter, and
spirited him to Nashville.

• • •

IN LATE NOVEMBER 1864, Confederate General John Bell Hood lost five of his generals and more than six thousand of his soldiers — two and a half times the Yankees' casualties — in the Battle of Franklin, which featured a Rebel charge as futile, bloody, and damaging to the Southern cause as Pickett's Charge at Gettysburg. After the battle, recalled Charlie Sandles, "there was a white man there helping with the wounded and dead boys. If he found one that he thought would not get well, he would hit that soldier on the back of his head and finish him up, then roll them all in a big hole together and pile the dirt over them. I did not help him much," Sandles recalled, "cause I'd got to where I would see spooks," so Sandles was told to "bury the dead horses that was killed."

TWO WEEKS LATER, Hood led what remained of his crippled, barefoot, and half-starved Army of Tennessee to within sight of Nashville's state-house and deployed his troops on frozen ground along a broken three-mile front. A few days before what would become known as the Battle of Nashville, a Northern chaplain "met an old Negro out near the picket line. He was bent with age and rheumatism, and his short hair was as white as a snow ball. He seemed to be out for a reconnaissance for his own benefit. I said to him, 'Well, what do you think? Will General Hood take Nashville?'"

"That's just it," the old man replied. "That's what I was studying on myself. And I reckon General Hood won't come to Nashville," he declared, "because he couldn't do justice to his self in here."

The old man was both right and wrong. Hood had committed his troops to an attack that could never succeed, from a position he could afford neither to defend nor to abandon. Nevertheless, Hood remained determined to attack.

"There am no fighting at first," a former slave named John Finnely recalled, "but before long they starts the battle." The cacophony "was awful: just one steady roar of the guns and the cannons." The windows "all shook out from the shakement of the cannons. There am dead mens all over the ground and lots of wounded, and some cussing, and some praying. Some am moaning, and this and that one cry for the water, and, God almighty, I don't want any such again. There am men carrying the dead off the field, but they can't keep up with the cannons." "It sounded like the cannons would tear the world to pieces," recalled a Nashville Contraband. "I could hear the big shells humming as they came. They cut off treetops just like a man cutting off weeds with a scythe. Big shells and little ones. Some were chained together and what not. You could hear them hit the ground and then burst."

By now, hundreds more Contrabands had swarmed into the city, many of them refugees from a camp in Pulaski that had been overrun by the Rebels. Tennessee's capital "was just packed with women and children, both white and colored," recalled a slave laundress from Franklin. "We were all huddled there together, slept together and ate together, and there was no distinction either in the food we received or the care we got. We all had to stay inside until the fighting was over." When a Yankee officer ordered everyone to drop to the ground, her mother thrust her head down with such force that it knocked out some of her teeth.

Just before one o'clock in the afternoon of December 15, a vastly superior Union force under the dogged General George Henry Thomas marched forward to sweep what was left of Hood's shivering army from the field. During the Battle of Nashville, William Walters heard "the boom of cannons one whole day," and the "rumble of army wagons as they crossed through the town. But there was nothing to see as the fog of the powder smoke became thicker with every blast of Secesh cannon. When the smoke cleared away, I watched the wounded being carried to the clearing across the road: fighting men with arms shot off, legs gone, faces blood-smeared: some of them just laying there cussing God and Man with their dying breath!"

FOR NASHVILLE'S CONTRABANDS, the Battle of Nashville would be not just another lesson in the horrors of war but a crucial test. Up to then, General George Thomas, a Virginian, had deprecated the fighting spirit of black men. Contrabands had applied to Thomas for weapons, but he had given them spades and shovels instead, and rounded up a thousand "loafing or unemployed Negroes or white men" to reinforce the city's defenses. Nevertheless, by 1864 the Union Army was actively recruiting black soldiers in central Tennessee, and as Thomas's troops advanced on Hood, eight black regiments took the field.

Outnumbered, outgunned, and outmaneuvered in one of the most decisive battles of the war, Hood's Army of Tennessee was decimated. Between his defeat and Sherman's devastating march through Georgia, the Confederacy would soon be reduced to defending "Richmond and its dependencies." The Union action at Nashville was so decisive, and the Rebel flight so complete, that there were relatively few casualties.

But on the Federal side of the equation, black regiments sustained some of the heaviest losses: 630 out of a Union total of 3,057. A Yankee chaplain recalled coming upon "the ranks of colored soldiers, filling a long trench dug on the hill side in front of our earthwork where the fiercest fighting occurred." General Thomas had himself owned slaves in Virginia, and at fifteen had been forced to flee his home during Nat Turner's slave insurrection. But now, touring the smoking battlefield, his horse stepping among the intermingled bodies of black and white troops, Thomas turned to his officers and declared that for him "the matter is settled; Negroes will fight."

And die. The cold was especially bitter that Nashville winter, and the Contrabands soon ran out of firewood. Families in tents were the first to suffer. One father begged for planks so that his children would not have to sleep in the trampled, half-frozen mud that lay six inches deep. In the weeks after Hood's defeat, about one out of every six — perhaps as many as 1,400 — Contrabands would die of exposure, disease, and starvation.

Part VIII

The East

1864

22

---◆◆---

"All That Killing"

Lee's Hen · *Spotsylvania* · *Henry Smith* · *Jane Tyler*
Cold Harbor · *A Yankee Hospital* · *Slave and Soldier Burials*
Paid Labor · *Marianna*

FOLLOWING ALONG IN an ambulance wagon, William Mack Lee, Robert E. Lee's slave cook, was hard-pressed to do his job. "In times of war, you get your victuals wherever you at. Army has to live on the country. But Marse Robert wouldn't let his men steal nothing." He always made his men "give a requisition" for whatever they took. Lee "had a commissary tent along, and a orderly to bring in food for headquarters. Only sometimes he'd get lost, or wouldn't bring in enough, and I'd have to get more somehow. I never exactly stole any food, but I caught a few chickens now and then," because the general "surely love chicken!"

THE ONE TIME that "Marse Robert ever scolded me in the whole four years that I followed him through the war, was down in the Wilderness." Two years earlier, Lee had acquired "a little black hen" and dubbed her Nellie. "She was a good hen, and laid mighty near every day. We kept her in the ambulance, where she had her nest." On May 4, the eve of the Battle of the Wilderness, "we was all so hungry, and I didn't have nothing to cook, that I was just plumb bumfuzzled. I didn't know what to do. Marse Robert, he had gone and invited a crowd of generals to eat with him, and I had to get the victuals." William had cooked "some flannel cakes, a little tea, and some lemonade, but I allowed as how that would

not be enough for them gentlemen. So I had to go out to the ambulance and catch the little black hen." He "hated for to lose her"; nevertheless, he "picked her good, and stuffed her with bread stuffing, mixed
with butter."

Somehow Lee recognized his prize hen when William "brung Nellie
into the commissary tent," for he turned on his servant "right before all
them gentlemen." "William," said Lee, "now that you have killed Nellie,
what are we going to do for eggs?" "I just had to do it, Marse Robert," he
replied. But Lee "kept on scolding me about that hen. He never scolded
about nothing else. He told me I was a fool to kill the hen what lay the
golden egg. It made Marse Robert awful sad to think of anything being
killed, whether 'twas one of his soldiers, or his little black hen."

The hen may well have been a surrogate for the thousands of Confederates Lee knew he was about to send to their deaths. On May 5, 1864,
Grant inaugurated his first sustained attack on the Army of Northern Virginia. Henry Smith arrived in Spotsylvania County on the second day of
the battle with his master, James E. Smith, of Company C, 4th Texas Infantry, and his comrade, B. L. Aycock. "Longstreet marched us at double
quick march for several miles," and by the time they reached the main
force, "General Lee's men was all wore out." Lee rode up "to the Texas
Brigade, and he made a talk that sure roused our boys all up." Then their
brigade commander "told us what General Lee done said. The boys went
into the battle line, and I gets sent to the ordnance wagons." Companies
C and E were posted at a battery near Lee, where, seated on his horse,
the general began to draw Yankee fire. "One of the Brigade boys see'd
where General Lee was getting right in plain view of the Northern skirmishers," Smith was told, "so one of the Texas boys, he gets hold of the
general's bridle rein, and he say 'Lee to the rear,' and that's one time the
general obeyed a private's command."

The Texas Brigade chased the Yankees out of a Union breastwork
constructed from "piled-up logs in the thick woods." Private Aycock "up
and goes to a tree that was forked near the ground right close to the
Northern lines," and fired at the retreating Yankees. "Then he looked
around" and saw that the five comrades who had been standing behind
him now lay "wounded or killed." The Texas Brigade "stayed right there
all day, and the next day buried their dead." Late in the night they were
ordered to march on Spotsylvania Courthouse to head off Grant. Smith
remembered how "the wagons, the artillery, the teams and the soldiers"
got so "mixed up on that awful dark night, that you can't tell nothing

about nothing, and every once in a while they'd stop, and down a fellow would drop to sleep in his tracks. One of the privates in Company C could not sleep, and he kept his self busy awaking the other soldiers up when they could make a move" of a few more steps. "They suffered all that night."

The Texas Brigade "gets where they told to, and they waits for Grant. The Northern soldiers just attack the Texas Brigade one place, and our boys just sent them back without no trouble at all. Everything is quiet a while," so Private David M. Dechard of Company E "decided to go over to the enemy's line and get close enough to hear what they going to do, and for him to see where they was." Soon Dechard returned carrying a pair of Yankee boots, "cause he done wored his out marching. Marse Dechard set down to try the boots on, and Marse Aycock standing watching, when something goes 'ping,' and Marse Aycock look at Marse Dechard, and he seen the boy open his shirt front. A ball had got between his ribs. In less than no time at all, that boy was dead, and he never did get to try on them boots what he need so bad."

The Yankees broke through where "the roads they made an angle about a half a mile from where the Texas Brigade was at," and what followed was so gory "the folks always call it, after that, the Bloody Angle." Smith tried to make his way forward, but his master ordered him back to the wagons. "All the time us boys getting fewer and fewer. Then General John B. Gordon drove the Northern soldiers back, and there wasn't no more fighting there." It was a Rebel victory, but a costly one, and for Lee a sign that Lincoln had finally found in Grant a commander who would fight.

JANE TYLER WAS one of forty slaves belonging to Dr. Wat Henry Tyler, whose plantation lay in Hanover County, Virginia. The doctor was the older brother of John Tyler, one of five former American presidents who had lived to see the nation plunged into a civil war they had done so little to avert. But Tyler had compounded his sins of omission by turning against the Union and joining the provisional Confederate government as a congressman.

Jane Tyler and her children lived in one of a double row of slave cabins behind the doctor's mansion, and had first laid eyes on the Yankees when Union cavalry cantered through the county in the summer of 1862. "But they soon went on," she remembered, "and they didn't do no harm." It was perhaps a mercy that Dr. Tyler died soon afterward, leav-

ing his plantation to his son J.C. For in the spring of 1864, Philip Henry
Sheridan's Union cavalry proved less benign as they scoured Hanover
County on their way to capturing the crossroads town of Cold Harbor.

"His men was quite troublesome, and we saw hard times. They didn't
tarry long, only one night; but 'they swept the deck and burned the
broom.' If a cavalryman come across one of the hogs that ran in the
woods, he'd kill it and throw it up on his horse and carry it away." The
Yankees tore "the clothes off my mother's line, and they took a new coun-
try-wove counterpane and a dress." They appropriated or destroyed all
the corn and fodder, and broke into the kitchen "and take the bread out
of the skillet. They come into our house and pointed to a featherbed." "Is
that your bed?" a soldier asked Jane's elderly mother. "Yes," she replied.
But the soldier chose not to believe her. "It's a blamed old Reb's bed," he
said, and carried it away.

Though Dr. Tyler had sent all of the family's gold-plated silver to
his brother for safekeeping, the soldiers barged into Tyler's mansion at
suppertime and "took hold of the tablecloth and pulled it off so everything on it went right down, and the china and glassware broke up on
the floor."

Young David Anderson was the slave of John T. and Frances Anderson, whose farm lay near the Tyler plantation. On a hot, dry morning at
the end of May, his master was "out in the garden with my mother and
four of us children picking strawberries. It was along after breakfast, and
he was fixing up some stuff to take to Richmond. By and by, my old Mistress come out to the garden." "Don't you hear it thunder?" she asked
her husband. "You listen to that roaring." "I don't see no cloud," he replied, "but that seems to be thunder or something." "He stood there listening and looking, and pretty soon he says, 'I certainly think a cloud is
rising somewhere. The sun is not as bright as it was a while ago.'

"Presently several men on big black horses appeared at the turn of the
road." "Hello! Fanny!" John T. called to his wife. "There's something going on." "We four children took for the gate. It was a big double gate in
front of the shop. We clumb up on it, and the men went past — bloobity,
bloobity, bloobity — as fast as they could ride." Soon a horde of Union
cavalry was "galloping down the road and through the fields in every direction," and infantry "running and carrying on" and tearing down the
fences.

"They had some of the prettiest, shiniest things at their sides: bayonets and swords. We children went out in the road to see all we could

see, and Mother had to run out and get us. We lived in a log cabin in Master's yard, and she took us there. She just screamed, she was so frightened. My old Mistress was wild, too. There was such a lot of mens and horses on the place, and they had come so sudden, and there was so much hollering and confusion" that Anderson's slaves "were all lost from each other." The soldiers rounded up most of John T.'s livestock and, to Anderson's horror, not only killed a young mule and an old horse "that was no good for their use," but all of the master's sheep and chickens.

As the Yankees set up camp in the woods across the road, "we was all so scared that in the night Old Master's people and the colored people" decided to flee. David Anderson's "mother lit some tallow candles to light our way," and masters and slaves crept through a "string of woods to another plantation."

AFTER SHERIDAN AND his Union cavalry had hunkered down at Cold Harbor, Grant prepared to defend this vital crossroads against Lee's advance. "When Grant's and Lee's armies got here," Jane Tyler recalled, "we kept watching which way they was moving, and the officers promised to tell us if there was any danger." On the morning of June 3, "it looked as if they might fight right on our place and tear things all to pieces. So the Union officers told us to take the children and every one and go away back in the rear." Most of the slaves "traveled on foot, and the women toted the children that couldn't walk." The battle was soon raging along a seven-mile front, and the Yankees were caught in a crossfire from the Rebels' zigzag maze of entrenchments. "Lord have mercy!" exclaimed Tyler. "It seemed like the guns shook the whole earth, and we could see the smoke rise as if there was a big fire. Thousands and thousands was killed" — at an hourly rate higher than in any other battle of the Civil War — "and if the Yankees captured a Rebel who could do anything at all to assist, they made him come and help the wounded."

ON MONDAY, JUNE 13, Grant withdrew his battered army to the James River, thereby giving Lee what would be his last significant victory of the war. "As soon as the Union army retreated back," Jane Tyler remembered, "most of the colored people went away with it. They didn't like being slaves," for many of them had masters "who drove them so, they fared mighty bad: *mighty* bad! So off they went with the Northern army, and some got killed and some didn't," and a "good many come back when the war was over."

The Yankees turned the late Dr. Tyler's house into a hospital. When Jane and her fellow slaves returned on June 12, "one of the wounded men was setting on the steps of the big house begging for water. I went to the well, which was right in the yard, and got some. He was leaning back, too weak to move, and I put my arm behind his head and gave him a drink. But the water and some blood come right out of a wound in his chest, and he fell over dead. Well," said Tyler, "I helped what I could." If she saw "a man suffering, I would give him water, and I made coffee and cooked and washed."

On June 14, after both armies had departed, Tyler and her oldest daughter "went on the battlefield. Hundreds of people were looking around there," including David Anderson, who came upon his mother's ripped-up feather bed lying in the woods. Others Tyler deemed "grave robbers" were "going along, pulling off coats and boots." Burial parties interred the dead soldiers "as fast as they could, and they tore the fences to pieces and used them to burn up the dead horses, and the old stinking beef, and the like of that."

Tyler and her daughter "come to where a lot of dead soldiers was buried. They was in great long trenches and not very well covered, and some hogs was down there eating of the dead bodies. Pretty soon a dog that belonged on our place ran past us with a man's foot in his mouth." "Oh, Mamma! Look what Tiger's got!" her daughter cried, and fell back in a faint. Tyler sent for her master "as soon as we got her in the house." "You deserve to lose the child," J. C. Tyler scolded her. "You had no business to take her to the battlefield." Jane Tyler "never did go to it no more."

AS SLAVES WERE often the first to venture out onto the field of battle after the armies withdrew, their testimony brims with grim accounts of their masters' fields littered with the dead and wounded. After the Battle of Jenkins' Ferry, in Grant County, Arkansas, Jane Osbrock's father "carried all us children and some of the white folks to see the battlefield. I remember the dead was lying in graves, just one row after another, and hadn't even been covered up." Cicero Gaulding and his master attended to the dead after the Battle of Senatobia, in Mississippi. "We dug a long ditch and laid them in," Gaulding recalled, "but Master would say, 'Don't bury no blue coat.'" "The poor soldiers were either buried or left lying on the field for vultures to consume." John Ogee recalled that he sometimes had to reassemble the corpses he found on the battlefield. "Some of them you could find the head but couldn't find no body, then sometimes

you could find the body and not the head." Ephraim Johnson of Mississippi performed an even grislier task, "helping to load carts of arms and
legs that army surgeons had removed at the hospitals."

Louvenia Huff's father was a Union teamster whose duties included
piling Rebel corpses into his wagon and "dumping them in the river," because "the Union soldiers wouldn't give the Rebels time to bury the
other side." Her father "took rations all but the times he hauled dead soldiers." "They make us pick up all the dead and burn them," recalled Jack
Harrison, who accompanied his master into the Union Army as a water
carrier and cook. "Master, he examine white soldiers that was not dead.
If he thought there wasn't a chance for him to get well, he take his
knife and cut the white soldier's throat. But sometimes he would shoot
him, so we could pile him on a fire or dig a great long ditch and pile them
in it. That was a terrible time," Harrison groaned. "All that killing for
nothing."

But some slaves seemed to take mass burials in stride. A Williamson
County slave remembered that at Murfreesboro, "we used to have to
bury a certain number of men every day. The burying ground was divided into sections, and we had to go out in the field, get our corpses, and
bury them." But he and a friend devised a system that saved them the
round-trip. "Some nights me and my partner used to go out in the field
and find two or three corpses that had been brought up by some others,"
then they would "take them to our grave, and bury them. In this way," he
cheerfully recalled, "we would get through and be gone to Murfreesboro
among the women before some of the rest got started." "When nobody
was looking," Jefferson Davis's former slave James Lucas "stripped the
dead of they money. Sometimes they had it in a belt around they bodies.
Soon I got a big roll of folding money. Then I come tramping back
home."

If some slaves seemed callous about disposing of soldiers' corpses,
they had good teachers. Many masters had buried their slaves without
a marker or a ceremony. "If a slave die, Master made the rest of us tie
a rope round his feet and drag him off. Never buried one; it was too
much trouble." When Mary Reynolds's fellow slaves died, the Kilpatricks
of Black River, Louisiana, had their survivors "cart them down to the
graveyard on the place and not bury them deep enough that buzzards
wouldn't come circling around."

"When a slave died he was just drug down there to a hole in the
ground and covered over with dirt," recalled Polly Shine, "but if some of

the white folks died it was terrible the way the slaves took on as well as the white folks." They did not have much choice. When a member of his master's family died, Willis Winn and his fellow slaves "had to go to the grave and walk round and drop in some dirt on him." But blacks were buried "any way. Dig a ditch and cover them up. I can show you right now," said Winn, "down in Louisiana where I was raised, forty acres with nothing but black folks buried on them."

Katie Darling's master would send a couple of his slaves off "to bury the body and tell them, 'Don't be long.' There was no singing and praying allowed, but just put them in the ground, cover them up and hurry on back to that field." "Once when some boys dug a slave's grave too short," David Byrd recalled, their owner "says to put back the body in the grave, and then he jumps into the grave hisself. Right on the dead he jumps and stomps till the body is smashed and twisted to fit the hole." Though Byrd's master "would let the Negroes form a ring around that Negro grave," and "bow our heads whilst Master would pray," Byrd reckoned a slave's passing hurt his master "worse, as he would be losing a valuable piece of property." But other masters were not so sentimental. Thomas Maguhee whipped several slaves for defying his order not to cry over a fellow slave's corpse. And a Georgia slave owner named Sam Kendricks attacked a group of slaves who had gathered to pray over the corpse of a little boy named Moses. He said if he ever heard Moses' father "preaching or praying round" in the "graveyard or anywheres else, he gwine lash him to death."

During the war, masters enlisted their house slaves in preparing white cadavers. Louis Hughes recalled trying to make his master's dead son look presentable. "He had lain on the battlefield two days before he was found," he remembered, "and his face was black as a piece of coal. I was there to assist in whatever way they needed," when a local doctor suggested they paint his face white. The procedure took all afternoon, and "it was not until late in the evening that his father and mother came down to view the body for the first time." After the corpse had been "all dressed, and the face painted, cheeks tinted with a rosy hue, to appear as he always did in life," Louis Hughes thought he looked "handsome."

FROM THE BEGINNING of the war, the Secessionist state of Florida had supplied the Rebels with much of their beef and salt. Hoping to interrupt the flow to the rest of the Confederacy, in February 1864, a Union force under General Truman Seymore invaded the state's interior, only to be thrown back by Confederate troops at the railway town of Olustee.

In September 1864, Union General Alexander Asboth set off on an expedition through northwest Florida to sweep away scattered Rebel cavalry and "collect white and colored recruits." As his men scoured the countryside, a Union trooper approached an eight-year-old Jackson County slave named Armstrong Purdee at the gate of his master's farm. "Boy," he asked Purdee, "does you want to go?" "Yes, sir," Purdee replied. The cavalryman then "moved one of his feet out of the stirrup and said, 'Put your feet in there,' which I did. At the same time, he reached for my hand and pulled me up on the horse, and placed me behind him and placed my hands about him." "Hold on," he warned Purdee. "Do not fall off."

Purdee spent the morning clinging to the trooper as he galloped from one plantation to another. Suddenly they heard gunfire, and "the Yankee that I was riding behind left the road and said to me, 'Hold fast. Do not fall.'" Somehow young Purdee managed to stay mounted as the trooper and his comrades "did not go around anything" but simply "jumped their horses over fallen trees" and anything else in their path. On the outskirts of Marianna two cavalrymen were shot from their saddles and taken to a nearby stream, where "water was poured on them. One was shot in the right breast, my attention being attracted by his groans and calling for water." As the expedition thundered into town, General Asboth himself was shot in the arm and the upper jaw, apparently by a sniper hiding in the local Episcopal church, which the Yankees immediately put to the torch. As the men inside ran out, the Yankees shot them down, but when news reached them that a substantial Rebel force was approaching from Georgia, they withdrew with some six hundred liberated slaves, including Purdee, who joined them on a steamboat bound for Fort Pickens on Santa Rosa Island, where his frantic father finally retrieved him. The Rebels would repeatedly repel Yankee expeditions into Florida, but each raid wrought such devastation that in the end Secessionist Governor John Milton, a descendant of the poet, holed up in his mansion, put a pistol to his head, and killed himself.

AFTER COLD HARBOR, David Anderson recalled, "the Yankees ran down this-a-way through the Chickahominy swamp and every direction, and the Rebels pushed off toward Petersburg as hard as they could rip." The widow Tyler moved to Richmond, taking with her "the oldest child from each of the slave families. That was pretty hard on us," Jane Tyler remembered, but there was nothing she could do. Her master "wanted to get out of the way of the army, and he went off with his family and left us with nothing. We just had to shift for ourselves."

They soon found employment with the Yankees, however, and for the first time in their lives they were paid for their labor. The Tyler house remained a Union hospital for the rest of the war, and the army "paid us for everything we did," said Tyler. "They paid us for work, and they bought peas, onions, lettuce, and such things from us. I've gathered many a lot of vegetables from the garden for them. Every Sunday the soldiers had meetings on the lawn: preaching, you know, for the hospital." Tyler fell in love with a drummer boy who "beat his drum to call the soldiers to the meetings." He promised her "that when the war ended, he was coming down South to see me, if he didn't get killed. I used to cook for him. I've given him many a mouthful to eat. He was mighty fond of corn-bread. So was all the soldiers. Oh! but we were glad when the cruel war was over!" Tyler exclaimed. "The white people said it was a civil war, but we slaves called it cruel."

23

"A Most Scandalous Thing"

CHARLIE MITCHELL WAS nine years old when the war began, and remembered his native Lynchburg, Virginia, as "a good-sized town." Woodruff's slave-trading yard "was about the biggest thing there. It was all fenced in and had a big stand in the middle where they sold the slaves. They sold them for a big price, handcuffed and chained them together," and led them off "like convicts. The yard was full of Louisiana and Texas slave buyers most all the time." A slave's "doom was done sealed if he was refugeed to Louisiana, cause that was where they beat them till the hide was raw, salt them and beat them some more."

It was here at this trading, transportation, and manufacturing hub that the Confederates established Camp Davis. "Located close to a big college there in Lynchburg," it soon looked "like another town." The Confederates "threw up a big breast-works out the other side of the college." Mitchell liked "to watch them drill the college boys there in town. They wore grey caps and suits in the winter and white suits in the summer. I didn't know till after surrender what they was drilling them for. General Shumaker was Commander of the Confederate Artillery, and killed the first Yankee that come to Lynchburg." Mitchell recalled that "lots of Confederate soldiers passed through Lynchburg going to Petersburg."

PETERSBURG MIGHT HAVE fallen as early as June 1864 had the Yankee attack on its inadequately manned fortifications been pressed. But even after breaking through the Rebels' first line of defense, Benjamin Butler's corps proceeded so cautiously as to allow the Rebels time not only to withdraw to their heavily fortified inner works but to receive reinforcements from Lee. The Rebels inflicted more than 8,000 Union casualties, four times the number of Confederates the Yankees had initially attacked. Butler's bungling necessitated a siege, which would last ten months and cost some 42,000 Union and 28,000 Confederate casualties.

On June 17, as Butler opened fire, Major General David Hunter attempted to attack Lynchburg's railroad and canal depots. "Once some Yankee soldiers come through close to Lynchburg," said Charlie Mitchell, and when Confederate General Jubal Early's corps arrived by rail, "there was a scrimmage between the two armies about two miles from town. It didn't last long," however, and Hunter withdrew into West Virginia. "I hear folks say that they found several blue jackets of the Yankees where they fought after the scrimmage was over."

IN JULY, JUBAL EARLY tried to divert Grant by mounting an attack on Washington. After winning a skirmish at Monocacy Bridge on the ninth, he reached the outskirts of the capital. Two days later, he menaced Fort Stevens, the most formidable of the bastions that guarded the city.

A freedwoman named Elizabeth Thomas hoped she would be protected from Rebel attack in her home behind the fort. But as Early approached, the Yankees decided to tear her house down and use her basement as part of a hastily dug 130-foot outer entrenchment. Thomas tried to plead with them to spare her home, but "the soldiers camped here at this time were mostly German," she recalled, "and I could not understand them, not even the officers." It was only when "they began taking out my furniture and tearing down our house" that she understood.

On July 12, Thomas sat weeping with her baby in her arms amid "what furniture I had left," when a "tall, slender man, dressed in black," came up to her. "It is hard," the man said, "but you shall reap a great reward." Thomas looked up, and "it was President Lincoln," she declared, adding that "had he lived, I know the claim for my losses would have been paid."

Soon afterward "an officer came prancing along and said, 'All you people must get out of here. We're going to form a line of battle.' This was back of the fort. Then the artillery came with their fine guns, and some sailors. The next thing we knew, the Rebel cannon balls came howling over our heads, and women and children were running in all directions." Thomas found shelter in a stable, and "rebel bullets pattered against it like hail." But while peering out from between the wall boards, she spotted Lincoln again, "standing on the fort," as a bullet felled a man beside him. An officer "made Mr. Lincoln get down behind the fort. But Lincoln was very tall," she said, "and kept peeping over the top at the woods from which the Rebels were firing."

Lincoln had assured Grant that he could defend Washington against the Rebels with "hundred-day men and invalids." Now Elizabeth Thomas watched as "a lot of sick men from the hospitals marched out and took charge of the cannon on the fort. And the way they shot at General Early's men was something awful. The guns on the fort set fire to many houses in front of them. Presently the Rebels stopped firing their guns and then the Union soldiers all yelled" and "charged down the slope," and the Rebels never threatened Washington again.

"THE WAR MADE us lots of trouble," recalled a freed black girl who had hired herself out to the Cooley family. They were the latest owners of Belle Grove, once a bright blossom in the diadem of plantations that adorned the Shenandoah Valley, but now a battered and all but discarded husk. Many of the plantation's slaves had "run off North, and a great many others were taken up the country by their masters out of the way of the army." But a hired slave girl had remained behind with her family "to keep everything together what we could."

Yankee soldiers encamped along nearby Cedar Creek "would carry off considerable outdoor stuff unbeknownst to us, and they would come into the house and look around and take what they pleased: victuals, flour, anything." But her people "didn't interfere with them," for they were "glad if they took the stuff and did us no other harm." It was the girl's experience that Yankees and Rebels "acted a good deal alike about stealing and destroying," and by the fall of 1864 "we couldn't hardly tell which from which because the Southerners would have on old blue clothes that they'd got off the camp, I suppose."

In Middletown, less than two miles from Belle Grove, a free girl named Serena Spencer was still in bed when an elderly slave from across the street "come rapping at Mother's door and called to her: 'Get up, Henrietta, get up! They're fighting!' Mother roused up us children, and we could hear the guns at Belle Grove going pop, pop, pop, pop!" Spencer's mother was "most scared to death," but her three-hundred-pound father, Abe, "toddled around lively for a little while," trying to see what was going on.

The Union Army's 8th and 19th corps were comfortably encamped at Belle Grove, where the hired girl had had to share her cabin with Union scouts. They might have averted what was to come if they had done their job, but now, in the early hours of October 19, Lieutenant General Jubal Early descended on them with a force of 21,000 Rebels.

At the first sputter of gunfire, the scouts "bounced up" and "rolled out of the house in a hurry," the hired girl recalled. "I run and looked out, and then I shut the door. It was already daylight and the fighting had begun. The Confederates were driving the Union men across the field down below the house. We kept as far back in our cabin as we could, and we set there not knowing when we'd be killed. It was too late to get to the big house."

The Yankees tried to form a line "back of a wall side of the Belle Grove house, but Lord! they didn't stop there long; in a little while the guns wasn't firing right around us no more. So I went to the door and looked out. The tents that had been in the yard were all gone," and the surrounding yard "looked just like new ground with the stumps on it," for men were lying "about over the fields every which way."

By now the stunned Federals were a mile and a half down the road, fleeing through Middletown with the Confederates in hot pursuit. "The Yankees come rushing through here with the Rebels right after them and knocking them in the head," Serena Spencer recalled. "The wounded men were crying, 'Oh Lord, oh Lord!' There was shooting all along this pike, and lots of bullets went through the upper part of our cabin."

But in afteryears Spencer would confess that she had "enjoyed it. I was small and didn't understand the danger. I thought it was the finest thing that ever was, and my folks couldn't hardly keep me in. Father and the others was all laying down flat on the floor by the chimney. But I wasn't a bit scared," and she romped back and forth across the street, "busy as a bee. The bombshells was coming over, and I just thought it was grand." After one of them landed in her mother's garden, Spencer rushed down to Main Street in time to see "a Yankee shot on a horse. He reeled first this way, then that, and fell off, and his saddle was covered with blood."

Returning at last to the house, Spencer rushed upstairs to the loft and stuck her head through a window to watch the battle. "A Union soldier had hid by the Episcopal church which was just beyond our cabin, and he was taking aim at a Rebel on the corner. But the Rebel went around onto the next street out of range, and the Yankee looked up and saw me watching him. Then he pointed his gun at me." "Take your head in," he commanded, "or I'll shoot you." But the hole in the window "was so small that my chin wouldn't go through without I turned my head side-ways." "Don't shoot!" she begged. But the Yankee "just laid back and laughed." "Little girl," he called to her, "I'm only funning."

"There was an uproar all that day," and in the afternoon two Rebels staggered into the Spencers' cabin and threatened to shoot Serena's mother for refusing to feed them. Because "some soldiers were so auda-cious they'd just as soon shoot you as not," especially if you were a free black, she told them that she and her family were the slaves of a white family across the street. "I don't believe it," one of the soldiers snarled. "You're a liar." But just as the confrontation seemed to approach full boil, Serena's mother heard a commotion in the street and rushed to the door. "Gentlemen," she announced after peering up and down the road, "you better get out of here. The Yankees are on the next street." "No, they're not," the Rebels snapped back. "We done whipped the Yankees this morning, and we're not bothering about them no more."

But Henrietta Spencer was not bluffing, for in the meantime Major General Phil Sheridan had arrived from Winchester, rallied his troops, and launched a massive counterattack. "We'd got news that they were coming," recalled the hired girl at Belle Grove, "and we had all gone to the cellar of the big house where the cooking was done, and the rooms down there were nice and large and had rock walls. I didn't feel much like keeping quiet when I could hear those wounded men groaning in the yard, even if the battle was going on. So I just spent my time walking from one door to another and peeping out."

THOUGH THE REBELS planted their artillery "in the orchard behind," Sheridan's men had "come so sudden that when the artillerymen tried to hitch horses to the cannon to drag them away, the horses got tangled up, and the men couldn't get the guns started," which was when Henrietta

Spencer had first "heard the Yankees backing the Rebels" through town. The two stunned Rebels looked out the door and then rushed to join their comrades as they rapidly fell back. But a Federal cavalryman cut them off and "captured the two rascals."

Mrs. Spencer had long endeared herself to the Yankees as a cook. She "baked bread for them," her daughter remembered, "and made up a little nourishment such as cakes and custard, and they used to double-pay her. They thought the Southern cooking was fine," and now a succession of her customers returned to shake Mrs. Spencer's hand. "Glad to meet you, Aunty," they said. "You see we're back on our old ground once more."

"It wasn't quite dark when they called, and they hadn't hardly gone" when a Confederate private named Charles W. Matthews "come busting in our door. He was a poor, raw-boned, consumptive young strip of a man who was one of our white neighbors." A Yankee patrol had spotted him running down the street in his butternut uniform. "Aunt Henny!" he cried as he burst in. "Uncle Spencer! Save me!"

Thinking fast, Abe Spencer hid Matthews up the chimney and told the boy's pursuers a shrewd version of the truth: that he and his family hadn't "seen nobody but what we knowed." The Spencers kept "Charlie up the chimney till after night," after which "it was a job to get him out. Father had to take hold of his legs and pull him down. His coat was all slid up around his shoulders," and his clothes "was all full of pot-black, soot, and stuff, and his hair was standing up just like bristles. If the Yankees had caught him, they'd have killed him," Serena said, judging by the treatment accorded a Rebel woman who was captured while "scouting around" in a Confederate uniform. "They hung her in some woods right out on the edge of town. She wore the men's clothes over her dress, and they pulled them off, and those clothes laid there on the ground in the woods till they rotted."

That evening, Spencer and her aunt were walking to their barn when "I heard something moving near the woodpile where there was lots of leaves. It was a scrambling sound." Spencer clawed at a heap of leaves "and found a little fellow with yellow stripes on his pants" who turned out to be a Rebel artilleryman shot in the head. "The leaves was sticking all over him, he was so bloody." Spencer ran off to summon a doctor, and though the soldier seemed delirious, "while the doctor was washing the blood off" he mumbled something. The only word they could make out was "Mother." "He said that twice," and died the next night.

The Yankees suffered 5,665 casualties at Cedar Creek, almost twice as many as the Confederates they had outnumbered three to two. But Sheridan had all but brought the Civil War in the Shenandoah Valley to a close with a victory that, with the fall of Atlanta the month before, would win Lincoln a second term. The Yankees returned to Belle Grove, where Sheridan took up residence in the mansion house. "The yard looked right frightful," recalled the hired girl. "There was so many men."

In Middletown the next morning, Abe Spencer took his daughter's hand and together they inspected "a field where there had been some very hot fighting." Near their house, "right over a fence," they came upon a dead Yankee "with the top of his head shot off. His brains and scalp were in his hat. Oh!" Serena Spencer would exclaim half a century later, "it was the most scandalous thing I ever saw in my life the way men was shot to pieces."

"THE BIG OFFICERS in the South and in the North was scheming to get to Richmond," recalled Henry Smith. "General Lee sent the Texas Brigade and some cavalry to keep Grant's men from getting the railroads that run from Richmond to the South and over which the people in Richmond and the soldiers got their supplies. The Brigade beat the Northern soldiers to the place and kept the North from getting the railroad," until August 18, 1864, when Grant tore up this vital supply line between Richmond and Petersburg. "In consequence," wrote James Smith, "much of the Rebel munitions of war and supplies had to be run over a distance of sixteen miles, and then transferred to the cars. Everything that could be used for carrying purposes was pressed into their service." But by now horses and mules had become so scarce that "Negroes were hitched to the wagons," Smith recalled, "and it was said made better time than when horses were used. They would go on their way, singing and joking; and, after a half-hour's intermission at certain places, would push onward as fresh and lively as ever."

BY NOW THE Federals were putting slaves and runaways to better use. As strangers to the South, the Yankees found them invaluable "on account of their thorough knowledge of the country: its ways and resources: its wood, water, fuel, game: and also of the habits of the enemy. Nothing escaped them," wrote James L. Smith. "They'd tell today what happened yesterday thirty miles off" and risk their lives to pass on information to Union engineers, cartographers, agents, and scouts. "Contraband pioneers, armed with sharp axes, would go on expeditions through the woods, under cover of the carbines of the cavalry, hewing away the heavy timber, and preparing the road for the advance." They took special pleasure in killing anything resembling a dog, and on many Virginia plantations "could be seen the lifeless bodies of bloodhounds whose deep baying would no longer be heard about the swamps, indicating the close proximity of pursuers" chasing down runaway slaves.

The pioneering detective Allan Pinkerton once crept into Memphis disguised as a Southern merchant. "Here," he wrote, "as in many other places, I found that my best source of information was the colored men who were employed in various capacities of a military nature which entailed hard labor." Pinkerton "mingled freely with them, and found them ever ready to answer questions and to furnish me with every fact which I desired to possess."

Spying entailed grave risks. "Many with even a word or a look of the least information, both white and black, have gone to their long home," recalled Henry Smith. After witnessing how Union soldiers treated a suspected Rebel spy, Smith "never gave any information either to Rebel or Union men," though "when he thought prudent," he would "aid the Union men all I possibly could." According to Virginia Hayes Shepherd, a Virginia freedman named James Bowser deserved to be ranked with Nathan Hale. Caught spying for the Yankees, he and his son were dragged into the woods. There a mob of slaveholders beat them, beheaded Bowser, and spared his son's life only so he could "carry the news of this ghastly example back to the other Negroes." Confederate scouts in South Carolina used to impersonate Yankees and persuade slaves to show them where the Rebels were encamped. Then, as soon as they obliged, the scouts would seize and lynch them.

The great slave rescuer Harriet Tubman went south during the war as a Yankee nurse and spy. "She was often under fire from both armies," wrote her biographer, and "led our forces through the jungle and the swamp." Tubman "gained the confidence of the slaves by her cheery words, and songs, and sacred hymns, and obtained from them much valuable information." William Webb "was made a spy for the Rebels," but took the job only to acquire all the information he could and share it with the Union Army. He had "stayed with the Rebels long enough," he said, and "learned all I wanted to know, and I knew they did not wish me much good will."

On August 26, 1863, as Union forces laid siege to Charleston, "an escaped Negro slave came in saying that the citizens of Charleston, many of them, wished to have the place surrender" rather than brave the Yankees' incendiary shells. "He said further, that some of our shells have come into the city going beyond the burnt district, and that they had set on fire a cotton shed."

When General Robert Sanford Foster "wanted two scouts to search the neighborhood thoroughly," Vincent Colyer recommended two freedmen. "After four days' absence they returned," wrote Colyer, "having been over a circuit of forty-five miles, part of the time in a heavy storm, through woods and swamps, in Negro cabins, et cetera, and relieved the minds of the Commander by their full and satisfactory report." Back in December 1862, William Henry Singleton had run away from the 1st North Carolina Cavalry and found a job as the servant of the commander of the 10th Connecticut Regiment at New Bern. Suspected by some of being a Rebel spy, he got a chance "to convince them of my honesty" when Yankee pickets brought a stranger into camp "as a suspicious person." Singleton identified him as Major Cornelius Richardson of Singleton's old regiment. But General Foster's adjutant "told me I must not be too positive about this man, because he was a Union man. My reply was, 'If I am not correct, you can cut my throat.'" After the Yankees confirmed both Singleton's and Richardson's identities, they brought Singleton before General Foster, who asked him the best way to move on the Rebels. Singleton suggested a route, and went so far as to tell Foster that if he were in command he would take the Rebels with a flanking movement by way of the Trent River. But Foster "did not accept my proposition and attacked directly, with the result," he said, "that they were repulsed."

IN THE FALL of 1864, Union forces under Major General Alfred Terry set out to test the Rebel defenses around Richmond. "One dark night in early October, us was ordered to move," recalled Henry Smith of General John Gregg's Texas Brigade. His ailing Rebel master had been wounded the previous July and now had to be transported in a wagon. "The Brigade was put on a place on the Darbytown Road" and ordered to countercharge the attacking Yankees. During the course of the day, General Gregg was shot through the neck and killed, and "somehow Marse Jim, he gets a gun and gets into the middle of things." Though the Rebels chased the Yankees back to their entrenchments along New Market Road, "a lot of our boys didn't come back. After dark some of them come back to where us was behind the lines, but there wasn't no Marse

Jim." So Smith crawled out onto the battlefield, only to find his master's perforated corpse. "I gets him up cross my shoulder, and brings him back and buries him, and then this boy gets a mule and a little grub and some of Marse Jim's things, and then I gets into a awful time," making his way back to Texas. "But I finally gets to the old master and tells what I has to and gives what I could keep of Marse Jim's things to the folks."

The siege of Petersburg wore on, thinning Lee's forces by gunfire and starvation. James Drumgoold had been "sent away to the war to keep his master at home, and we did not hear from him for a long time," wrote his sister Kate. "But we made up our minds that if he did not get killed, he would go over to the Northern side as soon as he should get the chance." Drumgoold "did try to get away, but he was caught and locked up in Richmond, and for a while we heard them say that he would be killed. But God was there to help him, so he came out all right and went to work on the breastworks," and, on his second try, "he got over on the Northern side."

As his master's body servant, Benjamin Johnson "didn't have to fight any at all," only "stood in the door of the tent and watch them fight. It was terrible. You could hear the guns firing and see the soldiers falling right and left. All you could see was men getting all shot up. One day I see'd one soldier get his head shot off from his body. Others got arms and legs shot off, and, all the time, all you could hear was the guns going bam, bam, bam." One morning, "I was leaning against the side of the tent with my hand stretched out," when suddenly "a load of grape shot from the guns hit me in the hand and the blood flew everywhere." Johnson recovered the use of his hand, but the father of a slave named George Johnson testified to the perils of serving Richmond's defenders by losing his left leg to a Yankee shell.

WILLIAM ROSE WAS astonished by the braggadocio of the Confederate troops he and his father saw pass along on a trestle at Ashepoo Junction, South Carolina. It was "near the end of the war," when Grant was "before Richmond" and "Sherman was marching — tump-tump — through Georgia. When I get to the junction the train start to come in. What a lot of train! The air fair smoke up with them. They come shouting in from Charleston, bound up-country. One engine in front pulling, one in the back pushing, pushing, pushing." The train was loaded down with soldiers, "thick as peas," and as they rode along the trestle, "one pick a banjo, one play the fiddle. They sing and whoop, they laugh; they holler to the people on the ground, and sing out, 'Good-bye.'" "Well, boys," cried one, "we going to cut the Yankee throat. We on our way to meet him, and he better tremble. Our gun greased up, and our bayonet sharp. Boys, we going to eat our dinner in hell today!"

The Rebels were going "to face bullet," Rose recalled, "but yet they play card, and sing and laugh like they in their own house." It was "the most wonderful sight" Rose ever saw: "all them soldier, laughing light, singing and shouting that way, and all riding fast to battle." Rose turned to his father and asked how men could be so bold when they knew they were "going down to die." "That ain't nothing," his father replied. "They-uns used to that. Ain't you know soldier different?" "Pappy," asked Rose, "you hear them talk about 'eat dinner in hell'?" "They been in the army long time," answered his father as the train passed by. "They don't study hell anymore."

But many Rebel troops were reluctant to take any more risks in a cause they deemed lost. Nathan Best's master was a Rebel captain, and "weren't at Richmond" when it fell because he "got a furlough to go see about his mother, just a few days before. But he just done it to shun that heavy battle. He kept bushwhacking along, and we never did get to Richmond."

"There ain't never been nobody fighting like our Confederates done," a manservant named Tom McAlpin declared, "but they ain't never had a chance. There was just too many of them blue coats for us to lick." He had seen "our Confederates go off laughing and gay; full of life and health. They was big and strong, singing Dixie, and they just knowed they was going to win." But now they were "skin and bone, their eyes all sad and hollow, and their clothes all ragged. They was all looking sick. The spirit they left with just been done whupped out of them. But it took them Yankees a long time to do it."

For its part, the Army of the Potomac that laid siege to Petersburg had lost most of its best and bravest troops in previous campaigns, and now consisted in large part of conscripts, bounty men, and substitutes who were equally reluctant to risk their lives on the orders of commanders they no longer trusted in a war so nearly won. Among the exceptions were many of the more motivated (and imperiled) black troops. During the Petersburg siege, a missionary visited several in a Union hospital. "The colored soldiers excel in jollity," she reported. "One man, who had lost his arm, said to me, 'Oh I should like to have it, but I don't begrudge it.' Another said, 'Another arm robbed. Well, there's one thing, 'twas in a glorious cause, and if I'd lost my life I should have been satisfied. I knew what I was fighting for.' 'It was my effort to take Petersburg,' said a third, 'and I worked as hard as I could.'"

Josh Miles recalled a song he heard black troops sing as the siege wore on. "Would you like to hear my song? / I'm afraid its rather long / Of the 'On to Richmond' double trouble? / Of the half a dozen trips / And the half a dozen slips, / And the latest busting of the bubble? / Pull off your coat and roll up your sleeve," ran the chorus, "For Richmond am a hard road to travel."

Part IX

Sherman

1864

24

---◆---

"Ain't Gonna Be Long Now"

Sherman • Meridian • Columbus • Atlanta • Slaves' Welcome
The Wrong Uniform • Milledgeville • "War Is Hell"

G RANT'S STAUNCHEST ALLY, William Tecumseh Sherman, had stuck by his friend when Grant was accused of insubordination and drunkenness, just as Grant had defended Sherman from allegations that he was mad. Before departing for the Eastern Theater to take overall command of the Union Army, Grant had entrusted his Division of the Mississippi to his ferocious and irascible old friend. With the western corps of the Union Army at his disposal, he would cut a broad swath running from Tennessee to the Carolinas.

IN EARLY 1864, Sherman marched out of the West to attack the railway town of Meridian, Mississippi. "When word come that they was coming, it sound like a moaning wind in the quarter," recalled Nettie Henry. "Marse Greer had done sunk all the silver in the duck pond and hid out the horses and cows" in a canebrake. "Everybody was saying, 'The Yankees is coming! The Yankees is coming!'" She and her playmates "was scared, but it was like Sunday, too: nobody doing nothing." So they took up the cry "and sort of sing-like, 'The Yankees is coming! The Yankees is coming!'"

But then the Confederates under Leonidas Polk evacuated Meridian, and the Yankees stormed in and "burn up seventy houses and all the stores." After Northern officers established their quarters in Henry's master's house, their men found all of Greer's caches of valuables and livestock. But at least "they left the house and didn't bother the family, because they called theyselves company. The good Lord knows Marse Greer didn't invite them! But the captain's being there kept the riffraff soldiers from tearing up everything," while elsewhere in the town "they tore up the railroad tracks and toted off everything they couldn't eat. I don't understand nothing about how come they act like that," Nettie Henry sighed. "Us ain't done nothing to *them*."

WILLIAM AND BETTIE LEWIS "were quite young when the Civil War broke out," but in their old age they remembered the day in April "when Columbus, Georgia, was attacked, captured, and subsequently burned by the Northern soldiers" under General James Harrison Wilson. Bettie was on the way back from town with her owner's family "when the first cannon fire from the Alabama side of the Chattahoochee was loosed on Columbus." The bombardment frightened them "nearly to death!" "The Yankees come," Abraham Chambers recalled, "and us heard the big guns way in Columbus, Georgia, and see'd the fire on Sunday night. I was on the swamp with eleven head of horses and some of Mistress' fine things from the house." Hearing the first shots, Rhodus Walton and his fellow slaves cried, "It ain't gonna be long now."

CUT OFF FROM their supplies by Union patrols and blockades, Atlanta's residents were already starving by the time Sherman reached the city's outskirts. Prices "was so high that you couldn't afford to buy nothing," recalled Ella Belle Ramsey, a slave of the Goldsmith family. "I remember one time Miss Goldsmith fuss cause they try to charge her five dollars for a little dab of sugar. I hear her say that somebody told her that they sell potatoes and carrots for a dollar each one."

Ramsey and her mistress nursed the wounded Rebel soldiers who crowded into the city from the Confederate lines. "Atlanta was crawling with soldiers then," she recalled. "They open a soldiers' hospital," but Ramsey "always hate to go there. It was just a little wood building with cots in it for the soldiers to lay on. But the men was always screaming and groaning and taking on, and it stuck in my ears." Even after she returned home, "I could hear them all night."

When news of Sherman's inexorable advance reached Atlanta, the Rebel authorities ordered all civilians "to get out of there and go someplace else." Those who "didn't leave had to be responsible for what happen to them. You see, both the Confederates and the Federals want the place," Ramsey explained. "I don't know why they want it, but they do." Ramsey's master told his slaves "he was sorry, but he got to send us to the country," which suited Ramsey, as she didn't "want to be in no place with all that fighting going on." So she was relieved to climb into Goldsmith's wagon and flee to his farm in Bartow County.

J. H. Hill was a child slave of Joshua and Emily Hill of Morgan County, Georgia, when the Yankees advanced on Atlanta. "We children hung out on the front fence from early morning till late in the evening, watching the soldiers go by. It took most of the day." The Yankees "carried provisions, hams, shoulders, meal, flour, and other food. They had their cooks and their servants. I remember seeing a woman in that crowd of servants" with a baby in her arms. "You children get off that fence," she shouted, "and go learn your ABC's." But Hill "thought she was crazy telling us that, for we had never been allowed to learn nothing at all like reading and writing."

William Ward recalled that "when Sherman reached the present site of Hapeville, he bombarded Atlanta with cannon." "That battle of Atlanta was the worst thing that's ever been," recalled George Strickland, whose master's farm lay just outside the city limits. "All the houses for a far piece just shook from the big guns. The Yankees camped in a big hundred-acre field close by. Then they rushed up to the house, kicked the gate down, took Mistress's trunk out and bust it open, hunting money. But they found none," and when the slaves wouldn't tell them where their master had hidden his horses, "they burnt the house down."

"Now that was some battle," exclaimed Elodga Bradford, who had tried to help his master, Private Charles Thompson Chamberlain of the Mississippi Light Artillery, fend off Sherman's attack. Bradford was a mess cook, but "sometimes, when the guns was quiet," he and his fellow slaves used to "get out and entertain the camp. Then we would all get to laughing and be right jolly. But most the time it was serious talk," he remembered. "We was losing too many men." Bradford was "right in the thick of it right from the start. Anybody who say I ain't seen heaps of killing and got deaf with all the noise, ain't telling the truth."

In the city, William Ward remembered, "the white residents made all sorts of frantic attempts to hide their money and other valuables. Some hiding places were under stumps of trees and in sides of hills." When Sherman entered Atlanta, he ordered the city evacuated and set ablaze. "Houses was burning in every direction," recalled Jim Stovall, "and Old Mistress's yard was illuminated." "It was a grand sight," said another slave eyewitness, "at least to us," though to the "poor folks that saw their homes go up in smoke, it wasn't so pretty. But, I tell you," he continued, "the people of the South needed some such of those as that; they needed to learn that war is a serious thing: no boys' play at all, nor fooling. And Sherman seemed to be the man for that kind of teaching."

During the battle, Bradford had become separated from his master, and sought him out after the Confederates had been routed. "But I find out they had took him prisoner. So I starts on my way back home." It took him "six weeks to walk back," and when he finally reached his master's plantation in Port Gibson, Mississippi, "I says to myself, I says, 'Elodga, you has been away from home long enough now. From now on, you is gonna rest your weary head, let your tramping feet relax, recline your poor pitiful body, and stay put in Port Gibson from now on.'"

Susan Mcintosh recalled watching Sherman's troops as they moved out of the city. "They marched up and down Marietta Street from three o'clock in the evening until seven o'clock next morning," and when they withdrew, "there weren't a house left standing in Atlanta what weren't riddled with shell holes." In the meantime, the Yankees rounded up slaves, including William Ward, and took them "as far as Virginia to carry powder and shot to the soldiers." They joined the thousands of Contrabands who had been falling into step with Sherman's army since the beginning of his campaign in early May, "doing any kind of work we were asked to do, but receiving no pay." Elijah Henry Hopkins followed Sherman as he "marched on toward Savannah; crossed over into South Carolina, went on through Columbia; and just tore it up" before working his way "on back into Georgia."

Though Ward "did not know whether Sherman intended to keep him in slavery or free him," other slaves were more sanguine. "One day a whole lot of Yanks came trooping up to our place, perhaps a thousand of them," recalled a Georgia slave. "They were known as 'Sherman's bummers,' but we found afterwards that most of them were the 101st Indiana regiment, commanded by Colonel Steele. They were a fine looking set of fellows, and we didn't have to be told that they were our friends. We welcomed them in as cordial a way as we knew how." Since the master and his family had "vanished as soon as the alarm came in that the dreaded Yanks were at hand," the slaves relieved the Yankees "of any necessity of taking anything by force, as we made all haste to present them freely with everything on the plantation that could be any use to them. Not only that, but the entire crowd — that is, the men and boys — volunteered to help carry away the property, particularly the mules. There were eight or ten of us 'boys,' and perhaps as many mules, and we all marched off together, happier than we ever had been before in our lives."

With the fall of Atlanta, many of the region's planters and farmers gave up all hope of retaining their slaves. J. H. Hill recalled how "Miss Emily called the five women that was on the place" and told them "they were free and could go wherever they wanted to." But she advised them "to stay around the house and attend to things as they had always done until their husbands come back, look after a place for them to stay," and then "rent from her if they wanted to."

BY MID-JUNE 1864, Sherman calculated that he had so weakened Joseph E. Johnston's forces that the time had come to attack the Rebels' entrenched position protecting the railroad approach to Atlanta. But he miscalculated, and 3,000 Yankee soldiers paid the price. To J. H. Hill's master's undying shame, Legree Hill, one of his own sons, was among the Union dead.

Legree "went to the war at the age of eighteen years." His mother had grieved over his going "because he was too young," but he "ran off and went" anyway, telling his mother that he would be "fighting against the Yankees," and hoped to "bring Lincoln's head back." When word reached his parents that Legree had been killed at Kennesaw Mountain, his father set off to find him among the Rebel dead. But he found his son buried instead "in the Yankee line, wrapped in a blanket" and "dressed like a Yankee, in their uniform. Of course," J. H. Hill noted, "nothing much was said about it, as I remember, cause he wasn't supposed to be a Yankee at all."

When a Yankee squad arrived at the William Glenn plantation in Oglethorpe County, Georgia, "everything was quiet and still as could be" except for Martha Colquitt's grandmother "singing and shouting" up in the loom house, where she had been incarcerated for several days as punishment for disrupting a Baptist meeting with her enthusiasm. "Them mens grabbed the axe from the woodpile and busted the door down, went in and got Grandma," and asked the old woman "if she was hungry." She allowed that she was, so "they took that axe and busted down the smokehouse door and told her she was free now, and to help herself to anything she wanted, because everything on the plantation was to belong to the slaves that had worked there. They took Grandma to the kitchen, and told Ma to give her some of the white folkses' dinner." "But the white folkses ain't et yet," Colquitt's mother protested. "Go right on," the Yankees said, "and give it to her: the best in the pot. And if they's anything left when she gets through, maybe us will let the white folkses have some of it."

Sherman's "bummers" apparently entered Georgia's capital of Milledgeville in an antic mood. They poured molasses down the organ pipes of St. Stephen's Episcopal Church to "sweeten" its tone and held a mock meeting of the state legislature to "repeal" Georgia's ordinance of Secession. "Did they ruin everything!" Snovey Jackson exclaimed. "Why, Milledgeville was just tore up. It weren't nothing more than a cow pasture when the Yankees got through with it."

Former slaves could be philosophical about Sherman's depredations, even when they were themselves among its victims. His soldiers "took my grandmother's cattle with the rest," mused Louis Joseph Piernas, "but the Yankees had to eat, and it was war. You know Sherman said, 'War is hell,'" and when Piernas was interviewed in the 1930s, it was still "that way in China and Spain." The Yankees "had to subdue our country," recalled Adaline Johnson of North Carolina, and that was why "they took everything they could find."

25

"What They Care?"

Hardened Hearts · Yankee Depredations · Raids · Abductions
Treasure Hunting · Bees and Hornets · Rape
Betraying Runaways · Comeuppance

B y 1864, MANY OF THE fresh young Yankees who had approached slaves in the early months of the Civil War as kindly liberators had either been killed or come to blame the slaves themselves for the war and all its horrors. The ever-mordant James Thomas believed that many Yankees were less interested in helping slaves than in humiliating their masters. They would urge a slave "to get away just to laugh at the discomfiture of his owner." Other soldiers envied masters for having had "too good a time" living off their slaves' labor, while others wanted to destroy the Peculiar Institution "because it would offer a better and larger field for white people."

During the later stages of the war, Union depredations increased — a function of hardening hearts, opposition to the Emancipation Proclamation, outrage at the enlistment of black troops, and growing fears that liberated slaves would overrun the North. Sherman's campaign compounded these factors by leaving the West's defense to black troops and white Southern Unionists, many of them Confederate deserters with little sympathy for black people. And overarching all of that was Sherman's own express policy of leaving a wide path of ruination in his wake.

Many individual Yankee soldiers, some of whom were slaveholders, did not see themselves as part of some abolitionist crusade. "You nasty, stinking rascal," Sam Ward's mother once scolded a Yankee forager. "You

say you come down here to fight for us, and now you're stealing from us."
"You're a god damn liar," replied the Yankee. "I'm fighting for fourteen
dollars a month and the Union."

"We helped raise that meat they stole," said Peter Brown of Mississippi. "They left us to starve and fed their fat selves on what was our living." "When the Yankees come, what did they do?" asked Henry Jenkins.
"They did them things they ought not to have done," he said, paraphras-
ing the General Confession of the Episcopal Church, "and left undone
the things they ought to have done." Descending like Vikings on their
masters' plantations and ransacking slave quarters as well as mansion
houses, most Yankees were not out to endear themselves to anybody.

LETETIA CUSTIS OF Alabama painted a terrifying picture of a Yankee
raid. Custis was sitting at her loom when her master's daughter looked
out the window and exclaimed, "'O-o-oh! Hannie! Just look down yonder!' 'Baby, what is that?' I says. 'Them's the Yankees coming!' 'God help
us!' I says, and before I can catch my breath, the place is covered." The
Yankees' boots "sounded like muttering thunder," and the "swords hanging on they sides" were "singing a tune whilst they walk. A chicken better
not pass by. If he do, off come his head! When they pass on by me, they
pretty nigh shook me out of my skin. 'Where's the mens?' they say, and
shake me up. 'Where's the arms?' They shake me till my eyeballs closing
up. 'Where's the silver!?' Lord! Was my teeths dropping out! They didn't
give me time to catch my breath. They took them Enfield rifles, half as
long as that door, and bust in the smokehouse window. They jack me up
off of my feet and drag me up the ladder and say, 'Get that meat out.' I
kept on throwing out Miss Mary's hams and sausages till they holler,
'Stop.' I come backing down that ladder like a squirrel, and I ain't stop
backing till I reach Miss Mary. Yes, Lord! Them Yankees loaded up a
wagon full of meat and took the whole barrel of molasses! Taking that
molasses killed us children! Our mainest amusement was making molasses candy" and cakewalking around with it. "Now that was all gone,"
Custis said. "Look like them solders had to sharpen they swords on everything in sight. The big crepe mullen bush by the parlor window was
blooming so pink and pretty, and they just stood there and whack off
them blooms." After they left a day later, Custis recalled, "the whole
place was strewed with mutilation."

Others were shocked by the Yankees' sheer brazenness. In Nashville a slave came upon a Yankee stealing vegetables from his master's garden. "I's gwine to tell Marse Charles," he warned the soldier. "Damn your Marse Charles," the Yankee replied. "What do I care?" Such encounters left a bad taste in slaves' mouths. Speaking of the Yankees, Sarah Virgil of Georgia "surely did hate them things." Johanna Isom of Mississippi bitterly recalled how "them good-for-nothing white trash rode up to our house and took Miss Sallie's best home-spun blankets and put them on they horses for saddle blankets" or "wrapped them round they legs. And then they took her fine silk dresses and put them on with hoops and all, hopped on the horses and galloped away singing, 'Yankee Doodle Dandy / Buttermilk and brandy.'"

"Them Cavalrymen would come riding through tearing up the whole creation, and taking everything they could snatch and grab," recalled Glasgow Norwood. "I tell you all, they was terrible." Lincoln may have "freed us," said Patsy Perryman, "but I never liked him because of the way his soldiers done in the South."

"WHEN THE YANKEES come through here," recalled Mandy Leslie of Alabama, "they took my mammy off in a wagon, and left me right side the road, and when she try to get out the wagon to fetch me, they hit her on the head, and she fell back in the wagon and didn't holler no more. They just drive off up the big road with Mammy lying down in the wagon." Leslie assumed they had killed her, "cause I ain't never see'd her no more. Uncle John Leslie and Aunt Josie and all they children come along in the wagon, going up North, and they said they found me standing the side the road crying for my mammy. Aunt Josie, she say: 'Poor little tad, you going with us. Us ain't got much, but us can't let you die.' And Uncle John, he say, 'Poor child, us mustn't leave her this way.' He lift me up in the wagon and us drive till the mule give plumb out."

"While I was at the mill," recalled James Henry Nelson of Alabama, "a Yankee soldier riding a white horse captured me and took me to Pulaski, Tennessee." Nelson was "no size," he said, "and I don't think he would have took me if it hadn't been for the horse." "They took my oldest brother," recalled Charlie Rigger of Arkansas. "He didn't want to go. We never heard from him. He never come back."

"What they care about you being white or black?" asked Lucindy Allison. "Thing they was after was filling theirselves up." If the Yankees "wanted a colored man to go in camp with them and he didn't go, they would shoot you down like a dog. Ma told about some folks she knowed got shot in the yard of their own quarters."

YANKEES "USED TO point the gun at me just to hear me holler and cry," Neely Gray remembered. "I was scared of them." "One day a Yankee officer tied his riding horse to one of the best apple trees in the orchard," recalled a slave named Isaac. "The horse he begun to bite the bark on the tree. So I said, 'Mister, that's a mighty good horse-apple tree your horse is biting; he'll kill it.' The Yankee give me a most searching look and said, 'You think more of a damn apple tree than I do of a man's life.' He stood close to me with his sharp shooter, his neck as red as any rose, all ready to put my candle out at any minute. You better believe I chased myself away from there. After that, I said no more about tying horses to apple trees."

A Tennessee slave remembered how the Yankees beat the slaves on his master's plantation, "but we would dodge. Mother would take the baby and lay her in the cornfield to hide him, and then lay down close by him." Yankee cavalry, just for sport, used to chase Tennessee field hands into the woods. "I remembers a storm us had," said Cornelia Robinson of Alabama. "I calls it a hurricane; but it was really the Yankees coming through." One slave boy was so terrified that when he went off to round up cows for the Yankees but couldn't find any, "he laid down in a hollow stump and nearly froze to death. They had to thaw him out" in a creek. "But he was powerful sick," and he "weren't no account for nothing after that." A party of Northern soldiers tied an Alabama mistress's senior slave to a tree "and whipped him with their bridle, because he wouldn't tell where Old Mistress hid things." When he still refused, "they set the barn on fire, and they set the crib on fire, and burned it up with everything Old Mistress had in the world. When she fetch anything out of the house, they flung it back: even her little children's pictures, what was dead."

Some slaves regarded the Yankees as lower class. "Now, if you please," an elderly house slave remarked as his fellow slaves rushed to greet the Yankees, "look at the poor white trash" they were "running after. If they was in the gutters," the Yankees "wouldn't pick them up, unless they wanted them to fight for them. I tell you now they won't get me," he assured his mistress. "And I thank God I know who my friends are."

TO FORCE MASTERS and slaves to reveal the whereabouts of their valuables, a few Yankees inflicted a common military punishment on civilians. "The Yankees wasn't so good," Everett Ingram remembered. "They hung my mammy up in the smokehouse by her thumbs" with the "tips of her toes just touching the floor, cause she wouldn't agree to give up her older childrens. She never did, neither." "One time the Yankee soldiers took young Master Henry and hung him up by the thumbs and tried to make him tell where the money was. Master Henry's little brother Jim and me run and hid. We thought they was gonna hang us too." "They hung old Master up by his two thumbs to make him tell where his money was," recalled Jeff Allen of Macon County, Alabama, "but he wouldn't talk." On a second raid, "they hung Master up by the neck to try to make him tell, and he still would not talk, so they said, 'Won't you take supper with us?' and Master said, 'No.' So then they said, 'Let him down. I expect his damn neck is pretty sore.'"

On their raid through Lee County, Alabama, the Yankees spotted some local men up the road and ordered them to halt. "The mens wouldn't stop," so the Yankees aimed their guns at them and were preparing to fire when "two white ladies threw a white flag." The Yankees lowered their rifles but abducted a local man named John Edwards and carved "a cross on his wrist." The Yankees put "Lake Brown and Clarence Bush out in the swamp to die," Paul Smith remembered, "but they got well, come out of that swamp, and lived here for years and years."

"I tell you them Yankees was mean," Frank Larkin recalled. "Used to shake old mistress and try to make her tell where the money was hid. If you had a fat cow, just shoot her down and cook what they wanted." "They tore our gate down and asked Mistress Jane for our keys," said Jefferson Davis Nunn. "She wouldn't give them the keys, so they shook her by the hair." Nunn's Alabama master had been ailing when he hid from the Yankees "behind a log." After they left he returned to bed, but he never rose again "and didn't live but about four months." Matt Brantley of Arkansas watched as "the Yankees burnt Boss Henry's father's fine house, his gin, his gristmill, and fifty or sixty bales of cotton, and took several fine horses. They took him out in his shirt tail and beat him, and whooped his wife, trying to make them tell where the money was. He told her to tell." "One time some Yankees come. I run hid around Miss Betty's long dress," recalled Ida Rigley of Virginia. "She was crying. They was pulling her rings off her fingers." Because she had been "good and kind to me," or at least as "good as I wanted," Rigley "sassed" the Yankees and told them to stop. They were unmoved. "I shoot your head off," one Yankee snarled back.

Centuries of servitude had taught slaves what whites were capable of visiting on blacks, but now the war was teaching them what whites were capable of doing to one another. Hallie Halsey, the slave daughter of her master, watched as Union soldiers gleefully hectored her white half brother to death. "Young man," they said, "can you ride a young horse?" "They gathered him and took him out and brought him in the yard," where they rode him on a rail, beat him, and literally "scared him to death." Everyone "grieved about the way they done their young master, one of my father's own children." Ike McCoy's parents told him that their master tried to hide from the Yankees by locking himself in a closet, but "the Yankees found him, broke in on him and took him out and they nearly killed him beating him so bad." The master then announced he was leaving his farm, but he "didn't live long after that." The sheer shock of the Yankees' approach was enough to kill some masters. "When them Yankees come," Minerva Meadows remembered, "it was on Sunday, and Mr. Lonney Combs dropped dead, he was so scared."

"Men in blue clothes came and put a rope around my marster's neck," Elizabeth Hines remembered. They led him through the slave quarters and demanded to know where he was hiding his bondsmen. "He told them, Texas. They said, 'Get them and free them,' or they would hang him." He ordered his slaves to return, but then "committed suicide because he had lost all his money." Rosa Simmons's master was so terrorized by the Yankees that for the rest of his life, "if he saw any kind of a white man coming down the road, he run in the house and hid between the feather bed and the mattress."

IT WAS LITTLE wonder that some slaves would recall with satisfaction and even amusement the fates of the more hapless Yankees who raided their masters' farms and plantations. After a Union trooper ran a blade through a goose, "she started hollowing and fluttering till the horses, nearly all of them, started running, and some of them bucking. Three of them horses throwed them sprawling." An Alabama slave recalled how a Yankee rode his horse over a beehive, "and Man! them bees and them Yankees sure did gallop! In about a minute there weren't no Yankees nowhere except down the road where the dust just fogging up!"

Wadley Clemons's owner kept "thirty hives of bees in one long row, and one Yankee run up to the first hive and jump in it head first, and the bees stung him till he died. The others pull him out and took him to the well and poured water over him, but he stayed dead, so they just dug a hole down by the side of the road and bury him in it."

Leslie Custis recounted what befell a Yankee sergeant who "run his bayonet clean through Miss Mary's bestest feather bed and rip it slam open! With that, a wind blowed up and took them feathers every which way from Sunday. You couldn't see where you's at." The sergeant "just throwed his head back and laugh fit to kill hisself. Then first thing next, he done suck a feather down his windpipe! Lord, honey, that white man sure struggled! Them soldiers throwed water in his face. They shook and rolled him over, and all the time he's getting limper and bluer. Then they jack him up by his feets and stand him on his head. Then they pump him up and down," shaking him "till he spit. Then he come to." Afterward, that particular raiding party "didn't cut no more mattresses," Custis recalled.

One bold slave boy tried to wreak vengeance on a squad of Yankee raiders. Hammett Dell had always enjoyed throwing rocks, and had become skilled at hitting distant targets. "We got our water out of a cave," he recalled, and "one day I going to the cave after water" when he "spied a hornets' nest in a tree long the lane." Knowing that the Yankees would "be along back for something else," Dell waited awhile in the woods, and "it wasn't long, sure enough, they come back and went up to the house." So Hammett "got a pile of rocks in my hands," and when "they come by galloping, I throwed and hit that big old hornets' nest. The way they piled out on them soldiers!" Dell proudly recalled. "You could see them fighting far as you could see them with their blue caps, the horses running and bucking." Dell ran back to the house to boast to his master "how I hit that hornets' nest with the first rock I throwed." But his master "scolded me, for he said if they had seen me they would have killed me. It scared him. He said, 'Don't do no more capers like that. Don't do nothing to them to aggravate them.'"

THOUGH LONG SUBJECTED to the assaults of their masters and overseers, female slaves had a special horror of rape at the hands of the Yankees. In Georgia "there was a heap of talk about the scandalous way them Yankee soldiers been treating Negro womans and gals." Black women were "a-feared to breathe out loud come night," Rufus Dirt recalled, "and in the day time they didn't work much cause they was always looking for the Yankees." To protect their womenfolk from rape, a group of black men on one Southern plantation placed all of them in one building and posted a guard outside.

"There were soldiers in the woods," recalled Julia Francis Daniels of Texas, "and they had been persecuting an old woman on a mule." Convinced they would come for her next, "I got so scared I couldn't eat my dinner. I hadn't got any heart for victuals." "Wait for Pa," her brother told her. "He's coming with the mule, and he'll hide you out." So Julia "got on the mule in front of Pa, and we passed through the soldiers, and they grabbed at me and said, 'Give me the gal! Give me the gal!' Pa said I fainted plumb away," but he got her through.

One night a slave listened as soldiers pursued a slave girl who had ventured off. They could hear her screams in the distance, and in the morning found her lifeless body. The only event during the war that Amanda Styles of Georgia could recount was the day the Yankees carried off her mother; she was never heard from again. Bessie Lawson's mother "went to take something to a sick widow woman for old mistress," but she was captured by Yankee soldiers encamped nearby and "never got back for a week." Though the Yankees "whooped Mama" and "she was afraid to try to get away," when her captors went off on a scout she got permission to "ride a little old broken-down horse" to a nearby thicket to collect "some black gum toothbrushes." As soon as she was out of sight, she cut through a pasture and returned home, where "one of the colored boys took the horse back nearly to the camps and turned him loose." But by then the Yankees had impregnated her, and "before my own papa got back" from serving his master's kin in the Rebel army, Lawson recalled, "she had a white child."

Rape was a means not merely of satisfying lust but of showing slaveholders that they were powerless against their foe. In a letter to Lincoln, B. E. Harrison of Virginia recounted how Yankee raiders spotted his black servant girl standing a few yards off. One soldier chased her, raped her, and dragged her back to Harrison's yard where, in full view of Harrison's wife and nieces, she was gang-raped by "seven or eight more soldiers." Private Adolph Bork of the 183rd Ohio Infantry was tried for the rape of a nine-months-pregnant "woman of color" named Susan. She testified that Bork threatened "he would blow me to pieces" with his revolver "if I didn't let him do it." Susan "got up to go out." But Bork ordered her to stay, and "put a hand on my breast and pushed me on the bed." "If you don't do what's right," he told her, "I'll bust you open," and he raped her.

When Yankees arrived at Somerset plantation in North Carolina, one of them cornered a thirty-five-year-old mother of four named Lovey Harvey in the cookhouse and raped her at gunpoint. Patrick Manning of the 8th New Hampshire Infantry tried to assault a slave named Clara Grier. "He took hold of me," she testified, "and attempted to throw me down, and I hollered, and he kicked me. He asked me if I wanted five dollars. I said no. He asked if he could stay with me. I said no. I am a quadroon. He was drunk." Manning was court-martialed and acquitted, but received three years at hard labor with a ball and chain for a series of other crimes.

Many assaults on black women went unreported, but not every Yankee rapist escaped punishment. A Pennsylvania saddler in McMinnville, Tennessee, barged into the home of Mrs. Jane L. Young, knocked her down, and "did then and there, feloniously and against her will, attempt to commit a rape upon the person of 'Sally,' a Negro woman in Young's employ." A military court condemned the saddler to a penitentiary for the remainder of the war, with a twelve-pound ball chained to his leg. Others were given sentences ranging from two years' hard labor to life imprisonment. One became the victim of mob justice: in Yorktown, Virginia, black vigilantes shot to death a Union sailor for attempting to force himself on a black girl.

Assaulted by Rebels and Yankees alike, some slave women became prostitutes. "My scout party met up with four titless half-breed girls who had been well used by the Rebels," a soldier wrote from New Mexico. "They were so lived up from their battles they offered us their favors at prices unheard of by the girls at Fort Craig. After much pleasuring, we found that the invaders had paid them off in Rebel money. This we bought. Back in our camp, we sold it as souvenirs so dear that we had our pleasure and a lot of money for more pleasure." A young Union soldier wrote his wife about the black prostitutes he encountered. "I was out the other night and see some big lusty ones, but did not derst to touch them." In Virginia, black troops were assigned to patrol the Contraband camps to keep white soldiers away from black women.

KEEPING FORMER MASTERS away was another matter. Some Union commanders accepted bribes in exchange for allowing masters to enter the camps and reclaim their runaway slaves. This was a special problem in Union-occupied portions of Kentucky, to which slaves fled thinking they would be free. But because Kentucky's neutrality exempted it from the Emancipation Proclamation, they discovered too late that they were still subject to the old code, which not only deemed them slaves but illegal immigrants.

In 1863, a prominent Nashville slaveholder tried to retrieve one of his slaves as she left a black church, but a mob of outraged blacks forced a passing provost guard to arrest him. In General Thomas's camps local whites who tried to fetch their slaves were subjected "to some humiliating treatment — such as riding the rail horse, or carrying a barrel up the hill and rolling it down again, and they would continue this process for hours." But many slave women did not regard the camps as safe and labored hard to afford other housing. Jennie Jackson of the Fisk Jubilee Singers recalled how her mother worked as a laundress so she could rent quarters in the yard of a family of local whites.

SOME SLAVES REGARDED Union raids as a comeuppance for bad masters. "Now take the Combinders," said Clara Walker. "They was on the next plantation. They was mean. Many a time you could hear the bullwhip, clear over to our place: PLOP, PLOP." If one of their slaves died, "they just wrapped them in cloth and dig a trench, and plow right over them." When the Yankees carried off their slaves, "Mistress Combinder, she holler out, and she say, 'What my girls gonna do? They ain't never dressed theyselves in they life. We can't cook. What we do?' And the soldiers didn't pay no attention. They just marched them off. And old man Combinder, he lay down, and he have a chill, and he die."

"When the soldiers came through," Julia Haney recalled, "there was an old Rebel eating breakfast at our place. He was a man that used to handcuff slaves and carry them off and sell them. When he heard that the Yankees were marching into town with all their bayonets shining, it scared him to death. He sat right there at the breakfast table and died."

While Federal troops were helping themselves to her possessions, an Alabama slave owner named Hammond "tried to remonstrate with them, but they just laughed" and reminded her that it was Southerners who had "fired the first shot at Fort Sumter," and it was Southerners who would pay the price.

Part X

East and West
1865

26

---◆---

"I Have Seen Father Abraham"

Selma · Richmond II · Slave Marts · Lincoln Tours Richmond
Appomattox · Answered Prayers

TWENTY-SEVEN-YEAR-OLD John Smith had the satisfaction of seeing former slave catcher and slave dealer Nathan Bedford Forrest suffer his most conclusive defeat. Smith had become "kind of puny" after minié balls punctured his side and his legs at Cedar Creek. He had fled the battlefield in such a hurry that the wounds had closed before the balls could be extracted, and he would carry them for the rest of his very long life. But after Smith's master was killed at Blue Mountain, the Yankees scooped him up and put him to work as a groom for General James H. Wilson. "I took care of General Wilson's horse," Smith recalled. "But I didn't like they ways much. He wanted his horse kept spic-and-span. He would take his white pocket handkerchief and rub over the horse, and if it was dirty, he had me whupped."

On April 1, 1865, "I was with General Wilson when he took Selma against General Forrest." As Smith rode along in an artillery wagon, he watched as Wilson attacked Forrest's defenses in three columns, inflicting 2,700 casualties, more than half the Rebel garrison and over eight times the Yankees' casualties. The town was filled with mansions, factories, and warehouses, but after Forrest fled, Wilson's men "set fire to all them things."

Aaron Willis was a seven-year-old boy "when them Yankees come" to Selma. "My mama hid me in the smokehouse" and "made my pallet on a box of meat. When they broke in there and found me, my mama told them I slept in there, and that there wasn't much meat in there. Then they look in the box and find that meat and took what they wanted of it." The next day, when Willis "told Old Master that I tried to save his meat," he gave him two bits. "I bought tobacco with it," Willis remembered, because "I used tobacco when I was little. My grandpa learned me to chaw and raise my own tobacco," which he continued to do into the 1930s.

From her master's farm a few miles down the road from Selma, Dinah Allen "could see the light from Selma and could hear the guns shooting." A week later, on "the night of the surrender," Allen was sitting on the porch nursing her master's grandson when she saw Yankees approaching down the road. "Howdy, lady," one of them called out. "Didn't you know you are free, and your 'master,' as you call him, can't beat you anymore?"

BY THE SPRING of 1865, the "hard road" to Richmond was nearing its end. On April 1, Sheridan conquered the crossroads at Five Forks and captured 5,000 Rebels. Its defense "at all hazard" had stretched Lee's line to the breaking point. His army dwindling, cut off from supplies, frustrated by long months on the defensive, the next day Lee decided to evacuate Petersburg and Richmond.

His wife, Mary, had remained in the Confederate capital for much of the siege. Early in the year, she had summoned her maidservant, Martha Parke, from Arlington to help her fellow slave Amanda Lee to wait on her. On April 1, she said, "Martha, Richmond is going to fall tomorrow." And, "sure enough, the city surrender to the Yankees next day." But not before the Confederates had put much of the waterfront and the business district to the torch.

The news swept across the country. "When we heared that Grant took Richmond," recalled Mary Barnes of Maryland, "the poor white folks was just as glad as us." "I was fishing with Pappy," recalled Mittie Freeman of Arkansas. "All of a sudden cannons commence booming: it seem like everywhere. You know what that was? It was the fall of Richmond. Cannons was to roar every place when Richmond fell. Pappy jumps up, throws his pole and everything, and grabs my hand, and starts flying towards the house. 'It's victory,' he keep on saying. 'It's freedom. Now we's gonna be free!'"

THE SIGNIFICANCE OF Richmond's fall was compounded by its notoriety as a slave-trading center. Before the war, twenty-eight men had openly advertised themselves as slave traders, and dozens of other self-described "auctioneers," "merchants," and "commission agents" principally depended on the trade. In fenced-in pens, on courthouse steps, in basements and warehouses, agents auctioned off as many as two hundred slaves a day, most of them to speculators who would transport them west, where Virginia slaves were prized.

Louis Hughes's master, Washington Fitzpatrick of Charlottesville, had brought Hughes to Richmond, "expecting to sell me. But as the market was dull, he brought me back and kept me some three months longer." At last he told Hughes that he had hired him out for a year to a Richmond boatman. "My son, be a good boy," his mother told him. "Be polite to everyone, and always behave yourself properly."

But Fitzpatrick was lying. His real purpose was to send Hughes to Richmond and sell him. As soon as Hughes reached the capital, a local speculator named George Pulliam "came to the boat and began to question me, asking me first if I could remember having had the chickenpox, measles or whooping-cough. Then he asked me if I did not want to take a little walk with him. I said, 'No.' 'Well,' said he, 'you have got to go. Your master sent you down here to be sold, and told me to come and get you and take you to the trader's yard.' I saw that to hesitate was useless; so I at once obeyed him and went." After several hellish weeks in Pulliam's slave yard, Hughes was bought by a plantation owner and transported to Pontotoc, Mississippi. He never saw his mother again.

William Robinson recalled spending weeks in a Richmond slave pen. "During this time I saw hundreds of mothers separated from their children. I heard the wail of many a child for its mother, and of the mother for her child." He once saw a mother who had been separated from her husband jump from the boat that was carrying her and her children away. She leaped into "the deep water" of the James River "with her baby clasped in her arms and the little girl handcuffed to her." Their corpses were retrieved the next day.

William Kinnegy of North Carolina recalled how a Richmond slave trader "made us strip stark naked; the women in one part of the room, the men in another; a rough cotton screen separating the two sexes. We were stood off at a short distance from our purchasers, and our physical condition fully considered and remarked upon, holding up our hands, turning round, and then we were sold accordingly. They did not call us 'people,'" he remembered, "but 'stock.' I had been used in North Carolina to the title 'droves of people,' but there in Richmond, they called us 'droves of stock,' 'heads of stock,' &c."

Will Ann Rogers was a young woman when her mother and grandmother were sent off to Richmond to be auctioned off. When a trader
sold Rogers's mother, her grandmother "fainted or dropped dead; she
never knowed which," for though Will Ann's mother tried "to go see
her mother lying over there on the ground," her new owner, Ephraim
Hester, forbade it, and "drove her off like cattle," and that was "the last
she ever knowed of any of her folks."

A Virginia slave named Emma Bolt wrote a letter saying that she had
never before dared to hope she might be free. "The man I lived with is
named W. W. Hall. He says that we belong to him in hell. He had sold my
brothers and sisters and would have sold me — and mother, and father
— if he could, for he had us sent to Richmond to sell." He told Bolt "that
the Yankees was all black, had four legs like a horse and one eye before
and one behind, and a horn on each side." A slave trader, Hall predicted
that long after the war was over he would still "be doing the same business. He says that the Rebels will be here in May. Thank God that the
Yankees come to Richmond" on Saturday, Hall said, for "he was going to
send us to Richmond the next Monday."

On April 3, after the Confederates had departed, a black correspondent named Thomas Morris Fletcher visited several of Richmond's
abandoned slave pens. "The jailors were in all cases slaves, and had been
left in undisputed possession of the buildings. The owners, as soon as
they were aware that we were coming, opened wide the doors and told
the confined inmates they were free." But they "could not realize it until
they saw the Union army," and "even then they thought it must be a
pleasant dream. But when they saw Abraham Lincoln," Fletcher reported, "they were satisfied that their freedom was perpetual."

ON APRIL 4, Lincoln arrived at Richmond's charred waterfront. "Would
you like to see the man who made you free?" a war correspondent named
Charles Carlton Coffin asked a crew of fifty black bridge builders. "Yes,
Master," one of them replied. "There he is," said Coffin, pointing to "that
man with the tall hat." "Be that Master Lincoln?" Coffin assured him that
it was. "Hallelujah!" cried their leader. "Hurrah, boys, Master Lincoln
come!" "He swung his old straw hat, slapped his hands and jumped into
the air," and "in an instant the fifty Negroes" took up the cry, and "ran towards the landing, yelling and shouting like lunatics. I could hear the cry
running up the streets and lanes, 'Master Lincoln! Master Lincoln!'"
Looking pallid and careworn, Lincoln held his son Tad's hand as he made

his way toward the abandoned Rebel capitol, "the crowd increasing every moment" and "the cry of the delighted colored people rising like the voice of many waters." A slave woman jumped up and down, shouting, "Glory! Glory! Glory!" Another chanted, "Bless the Lord!"

As Lincoln rested for a moment before ascending Richmond's Capitol Hill, "an old Negro, wearing a few rags, whose white, crisp hair appeared through his crownless straw hat, lifted the hat from his head, kneeled upon the ground, clasped his hands, and said, 'May the good Lord bless and keep you safe, Master President Lincoln.'" The President "lifted his own hat and bowed to the old man," his eyes wet with tears. An old woman declared, "I know that I am free, for I have seen Father Abraham and felt him."

"There was so many people to meet him, he went up to the tower instead of in the State House," H. B. Holloway asserted. "He said, 'I did everything I could to keep out of war. Many of you agreed to turn the Negroes loose, but Jeff Davis said that he would wade in blood up to his neck before he would do it.'" According to Holloway, Lincoln asked for "all of the Confederate money to be brought up there, and when it was brought, he called for the oldest colored man around. He said, 'Now, is you the oldest?' The man said, 'Yes sir.' Then he threw him one of those little boxes of matches" and told him to set the Confederate currency ablaze. Holloway claimed Lincoln then addressed the sullen local whites in the crowd: "I am gonna disfranchise every one of you, and it will be ten years before you can even vote or get back into the Union."

Be that as it may, the President departed in the early evening, awkwardly stepping aboard a navy cutter for the return trip to Washington. "Just as he pushed off amid the cheering of the crowd," Fletcher reported, another elderly woman shouted, "Don't drown, Master Abe, for God's sake!"

The next day, the seamstress Elizabeth Keckley accompanied Mary Lincoln on a tour of Richmond. "The Capitol presented a desolate appearance," she recalled: "desks broken, and papers scattered promiscuously in the hurried flight of the Confederate Congress. I picked up a number of papers, and, by curious coincidence," one of them turned out to be a "resolution prohibiting all free colored people from entering the State of Virginia." Keckley had the satisfaction of sitting "in the chair that Jefferson Davis sometimes occupied; also in the chair of the Vice-President, Alexander H. Stephens. We paid a visit to the mansion occupied by Mr. Davis and family during the war, and the ladies who were in charge of it scowled darkly upon our party as we passed through and inspected the different rooms."

LEWIS ADAMS OF Crystal Springs, Mississippi, had been sent off to serve with his master's son, H. C. Stackhouse, in the 16th Mississippi Infantry, in a company that dubbed itself the Crystal Springs Southern Rights. "I was with the South," said Adams. "I loved her ways. My best friends was Southern boys." But after all their "hardships and the troubles — hungry and such, and so on: little bit of grub, and fighting guns — I says, 'It can't last long.' I sits down and thinks very sad-like, as my friends dead or dying, and I study Captain Seibe from my hometown and his boy, Jake Seibe, shot through the head; Lieutenant Carl Lindsay killed in battle; and I says, 'What the use of fighting?'" Then followed "months of hell" defending Petersburg and Richmond, until "that fine old man, General Robert E. Lee, say, 'Let's quit.'"

ELIZA WASHINGTON DEEMED Lee's April 6 defeat at Sayler's Creek, Virginia, "the awfulest battle you ever heard of. The men lay dead in rows and rows and rows. The dead men covered whole fields." Two days afterward, late in the evening of April 9, recalled Samuel Spottford Clement, "the field hands could hear the boom of cannon and the crack of musketry from the battlefield near Appomattox Court House. The old field hands prayed in concert that the Yankees might win the fight." Their prayers were answered. Though Lee's remnant tried to escape Grant's tightening grip, ranks of Union infantry brought their flight to a bloody halt.

At last, "General Lee said that there wasn't any use doing any more fighting," and surrendered at Appomattox Court House. Lee was "a tall man, fine looking and dignified," recalled Eliza Washington. "Grant was a little man and short." According to Lee's loyal cook, William Mack Lee, the general told "Unconditional Surrender" Grant, "You didn't whip me. You just overpowered me. I surrender this day 8,000 men." But "it shall not go down in history I surrendered the Northern Confederate Army of Virginia to you. It shall go down in history I surrendered on conditions. You have ten men to my one; my men, too, are barefooted and hungry. If Joseph E. Johnston could have gotten to me three days ago, I would have cut my way through and gone back into the mountains of North Carolina and would have given you a happy time."

Lee actually surrendered more than 28,000 men, and William Mack

Lee would concede that he never knew what conditions Lee might have actually demanded. "But I know these were Marse Robert's words on the morning of the surrender: 'I surrender to you on conditions.'" Perhaps within his slave's hearing Lee had rehearsed such a speech; but, in the event, Grant saved him the trouble by greeting his foe graciously and offering him far more generous terms than Lee was in a position to demand. "General Grant let all the Rebels keep their guns," said Eliza Washington. "He didn't take nothing away from them."

Fannie Berry was at Pamplin City, Virginia, as stray Rebel fugitives from the Army of Northern Virginia tried to fend off their pursuers. "The Yankees and Rebels were fighting, and they were waving the bloody flag, and a Confederate soldier was up on a post, and they were shooting terribly. Guns were firing everywhere" when "all a sudden" she heard the strains of "Yankee Doodle Dandy" and looked up to see Union soldiers approaching. "How far is it to the Rebels?" a soldier asked her. But she was too afraid to reply, because "if the Rebels knew that I told the soldier," they would have killed her. She told him she didn't know, but when he asked again, Berry darted behind her master's house and furtively pointed in the Rebels' direction.

A regiment of black troops marched up, and, according to Berry, as soon as the Rebels caught sight of them, they raised a white flag "as a token that Lee had surrendered. Glory! Glory!" Berry exclaimed. "Yes, child, the Negroes were free, and when they knew that they were free they — Oh! Baby! — began to sing: 'Mary don't you cook no more, / You are free, you are free. / Rooster don't you crow no more, / You are free, you are free . . .' Such rejoicing and shouting you never heard in your life." For Samuel Spottford Clement, it seemed that at last God had heard the prayers that slaves had "sent up for three hundred years."

27

—◆—

"The Plans of God"

Victory • Abraham Lincoln • Portents • Grief
Lincoln Pros and Cons • The Grand Review

O NE BY ONE, the rest of the Confederacy's armies began to surrender. In Rodney, Mississippi, Katie Dillon saw that the Rebels
camped across the street "had their guns all stacked. I was looking
and wondering what it was," until she "heard some of the older
ones say the war was over." In Baker County, Georgia, Elijah Henry
Hopkins watched the Rebels as "they stacked their arms. Looked like
there was a hundred or more rifles in each stack. They just come up and
pitched them down," for they had to "turn them over." In Culpeper, Virginia, Ephraim Robinson and the Southern soldiers he had served "cried
like babies." But as he made his way home, he gradually realized that he
and his parents were free, and "he was glad."

John Belcher of Lowndes County, Georgia, remembered that the
Yankees celebrated their victory near his master's house "by digging a
long trench in a nearby field and putting several barrels of loose powder
in that trench and setting it off. It blowed a big hole there, so big," he
said, "it was used for a fishing hole for years."

ON A MORNING five days after Lee's surrender, Elizabeth Keckley noticed that Lincoln's countenance "was more cheerful than I had seen it
for a long while, and he seemed to be in a generous, forgiving mood."
When his oldest son, Robert, entered with a portrait of Robert E. Lee,
Keckley watched as "the President took the picture, laid it on a table be-

fore him, scanned the face thoughtfully, and said: 'It is a good face; it is the face of a noble, noble, brave man. I am glad that the war is over at last.'"

That afternoon, a theater proprietor named Harry Ford was decorating the presidential box with flags and bunting for the Lincolns, who had arranged to attend that evening's performance of *Our American Cousin.* Ford ordered a black stagehand named Joe Simms "to go to his bedroom and get a rocking chair, and bring it down and put it in the President's box." So Simms toted it across the alley and installed it: "a chair with a high back to it, and cushioned."

That afternoon, Simms spotted a familiar duo ducking into a neighboring restaurant: a scenery changer named Ned Spangler and the voluble young actor John Wilkes Booth. By the time the Lincolns arrived at Ford's Theatre that evening, Simms had taken his place in the wing opposite the President's box, and Spangler just below. Between acts one and two, another prop man named John Miles looked out the window and saw Booth bringing a horse from the stable. Coming around to the back door of the theater, the young thespian summoned Spangler by calling his name three times, whereupon Spangler hurried across the rear of the stage to meet him. Meanwhile, Simms had stepped outside and spotted a young black stable hand named John Peanuts lying on a bench and, as he often did when Booth was in the neighborhood, holding the actor's horse.

After Simms had returned to "wind up the curtain, I heard the fire of a pistol, and, looking down, I saw Booth jump out of a private box down onto the stage, with a bowie-knife in his hand," and make "his escape across the stage." A former slave named Mary Jane Anderson, who lived behind Ford's Theatre, "saw Booth come out of the door with something in his hand, glittering. He came out of the theater so quick that it seemed as if he but touched the horse, and it was gone like a flash of lightning. I thought to myself that the horse must surely have run off with the gentleman." But then "there was a rush out of the door," and Anderson heard people calling out, "Which way did he go?" Anderson asked a bystander what the matter was. "The President was shot," he said.

ALL THROUGH THE WAR, Lincoln had received letters warning him about assassination. "But he never gave a second thought to the mysterious warnings," Keckley recalled. When the First Lady worried about his safety as he rode his horse to the Soldiers' Home or walked across the yard to the War Department, Lincoln would say, "What does any one want to harm me for? Don't worry about me, Mother, as if I were a little child, for no one is going to molest me." But now a dying Lincoln was being carried out of the bedlam of Ford's Theatre and across the street.

Slaves well knew how deeply their masters hated Lincoln. Benjamin Henderson's mistress had three grandsons who rode off to war vowing to "bring old Lincoln's head back and set it on the gate post for a target." George Womble's master said he was going to use Lincoln's skull "for a soap dish." Louisa Alexander reported that her master was "always abusing Lincoln, and calls him an old rascal," threatening that "if he had hold of Lincoln he would chop him into mincemeat."

Mattie Jackson's master once "searched my mother's room and found a picture of President Lincoln, cut from a newspaper." He asked her what she was doing with "Old Lincoln's" picture. "She replied it was there because she liked it. He then knocked her down three times, and sent her to the trader's yard for a month as punishment." Esther King Casey remembered that just after war was declared, she and her father were passing through Americus, Georgia, when they saw "Abraham Lincoln hanging from a noose in the courthouse square. Of course, it was only an effigy," but Rebel recruits had shot it "full of bullet holes before they left town."

"ONE DAY," wrote the future Colored Methodist Episcopal minister Monroe Franklin Jamison, "the white folks received good news from the war, and things about the house wore a different appearance." His master, Alford Shorter, "was everywhere, cheery and lively." "What's the news?" Jamison asked him. "Why, old Lincoln is dead!" his master exclaimed.

Shorter's "good news" plunged his slaves "into the deepest gloom," as if their spirit had died with Lincoln. On the rainy morning the President died, a desolate Navy Secretary Gideon Welles encountered hundreds of newly liberated blacks gathered outside the White House, "weeping and wailing their loss." Though he had met many a strong man who "wept when I met them," the crowd's "hopeless grief" affected him "more than almost anything else." "The death of the President was like an electric shock to my soul," wrote Mattie Jackson, one of the thousands of mourners who walked past Lincoln's coffin as his funeral train paused in Indianapolis on its journey to Springfield, Illinois. "I could not feel convinced of his death until I gazed upon his remains, and heard the last roll of the muffled drum and the farewell boom of the cannon. I was then convinced that though we were left to the tender mercies of God, we were without a leader."

John Eubanks and William Lattimore recalled how "all the soldiers had wreaths on their guns" and wore "that black band around their arms." "The whole country was draped in mourning," wrote James L. Smith, and "every eye was dimmed with tears. Pen cannot begin to describe the sadness. Deeply the people felt the loss of one whom they loved as a father." America had lost "a pure patriot; humanity a tried friend; freedom a great champion," for Lincoln's heart "could be touched by all classes of the nation, from the highest to the lowest." And now he had been "stricken down at the time when his great wisdom was so much needed in bringing his distracted and blood-drenched country" into safe harbor.

In their grief and shock, black people believed, with some justification, that Lincoln's assassination was part of a conspiracy against them. H. B. Holloway claimed he had looked "right in Lincoln's mouth when he said, 'The colored man is turned loose without anything. I am gonna give a dollar a day to every Negro born before Emancipation until his death: a pension of a dollar a day,'" which was why Southern whites wanted him killed. "It's gonna be an awful thing up yonder," Holloway warned, "when they hold a judgment over the way that things was done down here." When the Civil War was over, "and they didn't fight any longer," said Lizzie Barnett, Lincoln set the slaves free "and then got assassinated for doing it," just as President William McKinley would be assassinated after the Spanish-American War for trying to get black people "a slave pension." "If you will notice," said Belle Garland Myers Caruthers, "all the Presidents that have been assassinated were Republicans."

Some felt as though Lincoln had abandoned them. An interviewer once asked Billy Abraham Longslaughter of Virginia why he credited Grant and not Lincoln with freeing the slaves. "Well, I tell you, white folks: Mr. Lincoln didn't live long enough to help us," because he "went to the Ford's Circus and got shot." "Abraham Lincoln started heap of things he didn't finish," said Jerry Eubanks. "Nobody ever went back where he left off." Joe Rollins recalled the slaves saying that Lincoln would give them a home. But then "he dead, and ain't give us no home."

Louis Meadows of Alabama thought God had punished Lincoln for his hubris. "When Mr. Lincoln was killed, us didn't think us would go back to slavery, cause us done been turned free. We had took the oath that as long as there was breath in the body or blood in the veins, that never again would we go back to slavery." Meadows conceded that "things was hurt by Mr. Lincoln getting killed," but he "lost his life cause he promised more than he could ever rightly hope to do. That where folks make mistakes," he said, "in biting off more than they can chew."

FORMER SLAVES WERE divided in their opinion of Abraham Lincoln. Hannah McFarland "didn't care much about Lincoln. It was nice of him to free us," she had to admit, "but of course he didn't want to." "Old man Abe Lincoln was a fine old man, and I liked him," said Tishey Taylor of Missouri, but "he never freed us," only "told us how." Some blamed Lincoln for their hardships after Emancipation. "Lincoln was a fine, conscientious man," one former slave conceded, "but he turned us out without anything to eat or live on." During the first winter after the war, almost every Negro "in the world cussed old Abraham Lincoln."

"Abraham Lincoln gets too much praise," contended Alice Douglass. "I say, 'Shucks, give God the praise.'" George Strickland agreed. "It was the plans of God to free us," he said, "and not Abraham Lincoln's." "Lincoln got the praise for freeing us, but did he do it?" asked eighty-one-year-old Thomas Hall. "He give us freedom without giving us any chance to live to ourselves. And we still had to depend on the Southern white man for work, food, and clothing. And he held us, through our necessity and want, in a state of servitude but little better than slavery. Lincoln done but little for the Negro race, and from a living standpoint, nothing. White folks," Hall continued, "are not going to do nothing for Negroes except keep them down. Harriet Beecher Stowe, the writer of *Uncle Tom's Cabin*, did that for her own good. She had her own interests at heart, and I don't like her, Lincoln, or none of that crowd."

But most would revere the memory of the martyred Great Emancipator. "I thinks that Abe Lincoln was a mighty fine man," said William Henry Towns. "Some say that Abe wasn't interested so much in freeing the slaves than he was in saving the Union." But for Towns, it didn't "make no difference if he wasn't interested in the black folks," for he "sure done a big thing by trying to save the Union," for without the Union there could have been no freedom. As an old man during the era of Jim Crow, Towns didn't "like to talk about this that have done happened. It done passed, so I don't say much about it, specially the presidents, cause it might cause a disturbance right now." But he would say this: "All men means well, but some of them ain't broad-minded enough to do anything for nobody but themselves. Any man that tries to help humanity is a good man."

Mattie Jackson admired Lincoln for his capacity to grow, for had he "considered it too humiliating to learn in advanced years, our race would yet have remained under the galling yoke of oppression." "Lincoln?" asked Nancy Gardner of Oklahoma. "Now you is talking about the Negro's friend! Why that was the best man God ever let tramp the earth!" "I bless God about Abraham Lincoln," Sarah Wilson declared. "If he give me my freedom I know he is in heaven now." London Law Hemmett thought Lincoln was "the greatest man that ever lived."

In some slaves' pantheon, Lincoln attained biblical stature. James Southall called him "God's emissary." Others said he was "next to the Lord," "next to God," "partly God." Annie Young thought Lincoln was greater than Moses. "He done more for us," declared Charles Willis, "than any man done since Jesus left." "Lincoln was a durn fool man," said George W. Harmon, "but he was better than John the Baptist: next to Christ." William Watson was "glad to the Lord I am free and serving the Lord and Abe Lincoln's spirit. That's how much I love that man."

EVEN THE TRAGEDY of Lincoln's assassination could not altogether smother the North's joy in its monumental triumph over Secessionism, nor African-American jubilation over slavery's end. A black mule driver for the 101st Indiana Infantry recalled that early in the morning of May 24, 1865, the Contrabands of Washington, D.C., "were wide awake: anything for a display, and turnout, and excitement." To boost the morale of a people still grieving for not only Lincoln but their fallen kith and kin, President Andrew Johnson had ordered a Grand Review. The muleskinner's commander, Major George Steele, gave him the honor of leading the pack mules immediately behind his regiment's ranks. "I thought the year of jubilee had come sure," the muleskinner remembered. "Lots of the officers — and our colonel was one of them — wanted new uniforms," but they were ordered to march in their battle fatigues instead. "So we marched through the streets of the great city without hardly waiting to brush off the dust. And I brought up the rear of the 101st Indiana with the same old pack mule I had led for many a weary mile through a portion of the state of North Carolina and Virginia." The procession stretched for twenty miles and took two days to pass, and "the folks that saw this review say it was the grandest sight ever seen on this continent." Although the muleskinner couldn't see much of the parade from behind his regiment's ranks, "I was happy."

28

---◆---

"A Tired Old Man"

Jefferson Davis · Alexander Stephens · Davis's Decline
Harbingers of Victory · Coming Home · Ruin
Dreams of Master

J AMES LUCAS REMEMBERED, "plain as yesterday," when Lincoln "got killed, and how all the flags hung at half mast. The North nearly went wild with worrying and blamed everybody else. Some of them even tried to blame the killing on Marse Davis."

Henry Walton's father, whose mistress had whipped his wife to death, had accompanied his master into Rebel service. His master was mortally wounded, and on his deathbed he bequeathed his servant to Jefferson Davis's secretary, Micajah H. Clark. "On the day of the surrender," said Walton, "my papa carried the news of the surrender to Captain Clark, who told him to shut up and not say anything about it, as President Davis would have him shot." Even after Joseph E. Johnston surrendered his Army of Tennessee on April 26, Jefferson Davis refused to admit defeat and set out to unite whatever regiments remained in the field and join forces in Texas with Kirby Smith. There, in "country abounding in supplies, and deficient in rivers and railroads," he intended to continue to wage war "until our enemy, foiled in the purpose of subjugation," would "acknowledge the Constitutional rights of the States, and by a convention, or quasi-treaty, guarantee the security of person and property."

Davis's wife, Varina, had once predicted to Elizabeth Keckley that she would accompany her triumphant husband to Washington, D.C., as the nation's First Lady. But now, after Union soldiers hunted Booth down and killed him, she found herself accompanying the nation's most wanted fugitive as he made his way through the Carolinas and performed his last presidential duties in the little town of Washington, Georgia. For six days the Davises trudged on, accompanied by their four children, Confederate Postmaster General John Henninger Reagan, Governor Francis Richard Lubbock of Texas, assorted relatives and military officers, and a squad of cavalry escorting a small caravan of wagons and ambulances.

After Richmond's fall, Lincoln had expressed some ambivalence about capturing his Secessionist opposite number; perhaps, he suggested half in jest, it might be less troublesome to let Davis flee the country. But suspecting Davis of backing Booth's conspiracy, the Federal authorities now deemed his capture a necessity.

According to a story Ohio freedman Elmore Steele enjoyed telling his descendants, Captain George W. Tool of the 50th U.S. Colored Infantry received orders "to be on the lookout for Jefferson Davis." Tool had been informed that Davis "would stop at a wayside inn" with a small party of his loyalists, including "a little boy attendant, about fifteen years old." Assuming that Davis had donned a disguise, Tool sent Steele to the inn to bribe the boy into identifying the fugitive as he ate his supper. "When they sit down to eat, the colored boy tucked the napkins under their chins" and, by arrangement with Steele, "pull Jefferson Davis's twice under his chin before tucking it in." Steele "watched close," then returned to report what he had seen. But by the time Tool's company reached the inn, Davis, if indeed it was Davis, had fled.

The fugitives traveled through middle Georgia like gypsies, and on May 10 camped a mile north of Irwinville. "Folks said he had the money train," Tim Thornton remembered, "but I never see'd no gold, nor anybody what had any." Marie Sutton Clemments thought she had an explanation. From her mistress's yard in Lincoln County, Georgia, just across the South Carolina line, she had seen "five wagons come by. They said it was Jeff Davis's wagons. They was loaded with silver money. Somehow the folks got a whiff of it and got the money out." In fact, the wagon train's Rebel guards had opened it, demanding their pay.

John Rogers was told that "some of the Darkies what had gone over on the Yankee side betrayed the president" as he camped by a spring near Irwinville. Addison Ingram claimed to have been an eyewitness to Davis's capture. After the Yankees caught him, a story would circulate that Davis had tried to sneak off disguised in women's clothing. His defenders said "it weren't so about that dress affair," said Ingram, "but it sure God was! He done had a gal's dress on right over his man's britches, and it was his foots in man's shoes what give him away. Just when he done lift his feet to hand, the skirt tail catch on his shoe strop!"

The story lent Davis's flight a certain symmetry, for after the election of 1860, Lincoln had crept into Washington in disguise. But whether Davis intentionally impersonated a woman or, in his haste and exhaustion, grabbed his wife's robe instead of his own, is subject to debate. (Years later, Elizabeth Keckley would recognize Davis's robe as her own handiwork.) In any case, as the Yankees closed in, Varina Davis added a shawl to his ensemble and sent her mulatto slave to accompany him with a bucket, apparently in hopes they might pass as two slaves fetching water from a spring. But Davis's boots and spurs did indeed give him away, and with the exception of a couple of Rebel officers who managed to hide from the Yankees in the woods, Davis and his party were rounded up and transported to Macon.

WHILE HIS CAPTORS were at it, they swung south to pluck Alexander Stephens from his plantation, to which Davis's estranged vice president had retired when he judged the cause was lost. The Yankees imprisoned Stephens for five months, during which he continued to insist, in his diary, that anyone trying to address the race question must regard black inferiority as "a fixed invincible fact." He warned that should Lincoln's egalitarian principles be followed, "it would end in the extermination or the driving from the country of one or the other of the races." And yet in his dreams the little planter conjured his servant Pierce, well dressed and promising "never to leave me," for Stephens had been, or so said Pierce's phantom, "the best friend he ever had."

AFTER PASSING THROUGH a gauntlet of jubilant but derisive Yankee soldiers, Davis and his family were cordially received by General James H. Wilson. But for almost two years, Davis would languish in prison at Fortress Monroe, where a vengeful General Nelson A. Miles would oversee his incarceration, and occasionally place him in anklets and leg irons, ostensibly to prevent his escape. In a letter home to Varina, Davis protested that the wearing of chains "are orders for a slave, and no man with a soul in him would obey such orders." In 1870, Davis's old seat in the U.S. Senate was occupied briefly by Hiram Rhoades Revels, a free black from North Carolina who had spent the war organizing black regiments for the Union Army.

That autumn, Florida Hewitt was going about her duties at Brierfield plantation when she heard somebody shout, "Here comes Marse Jeff!" She looked down the long, overgrown drive to the Davis mansion and saw a rider approach. But if he was Jefferson Davis, he "no longer sat superbly erect, but drooped and sagged like a tired old man." One of his eyes "glittered blindly" as he reined his horse to a halt. After distributing a bundle of shoes among Hewitt's children, he painfully made his way into her shack. Sitting with her "knee to knee," he recounted "his capture and imprisonment, pulling up a trouser leg to show the bruise of shackles on his emaciated shanks." By then Davis's late brother Joseph had sold his plantation to a capable family of former slaves named Montgomery. Thus, "on this visit, the outlawed President of the Confederacy was the guest of Negroes in his former home." When the Montgomerys could not sustain the plantation, Davis would resume proprietorship, but he proved too feeble for the task. Leaving his shrunken plantation in the care of a white overseer named Trainer, Davis moved to Beauvoir, on the Mississippi coast, to write his memoirs.

"Late in 1889," wrote Florida Hewitt's interviewer, "he returned to Brierfield for the last time, eighty-one years old and so weak he could scarcely totter across the stage plank. The manager, Mr. Trainer, met him with a wagon whose joltings caused him torture on their ride of two miles. He was very ill, and Mr. Trainer sent a Negro to hail a steamboat." Miles Stone recalled "how tenderly they laid Mr. Davis on a stretcher. Four Negroes bore him to the steamboat," bound for New Orleans, where he died soon afterward. Though he apparently succumbed to malaria, a rumor circulated among the slaves of Georgia that a black cook "put poison in Jeff Davis's something-to-eat, and that was what killed him."

"I never did hitch my mind on Jeff Davis," said Mary Colbert. "He had his time to rule." "No doubt" Davis thought he was "doing the right thing," Minnie Davis would politely concede. But "to be frank," ventured George Miller, he "lacked wisdom in so great an undertaking" as rebellion.

SOME SLAVES HAD seen the Rebel defeat coming from a long way off. Every time Ann Drake's master returned from the front, she noticed a decline in the quality of his mount. "When he left he ride his big black mare, and when he come home he was riding a speckled horse named Buford. Then he went away again, and when he come back he was riding a mule named Ginny." George Washington Miller saw the South's defeat coming when he observed that Rebel soldiers no longer traveled light, ready for battle, but carried large packs. "I was in the Carolinas when news of freedom came at the death of Lincoln. We was looking for it," he said, "because the Confederates had so many backsacks."

As "the times changed from slavery days to freedom's days," Annie L. Burton was "mystified to see such wonderful changes." But as the days "glided by," she would see "my master and mistress in close conversation, and they seemed anxious about something that I, a child, could not know the meaning of." But after a few weeks, "I began to understand." Night and day, and one by one, all the slaves began to run off, "until there was not one to be seen. All around, the plantation was left barren. Day after day, I could run down to the gate and see down the road troops and troops of Garrison's Brigade, and in the midst of them gangs and gangs of Negro slaves who joined with the soldiers, shouting, dancing and clapping their hands." As they trooped home, dozens of Negro soldiers "discarded their uniforms for the gaudier clothing that had belonged to their masters in former days, and could be identified as soldiers only with difficulty."

On April 9, 1865, Henry Banner's Virginia master emerged from his house and announced, "General Lee's whipped now, and damn badly whipped. The war is over. The Yankees done got the country. It is all over. Just go home and hide everything you got. General Lee's army is coming this way and stealing everything they can get their hands on." "For three weeks steady after the surrender," recalled John W. H. Barnet of Louisiana, "people was passing from the War, and for two years off and on, somebody come along going home; some rode and some had a cane or stick walking. When a troop of discharged Rebel cavalry came to her cabin, George Washington Miller's mother "cooked from midnight till next evening. Some of them was crippled up and some of them didn't have no clothes on: just wore off them. When they left, they blowed the bugle for the signals, just like they did coming up."

"The funniest sight" that Eliza White "ever saw was when the soldiers came from war, all of them coming down the road with sticks cross they backs and holding to them with their hands all just alike, and it did look so funny." "The day surrender come," Allen Williams "never see'd the like of guns and soldiers half starved and naked. They was running low of rations when the war ceased." Cheney Cross remembered when Captain John W. Purifoy of the 44th Alabama Infantry "come on in home from the war." The captain "didn't exactly favor his self then, cause when I see'd him coming round the house he look so ragged and ornery" that Cross took him for the devil himself. Cross ran out "behind the smoke-house, and when I got a good look at him through a crack, it look like I could recognize his favor. But I couldn't recall his name to save my life. Lord, he's a sight! All growed over and bushy! You couldn't tell if he's man or beast. I kept on looking whilst he's coming round the corner, and then I heard him say 'Cheney, that you?'"

"When the war done gone, Old Master he come, with one of he arms shotten them off. Old Mistress, she cry, she so glad to see him. And Uncle Jude, he run and hug Old Master, and us all cry and take on, we so glad Old Master come back and so sorry he arm shot off." Roxy Pitts's master "got killed in Virginny, they said, and he didn't never come back home. And them what did come back was all crippled up and hurt."

Some dead men did return, however. A farmer named Glover often visited Willie Blackwell's owner, and as a boy Blackwell used to meet Glover's horse in the drive and open the gate. Then Glover would reach down and heft him onto his horse and ride with him to the house. One day Glover turned up and, as usual, Willie opened the gate, but Glover made no move to lift him. Bewildered, Blackwell saw that Glover's boot was spattered with blood and ran off to summon his master. But Glover "done been shot on the way over, and am done dead when I's open the gate for him."

It fell to slaves to break bad news to returning soldiers. "One day in '65, young master came home." Belle Garland Myers Caruthers "knew when I heard his footsteps on the porch that he was awful downcast. The war was over, but we didn't know it till he came home. He came to his mother's room, and I met him at the door. He said 'Belle, where is Ma?' And I said, 'She died one week ago today.' He just turned away without a word and walked the floor all night."

Easter Reed feared that all four of her master's sons would be killed in the war. "And they did get hurt. When they come home they was sick," and Reed "had to fan the flies off of them." But they died "soon after they got back home." George Morrison's uncle survived his service as a cook for the Confederate Army, but when "he came back, he wasn't happy in his mind like my pappy was."

It took Tom Siggers's family two months and six days to get to Mississippi from Texas. "In their travels, they passed through scenes of great desolation: towns had been burned and the country laid in waste during the war." Siggers was impressed by the "huge piles of grape shot piled on the bank of Red River." As George Washington Miller led his family back to Mississippi from South Carolina, some places they passed "was so strong with stink from battles fought and dead bodies left, we had to hold our noses." When the Rebels returned to east Texas, recalled John Love, "they finds all they cattle stoled or dead," and "the plantations all growed up in weeds and all the young slaves gone." The railroads "was all run down, and not safe to use; the factories and the mills was most of them closed. Times was hard and no money, and if there wasn't plenty wild animals everybody done starve."

Slaves were dismayed, delighted, or simply astonished by how quickly the mighty had fallen. "Old Master, he didn't go to the war," said Theodore Fontaine Lewis of Alabama. "He too old to go, so he stays home and make corn and fodder and oats, and sends them to the soldiers out killing Yankees. One day the Yankees come along and burnt up everything on the place" except the slave cabins. His master "went off somewhere when they come; and, when he come back," he had to live in one of the cabins until he could build himself a new house. "But the new one," Lewis noted, "wasn't big like the old one."

Vice President Stephens's brother "was one of these die-hard Southerners. He did something, and they arrested him. It made him so mad," he mounted a horse "and fell off and broke his neck." They called it an accident, but Claiborne Moss believed "he really killed himself." "The one surviving son" of Annie Row's Texas master "returned to the farm, shut himself in a shed, and cut his throat," leaving a note saying "he not care for to live" because the slaves were free.

Some masters failed to comprehend how steeply their fortunes had declined with Emancipation. Isaiah Green's family remained on the Willis plantation until their owner's extravagance forced them to move. "He ran through 3,000 acres of land, and died on rented land in Morgan County." Adam Singleton of Alabama watched the fortunes of his master, George Simmons, take a downward spiral after the war. Simmons had been "mighty rich before the war, but after the war he was mighty poor." When Simmons "come back home, he sat on the front door steps with his head down nigh all day, just thinking and thinking." Singleton's mistress "got sick and on the bed for a long time and died," whereupon

"Simmons, he took to drink mighty hard and got cross with the Darkies, and wouldn't pay them for work."

Henry Clay Bruce's master "had been reared in the lap of luxury, graduated from college, then had studied law, and never earned a dollar to defray expenses," but now he "came home penniless, and with health gone, to find his father dead, his Negroes freed, and stock stolen." In early 1865, Bruce "visited my old master and found him greatly disheartened and hard-pressed. He told me that he wished I had kept the horse, for he would have been better satisfied, as it had been taken from him by the thieves, dressed for self-protection in the uniform of Uncle Sam."

Walking through Richmond soon after Lincoln's visit, the black abolitionist propagandist William Wells Brown observed several white men wearing "long, black cloth cloaks, beneath which was a basket. Into this they might be seen to deposit their marketing for the day. I noticed an old black man bowing very gracefully to one of these individuals" and asked who the white man was. The old man answered that the man had been a major in the Confederate Army. "He was very rich before the war," he continued, "but the war fetch him right down, and now he ain't able to have servants. He's too proud to show his basket, so he covers it up in his cloak."

"The last time I see'd the home plantation," recalled William Colbert, "I was standing on a hill. I looked back on it for the last time through a patch of scrub pines, and it look so lonely. There weren't but one person in sight: the master. He was setting in a wicker chair in the yard looking out over a small field of cotton and corn." There were "four crosses in the graveyard in the side lawn where he was setting, over the graves of his sons who'd been killed in the war."

Their masters would haunt slaves for the rest of their lives. Frances Kimbrough swore that while working in the field a few weeks after her young master's death she saw his ghost "leaning against a pine tree, watching us free Negroes work." "After the war was over," Thomas Brown recalled, "my mama and daddy moved to Nashville, at a place called Dutch Town," from which "they could look down the river and see Old Master's plantation." In his old age Albert Cummings told a visitor that his master still came to him in his dreams. "And he always appears without food and raiment, just as the South was left after the war."

29

---◆---

"The Row's End"

IT WAS IN THE MIDST of such ruin that masters first officially notified their slaves of what most had long concluded from the shouts of passing Yankee soldiers, the whispers of runaways, and the grumblings of their masters: that the Confederacy's defeat had put an end to their servitude. All through the South, the same scene played itself out. Masters and mistresses called their slaves together and, sometimes with a Union soldier standing by as a witness, read aloud a proclamation that they would then translate for their slaves as, "You are as free as I am."

Aaron Carter recalled a typical scene. "Master call us all over to the big, long porch and say, 'You is all set free. Those want to stay can stay, those want to leave can leave.'" "Ginny," Mandy Jones's master told her mother, "you-all don't belong to me no more. You and Wesley and the childrens: you just belong to yourselfs." "I don't knows how long Master had the notification," Abe McKlennan recalled, "but, like it was today, and then all next day, all next morning pass by. Finally Master Burkett come out the fields up to us and yell to us to all gather around." "Well," Burkett told them, "now you is all free! Just as free as I am. Don't belong to me, or no one: onliest yourselves." "Weren't nobody say nothing," McKlennan remembered. "Only stand there."

Such reticence was understandable. Toy Hawkins's master did not inform his slaves that they were free until the fall. When a slave woman "what was down by the spring washing clothes started shouting, 'Thank God-a-Mighty! I's free at last!'" her master "come and knocked her down," and she "fainted dead away then, because she wanted to holler so bad and was scared to make a sound."

No one could blame her. "I was riding on my horse over to Columbus to carry some clothes to the soldiers," recalled Pet Franks. "On the way back I heard a bell ringing, and I think it must be a cow strayed off. But when I look, I sees a Negro man with his hands in a iron halter up above his head, and a bell strung between them. He say his master had beat him, and then for two days had kept his hands and feet nailed to a board — you could see the nail holes, too — and then had put his arms in that halter and turn him loose. He say it was all because his master heard tell that he say he would be glad if the Yankees won the war so as he could be free." "All of the slaves on the plantation were glad when they were told that they were free," recalled George Lewis, "but there was no big demonstration, as they were somewhat afraid of what the master might do." When Addie Vinson's mistress gave her slaves the news, "the Negroes started hollering, 'Thank the Lawd, us is free as the jay birds.'" But just then "a white man come along and told them Negroes" that if he heard them say that again, "he would kill the last one of them."

BUT NOTHING COULD contain a freed slave's joy for long. Some of the most exuberant celebrations occurred among slaves who learned about freedom while laboring on their masters' crops. Mariah Jackson and six other slaves were carrying a heavy log out of a field they were clearing when "a great big white man come, jumped up on a log and shouted, 'Freedom! Freedom!' They let the log they was toting down" and rushed to their master's house, where "they cooked and ate and thanked God. Some got down and prayed, some sung. They had a time that day. They got the banjo and fiddle and set out playing," and some of them "got in the big road just walking." When white men told Eda Harper's mother-in-law that she was free, "she dropped her hoe and danced up to the turn road and danced right up into Old Master's parlor. She went so fast a bird could not have held on to her dress tail. That night she sent and got all the neighbors, and they danced all night long."

Jacob Stroyer's father had often spoken of the year of Jubilee. "In the dark days of slavery, he said to Mother, 'The time will come when this boy and the rest of the children will be their own masters and mistresses.'" Stroyer's father died "six years before that day came," but his mother lived to see it. Elderly slaves had prayed as much for their descendants' freedom as their own. "The slaves would go to the woods at night where they sang and prayed," recalled George Womble of Georgia. "Some used to say: 'I know that someday we'll be free, and if we die before that time, our children will live to see it.'" Lucretia Alexander recalled that when a Union officer "who had his arm off at the elbow" pointed to an elderly black man and called out, "You're free as I am," the "old colored folks, old as I am now, that was on sticks, throwed them sticks away and shouted."

"Uncle," a Union officer remarked to a jubilant old slave, "freedom will do you no good, for you are just on the edge of the grave." "I know that, Master," the old man conceded. "I knows that well enough. But I've got my boys, and I bless you all, cause you give them free." When Dashwood Ward offered to allow his old slave Uncle Fendall the option of remaining with his Secessionist master, he answered, "Master Dash, this here might be a mistake, and then these Rebs might go back fighting again, and we might not have but four or five days' freedom. I's gonna take the first day, cause I done prayed all my life for it. So goodbye, Mr. Dashwood Ward."

Some slaveholders took advantage of their former slaves' sense of decorum and never did notify them of their liberation. "They say all the colored people's free," an elderly slave told a visitor to Salisbury, North Carolina, in late 1865. "They do say it certain; but I'm going on same as I always has been," because his mistress "never said anything to me that I was to have wages, nor yet that I was free; nor I never said anything to her. You see, I left it to her own honor to talk to me about it, because I was afraid she'd say I was insulting to her and presuming, so I wouldn't speak first. She hasn't spoke yet."

Demanding to know why Harry Bridges's master had not yet told his slaves that they were free, a Yankee patrol ordered him "to send for the Negro men who were working on another part of the plantation. When all the slaves had assembled, the Union men told them of their freedom. One negro woman, who was unable to believe the news, asked if they might leave the plantation at the moment to go where they wished, and of course she was answered in the affirmative, much to her surprise." Bridges recalled that his master "planned to have the negroes finish that year's crop," but that day Bridges's mother "took her few belongings and her five children, three others having been previously sold, and left."

SOME MASTERS PURPOSELY delayed informing their slaves of their freedom as long as they could. "I reckon they was right smart old masters what didn't want to let they slaves go after freedom," Beatrice Black recalled. "They hated to turn them loose. Just let them work on. Heap of them didn't know freedom come. I used to hear tell how the government had to send soldiers away down in the far backcountry to make them turn the slaves loose." Rosetta Davis's people "didn't know it was freedom till three or four months," when a man "come along and said he was going home, the War was over. Some of the hands asked him who win, and he told them the Yankees. They got to inquiring and found out they done been free."

Rachel Hankins's master didn't tell his slaves they were free until June 19. For years afterward, "every 19th of June he would let us clean off a place and fix a platform and have dancing and eating out there in the field." Though Joe McCormick's people were told of their freedom in May, "the Negroes were not really free until December, when all the crops had been gathered. During those months the master paid them nothing for their labor, but they were fed and clothed as usual. Then the slaves began to leave. They did not bid the master farewell but would slip away, a few at a time. Finally, all of them left except one woman who was the cook." Henri Necaise didn't find out he was free until his master "started to whup me once, and the young master up and says, 'You ain't got no right to whup him now. He's free.' Then Master turned me loose."

"After the slaves were set free, any number of them were bound over and kept," recalled George Womble, who had himself unwittingly scrawled his mark on what turned out to be a contract binding him to his master's family until his twenty-first birthday. But even then his master would refuse to let him go. His mistress tried to help him escape, but he was soon discovered holed up at the home of an elderly white woman who had befriended him. "A rope was tied around his neck, and he was made to run the entire way back to the plantation while the others rode on horseback." When eleven-year-old Gabe Butler's fellow slaves were set free, the sheriff of Amite County, Mississippi, "come and made me over to my Mistress, and I was a slave for three years after the surrender," until an elderly woman "see'd the Judge, and she got some papers and come got me and set me free." After freedom was declared, George

Eason of Georgia "was still held in bondage and hired out by the day."
He ran away and located his father, "but was found and brought back."
He would not be released from bondage until 1867.

THERE HAD BEEN so many false alarms during the war that some slaves
had taken to dismissing the constant rumors that they would soon be
free. "I guess we must have celebrated Emancipation about twelve times
in Hornett County," recalled Ambrose Douglass. "Every time a bunch of
Northern soldiers would come through they would tell us we was free,
and we'd begin celebrating. Before we would get through, somebody
else would tell us to go back to work, and we would go." When asked
what he did after his master told him he was free, a Georgia slave named
Willis replied that he "went down to Augusta to the Freedmen's Bureau
to see if it was true."

Tom Robinson also greeted the news with disbelief. "Mr. Dave come
down into the field, and he had a paper in his hand. 'Listen to me, Tom,'
he said, 'listen to what I reads you.' And he read from a paper all about
how I was free. You can't tell how I felt. 'You're joking me.' I says. 'No, I
ain't,' says he. 'You're free.' 'No,' says I, 'it's a joke.' 'No,' says he, 'it's a law
that I got to read this paper to you. Now listen while I read it again.' But
still I wouldn't believe him. 'Just go up to the house,' says he, 'and ask
Mrs. Robinson. She'll tell you.' So I went. 'It's a joke,' I says to her. 'Did
you ever know your master to tell you a lie?' she says. 'No,' says I, 'I ain't.'
'Well,' she says, 'the war's over and you're free.' By that time I thought
maybe she was telling me what was right. 'Miss Robinson,' says I, 'can I
go over to see the Smiths?' (They was a colored family that lived nearby.)
'Don't you understand?' says she. 'You're free. You don't have to ask me
what you can do. Run along, child.' And so I went. And do you know why
I was a-going? I wanted to find out if they was free too. I just couldn't
take it all in. I couldn't believe we was all free alike. Was I happy? Lord.
You can take anything, no matter how good you treat it, it wants to be
free. You can treat it good and feed it good and give it everything it seems
to want. But if you open the cage, it's happy."

"We was under hard task-masters," said George Young of Alabama. "I
was under burden and bound." But now "people shouted and rejoiced,"
Parrish Washington remembered, because their "heavy load had fell
off." "Lots of colored folks seem to be rejoicing and sing, 'I's free, I's free
as a frog,'" said Lafayette Price, "because a frog had freedom to get on a
log and jump off when he please." That might explain the reaction of a

slave woman Anna Woods remembered who "jumped up on a barrel, and she shouted. She jumped off and she shouted. She jumped back on again and shouted some more. She kept that up for a long time, just jumping on a barrel and back off again."

Masters often garnished their proclamations of freedom with advice. "The Yankees and some of our leading colored men got up and spoke, and told the Negroes, 'You are free now. Don't steal. Do honest work, make an honest living to support yourself and children.'" When Julia Terry of Lynchburg, Virginia, told her slaves they were free, she enjoined them "to remember that she had always taught us to be good, honest and truthful and not be sassy to white folks." Hannah Chapman's master told his slaves "not to steal nothing, and to be honest."

The day she found out she was free, a teenage Annie Griegg was doing laundry at a spring. "I had one pot of clothes to boil, and another just out of the pot to rub and rinse," when a fellow slave summoned her to her mistress's kitchen. Griegg told the girl to get a pot of water boiling to scald some chickens while she finished the wash. By the time she returned to the house, however, "Mrs. Field had a handful of switches corded together to beat me" for disobedience. But Griegg threatened to defend herself against her mistress with "the pan of boiling water to scald the chickens in. She got scared of me, told me to put the pan down. I didn't do it." So her mistress "sent to the store for her husband. He come, and I told him how it was," at which point Fields turned on his wife, saying, "Mary Agnes, she is as free as you are or I am. I'm not gonna ever hurt her again, and you better not." "And that," said Griegg, "is the first I ever heard about freedom."

The first evidence Sally Dixon saw that the war was over was "a big music boat came up the Mississippi River. The band was playing, and everybody on it was singing, 'We done hung Jeff Davis to a sour apple tree.'" "When us was freed," Frank Menefee's people sang, "I's going back to Dixie / No more my heart to wander. / Never see my master no more."

In 1865, Turner Jacobs was "just a happy kid" who had never been whipped. He "didn't care much" about Emancipation, but he was "glad now," he told his interviewer, "cause I's a Christian, and it ain't in the Good Book for us to be slaves." The youngest children did not know what to make of freedom. "The band was playing and flags was flying about," recalled Gus Askew, but "us little Negroes didn't get no joy out of it. Mr. Lincoln done said we was free, but us little Negroes was too scared to listen to any band music, even if the soldiers had come to set us free. Appears like us was always getting in somebody's way in them days and getting scared of something. But we went on away from the soldiers and had a good time amongst ourselves, like we always done when there wasn't any cotton picking." "When the soldiers came, we run and hid," recalled Dicey Thomas, "and the soldiers came and poked their bayonets under the bed and shouted, 'Come on out from under there. You're free!'"

Some children were not so much frightened by the prospect of freedom as disappointed. Charlie Hudson recalled feeling all "burnt up" by the news, because he would no longer "have the privilege of riding behind Miss Betsey on old Puss no more when she went to meeting." "I was mighty young," said Ned Chaney, "and children with plenty to eat is free anyhow. Tell them they gonna be free don't make no impression on them; they already free as they wants to be."

Masters had been lying to their slaves for so long that when they declared their slaves free, even the children did not believe them. Sally Crane of Tennessee "got scared and thought that the speculators were gonna put me in them big droves and sell me down in Louisiana." "You fool," said her mistress. "You are free. We're gonna take you to your mammy." But Crane was convinced that "they was carrying me to see my mother before they would send me to be sold in Louisiana."

For young Hattie Sugg of Mississippi, freedom meant she could at last "comb my hair just like the white girls." "When the soldiers in them blue uniforms with gold buttons come" to tell her fellow slaves they were free, young Dolly Whiteside told herself, "I'm going have some buttons like that some day." But other children would learn the meaning of freedom from their parents. Annie Price's father told his mistress "that he did not want to remain on the plantation any longer than it was necessary to get his family together," because "he wanted to get out to himself so that he could see how it felt to be free." As young as she was, Price "felt very happy, because the yoke of bondage was gone, and she knew that she could have a privilege like everybody else."

Tim Haynes was six years old "the day we was set free. My old mistress, Miss Becky Franks, come in and say to my mother, 'Addie, you is free this morning,' and commenced crying. She give my mother some jerked beef for us. I know I run out in the yard where there was eighty Yankee soldiers, and I pulled out my shirt tail and ran down the road kicking up the dust and saying, 'I'm free, I'm free!'" But his mother called after him, "You'd better come back here!" For children, of course, freedom did not mean freedom from their parents. "What is freed?" Ann Drake asked her mother. "If I give you a backhand slap, you brat," she answered, "I'll teach you what 'freed' is."

FOR THE WORST-TREATED SLAVES, freedom's most immediate bene-fit was an end to the lash. Lewis Favor had "prayed all of the time be-cause he never wanted to be whipped with the cowhide, like others he had seen." Alex Montgomery's folks "wanted to be set free so Mr. Hodge wouldn't whup them any more." "Just before freedom come," James Bolton remembered, Sherman's men rode through "and told us that the bull-whups and cowhides was all dead and buried." The first thing Hestern Norton's Mississippi master did after he declared his slaves free was "whitewash the bull whip and hang it on the side of the house." "No more driver's lash for me," liberated slaves would sing. "No more, no more."

MANY MASTERS COULD not hide their bitterness and grief. Frank Fikes's owners had not been "mean to us at all until after surrender." But then "they got mad at us because we was free, and they let us go without a crumb of anything, and without a penny, and nothing but what we had on our backs."

Henry Lewis McGaffey's master did not take his slaves' jubilation with grace. Their singing and praying made Otis McGaffey so angry that "he drive them out of his sight." "Well, you black bastard," said Charlie Sandles's master, "you are free. You can do just as you please," and he gave Sandles fifty cents. "I began to dance and shout," Sandles recalled, "and you know he like to have whipped me." Margaret Goss's master ac-idly told his slaves, "The damn Yankees have come and set you free. I hope you are satisfied."

"You are all free, just as free as I am," Mingo White's master declared. "Now go and get yourself somewhere to stick your heads." But this sneering adieu did not have the desired effect on White's mother. "Just as soon as he say that, my mammy hollered out, 'That's enough for a yearling!' She struck out across the field to Mr. Lee Osborn's to get a place for me and her to stay." After proclaiming his slaves' liberty, H. H. Edmunds's master "told the slaves to resume their work. Since I was free," said Edmunds, "I refused to do so, and as a result, I received a ter-rible licking. I mentally resolved to get even some day, and years afterward, I went to the home of this man for the expressed purpose of seeking revenge. However, I was received kindly, and treated so well, that all thoughts of revenge vanished, and for years after, my boss and I visited each other in our homes."

HARRIET GRESHAM OF Florida recalled for her interviewer the brave face her mistress put on when the day came to notify her slaves. Her mistress "was very frightened, but walked upright and held a trembling lip between her teeth" as they waited one last time for her to sound the horn that had summoned several generations of human chattel to and from work. But others were more labile. Andrew Jackson Gill recalled that his mistress "stood there tall and straight, and tried to smile. But I see'd a tear a-trickling off her nose, and pretty soon we was all crying together." As Ida Rigley's mistress watched her slaves "put their beds and clothes" up on Union Army wagons and follow the Yankees down the road, she said, "They need not follow them off. They are already free." "The way she said it," Rigley remembered, "like she was heartbroken, made me nearly cry." Harry Bridges of Pike County, Mississippi, recalled seeing his mistress "falling across the bed in tears and asking her husband what they were to do."

Many masters were equally distraught. "Old Master never did tell us we was free," Emma Jackson remembered. "He called us up to tell us, then every time he would start to tell it, he would bust out and cry." "It was fodder pulling time when Marsa come told us we was free," said Frances Willis. "When he got close enough, I could see he was crying. Before he had been there long, he told us we was just as free as he was and could leave if we wanted to." "One day, I's walking by the house," recalled Walter Rimm, "and I's see the master setting on the porch. I's thought him am mad, cause his face am all screwed up." Rimm became scared "cause I's always doing something for to get the whuppings. But him am grieving. All us colored folks crowds around the porch and am some surprised, cause the master am crying. Him never cries except at some of his folks' death, so we childrens says some of his folks am dead."

Jake Dawkins's master not only "was too old to go to the war" but almost too drunk to notify his slaves. "Negroes," he slurred, "I hates to tell you, but you is as free as I is." The news affected Mahalia Shores's master even more violently. "Master Jim was setting on the porch. Tom Chapman was his overseer. They rung the big farm bell and had the oldest Negroes stand in a line and us little ones in front so we could all see. Tom Chapman read the paper and stood by the soldier," after which Master Jim "vomited and vomited."

THE DAY THEY told Carrie Hudson that her people were free, a white man named Bruce of Elbert County, Georgia, asked, "What you say?" When they "told him again that all the Negroes was free, he bent hisself over, and never did straighten his body no more. When he died, he was still all bent over," just to "show the world how he hated to give his Negroes up after they done been set free."

When the time came to notify her slaves of their liberation, James Reeves's mistress had been ill for some time and "was just able to come to the door and deliver that message" to her assembled slaves. Speaking through her senior slave, Henry, because she was "too full" to address them all, she told them they were free. "Three weeks after that time, they brought her out of the house feet foremost and took her to the cemetery. The news killed her dead."

Dwindling away after the shock of the Confederacy's defeat, Cora Shepherd's master "call us all into the room" and "lay there looking at us. 'All my little Darkies,' he said, and I never will forget that: us all standing round looking at him so sick. 'I hate to see you all scattered, but as long as you live, I want you to stay here, and when you buried, I want you buried on the Walden premises.'" "Us don't want you to die, Master!" his slaves cried. "Us won't get no more shirts!" At this he "bust out in a cry, and all us children bellowed too. 'I am born to die,' he told us," and expired soon afterward.

This matter of clothes loomed large. When Allen Williams's master told him "the damn Yankees is freed you," "he grabbed me by the arm and pushed my sleeve up and pointed to my skin, and say, 'Allen, my daddy give a thousand dollars in gold for that, didn't he?' 'He sure did,' I told him. Then he say, 'Didn't my daddy give you to me, and didn't I put them clothes on you?' 'Sure enough you did,' I say to him. Then Master George say, 'Yes, and the damn Yankees took you away from me. But them is my clothes.' Then he made like he was gonna take my clothes away from me, and we scuffled all around the field." But Rube Witt's fellow slaves could not rid themselves of their slave clothes fast enough. "You'd ought to see'd them pulling off them croaker-sack clothes when master says we's free," she said. A Georgia slaveholder named Huff could not bring himself to tell his slaves they were free because "he hated the thought of a Negro being able to wear a starched shirt."

FREED SLAVES AND former masters tried to puzzle out their new relationship. As Isaiah Green's mistress tearfully stood by, a Yankee officer told her slaves that if she "calls you 'John,' call her 'Sally.' You are as free as she is, and she can't whip you any more." Sarah Jane Patterson remembered hearing a freed slave ask if freedmen still "got to say 'Master.'" "Somebody said, 'Naw.' But they said it all the same. They said it for a long time."

It was hard for former slaveholders to comprehend that they could no longer rule with the same old coercive impunity. Shang Harris's mistress threatened to chop off the arms of any freed slave she caught fighting, but her husband intervened. "Arms cut off?" he said. "Huh! You get yours *broke* off if you don't hush." After freedom, Hannah Austin's mistress "called me asking that I come in the yard to play with the children. I did not go," Austin recalled, "but politely told her I was free and didn't belong to any one but my mama and papa." And as she "spoke these words, my mistress began to cry." Emmaline Kilpatrick's master demanded that any of his former slaves who remained with him would have to "promise him to be good Negroes and mind him like they always done." But two "brash good-for-aught-things" refused. Alex McKinney's master "told us we was free soon after the surrender," but he continued to whip "every one of us: from the biggest to the least."

Alec Pope's master, Mordecai Edwards, "was pretty good," though "not too good. He tried to make you do right, but if you didn't he would give you a good brushing. When Old Master told my pa and ma us was free and didn't belong to him no more," he said "he couldn't brush the grown folks no more, but if they wanted to stay with him he would brush they childrens if they didn't do right." Pope's mother told him "he weren't going to brush none of her childrens no more." When Richard Parrott's master ordered his mother off the plantation without her children, she refused to go for fear he would bind them to him until their twenty-first birthdays. His mother "kept the family together until the husband's return; then they left the plantation together."

"After the war ended and us was freed," said Tony Cox of Mississippi, "us had a hard time getting adjusted, and making a way for us selves." "We did not know a thing," recalled John McAdams of Texas. "Could hardly buy our own groceries. As slaves we did not have all that to do, as that had rested on Master's shoulders, and I did not think that I would ever have that to do. But I did. So it was hard on me when I found out that they would give me money for my work, and I had all that to do myself."

FOR SLAVES WHO had never been paid for their labor, money was a puzzle, and whites were not above taking advantage of their ignorance. One of their tricks was to pay them in Confederate dollars. "The war is over," Lucindy Hall's master told her, "and you can lay in bed now and sleep till ten o'clock if you wants to. You gonna work for wages from now on." So Hall "commenced dancing and shouting and knocking down the corn, I was so happy. They paid me to stay in the house," and she thought she "was white" because she was "getting paid to work." But her former master "paid me in money that wouldn't pass; it wasn't no good." "During the War, Jeff Davis gave out Confederate money," said Lucretia Alexander. "It died out on the folks' hands. About twelve hundred dollars of it died out on my father's hands." Henry Banner found a sack of money in the street and tried to spend it on groceries. "My goodness, Henry," said the clerk, "that money's no good. The Yankees have killed it." And here Banner "had done gone all over the woods and hid that money out," and now "all our money was dead."

But many slaves who had worked for the Yankees had been astute enough to accept and save Union greenbacks. In the wartime South "you couldn't pay for a dime's worth even with a five dollar bill of Union money then," Julia White recalled, but Yankee soldiers had kept "telling my father to take all the greenbacks he could get and hide away." "Just wait," they told him. "Someday Confederate money won't be any good, and greenbacks will be all the money we had." But, to be on the safe side, he exchanged his dollars for gold, and "that's how my father got his money."

In children's hands, Confederate dollars became play money. "When peace was signed," recalled David Lee of Florida, "they give me lots of Confederate bills to play with." Dosia Harris found $8,000 worth of what she called "Jeff Davis's fodder," which "the whites throwed away after the War. Us children picked it up and played with it." Robert Heard's mistress "would have been powerful rich if Confederacy money hadn't have been so worthless. She had four loads of it hauled out of the house and dumped in a ditch." "My folks didn't have no money but that worthless kind," James Lucas recalled. "It was all they knowed about. When I grabbed some of it and throwed it in the blazing fire, they thought I was crazy, until I told them, 'That ain't money! It's no account!' Then I give my daddy a greenback and told him what it was."

THE VAGARIES OF economics in an ostensibly free South motivated hundreds of thousands of slaves to learn to read and write. Literacy was all that stood between freedmen and the kind of quasi-reenslavement to which many former masters contrived to relegate them. One night, a literate Robert Cheatham was invited to meet "a fine looking white man who was talking to the slaves when I got down there. He was telling them that a rich man in a northern state had put up a large amount of money to spend on educational material for the Negro youths." "All you negroes have to do is sign up these papers," he told them, "and the books will be sent to you." But as they walked up to sign the papers, Cheatham asked his cousin to bring a torch over so he could read what they said. What he read was "not an order for books but a paper of indenture calculated to bind each of us to the services of some rascal. When we refused to sign the papers, the man galloped his horse away, and we never heard from him again. That," Cheatham concluded, "partially explains our longing for books."

THEN THERE WAS the law to contend with, for with Emancipation errant Southern African Americans no longer answered to their masters but the state. In the 1930s, Charlie Davenport cited the case of a drunken Negro who had been accused of shooting a white man. "If he gets caught, he'll be worse off than any slave, cause he'll have a ball and chain on his foot or else get his neck broke." Some slaves were slow to realize that their masters could no longer protect them from the law when they transgressed. A defiant young man named Philos was indicted for threatening to shoot someone named Arthur. Philos ran away, but reappeared three weeks later, "boasting that no white man could arrest him. He had been to the [Freedmen's] Bureau and knew the law; he was armed, and meant to go where he pleased." Nevertheless, he was promptly arrested and arraigned, and as he awaited trial he sent for his old foe Arthur. "Arthur," he said, "you know I's always hated you, and talked about you. But you was right when you told me not to get into no such troubles as this." "I told you you didn't know nothing about law," Arthur reminded him; "that no law allowed you to carry on mean." The judge in the case complained that he could not get Philos to understand "why a word from his employer isn't enough now to release him, as it would have done while he was a slave."

It did not take long for slaves to realize that just because they got freedom did not necessarily mean they got justice. "Yes," a former slave in Raleigh, North Carolina, conceded to a visitor, "we are ignorant. We know it. I am ignorant for one, and they say all Negroes is. They say we don't know what the word 'constitution' means. But if we don't know enough to know what the Constitution is, we know enough to know what justice is. I can see for myself down at my own court-house," where "they've got a figure of a woman with a sword hung up there. I don't know what you call it: 'Justice'? Well, she's got a handkerchief over her eyes, and the sword is in one hand and a pair of scales in the other. When a white man and a Negro gets into the scales, don't I know the Negro is always mighty light? Don't we *all* see it? Ain't it so at *your* courthouse?"

LIBERATION SET off a mass exodus from slaveholders' farms and plantations. "I remembers the day well when Master told us we was free," recalled Julia Bunch. "About 200 Yankee soldiers come, and they played music right there by the roadside: the first drum and fife music I ever heared. Lots of the Negroes followed them on off with just what they had on."

After an Arkansas overseer announced that the slaves on his employer's farm were free, and that they could either leave or remain and work, his employer's slaves "left like when you leave the latch gate open where is a big litter of shoats, and they just hit the road and commenced to ramble. They stole mighty nigh all the mules and rode them off." "After we was freed," recalled George Taylor, "Old Master come out in the yard and got in the middle of all of us, and told us that the ones that wants to stay with him, to stand on one side, and the others to stand on the other side. So my paw got on the side with those who wanted to leave, and us left Old Master and paddled down the river in a paddling boat." Although her owners were reputedly kind, Amanda Tellis was told "to pretend she had a chill, and go to her mother's cabin. So she did as she was told. When she reached the cabin, her mother, brothers and sisters each had a pillow slip, filled with clothes. She was given hers, and they ran away to Mt. Vernon, Alabama." An Alabama house slave named Mary Ella Grandberry recalled that her master's field hands lingered for a couple of weeks, "and then one morning I woke up and all of them had left during the night. I was the only Negro left on the place. I cried and cried, mostly because I was just lonesome for some of my own kind to laugh and talk with."

Most freed slaves remained in the South. "I had sort of learned to like to stay down here," recalled Elmo Steele, "especially when I met and fell in love with the gal I married. I was thirty three years old when we married. I's never lived in the North no more. I kind of wanted to see things thriving, anyway," and see "the South rebuilt."

30

---◆---

"Nowhere to Go"

*A Void • Returning Home • At a Loss • Hunger • Devastation
Forty Acres and a Mule • Betrayals • Worth the Price*

F OR MANY FIELD SLAVES, the material benefits of freedom were manifest. No longer would they have to live packed into quarters, wear nothing but rags, go barefoot in winter, eat out of troughs, work from before dawn until after dusk without even the prospect of pay. But for the more connected house slaves, freedom meant exile from the relative comfort of their masters' homes. Even those who chose to remain with their former owners as servants found that the war had destroyed their masters' former prosperity. In either case, masters could no longer protect their former chattel from outsiders. For many liberated slaves, stepping into freedom was like tumbling into a void.

"SOME WAS GLAD and some was sorry," Wheeler Gresham recalled. "They all was at a wonder: at the row's end. Didn't know where to go." Some balked at leaving their homes and losing what little they had acquired as slaves. "Some left," recalled Squire Irvin, "but most of them stayed. You know how folks is. They thinks they wants to do something and when they finds out they can do it, they are not so anxious as they thought they were."

"When the war ended," wrote Celestia Avery's interviewer, "Mr. Heard visited every slave home and broke the news to each family that they were free people, and if they so desired could remain on his plantation." But most of his slaves fled, "for old man Heard had been such a cruel

master everyone was anxious to get away from him." Abused by their
husbands, shamed by their menfolks' assignations with female slaves, some
mistresses joined in the exodus. "Old Marse had always been so hard to
get along with till when the war ended and the slaves all left him and everything was upset. Old Missus, she up and left them too. He had married
her from away off somewheres, and she went back to where she come
from. And I don't blame her."

Ambrose Douglass had never known what to make of the war. Though
some of his friends joined the Union Army, since Douglass "didn't know
who was going to win," he had decided not to "take no chances." But
when freedom was finally declared, "I didn't take no chances on them
taking it back again," and he "lit out for Florida." The night they heard
they were freed, Easter Jackson's people "went up to the 'Big House,'
worried and asking, 'Young Master Tom, where is we going? What is we
gonna do?' Young Master Tom said, 'Go on back to your cabins and go
to bed. They are your homes, and you can stay on here as long as you
want to.'"

BUT MANY OF "the colored folks didn't know how to take care of themselves," Temple Wilson observed. "Just snatched from savages into slavery and then freed, with no book learning nor money nor nothing, and
set down in the Southland where everything was ruined for anybody."
Men and women who had labored so long for so little believed they had
been abandoned by their masters. "Old Jeff Davis said when the Negroes
was turned loose, 'Divide up your knives and forks with them.' But," said
Evelina Morgan, "they didn't do it." After the surrender, a Yankee told
John Belcher's master to give his Negroes "half they made so they can
have something to live on." But all his master gave Belcher was an "old
mule that was crippled and no account."

"They were not any farms or plantations divided among the Negroes,"
John McAdams recalled. "Neither did our owners give us any money
or anything else. At times they hardly gave us work to do. Then half of
them would not pay us when we worked, because they knew they did not
have to pay us, and we could not make them pay us. Sometimes they
would give us their old cast-off clothes," but "that we could not eat, so
that made us have to steal lots so as we could feed our kids." But even
if one believed that the South owed them at least the tools of survival,
"who was gonna give it to them?" asked J. T. Tims of Arkansas. "The

Rebs? They didn't give them nothing but what they could put on their backs; I mean lashes."

SOME FELT EQUALLY betrayed by their liberators. After the Yankees left, all that many slaves had to thank them for "was a hungry belly and freedom." "The Government's gonna send you some money to live on," Ella Wilson remembered being told. "But the Government never did do it. I never did see nobody that got it. Did you? They didn't give me nothing and they didn't give my father nothing. They just set us free and turned us loose naked." Jake Goodridge was skeptical from the first. "The Yankee soldiers give out news of freedom. They was shouting around. I just stood around to see what they going to do next. Didn't nobody give me nothing. I didn't know what to do. Everything going. Tents all gone, no place to go stay, and nothing to eat. That was the big freedom to us colored folks. *That* the way white folks' fighting do the colored folks."

Wylie Nealy was equally bitter. "Everybody was proud to be free. They shouted and sang," but then "they was told to scatter and nowhere to go. Cabins all tore down or burned. No work to do. There was no money to pay." "They went wild," Casper Rumple remembered, "walking and whooping up and down the road. They found out when they nearly starved they had got the bad end of the game somehow."

THE SHOCK OF liberation and its attendant hardships killed some slaves as well as their masters. Belle Buntin's mother "soon died after the surrender. She died at Batesville, Mississippi. Lots of the slaves died; their change of living killed lots of them." "When freedom come, folks left home, out in the streets, crying. Praying, singing, shouting, yelling, and knocking down everything," recalled Patsy Moore. "Some shot off big guns," but then "come the calm. It was sad then. So many folks done dead. Things tore up and nowheres to go. Nothing to eat, nothing to do. It got squally. Folks got sick, so hungry. Some folks starved nearly to death. Times got hard." Her mother "was a cripple woman" and her father "couldn't find work," so they all "went to the washtub," for laundering was "the onliest way we all could live." Thomas Ruffin "used to dig up dirt in the smokehouse and boil it and dry it and sift it to get the salt to season our food with. We used to go out and get old bones that had been throwed away and crack them open and get the marrow and use them to season the greens with. Just plenty of Negroes then didn't have anything but that to eat."

The freed slaves who flocked to Union camps after the war "weren't used to the stuff the Yankees fed them," recalled James Lucas. "They fed them wasp-nest bread instead of corn-pone and hoe cake, and all such like. They caught diseases and died by the hundreds, just like flies. They'd been fooled into thinking it would be good times, but it was the worst times they ever seen. 'Tweren't no place for them to go; no bed to sleep on; and no roof over they heads. Them what could get back home set out with they minds made up to stay on the land. Most of they mistresses took them back, so they worked the land again. I means them what lived to get back to they folks was more than glad to work! They done had a sad lesson."

Some pinned their hopes on Queen Victoria, whose dominion in Canada had afforded runaways a refuge from slavery. Negroes in Louisiana believed that Her Highness had "sent a boatload of gold to America to give the free men," Willis Winn remembered, "but we never see'd any of it." William Porter heard that Victoria had "offered to buy the slaves and raise them till they were grown, then give them a horse, a plow and so many acres of ground. But the South wouldn't accept this offer."

LIBERTY "WAS PICTURED pretty to some," recalled Myra Jones of Mississippi; "all about us a getting land, mules and the like." In January 1865, General Sherman had issued Special Field Order No. 15, which reserved "the coastal islands south of Charleston south, abandoned river rice plantations up to thirty miles inland," and the country bordering St. Johns River, Florida, for the settlement of former slaves who had been liberated "by the acts of war and the proclamation of the President of the United States." Slaves in these areas were deeded forty-acre lots and promised mules and horses from the army's surplus stock. By summer, the government had distributed some 400,000 acres among about 40,000 former slaves.

Promulgated by Yankee soldiers, word of this largess swiftly spread, until "forty acres and a mule" became a common expectation among freed slaves throughout the South. Sam McCallum of Mississippi was so confident about it "that I picked out my mule. All of us did." But the order was never officially extended beyond the southeastern coast, and few slaves were deeded slaveholders' abandoned lands.

"That old story about 40 acres and a mule" made Boston Blackwell laugh. "I never knowed any person which got it. The officers telled us we would all get slave pension. That just exactly what they tell. They sure did tell me I would get a parcel of ground to farm," but "nothing ever hatched out of that, neither." For veteran black soldiers the disappointment was especially cruel. A returning veteran told his fellow freedmen that Yankee recruiters had promised him "forty acres and a mule," but "all he got was a suit of blue clothes," Ebenezer Brown remembered, "and he come home on foot, because they took his pony."

"The Yankees passed as our friends," Isaac Stier recalled, "but they was poor reliance. Some of them meant well towards us, but they was mis-told about a heap of things. They promised us a mule and forty acres of land. Us ain't seen no mule yet. Us got the land all right, but it wasn't no service. Fact is, it was way over in a territory where nothing would grow." The Yankees gave James Lucas "one hundred and sixty acres of land, but it weren't no account. It was in Mt. Bayou, Arkansas, and was low and swampy. 'Tweren't your land to keep lessen you lived on it. You had to clear it, drain it, and put a house on it. How I gwine to drain and clear a lot of land with nothing to do it with? Reckon somebody living on my land now."

Even rich, cultivated land could not guarantee a freedman's prosperity. "Soon's freedom come," Amos Lincoln's parents squatted on one hundred acres of "good" and "high" government land. But one night "somebody come shoot him in the back" and chased off his wife and children. "I had a lot of property in the past," recalled a Mississippi freedman named Edmond Bradley, "but they rogued me out of it. My grandmother was Celestine Ladnier. She owned a lot of property along the beach at Pass Christian, but Lawyer Henderson got hold of it." And though Lu Perkins's Texas master bequeathed two hundred acres to her father, "his boys wouldn't let him have it."

This was not the freedom they had imagined. John McAdams of Texas "expected different from what I got out of freedom, I can tell you. I knows one thing: I was not expecting to be turned loose like a bunch of stray cattle. But that is exactly what they done to us." Slaves "wanted freedom," said Henry Nelson, "but they didn't know how it would be. They didn't know it meant set out." "They tell us we's free," Walter Calloway observed, "but we ain't never been what I calls free. Cause Old Master didn't own us no more, and all the folks soon scatter all over. But if they all like me, they still have to work just as hard, and sometimes have less than we used to have when we stay on Marse John's plantation."

"They had a mighty hard time while they was slaves," said Alex Montgomery, "and then they had nothing but hard times ever since they was
set free. We knowed nothing but hard times all our lives."

Freedmen attributed the North's broken promises to the death of
Lincoln. "Some said they wouldn't have to work any more," Gabe Butler
recalled, "cause Mr. Lincoln would give them everything." But when
Lincoln was killed, "they knowed the jig was up." "The only thing we got
was pure air to breathe," said Evie Herrin. "They ain't given us nothing
else to this day." "I've paid taxes on every one of you," said Jerry Cook's
master, "and I've paid high, too. Now they say that money is to be appropriated to take care of you, and I hope it will." But Cook "ain't seen none
of that money to this day."

"IF WE HADN'T have had to work and slave for nothing," argued William Henry Towns of Alabama, "we might have something to show for
what we did do, and wouldn't have to live from pillar to post now." Mary
F. McCray asserted "that had proper steps been taken and careful observations made of the condition of affairs in the South at the close of the
war, the Negro race would be seventy years in advance of the position it
occupies to-day. The bloody war resulted in envy, hatred, strife, malice
and prejudice between the black and the white, which is sin of the worst
nature."

After the war, the rich "got many of the poor whites on their side." At
first, "the poor white people felt that their interests lay with the Negroes:
for the first time they had voting rights, and schools for their children.
But the landlords kept poisoning their minds, saying 'You're voting with
Negroes. You're lining up with Negroes,'" and thus the rich landholders
"split many of them away from their own best interests."

Charlie Davenport blamed his people as much as their former masters for the freedmen's plight. "The colored folks ain't made much use of
they freedom," he judged. "They is all in debt and chained down to
something, same as us slaves was." Davenport had concluded that there
was "no such thing as freedom. Us is all tied down to something."

FOR ALL THE hardships, injustices, and betrayals, however, most cher-
ished their freedom no matter what the cost. "When Lincoln freed
us, we rejoiced," recalled Edna Boysaw, "yet we knew we had to seek
employment now and make our own way." Most slaves, declared Reverend William Henry Rooks of Arkansas, "didn't expect nothing but free-

dom. Just freedom! In Africa they was free as wild animals," and then, under slavery, "they was so restricted. Just put in bondage for no reason at all." Freedom meant the right simply to be themselves. Though Dave Weathersby had been told "we'd get property, and some talk of equality with the white folks, that didn't strike us so much as us Darkies just wants to be Darkies amongst ourselves."

Just after the war, a visitor asked some Contrabands if they wouldn't be just as free at home as they were in a Union camp. "But I's want to be free man," said a man who was patching a hole in the abandoned tent in which he lived. "Come when I please, and nobody say nothing to me, nor order me round." "The Lord told we to come here," said another. "The Lord; him'll take care of us now." "It's mighty good to do just as you please," said Rachel Adams, who preferred living on "bread and water" than that she belong to someone who "treat us bad to slave for." "All Negroes would rather be free," William McWhorter asserted, "and I ain't no different from nobody else about that." "It was God's blessing to the black peoples," said Louis Meadows, "to come out from bondage; to belong only to theirselves and God; to read about what's going on in the world and write and figure for theirselves," and get "ready to rest when the judgment day comes about."

31

"I Got My Own Again"

Retrieving Kin • *Separation* • *Abandoned* • *Perils*
Tragedies • *Vengeance and Reconciliation* • *Reunion*

OVER THE DECADES that followed the Civil War, the freedoms former slaves had gained would be constricted to the point of suffocation, until their descendants found themselves trapped in a mutation of the Peculiar Institution: a white supremacist snare of poverty, fraud, debt, terror, and disenfranchisement. So for many former slaves the most enduring legacy of their emancipation was the opportunity it afforded them to reunite families long shattered by slavery. As soon as the guns fell silent, long-lost mothers and fathers, children and grandchildren, turned up at their past masters' gates to retrieve their kin.

"My brother Frank slipped in the house where I was still staying," recalled a house slave named Dora Franks. "He told me us was free and for me to come out with the rest. Before sundown there weren't one Negro left on the place." In mid-May 1865, Ike Woodward's "white folks sent me to the well down in the valley below the house to get a bucket of water. When I started to draw the water, I saw my brother coming through the woods riding a blazed-face mare. He never said a word but galloped to the well, picked me up and put me on the horse with him and carried me from Master Conners."

THE NORTH'S VICTORY had fitfully reunited a divided nation, but for many slaves it resulted in the recovery of their lost relatives and, by extension, their identities: a reunion with their own humanity. Before the

Peculiar Institution had run its course, masters had prided themselves on the young their slaves produced, exhibiting them to visitors like prize calves. "It is remarkable the number of slaves which may be raised from one woman in the course of forty or fifty years with the proper kind of attention," exulted a Mississippi planter named William B. Trotter.

"If the woman didn't have any childrens," recalled Sylvia Watkins of Nashville, "she was put on the block and sold and another woman bought. You see, they raised the childrens to make money on, just like we raise pigs to sell." "My maw say she took with my paw, and I's born," said Lulu Wilson, "but a long time passed and didn't no more young ones come. So they say my paw am too old and wore out for breeding, and they want her to take with this here young buck." So her master sent his "hounds on my Paw and run him away from the place, and Maw always say he went to the free states. So she took up with my step-paw, and they must have pleased the white folks" because together they would produce nineteen children.

Perhaps it was a mercy that some slave children had been too small to understand when their parents were taken away from them. Mandy Tucker "was large enough to know when they took my parents to Texas, but I didn't know how serious it was till they was gone. I remember peeping through the crack of the fence, but I didn't know they was taking them off." Henri Necaise of Mississippi "never knowed my mother. I was a slave, and my mother was sold from me and her other childrens. They told me when they sold her, my sister was holding me in her arms. She was standing behind the Big House peeking around the corner and seen the last of her mother." Necaise was told that as a small child "I used to go to the gate hunting for my mammy," and "used to sleep with my sister after that." Before young Laura Clark was taken away by a speculator, her mother climbed into his wagon and made an elderly slave promise she would "take care my baby child, and if I never sees her no more, raise her for God." Then her mother "fell off the wagon where us was all setting and roll over on the ground just crying," Clark recalled. "But us was eating candy what they done give us for to keep us quiet, and I didn't have sense enough for to know what ailed her. But I knows now, and I never see'd her no more in this life."

Louis Hughes's illegally enslaved wife and family had been sold away from him by Nathan Bedford Forrest. Another slave named Priscilla Parker, along with her sister and three brothers, were also separated from their mother and transported to Forrest's Memphis slave pen, where the future cavalry commander sold her sister to a New Orleans trader; a brother to a man in Covington, Kentucky; another to a man in Lebanon, Kentucky; and the third to a man from Louisiana. After Parker herself was sold to a man from Paducah, Forrest was "right well pleased" by her sale, "and say he done made three hundred dollars on me."

"My grandmother on my mother's side had 21 children," recalled George Johnson, "and my mother said none of them ever knew where one another was, because every one of them was sold to different ones of the whites," and since all of them took their new master's name, "naturally nobody could find them. My mother said almost all the time around my grandmother's cabin there was weeping and wailing every day or so when they'd come to buy some of them."

When twelve-year-old Lucy Thurston's master announced that he had sold her mother, "Mammy don't make no fuss because she know better. She only say, 'Where am I going, Master?'" "You and Lucy be sold to Master Ballot," he replied. The next day, Ballot hustled them onto a boat bound for New Orleans, where he promptly put them up for sale "on the slavery block, and bade us twist and turn and show our teeth. Master Dickey bid on Mammy, but some other man outbid him, and my Mammy was sold away from me. I cried and cried, but it weren't no use. Master Dickey took me to Covington, Louisiana, and I work out in the fields." After Boston Blackwell's mother was sold away from him, his sister was "the onliest of all my people I ever see'd again."

MANY OF THE slaves who fled to the Union lines were never seen again. Some were killed, of course, either in battle or in ambushes as they headed home; many died of disease; others returned to find that their families had been scattered by slave traders and refugeeing masters. Still others simply would not go back to the scenes of their bondage, to a region devastated by war, to a South where discharge papers from the Union Army could get a man killed. Neither of the fathers of Anna Baker and Ed Williams of Mississippi returned, and they never "knew much" about them. "When them Yankees come through they got one of Master Fox's best horses and took my brother Limuel with them too," said Phillis Fox, "and I ain't never see'd or heard tell of him no more."

Some slave marriages would not survive Emancipation. "When we was freed," recalled Primous Magee, "the slaves that was married all had to get a license and be married over again. My pa quit my ma when he found this out, and wouldn't marry her over again. A heap of them quit that way. I reckon they felt free sure enough, as they was freed from slavery and from marriage." Forced to breed together, Mollie Dawson's "mother and father never did loves each other likes they ought to, so they separated as soon as they was free."

To their wives, and perhaps especially their children, it sometimes did not matter whether their menfolk found freedom or took up arms in a noble cause; they had abandoned their families. Gabe Butler denounced his father for running away: "After the Yankees come down there, my pappy stole Missus's finest horse and run way and joined the Yankees." He believed his father "ought not to done that cause he was Mistress's favorite slave. We never see'd him again, but heard one time he was in Vicksburg." "Most of the Negro men on Mr. Alford's plantation ran away and went to Yankees," recalled Ann May of Mississippi. "My husband went to them; he went on to Mobile, and I never saw him for many years," until "he come back and died in 1870 with small pox." "My pappy left the night the Yankees took Selma," recalled Irene Poole of Alabama. "It was on Sunday, and I ain't see'd him since."

Abandoned women and children preferred to believe that their menfolk did not return because they had been killed. "I guess my daddy was killed in the war," recalled Jonas Boone of Arkansas, "for he never come home when my uncles did." Liddie Aiken remembered seeing the Yankees come by near Mobile, "and every one of the men and boys went with them but Uncle Cal." Liddie's mother "said she never seen but one ever come back," and "thought they got killed or went on someplace else." Some told their children that their fathers had been kidnapped by the Yankees and held in bondage above the Mason-Dixon Line. Gus Williams of Arkansas "never seen my daddy cause the Yankees carried him away during the war" and "took him away to the North."

Others simply accepted their menfolks' disappearances as mysteries of war. Cella Perkins's father "went to war with his master, and he never come back to Mama. She never heard from him after freedom. He got captured and got to be a soldier and went away off. She didn't never know if he got killed or lost his way back home." "My Pa, he go off to fight," Rachael Santee Reed remembered, "and we ain't never knowed" where he went "or which side he was fighting on."

Former slaves recalled the dilemma facing abandoned wives and mothers. During the Union occupation of Pine Bluff, Arkansas, "twelve men went round back and forth through the county" telling slaves "they would have to marry over again. But my ma never had a chance to see the old man any more. She didn't marry him over again, because he didn't come back to her." Tom Hunley's father "and some other colored men went off with the Yankees." His mother stayed behind, waiting for him, but "my pappy never did come back no more after that."

Women disappeared as well. Roxy Pitts's mother took the opportunity the war provided to return to her tribe. "My mammy was part Indian, and Old Master couldn't keep her home nor working neither; she always running off and stay out in the woods all night long." When her daughter "was a little gal," Roxy's mother "runned off again and left a teeny little baby, and never did come back no more. They said she gone where the Indians is. That was after the war, and Pappy had to raise that little bitsy baby his self. He took it and me to the hotel where he working, and kept a bottle of sweetened water in his shirt to keep warm to give the baby when it cry."

"FAMILY TIES ARE held sacred to the Negro as to the white man," said Robert Cheatham of Kentucky. "Husbands are loyal to their wives and children although for hundreds of years it had been the privilege of the masters to separate families." "Have you any children?" a missionary asked an old slave woman in Norfolk, Virginia. "No, honey," she said, "no I hasn't. And yet, Missus, I has. Fourteen children I's raised and hugged in these old arms; and sometimes I thinks I feels their little hands on my cheeks. But they's all gone. I don't know where they are." And even if she were dying in the corner of the mission hall, "there wouldn't be one to bring me a cup of water."

But now "Emancipation called for a new chapter on the part of the colored people," said Mount Moore of Texas. "During slavery, when they went to sell you, if you had a wife, they sell you from her anyhow. If you had brothers and sisters they sold you from them." But in freedom "the colored people had a chance to get back with their folks."

During the war, Booker T. Washington's stepfather had fled to Unionist West Virginia and got a job in a salt furnace. "Soon after freedom was declared, he sought out my mother and sent a wagon to bring her and her children to West Virginia. After many days of slow, tiresome traveling over the mountains, during which we suffered much, we finally reached Malden, and my mother and her husband were united after a long enforced separation." "My step-paw never did like me," recalled Lulu Wilson of Texas, "but he was a fool for his own young ones," and "tramped over half the country, gathering up them young ones they done sold away."

Eliza Suggs's father left his blacksmith shop and joined the Union Army in 1864, only to be wounded and taken North by a Captain Newton, his commanding officer. "The thought uppermost in his mind was how to get his family from the South. For him to have gone after them, in person, at that time, would have been at the risk of his life." So he arranged for Newton "to go and find his family and bring them to him. This Captain Newton did, finding them not far from where Father had left them. Father now went to work with great zeal at his trade to earn money for the purpose of getting a home for his family. He was at last a free man, with his dear family — a free family, and living in his own free country."

Suggs's father was right about the risks involved in retrieving kin. "One day two young men called for passes for this purpose," reported the painter Vincent Colyer, who served as a superintendent of refugees in New Bern, North Carolina. "Their wives lived in the neighborhood of Kingston." Colyer gave them permission and armed them with a pistol to defend themselves. But three weeks later, "several refugees, arriving from Kingston, informed us that one of these young men had been shot, and taken prisoner. He had somewhat rashly exposed himself by visiting his wife in early twilight, and had been discovered by her master, who was a noted rebel, who laid wait for him, and when the young man emerged from his wife's cabin, he shot him. They bound him hand and foot, and placing him on a hand cart, drove him through the streets of Kingston to the town jail."

Some returning slaves found they had to reclaim their children from the husbands their wives had acquired in their absence. Beatrice Black's father-in-law came back to Arkansas after serving in the Union Army, only to find that his wife had remarried and borne three children. But unlike his replacement, "he had some money he made in the war" and bought forty acres of government land. So she returned to him, "raised all her thirteen children there," and even "brought Grandma back out here with them from Tennessee."

Other remarried slaves regarded the die as cast. Separated from her husband before the war, a slave woman had given up hope of ever finding him. So she remarried, only to catch sight of him "in a crowd of supposed strangers at the Rope-Walk" in Norfolk, Virginia. " 'Twas like a stroke of death to me," she said. "We threw ourselves into each other's arms and cried. His wife looked on and was jealous, but she needn't have been," for the two separated former slaves resigned themselves to their new circumstance and bade each other goodbye.

Mothers who had been sold or sent away also returned to retrieve their children. "Many white folks loaned their slaves to Secessioners to help build forts all over the state," recalled Cora Gillam of Arkansas. "They was building forts to protect Little Rock," as Union Major General Frederick Steele commenced his campaign to rid Arkansas of Rebels. The Confederates "didn't only take the best looking men," said Gillam; "they took the best looking women, too," including Gillam's mother. She feared she would never see her mother again, but when the Yankees took Little Rock, and "all the other slaves went on somewhere else," Gillam's mother "came back here to me. She said that she wouldn't have come back herself, if it hadn't been that we children were there."

Masters and mistresses did not give up their former slaves easily. Some persuaded their departing slaves to leave their youngest children with them so they could be cared for while their parents looked for jobs and new homes. Mistresses pleaded that they had promised their parents, perhaps, or a dead slave woman, that they would always look after little So-and-So, and refuse to give the child over to the parents. "After the War, Ma and Pa stayed on with Marse Hamp a long time," Mahala Jewel remembered. "Mistress died when I was just a little child, but she had done willed me to Miss Mary," and told her always to take care of Mahala. "Miss Mary stayed right on there with Marse Hamp," and little Mahala stayed with Miss Mary, but "my ma and pa had done left, and I ain't never heared nothing more from them since they went away."

"I never see'd my father after the closing of the war, recalled Maggie Westmoreland of Louisiana. "He had been refugeed to Texas and come back here, then he went on back to Mississippi." By then he had sired eleven children by Westmoreland's mother, but she remarried and bore six more. "When my stepfather was mustered out at De Valls Bluff he come to Mrs. Holland's and got mama and took her on with him," but her parents "gave" Westmoreland to her mistress's daughter.

"Soon as my daddy hear them firing off for the surrender," recalled Letetia Custis of Alabama, "he put out for the plantation where he first belong. He left me with my mistress at Pine Flat, but it weren't long till he come back to get me and carry me home with him." Her mistress "didn't want to part from me," however. "She say, 'Stay here with me, and I'll give you a school learning.'" She commanded a servant to go and buy Custis "one of them Blue Back Websters, so I can educate her to spell." But Custis's father was unmoved. "Her mamma told me not to come home without her," he told her, "and she has to go with me." Custis would never "forget riding behind my daddy on that mule way in the night. Us left in such a hurry, I didn't get none of my clothes hardly, and I ain't see'd my mistress from that day to this!" Some young house slaves preferred the comforts of their former masters' homes to the hardships of a freedman's life. "After the war was over, my pa, he comed up to our house and got my ma and all us children and carries us down to his master's place," but Susan Matthews "didn't want to go cause I loved my mistress, and she cried when we left."

ANOTHER OBSTACLE TO reunion was the slave owner who bitterly contrived to keep slaves ignorant of their relatives' whereabouts. Eliza Suggs's mother had spent the war in her mistress's house, pining for her husband, James, who had run off to join the Union Army. "As to any direct word from her husband, she had none," Suggs recalled. "He wrote her letters but they were destroyed. Many a false report concerning him was conjured up and poured into her ears by her unfeeling mistress, who would come into the kitchen, light her pipe and sit leisurely down to rehearse to my mother what she had heard about 'James,' every word of it the product of her own fertile imagination, and told purely for the purpose of making Mother miserable." Lighting her pipe, her mistress would begin by saying, "Well, I heard from James today. The 'Yankees' have got him." "And then would follow some horrible recital of how the 'Yankees' had him chained to an anvil block and were starving him to death, or something else equally consoling. At such times mother would calmly answer, 'Oh, well, he is as well off there as he would be here.'"

But as the war drew to a close, her mother's mistress returned them from Georgia, to which they had been refugeed, and summoned two of Eliza's siblings. When the Confederates surrendered, "Mother could see so clearly the hand of God in the restoration of her children in His own appointed time and manner," for had they remained in Georgia until the end of the war, "it is very doubtful, humanly speaking, as to whether she would ever have seen them again." Even so, her mother had "eight brothers and sisters, and cannot tell where one of them is today."

AFTER THE WAR, black papers ran hundreds of "Information Wanted" ads inquiring after the whereabouts of long-lost kin. A single issue of Nashville's *Colored Tennessean* contained twelve advertisements seeking the whereabouts of twenty-five relations: Augustus Bryant and his wife, Lutitia, sought their five children, ages eight to twenty, whom they had not seen in five years; Eliza Van Ratlie sought her two sons, who had been sold in Nashville to a trader and taken to Virginia; and so on. At black church services preachers routinely relayed inquiries after relatives separated by slavery and the war. Ira Jones's mother was sent from Kentucky to Mississippi to be sold, but she "later found her relatives in Kentucky by writing to her former church." And ten years after the war, Charles H. Williams located his mother by means of the black Catholic grapevine in Kentucky.

But "most of them," declared Tines Kendricks, "never got together again even after they was set free." "And for this reason," wrote Eliza Suggs: "so long as the slaves were considered property, each owner naturally looked after his own belongings and kept them together. After the slaves were freed, however, no one cared what became of them. And so it was at the close of the war, that many families were separated and were never reunited." The tendency of freed slaves to rename themselves, their youth at the time they were separated, the perplexities of illiteracy, the hostility of local officials, refugeeing, the difficulties of travel, and the destruction of public records lengthened the odds of ever finding a long-lost relative. "After freedom, a heap of people say they was going to name themselves over," recalled Lee Guidon. "They named theirselves big names, then went roaming around like wild, hunting cities. They changed up so, it was hard to tell who or where anybody was. Heap of them died, and you didn't know when you hear about it if he was your folks hardly."

BUT FREED SLAVES persevered. Maggie Porter of the Fisk Jubilee Singers had a fitful reunion with her older sister, who had been sent away to another plantation during the war. Porter's mother fled to Nashville, where she had hoped Maggie's sister might turn up someday "in the tide of homeless freedmen that in those days ebbed and flowed through every Southern city." One day when young Maggie was alone in the house, a woman turned up at the door asking for her mother. Having been instructed never to admit a stranger, Maggie refused to let her in. The woman protested that she was her long-lost sister, but when Maggie refused to believe her, her sister returned to Mississippi in tears, "and it was some time before she could get over the chill of this reception sufficiently to come make her home with her mother."

Malindy Smith of Mississippi remembered "seeing my Mammy crying once, and my oldest sister asked her what was the matter. She said, 'Your daddy gone to the war, and you won't never see him no more.'" But she was wrong, and "when he come back my mammy was sitting out where she could see away down the road and saw him coming. She tore out to running towards him, and us kids right in behind her."

The effect of such reunions on former slaves was profound. "We are frequently charmed," wrote the missionary Lucy Chase, "with the delicacy and tenderness with which Negroes express affection for each other. They know how to love, and how to remember. We sometimes witness the unexpected meeting of scattered members of a family. When the *John Tucker* was at the Craney Island wharf, a little girl who had wondered where she should go — as she had no friends to go with, or to go to" — strayed onto the deck of the steamer and found her father working as a boatman. A slave woman once approached Chase's sister, leading an eighteen-year-old girl with a disfigured face. "See my daughter?" she asked. "They sold her away from me when she was just old enough to rock a cradle, and see how they've done her bad! See how they've cut her up. From her head to her feet she is scarred just as you see her face." As Kate Drumgoold's mother made her way North with her family, she learned that a son whom she had given up for dead "was going to school; that the Northern people had teachers there in the South to teach them to read and to write." His friends "found Mother and got her to go to the place where he was, and sure enough there was her dead and lost boy, and the joy and love that came to that dear, loving mother and her only son on that day will never be known on this side of the grave."

A slave named Diana Wagner was separated on the auction block from her son "when he was a nursing baby," but he was told her name, and after Emancipation he eventually found her. "She said she was willing to die that the Lord let her live to see her baby again and had taken care of him through all these years." When Louis Hughes was reunited with his brother William, whom he had not seen since early childhood, "it seemed, and indeed was, wonderful that we should have met again after so long a separation." Looking into the faces of his wife and children, Hughes "seemed to have entered a new and broader life, and one in which the joys of social intercourse had marvelously expanded."

But for those who could not locate their kin, the wound was deep. John Adams of Virginia managed to reunite with most of his family, "but still I sorrow yet. My dear sister, Sallie Ann Adams, who was sold with brother Aaron, has not been heard from yet. But we still hope that God will bless us with that opportunity to meet her on earth. If not, this is our hope in the last days."

The convergence of far-flung relatives sometimes resulted in tragedy. Cora L. Horton's grandmother used to tell her a story about a woman who, long before the war, had been separated from her little boy. After the war, she married and started a new family. Then one day "she and her husband got to talking about old slave times. She told him about how she had been sold away from her baby son when he was a little thing. She told him how he had a certain scar on his arm." But her husband had a similar scar, and when "he got to talking about slave times, they found out that they were mother and son. He left her and went on his way, sad because he didn't want to stay on living as husband with his mother. I don't think those people were held accountable for that," Horton told her interviewer. "Do you?"

Nor did Emancipation prevent subsequent separations. Richard Miller's mother was ambitious for her children. After the war, she enrolled them in school in Kentucky. "One day, when the children came home from school," his mother had gone "they knew not where." Eventually Miller learned that his mother had been abducted and transported to Texas. In 1871, Miller received a letter from her, and traveled to Texas to fetch her. She was not hard to spot, for she was an East Indian immigrant who had married a slave. "The last time I saw her, she was washing clothes at the branch," and "all I could remember about her was her beautiful black hair, and the cotton dress." Miller recognized her at once, and listened as she recounted stories of his boyhood. But before returning to Kentucky, he hunted down the man who had kidnapped her, "shot and killed him," and took her safely home.

RICHARD MILLER WAS not the only slave to return with vengeance in his heart. "The black man purchased two years previous at a good price was now hunting his former owners with a deadly weapon," wrote James Thomas. "People with Southern feeling said the country had gone to the devil." Levi Lindsay's master had been so cruel to him that "in anger one day he hit his master on the head. As punishment the master gave him two hundred lashes; and then, in the raw, he put salt and pepper. After Levi recovered from injury from the severe beating, he again hit his master on the head," but this time escaped to Canada. When Levi heard about the Civil War, he returned to the United States with the intention of killing his former master if he could. "But as far as can be found out," Haywood Patterson told his interviewer, "he did not succeed."

"Masters was afraid to meet their slaves after freedom," recalled a Tennessee slave, "cause some of them was so mean they was afraid they would kill them." Discharged black troops heading home would sometimes "pause on their trip at some plantation, ascertain the name of the meanest overseer on the place, then tie him backward on a horse and force him to accompany them." Such a fate befell "Messrs. Mays and Prevatt" of Florida, who were "generally recognized as the most vicious slave drivers of the section."

But many freed slaves balked at retaliating against their masters. A slave noisily denounced his master when the Yankees came, and demanded that they hang him. But when an officer offered to let the slave do the job himself, the slave demurred. "Uh, no," he said. "Can't do it. Can't do it. Can't see Master suffer. Don't want to see him suffer." A Union chaplain once overheard a black preacher beg the Lord to "shake Jeff Davis over the mouth of hell, but O Lord," he added, "don't drop him in!"

For some, it was enough to claim a measure of what they were owed and to tell their masters off. When the Yankees informed him that he was free, a Virginia coachman "went straight to his master's chamber, dressed himself in his best clothes, put on his best watch and chain, took his stick, and, returning to the parlor where his master was, insolently informed him that he might for the future drive his own coach."

Others found dignity in treating their former masters with courtesy. A Major Holden had regularly whipped his slave Henry, who promptly ran away and joined the Union Army. "He came back to the farm once at the head of a dozen soldiers," recalled Rachel Cruze. "Old Major was sitting in his favorite chair on the porch when he saw Henry coming with those soldiers, and he almost fell, he was that scared. So many times the slaves had returned to kill their masters, and poor Old Major thought Henry remembered that whipping. But Henry drew the men up in front of Old Major, and he said, 'This is my master, Major Holden. Honor him, men.'

And the men took off their caps and cheered Old Major. And he nearly
fell again; such a great big burden was off his shoulders then." When
Henry commanded his men to stack arms, "they all stacked their guns together in front of Old Major," and they went into the house to see Miss
Nancy; and Miss Nancy sent out to have some chickens killed, and in no
time at all those men were all seated around the dining room table having a regular feast."

MARK TWAIN RECOUNTED a story he'd heard from a slave in New
Bern, North Carolina, whose son Henry had been sold away from her.
"By and by the years roll on and the war come," she told Twain. "My master, he was a Confederate colonel, and I was his family's cook. So when
the Unions took that town," she said, "they ask me would I cook for
them. 'Lord bless you,' says I, 'that's what I's for.'" One day she approached some Union officers in the parlor, "and I drops a curtsy, and I
up and told them about my Henry. They listening to my troubles just the
same as if I was white folks. And I says, 'What I come for is because if he
got away and got up North where you gentlemen comes from, you might
have seen him, maybe, and could tell me so as I could find him again; he
was very little, and he had a scar on his left wrist, and at the top of his
forehead." But "none of the gentlemen had run across him, so they
couldn't do nothing for me."

Raucous army balls were the plague of her existence in New Bern,
where one night she was especially "rasped" by the antics of a particular
black regiment. "I was just boiling! Mad? I was just *booming!*" And "they
was waltzing and dancing!" At one point, "along comes such a spruce"
black sergeant "a-sailing down the room with a yellow wench round the
waist" and "smiling at my big red turban, and making fun. And I ups and
says, 'Get along with you, rubbish! I weren't born in the mash to be
fooled by trash!'"

The cook's outburst stopped the young soldier in his tracks, and he
immediately ordered his comrades back to their quarters. The next
morning, as she was getting the officers' breakfast, "I was stooping down
by the stove, and I'd just got the pan of hot biscuits in my hand and was
about to raise up" when she saw the same young soldier's face "come
around under mine, and the eyes looking up into mine, and I just
stopped right there and never budged! Just gazed, and gazed. And the
pan begin to tremble, and all of a sudden I *knowed!* The pan dropped on

the floor, and I grab his left hand, and shove back his sleeve. And then I goes for his forehead" and pushed his hair back. "Boy!" she gasped, "if you ain't my Henry, what is you doing with this welt on your wrist and that scar on your forehead? The Lord God of Heaven be praised!" she exclaimed. "I got my own again!"

——◆——

"All Alike"

Lee · Arlington · Burials · Contraband Graves

R EGRETTING THAT HE had ever trained to become a soldier, Robert E. Lee tried to set an example for his countrymen by accepting defeat with grace and urging his men to return peacefully to whatever they could recover of their previous lives. While serving as president of Washington College — renamed Washington and Lee University in his honor — he suffered a heart attack in October 1870, and died in a delirium, issuing orders to his phantom generals. But the last words ascribed to him — "Strike the tent" — he would have addressed in former times to his body servant, William Mack Lee.

Another of the general's servants, Jim Parke, had spent much of the war hired out to dig forts for the Yankees along the south end of Lee's plantation at Arlington. One day a Union officer ordered him to dig two graves on his master's grounds, and thus Parke had the distinction of digging the first two graves in what would become Arlington National Cemetery.

"We buried two soldiers: one, he wore the blue; and the other the gray. We buried them side by side. And then — good Lord help us! — they commence to come. Bodies from the battlefields. Mostly from Manassas, and along the Potomac, and from hospitals."

After the war, Parke remained at Arlington as a government gravedigger. "See the big tombstones?" he asked a visitor on the eve of the Great Depression. "Generals. Officers. When they buried them, important folks turned out: horses and men marching, big speeches. And the little tombstones, all alike: common soldiers. I's carved out the last resting places for them all. When they get in the ground, they all alike: generals and private soldiers: all alike, sleeping in the same bed of ground." Though gravediggers came and went, Parke "worked on after they all scattered and gone, for Arlington's my home, where I's born and always lived. Besides that," he added, "I had a steady job, for big folks all time dying for the government, same as ordinary folks dying for the undertaker."

Starting with the graves near Fort Meyer Gate, he saw the cemetery rapidly grow, and as more corpses kept arriving, the diggers ran out of open space. One day an officer ordered Parke and his crew to get hold of some axes and "clear some ground." Old man Custis had never let anyone "cut down his trees, and Master Robert wouldn't let them be hit with an ax when I's tending the yards." But now "here we's going have to chop down the big oaks, and elms, and hickories. Made me most weep. But it had to be. Trees so thick it was a regular forest, so we chop down the trees. We had one Negro named Jack, and when we's chopping with the axes, he's singing so as we hit at the same time: 'Chop that tree-ee: Wham! Oh-ah bo-oys: Wham! Bossman say-ay: Wham! Chop that tree-ee!: Wham!' And when a big one crash, I'd think what Colonel Robert say to me: 'Jim, it takes a long time to grow a tree!'

"It took heaps longer to dig up trees and clear the ground than dig the graves," Parke recalled. "Dig round the roots; big tree crash down; fill up the hole; that's room for several graves." The first graves were dug "the best way": mounded over and sodded. But, to Parke's dismay, he and his crew were eventually ordered to tamp them all flat.

By the late 1920s, Parke had buried generals and admirals around his former master's grounds, as well as men killed in the Spanish-American War and World War I, as Arlington Cemetery became perhaps the nation's most hallowed ground.

There was one part of the cemetery, however, that few visited or even knew about. But Parke remembered. "During the Civil War," he told a visitor before his death in 1929, "we buried the colored men in a special place near the flats. 'Contraband' they called them: Negroes that were following the armies.

"We put them all there together," he said, "and they there yet."

AUTHOR'S NOTE

◆—◆

"We'll Talk This Story Over"

FOR THOSE SEEKING ancestors among these pages, and for those who want to dig deeper into these stories, I have appended an alphabetical directory of everyone I have directly quoted. In the case of former slaves, I have tried to determine their dates and places of birth, the names of their parents and siblings, the names of their owners, and in some cases additional biographical material.

More than half of the voices in this book come from a series of interviews with former slaves that were conducted during the 1920s and 1930s. Most of these were undertaken by the Federal Writers' Project of the Works Progress Administration, to which every American owes an enormous debt of gratitude. The following caveats do not diminish that debt, but it is important that the reader of these interviews and this book understand some of their limitations.

When I first came upon the anonymous interviews the pioneering sociologist Ophelia Settle conducted under the auspices of Fisk University in the late 1920s, I wondered why her subjects seemed to speak so much more candidly than most of the thousands of ex-slaves from all over the country whom the WPA interviewed in the late 1930s. One reason, I realized, was that Settle was black, whereas whites conducted most of the interviews — and not just whites, but in some cases relatives of the families that had held their subjects in bondage. Another reason was that, unlike Settle, the WPA did not grant their subjects anonymity: those who agreed to be interviewed had to provide their names and addresses and sometimes sit for photographs. One other reason was that by the time the WPA began its fieldwork, most of Settle's subjects had died, as had the vast majority of former slaves who had experienced bondage as adults.

Though the very act of selecting the witnesses who testify in these pages is an interpretive act, I have tried to keep my own opinions to myself. My role was more editorial than authorial — a matter of selection, organization, and segues. Otherwise, I let them speak for themselves.

Slaves' memories were no freer of conflations, omissions, evasions, and fabrications than anyone else's. Among the thousands of accounts I surveyed, there were some demonstrable whoppers masquerading as fact. But I learned from hard experience that even the most skeptical inquirers into the history of slavery must restrain themselves from dismissing the most outlandish stories as whole-cloth inventions, for the lives that many of these witnesses led were themselves so outlandish in their extremity. They were recalling a time when one out of every seven Americans and one out of every five Southerners was a slave; when whites bought and sold their fellow human beings, even their own children; when people were commonly relegated to eating from troughs like hogs; when grown men and women could be savagely whipped for the slightest infraction; when raping a black woman was not a crime; when mothers were denied the right to nurse, let alone name, let alone direct the destinies of their offspring; when America's unprecedented prosperity rode on the blood, sweat, and tears of millions of enslaved men, women, and children.

Every memory is a mixture of fact and fabrication, and how people mix the two, and in what proportion, can be as enlightening as the most fastidiously documented account. But the best of these witnesses tried hard to avoid the temptation of making things up. "I ain't going tell nothing but the truth," Jane Osbrock declared, because the "truth better to live with and better to die with." Asked one question too many, Orleans Finger told her interviewer, "I don't remember. I better quit talking now before I start lying."

MANY OF THE stories they told were stark and harrowing, and I did nothing to water them down. Nor did I try to counterbalance their experience of the terror of battle and the horror of its aftermath with tales of glory, nobility, and valor, for even those who fully understood the stake they had in the Union cause were bewildered by "why white people couldn't settle their differences without fighting" and horrified by their willingness to slaughter each other in such numbers.

I did bowdlerize this book in one respect, however, and that was by eliminating what has come to be called the N-word. It appears in grim profusion throughout the sources on which I have drawn. But the following exchange will, I hope, help to explain why this will be the only appearance it makes in these pages:

One day during the war, a missionary rebuked an elderly escaped slave for calling her fellows "niggers." "We are niggers," she protested. "We always was niggers, and we always shall be. Nigger here, and nigger there. Nigger do this, and nigger do that. We've got no souls. We's animals. We's black, and so is the Evil One." "You don't know that," scolded the missionary. "Yes I do," she replied. But the Bible doesn't say that the devil is black, the missionary persisted. "Well," the old woman replied, "white folks say so, and we's bound to believe them, cause we's nothing but animals and niggers. Yes, we's niggers! Niggers! Niggers!"

The preceding is more than any reader should have to endure, and a tragic demonstration of the word's corrosive effect on not only the people to whom it was applied but the reader as well. Sparing sensibilities is not the entire reason I decided to eliminate it, however. My decision also derives from my frustration in trying to puzzle out its use as recorded by the subjects' amanuenses. It is often impossible to determine whether former slaves employed the word in its derogatory sense or used it as a more neutral variation on the word "Negro." In fact, it is sometimes hard to judge whether they employed it at all, for it may just as likely have been introduced by their interviewers in an attempt to render their testimony in "Negro dialect."

Though eliminating this epithet may to some degree have blunted the interviewees' representations of the acts of verbal and psychological violence to which they were subjected, it does remove one more layer of fog, one more level of static, through which to learn about slavery and the war. Its profusion would have further dimmed an already dismal atmosphere, and for the sake of shedding more light than heat, and in consideration of readers who cannot read when they see red, I excised it entirely from this book.

STUDENTS OF SLAVE narratives will note that I altered the dialect form of many of the original interviews. Some WPA editors were so determined to present this material in what they deemed "authentic Negro dialect" that if they received an interview accurately transcribed in the "proper" English of the interviewee, they sent it back to be reworked with all the stereotypical usages with which black speech was represented at that time.

Perhaps more than any other group in our history, emancipated slaves put tremendous stake in education and wanted to write what they were taught to regard as proper English. "I think the press is inclined to treat the colored people unfairly," complained a former St. Louis slave named Susan Wright. "It appears to take a keen delight in reproducing their awkward speech. Editors should take into consideration the trials the colored people have passed through and the little opportunity they have had for self-improvement."

At a time when Americans did not so much think about race as exercise their reflexes, dialect was imposed promiscuously. Even the most self-improved African Americans did not escape the caricaturist's brush. The boxing champion Jack Johnson spoke elegantly, but he was always represented as expressing himself like a minstrel. George L. Knox recalled that when literate African Americans in Indiana submitted articles to white newspapers in perfectly grammatical English, editors would recast them in black dialect.

With breathtaking hauteur, a white interviewer for the WPA named William V. Ervin of Texas described a ninety-year-old former slave from Johnson County named Thomas Johns as boasting "an intelligence much above that of the average Negro, and which would even do credit to some ranks of the white race. He pronounces well most of the words he uses, and seldom misplaces one as to meaning, even occasional 'big' words." But this did not prevent Ervin from representing Johns as employing "de," "ol'est," "somepin'," "ketch," and on and on. (For consistency's sake, Ervin probably should have represented his own Texas self as saying "a intell'junce much 'bove that uv th' av'age nigrah.") "This is the first story we have had in which the client did not use any dialect," wrote Mary Colbert's interviewer. "Her grammar was excellent," she wrote, and added, as if by way of explanation, "Her skin was almost white, and her hair was quite straight."

It comes down to the old problem of representing speech in written form, which is in turn vastly complicated by the politics of what is white English and what is black English. The slaves spoke a vigorous English that employed its own conjugations and syntax. And for that reason I chose not to alter or "correct" any "whup"s or "ain't"s, or any idiomatic usages such as "I done remembers" or "that weren't nothing."

I am concerned, however, not so much with how they may have sounded but with what they said. I hope that what is represented in these pages as slave speech is at least as authentic as anything the old dialect forms ever accomplished, and far more immediate and accessible. All dialect achieved was to distance the reader from the speaker, to remind the presumably white and educated reader that he or she and most especially the transcriber were above the kind of quaint rhetorical lapses of the poor, uneducated black. It thereby made transcriber and reader accomplices in a caricature that was not only gratuitous and degrading but grossly inaccurate. Cleaning up these transcriptions may have cost them a measure of their theatricality, but I think something more important has been gained: the sensation of listening respectfully and without mediation while an ancestor is speaking.

"I SEE'D IN a dream a long time ago, honey," Susan Rhodes of Missouri assured an interviewer from the Works Progress Administration, "that one of these United States presidents was going to send folks around to get some of us slaves to tell our lives way back yonder, cause they wants to know about it from us ourselves and not what somebody else wants to say. And of course, the President was not old enough his self to know, and he wants to learn the truth about it all for himself, and he's right, honey. Yes, he is." After all, observed Charlie Sandles of Texas, Franklin Delano Roosevelt was "the only friend that the Negro has ever had elected since the one that freed us," and in their poverty some hoped the President would reward their cooperation with a boost in their pensions. "What's all this information you asking about going to be for?" asked Caroline Bonds. "Will it help us along any, or make times any better?"

Other former slaves feared not only that whatever they said could get back to the whites who still held such fearful sway over them and their families, but that it would expose them to the scorn and ridicule of their own descendants. "I have heard a heap of people say they wouldn't take the treatment what the slaves took," a former Nashville slave boldly began. "But they would've took it or death. If they had been there, they would've took the very same treatment." But then she grabbed her interviewer's arm. "Say, is there any danger in this talk?" she asked. "If so, I want to take back everything I said."

Some believed that the government that had freed them could reenslave them at any moment. Liza McGhee "was hesitant about talking freely," her interviewer reported, "as she feared the white people were planning to enslave her again." "I remember some things about old slave days," McGhee allowed, "but I don't want to say nothing that will get me in bondage again. I am too old now to be a slave. I couldn't stand it."

The result was that some former slaves, out of courtesy or caution, told their white interviewers only what they thought they wanted to hear: that they missed slavery, that they'd never heard of anybody getting whipped, that things had gone downhill for black people since Emancipation, that the Yankees had been cruel and their masters kind, that slavery was about all black folks were fit for. "I wouldn't have knowed it was slavery," said Nap McQueen, "if they hadn't told me so, I was treated so good." Ellen Butts recalled her mistress as a fountain of charity. "Come Sunday she done put a bucket of dimes on the front gallery and stand there and throw dimes" to the children, "just like feeding chickens."

Some of their nostalgia was undoubtedly sincere. It expressed not only a geriatric yearning for a return to their childhoods (when many of them had yet to be put to work as slaves) but also a harking back to a time when they ate regularly and could at least hope they could rely on their masters' protection — a time that for them compared favorably with the peril and poverty of the Jim Crow South. "There is not a great deal of difference in the way most of the Negroes lived and got along for a long time after the war," George Johnson contended. "Only the white man realized the true significance of freedom for the black man."

Some former slaves wondered why their interviewers weren't taking as much interest in the injustices of the Jim Crow present as they showed in the South's slave past. "Them was dreadful days!" Alice Lewis declared, but then "these is dreadful days, too. Old man Satan, he sure am on earth now." During the Depression, Willis Winn took a trip "to where I was raised, to see my old missy before she died." He encountered black people within "twelve or fourteen miles of that place" who still "didn't know they is free." And there were plenty more in Maryland "what is same as slaves, and has worked for white folks 20 and 25 years and ain't drawed a five cent piece: just old clothes and something to eat," which was just "the way we was in slavery."

"You want to know what they did in slavery times?" asked an outraged Alice Johnson. "They were doing just what they do now! The white folks was beating the Negroes, burning them and boiling them, working them and doing any other thing they wanted to do with them. Course you wasn't here then" to know about bloodhounds and bullwhips. But "the same thing is going on right now," she said. "If you don't believe it, go right out here to the county farm, and you find them still whipping the Negroes, and tearing them up, and sometimes letting the dogs bite them to save the bullwhips."

A little way into his session, Saint Johnson of Arkansas turned on his interviewer. "I've told you enough," he snapped. "I've told you too much. How come they want all this stuff from the colored people, anyway? Do you take any stories from the white people? They know all about it. They know more about it than I do. They don't need me to tell it to them. I ain't got nothing to say about politics. You know what the truth is. Why don't you say it? You don't need to hide behind my words."

Some white interviewers steered their subjects onto safer ground: an Uncle Remus territory of songs, hunts, festivities, arts and crafts, superstitions, and cures. Even if such subjects as miscegenation, whipping, breeding, and slave pens reared their ugly heads, editors sometimes excised them. Slaves wearied of the presumptuous and intrusive ignorance of the interviewers themselves. A white interviewer named Letha Hatcher described a former slave named Amy Domino as a "queer little shiny, black-skinned Negro woman, living with friends in northeast Jasper, in a crowded shack. She seems to have delusions of grandeur," Hatcher said. "When entering the house, she unceremoniously takes the only good chair available, leaving a topless nail keg or the bed for other visitors to sit upon." But how it must have pleased Amy Domino to perch Mrs. Letha Hatcher on a nail keg!

A few former slaves repaid their interviewers' condescension with sly disinformation. When a Texan named Winger Van Hook was asked to reel off some slave cures, it amused him to prescribe to his interviewer the following treatment for a sprained ankle: "Bathe the sprain with turpentine," he instructed, "light with a match and let it burn two minutes, then fan the flame with your hat."

Others professed indifference. "I don't know if it would've been better to have stayed a slave," said Cassie Blackmond Smith. "We've always had a living, and I don't care no more, cause me and the old man is living on borrowed time anyhow." "The whole world gone pass my judgment long ago,"

said Henry Anthony. "I just sets round to see what they say and do next."
"I've almost forgot about slavery days," Susan Mcintosh declared. "I don't
read, and anyway there ain't no need to think of them times now." "I could
tell much more about it, but I don't like to talk," said Dempsey Pitts. "Will be
gone pretty soon, and what I knows is going with me." "I can remember
heaps more about war days than folks thinks I can," said Edward Jones of Alabama, "because I don't discuss it with them. I made up my mind long ago
not to get in no argument with folks what ain't got no logic in their conversation, because it don't get you nowhere, and there ain't no argument against
ignorance."

A former black soldier explained why he would not discuss slavery.
"When the war was over," Mack Henderson recollected, "we colored men
were all called together and told not to ever talk of the past. We were told
this by our Union officers." "This is a new day," they were told. "Forget the
past. You are free men, but you are black men, and you have still a hard way
to go." So Henderson refused to "talk to nobody about what went on in the
army. It was a secret then, and to me it is a secret now." Nor would
Henderson say much about slavery, as it was "too long past." "I remember
lots about the war," said Willis Winn of Texas. "But can't tell you all, cause
every war have its secrets."

Memories of bondage were painful — sometimes too painful — to recount. According to her interviewer, Julia Rush was given to her white former playmate, "who was at the time married and living in Carrollton, Georgia. She was very mean and often punished her by beating her on her
forearms for the slightest offense. At other times she made her husband
whip her on her bare back with a cowhide whip." Rush's "young mistress
thought that her husband was being intimate with her, and so she constantly
beat and mistreated her," and cut off all of Rush's "long, straight hair." After
the cruel treatment she received, "Mrs. Rush says that the mere thought of
slavery made her blood boil."

"Many was the times during slavery that I'd get to thinking about being
slaves, and I'd sit down and cry and cry," said Maria Tilden Thompson of
Texas. "I would rather die than live through them days again." "My mind
ain't sprightly like it used to be," said Calline Brown of Mississippi, "and
heaps of things what went on when I was young, I forgets, and heaps of them
what I want to forget I can't. Them was terrible days."

"You can't get the whole story by reading the words in this interview," insisted Irene Robertson, a white WPA canvasser from Arkansas. "You have to
hear the tones and the accents, and see the facial expressions and bodily
movements, and sense the sometimes almost occult influence; you have to
feel the utter lack of resentment that lies behind the words that sound vehe-
ment when read. You marvel at the quick, smooth cover-up when something
is to be withheld, at the unexpected vigor of the mind when the bait is attrac-

tive enough to draw it out, and at the sweetness of the disposition. Some old
people merely get mellowed and sweetened by the hardships through which
they have passed," though sometimes Robertson wondered "if some of the
old folk don't have dispositions that they can turn off or on at will."

Perhaps Robertson, who would go on to write a ringing defense of slavery
("Slaveowners, as a rule, arranged for their Negroes to have all needed pleasure and enjoyment," etc.), was unable to recognize that the interview's au-
thenticity lay in the starkness of its substance and not in the courteous manner of its delivery. "I have noticed so many times," wrote Rachel Cruze, "that
when a colored person is telling of some real cruel treatment he has had at
the hands of his master, he seems to think it funny and laugh and laugh. I
can't understand it." Elizabeth Keckley, Mary Lincoln's freed seamstress,
suggested a possible answer. She recalled that her master "never liked to see
one of his slaves wear a sorrowful face, and those who offended in this particular way were always punished."

DESPITE ALL THEIR fears and hesitations, and the danger their candor
might pose, most former slaves proved eager to talk to the WPA. "Does you
mean that you is willing to set here and listen to old Neal talk?" asked Neal
Upson of Georgia. "'T'ain't many folkses what wants to hear" old black folks
"talk no more." "Most folks don't take up no time with old wore-out Negroes," Nancy Smith observed. "Them slavery days done been so long ago,"
said Gabe Emanuel of Mississippi, "I just remember a few things that happen then. But I's sure mighty pleased to relate that what I recollect." "We
weren't allowed to tell it then," Ella Marples told her interviewer when she
was asked about whippings, "but right then I say, 'If I ever get free, I going to
tell it,' and now I's telling you."

"The memories of slaves were simply wonderful," wrote the former slave
Henry Bruce. "They were not unmindful, nor indifferent, as to occurrences
of interest transpiring around them, but as the principal medium through
which we obtain information was entirely closed to them, of course their
knowledge of matters and things must necessarily have been confined within
a very narrow limit; but when anything of importance transpired within their
knowledge, they knowing the date thereof, could, by reference to it as a ba-
sis, approximate the date of some other event in question."

Slaves marked time by "the first fowl crow," "crack of day," "when the sun
stand straight," "when the shadows lay long," "at frog peep," "first star
shine," and "moonrise." Their calendars were marked by "young flood,"
"flood tide" or "ebb tide," "last moon" or "new moon." Years were divided by
seasons of snow, rain, heat; by plowing, sowing, and harvest cycles. And then
there were the extraordinary signposts by which they ordered their memories: "the big flood," "the big drought," "the year old Nat rose up," "the year

the stars fell," "the year of the comet," and so on, until the war came along to provide new signposts.

"Yes Lord!" exclaimed Matilda Hatcher. "I have been here so long I ain't forgot nothing. I can remember things way back. I can remember things happening when I was four years old!" "My mind kinder comes and goes," said Anthony Abercrombie of Alabama. "It's the things what happen in these days that's so easy for me to disremember," but he could "always remember about slavery time." "I remember it well," said Neely Gray of Arkansas. "I'm a person can remember. Heap a folks tell what other folks see, but I tell what I see." And yet it puzzled Smith Simmons how "all the little things stays with me better than the big ones do."

"You say you want me to talk to you about the experiences of my life?" asked Mollie Kinsey of Georgia when she was interviewed in 1940. "Is this something about *Gone With the Wind*?" she asked, for the movie had premiered in Atlanta the previous December. "I just knowed when you asked me to talk with you it was something about that. Well, that's all right," she said. "I wouldn't have mind telling you no-how if it was." But "Oh!" she exclaimed. "You is blessed to live in this day, and don't know the tortures the slaves went through!"

"I was ten years old at the Surrender, but I took notice," said Nettie Henry of Alabama. "Them was scary times, and when you is scared you takes trigger-notice." "Now, these are stubborn facts I'm giving you," warned Sam Word, "but they's true." "People been through what I been through," declared a slave from Tennessee, "they surely would be graduated."

A DIRECTORY OF WITNESSES

THE FOLLOWING IS an alphabetical directory of everyone, black and white, quoted in this book. Wherever possible, I have included biographical information culled from personal accounts and various historical and genealogical sources, including U.S. censuses and slave schedules and a range of maps, Civil War reference works, county histories, and the like. The testimonies of witnesses whose names are followed by state acronyms in parentheses are from the Federal Writers' Project's *Slave Narratives: A Folk History of Slavery in the United States from Interviews with Former Slaves,* which is arranged by state in George P. Rawick's multivolume compendium, *The American Slave.* The state acronyms refer not necessarily to the state in which the subjects resided during the war, but to the state in which they were interviewed in the 1920s and 1930s. Though most of these interviews are freely available on the Internet in searchable form at the Library of Congress's American Memory site, I have included the state designations to facilitate further research in the original sources.

First Names and Epithets Only

Anne in Egypt, ed., *Unwritten History of Slavery,* p. 184. **Anonymous** re the slave Leonard. Escott, *Slavery Remembered,* p. 122. **Anonymous** ("The Colored Woman at Headquarters") in Johnson, *Battleground Adventures,* pp. 392–95. Born ca. 1838. Her identity, like those of many of Johnson's subjects, was established on behalf of the author by the genealogist Jacqueline E. A. Lawson of Diversitudes and the Black Genealogy Research Group of Seattle, whose findings helped to persuade me of the basic accuracy of Johnson's transcriptions. **Charles** in Johnson, ed., *God Struck Me Dead,* pp. 33–34, 36, 49. **Dave** (GA). Born near Ellerslie, in Marris County, Georgia, slave of George Kilpatrick. **E.L.B.** in "The Story of a Contraband," *Stillwater* (MN) *Daily Gazette,* March 5, 1886. The 101st Indiana Regiment was commanded by Colonel George Washington Steele, later a congressman and the first governor of Oklahoma. **The Fighting Slave at Vicksburg** in Johnson, *Battleground Adventures,* pp. 217–23. **Isaac** in Capeheart, *Reminiscences,* p. 3. **Jane** (AL). Slave from Georgiana, Alabama. "I married Rufus, and us raise a big family right on Master's plantation, and out of our twelve childrens," she boasted, none had ever "seen the inside of the jailhouse." **Jule** in Haviland, *A Woman's Life Work,* pp. 274–75. **Mathis.** I have determined that the anonymous "Runaway Slave" I have named "Mathis" was the property of E. B. Mathis of Pond Springs, Walker County, Georgia. The ages of E.B.'s male slaves (eighteen, twenty, twenty, and twenty-one) fit "Mathis" and the three men who ran off with him, including Moses Mathis (incorrectly transcribed by Johnson as "Mose Matthews"), who appears in successive censuses in Walker County. The ages of E.B.'s youngest daughters, given by "Mathis" as twelve and fifteen when he hid them for his master during the war, jibes with the ages of his youngest daughters — eight and eleven — in 1860. The location of Mathis's farm at Pond Springs — about six miles from Pigeon Mountain and about twenty miles south of Chattanooga, Tennessee — also fits the location described by the "Runaway Slave" in Johnson, *Battleground Adventures.* **Susannah** in Egypt, ed., p. 315. **Tom** in Hepworth, *The Whip, Hoe and Sword,* pp. 178–79. **White officer** of the First Kansas Colored Regiment, quoted in Goodrich, *Black Flag,* p. 58. **William** in Armstrong, *Old Massa's People,* pp. 285–86. **Willis** (GA). Slave of Dr. Balding Miller on Rock Creek plantation in Burke County, Georgia.

A

Charlie Aarons (AL). **Anthony Abercrombie** (AL). Slave of James Abercrombie, whose farm lay "16 miles north of Marion, Alabama, in Bibb County." **Laura Abromson** (AR). Daughter of Eloise Rogers, who was born in Missouri and taken to Brownsville, Tennessee. Slave of Alex and Barbara Ann Rogers, who owned hundreds of acres and a cotton factory. **John Quincy Adams.** Claimed to have been born 1845 in Frederick County, Virginia, but also says his parents were living in the 1930s, so it is more likely he was born no earlier than the 1850s. Slave of George F. Calomese, who owned his parents and their twenty-five children. *Narrative of the Life of John Quincy Adams* was published in 1872 when he lived in Harrisburg, Pennsylvania. **Lewis Adams** (MS). Born 1824 in Illinois, sold in 1839 to Colonel Tom Dancy, near Houston, Texas. Around the same year he was carried from Illinois to Texas in a covered wagon by slave dealers named Bob and John Kirkendal, and eventually sold to Henry William Stackhouse of Hinds County, Mississippi. He died in 1930. **Rachel Adams** (GA). Born in Putnam County, Georgia, about two miles from Batonton. Daughter of Isaac and Amelia Little. "Pa, he was sold away from Ma when I was still a baby. There was 17 of us children, all but one of them girls." **William M. Adams** (TX). Born ca. 1843, slave of Jones Davis in San Jacinto County, Texas. **Liddie Aiken** (AR). Born near Mobile, Alabama. "My mother was born in southwest Georgia close to the Alabama line. Her mother come from Virginia. She was sold with her mother and two little brothers. Her mother had been sold and come in a wagon to southwest Georgia. They was all field hands." Her mother had two younger brothers, Henry and Will Keller. **George Washington Albright** (MS). Born in 1846 near Hollis Springs, Mississippi. "My mother and father were held by different owners, and when I was 11 years old, my father was sold to a man in Texas." **Jacob Aldrich** (TX). Born January 10, 1860, in Terrebonne Parish, Louisiana, the slave and grandson of Michelle Thibedoux. He lived in Terrebonne and St. Mary parishes until the Mississippi River flood of 1928, when he went to Beaumont, Texas. **Sam Aleckson** was born in South Carolina in 1852. Treated kindly by his owners and taught to read, he served in the Confederate Army throughout the war and wrote one of the milder accounts of life as a slave. Nevertheless, he concluded, "there is nothing good to be said of American slavery. I know it is sometimes customary to speak of its bright and its dark sides," but Aleckson "was not prepared to admit that it had any bright sides," unless you counted Emancipation. Aleckson, *Before the War,* pp. 76–78, 85–86. **Louisa Alexander** attended Oberlin College before the war. **Lucretia Alexander** (AR). Born near Hazelhurst in Copiah County, Mississippi. "My mother was born in Washington County, Virginia. Her first master was Qualls Tolliver. Qualls moved to Mississippi and married a woman down there, and he had one son: Peachy Tolliver. After he died, he willed her to Peachy. Then Peachy went to the Rebel Army and got killed." **Barney Alford** (MS). Slave of Edwin Alford of Mississippi, who "owned a big plantation right near the Louisiana State line." **Dinah Allen** (MS). Born ca. 1847 in Perry County, Alabama, one of eight "Hall children," owned first by Lee Walthall and then sold to Tom Bondurant. **Hannah Allen** (MO). Born in Harrison County, Missouri, in 1859 and raised in Georgetown, Scott County. Slave of John and Alice McWiggin, "who raised hogs, sheep, hemp, and darkies. He had about 830 darkies on the place." **Jeff Allen** (AL). Born March 16, 1862, in Macon County, Alabama, the slave of Lewis and Jane Allen, brother of Frank, Frederick, Marie, Sherman, William, Harriet, and Alice, and nephew of Nancy and Dennis Stodemine. **Allen Allensworth.** Born April 7, 1842, in Louisville, Kentucky, son of Phyllis and Levi Allensworth, slave of Mrs. A. P. Starbird and then her son Thomas. Paraphrased in Alexander, *Battles and Victories of Allen Allensworth,* pp. 173–74, 176. **Lucindy Allison** (AR). Born 1876, told her mother's tales of her servitude in Arkansas. **Serena Spencer Anchor** in "The Negro Village Girl," Johnson, *Battleground Adventures,* pp. 406–15. **David Anderson** ("The Slave Boy") in ibid., pp. 336–39. His identity was pinpointed by Jacqueline E. A. Lawson. **Mary Anderson** (NC). Born May 10, 1851, on a plantation near Franklinton, Wake County, North Carolina. "I was a slave belonging to Sam Brodie, who owned the plantation at this place. My missus' name was Evaline. My father was Alfred Modie and my mother was Bertha Brodie." **Robert Anderson** in Anderson, *From Slavery to Affluence,* p. 42. **Henry Anthony** (AR). "I was born at Jackson, North Carolina. My master and mistress named Jason and Batey [Betty/Elizabeth] Williams, but my pa's name was Anthony. My young master was a orderly sergeant." **George W. Arnold** (IN). Born April 7, 1851, in Bedford County, Tennessee, slave of Oliver P. Arnold. His mother was from Home, Georgia, and sold at auction at the age of twelve. **Jared Maurice Arter.** Re Crossroads combat: Arter says this was in the summer of 1863, but his location suggests that he would have witnessed these fights a year earlier. Arter, *Echoes from a Pioneer Life,* pp. 10–11. Born January 27, 1850, the slave of William Schaeffer, inspector of arms at the U.S. Arsenal at Harpers Ferry, whose farm lay near the junction

of Winchester Turnpike and Shepherdstown Highway, halfway between Harpers
Ferry and Charles Town, West Virginia. **Levi Ashley** (MS). Born the slave of Dan
McRainey, by the Atchafalaya River in Louisiana. McRainey died shortly after moving with his slaves to Wilkinson County, Mississippi, whereupon Levi became the
property of McRainey's sister and her husband, John Jones, who lived on "the old
Bacot place." **Gus Askew** (AL). Born in 1853, a slave of the Edwards family in Henry
County, Alabama. Brought to Eufaula just before the close of the war, he stayed on as
a blacksmith after the war. **Bill Austin** (FL). Born the slave of a Mr. Smith near the
line between Greene and Hancock counties, in Georgia. **Hannah Austin** (GA). Austin was born ca. 1854, the oldest child of Liza and George Hall; her master is given as
Mr. Frank Hall of Georgia. There is an F. L. Hall listed in Sumter with one older female slave, but a likelier candidate may be John F. Hall of Appling County, who
owned one sixteen-year-old and one four-year-old female slave in 1860. **Celestia
Avery** (GA). Born ca. 1862 in La Grange, Troup County, Georgia, slave of Peter
Heard. Granddaughter of Sylvia Heard.

B

Harriet Bailey. She turns up in the 1860 census in Mummasburg, just up the pike
from the Hartzell farm, where the narrator worked. She gives the year of her birth as
1843, as does a married Harriet C. Stanton in the 1910 through 1930 censuses, where
she is listed as living in Gettysburg itself. "Harriet" is the only black woman born in or
around 1843 who remained in Gettysburg for that entire period. Johnson, *Battleground Adventures,* pp. 187–91. **Anna Baker** (MS). Born ca. 1858, slave of a Mr.
Morgan, "about seven miles from Tuscaloosa, Alabama," and the youngest child in
her family. **Georgia Baker** (GA). Born the slave of Alexander Stephens, a mile and a
half from Crawfordville, in Taliaferro County, Georgia. **Charles Ball.** Born in Maryland in the late 1700s. Sold down to Georgia after it repealed its ban on slavery, he escaped twice, the second time to Pennsylvania, where he became active in the Underground Railroad. Ball, *Fifty Years in Chains,* pp. 19, 21. **General Lee Ballard** (AL).
Born November 18, 1861, in Clayburne Parish, Louisiana. Moved to Danway, about
eight miles from Opelika, Alabama, between West Point, Georgia, and Lafayette,
Alabama. Son of Wesley and Ursie. In 1938 he had at least eight living siblings:
Caline, Julie, Mike, Elick, Howard, Will, Jessie, and Lee. Slave of Jim and Mary
Monk. "Their children was: Lloyd, Lula, Mattie, Jimmie, Nathan, Mell, Rissie, Annie, Sudie and Sallie." **Samuel Ballton.** Born 1838, a slave field hand of Vincent
Marmaduke of Westmoreland County, Virginia. Ballton was interviewed in New
York in 1910. Blassingame, *Slave Testimony,* pp. 543–47. **Frederic Bancroft.** Born
in Galesburg, Illinois, in 1860, he attended Amherst and Columbia, where he lec-
tured briefly before becoming the librarian of the State Department. A retiring bach-
elor, he nevertheless scoured the South in search of slavery's vestiges, interviewing
traders and slave owners as well as former slaves. The annual Bancroft Prize in history is named in his honor. Bancroft, *Slave Trading in the Old South,* pp. 94–97.
Henry Banner (AR). Born ca. 1849 in Russell County, Virginia, and sold out of the
county during the war. **Mary Barnes** (MD). Born ca. 1844 in Charles County, Maryland, daughter of William N. Turner, younger sister of William and Sam Turner, slave

of Robert Ryan. **John W. H. Barnet** (AR). Born ca. 1856 in Clinton Parish, Louisiana. "My parents and four children was sold and left six children behind." Sold at New Orleans in 1864 to J. J. Gambol (Gamble?) of northern Louisiana. **Lizzie Barnett** (AR). Born a slave of Fannie Pennington near Nashville, Tennessee. **Emma Barr** (AR). Her mother was a slave of a Dr. Pope, ten miles south of Augusta, Arkansas, near where Emma was born. **Moses Battle** quoted in Cimprich, *Slavery's End in Tennessee*, p. 71. **Lura Beam.** Born in Marshfield, Maine, in 1887, she worked for the American Missionary Association from 1908 to 1919 at the Gregory Normal Institute in Wilmington, North Carolina, and the LeMoyne Normal School in Memphis, Tennessee, before becoming the association's assistant superintendent of education in the Deep South. She died in 1980. Beam, *They Called Them by the Lightning*, pp. 14, 183. **John Belcher** (MS). Born September 28, 1849, in Valdosta, Lowndes County, Georgia, slave of James Walker. **Charlie Bell** (MS). Bell's interviewer lists him as having been born in 1856 in Poplarville, Pearl River County, Mississippi, on the plantation of a Mr. Moore, but no such slave owner turns up in the 1860 slave schedules. **Nancy Bell** in Blassingame, *Slave Testimony*, p. 555. **Oliver Bell** (AL). Slave from Livingston, Alabama. **Willis Bennefield** (GA). Born 1835, probably near Augusta, Georgia. **Mrs. Elijah Berry** in Egypt, ed., *Unwritten History of Slavery*, p. 189. **Fannie Berry** (VA). Owned by Delia Mann(?) on Crater Road in Pamplin, Virginia. **Nathan Best** (MS). Born May 19, 1845, in North Carolina, slave of Henry and Rufus Best. **Beatrice Black** (AR). Born "below the city pump" in Biscoe, Arkansas. "My husband is a twin and the youngest of thirteen children. His twin brother is living. They are fifty years old today [August 6, 1938]. His mother [Dedonia] lived back and forth with the twins. She died year before last." **William Edward Black** (NC). Born January 1, 1846, in Charlotte, North Carolina. "My mother was Edith Black and my father was Morris Black and I had six sisters and four brothers. We were free people in North Carolina, but lived with and worked for the O'Neill family, members of the white race. Miss Rachael O'Neill married Mr. Major Daniel Black in 1861. He was from Mississippi and told her he had lots of money. She wanted to find out so she moved back with him and brought our family with her. When Mr. Major Black got to his home in Itawamba County, he enslaved us." **Boston Blackwell** (AR). "My borned name was 'Pruitt' cause I got borned on Robert Pruitt's plantation in Franklin County, Georgia. But Blackwell, it my freed name. After my mammy got sold down to Augusta, I was sold to go to Jefferson county, Arkansas." **Adeline Blakely** (AR). Born July 10, 1843 (based on census data) or 1850 (in interview), in Hickman County, Tennessee, and a year after her birth was taken by her owners, the Blakely family, to Fayetteville, Arkansas. Mrs. Blakely's maiden name was apparently Parks. The only "Old Man Parks" I could find in the 1860 census for Washington County was John Parks. Her name is consistently spelled "Adaline" in the census records. **Henry Bland** (GA). Born 1851 near "Ardenton"(?), Georgia, son of Martha and Sam Coxton. His father was born in Hancock County, Georgia. His mother was a cook, and she and her mother were brought to Georgia by a speculator. Slave of a Mr. "Coxton" (James W. Coston of Washington County?). **Peter Blewitt** (MS). Born December 11, 1850, in Galveston, Texas, son of Peter and Hannah Blewitt, grandson of Jason and Lucy Horne. Slave of John Horne, who sold his father to Henry Blewitt in Newton County, Texas. **Emma Bolt (Colt?)** in Swift, *Dear Ones at Home: Letters from Contraband Camps*, p. 107.

James Bolton (GA). Born ca. 1852. Son of Whitfield and Liza Bolton. His brothers were Thomas and John, and his sister was Rosa. Slave of Whitfield Bolton near Lexington, in Oglethorpe County, Georgia. **Caroline Bonds** (AR). Born March 20, 1866(?), in Anderson County, North Carolina, daughter of the former slaves of the Hubbard family. **Rhoda Bones** (MS). **Tom Bones** (MS). Born free in Charles City County, Virginia, near the Chickahominy River. Conscripted by the Confederate Army to fish for shad in the James River. **Jonas Boone** (AR). Born March 15, ca. 1851, in Cornerville, Mississippi, slave of Mrs. L. D. Hewitt. His grandfather was the slave of the pioneer Daniel Boone. "Mr. John Boone's and Miss Mary Black's grandpa, and I was named Boone for him, my granddaddy." **Alec Bostwick** (GA). Born ca. 1861 in Morgan County, Georgia, son of Martha and Jordan Bostwick, sister of George, John, and Reece. "There weren't but one gal, and she died when she was little." **Elizabeth Hyde Botume.** From 1864 to 1902, she worked on the South Carolina sea island of Port Royal and was one of the first Northern teachers of freed slaves. Botume, *First Days Among the Contrabands*, pp. 13, 128. **Joe Bouy** (MS). Born ca. 1848, three miles from Caseville, Mississippi. Slave of John Bouy. **Rivana Boynton** (FL). She said she was born in 1850, the slave of John and Mollie Hoover, who owned a large plantation between Savannah and Charleston, near the Georgia line. **Edna Boysaw** (IN). "When the Civil War ended, I was living near Richmond, Virginia. I am not sure just how old I was, but I was a big, flat-footed woman." **Elodga Bradford** (MS). Son of a freedman and a slave woman, he had eleven brothers. Slave of Dr. Charles Thompson Chamberlain (1815–1871) of Port Gibson, Mississippi, who moved to Natchez at the beginning of the war and is listed as owning sixty-six slaves in Jefferson County in 1860. He served in (Captain Pat) Darden's Company, Mississippi Light Artillery. Born in 1854, Darden's son George Earl became a leading political figure in Oregon, serving as senator and governor. He died in 1928. **Andrew Bradley.** Private William Bradley served under Captain Edmund Cowan and First Lieutenant J. M. Truittin in Company G of the 14th South Carolina Infantry, which sustained 145 casualties at Chancellorsville. Armstrong, *Old Massa's People.* **Edmond Bradley** (MS). A "French 'Creole' Catholic mulatto," born free in 1842 at Pass Christian, Louisiana. **Jacob Branch** (TX). Born 1851, slave of the Van Loos family in Louisiana, who sold him as a baby to Elisha and Eliza Stevenson of Double Bayou, Texas. **Matt Brantley** (AR). Born in Dallas County, near Selma, Alabama, slave of Mary Ann E. and W. "Ephraim" (Rasco). His parents were Lucindy Rasco and Silica Brantley, a slave of Warren A. Brantley. **Ellen Brass** (AR). Born in Greene County, Alabama. "I was about four years old when I came from there . . . I growed up in Catahoula, Louisiana." Daughter of Lee and Caroline Butler. **Wiley Brewer** (MS). Claimed to be 130 years old in 1937. Slave of Raleigh Brewer, a Virginian who settled close to Macon, Georgia. **Harry Bridges** (MS). Born a slave of Major Sartin, a prominent planter and slave owner of Pike County, Mississippi. **Della Briscoe** (GA). Slave of David Ross, who owned a large plantation in Putnam County, Georgia. **Henry Broadus** (TX). Born on a farm near Mobile, Alabama, in March 1860, slave of Churchill Jones, who refugeed him to Marlin, Texas. **Calline Brown** (MS). Born 1832, the slave of a family named Howard, near Rockport in Copiah County, Mississippi, who gave her and some adjoining acreage to a Miss Mullen. Forty-five-year-old Mary Mullen is listed as owning four slaves. No Howards listed in the 1860 slave schedule for Copiah County, nor anywhere in Mississippi. But

living next to Mary Mullen, according to the 1860 census, is a poor farmer named
Murrah, owner of three slaves. "Murrah" may have been misheard or misremem-
bered as "Howard." **Ebenezer Brown** (MS). Born ca. 1857, "about twelve miles
south of Liberty, on the road that goes from Liberty to Jackson, Louisiana," slave of
Bill McDowell, who was "mighty tough on his slaves." **Elcie Brown** (AR). Born ca.
1852 near Centerville and Clinton in Yell County, Arkansas, slave of Johnnie Reeves
and his son Henry L. Reeves. **George Brown** (AR). Born 1854 in Marengo County,
Alabama, slave of Jim and Sarah Williams Hart. "Good to me? I'd rather let that
alone. Plenty to eat? I'll have to let that alone too." **Gus Brown** (AL). Body servant of
William Brown of Richmond, Virginia, who fought alongside Stonewall Jackson. **Peter Brown** (AR). Born March 1, 1852, slave of David Hunt on Woodlawn plantation
in Jefferson County, Mississippi. After Hunt's death in 1861, the plantation was managed by his widow, Ann Ferguson Hunt. **Rina Brown** (MS). Born ca. 1853 in Franklin County on the Homochitto River, about forty-five miles from Natchez at a settlement now named Monroe, Mississippi. Slave of Mr. John F. and Atlanta Lea, brother
of Rose, Chaney, and Prustess — all dead by 1937. **Thomas Brown** (MS). "Born the
son of William and Fanny Anderson, slave of Matt Anderson, maternal grandson of
Fanny, who was part Indian from "the mountains of Virginia." When Mattie, his
young mistress, married a Mr. Brown, her father gave her Thomas's parents. **William
Wells Brown.** Born 1814 in Lexington, Kentucky, slave of his father, George Higgins. Brown escaped in 1834 and became a conductor on the Underground Railroad
and a featured speaker for the American Anti-Slavery Society. He wrote several
books before his death in 1884. Brown, *My Southern Home,* p. 202. **Henry Clay
Bruce.** Born 1836, slave of Lemuel Bruce. Sold at the age of eight to Jack Perkinson
of Keytesville, Missouri. Hired out to different people, and returned with Perkinson
to Virginia in 1847. After the war, he and his wife moved to Leavenworth, Kansas. He
died in 1902. Bruce, *The New Man,* pp. 12, 36–39, 105–6, 111. **Julia Bunch** (GA).
Slave of Jackie Dorn of Edgefield County, Georgia; given as "a wedding gift." **Belle
Buntin** (AR). Born in Oakland, Mississippi, slave of Johnson and Sue Buntin. "They
had two children: Bob and Fannie. He had a big plantation and four families of
slaves." **Jeff Burgess** (AR). Born ca. 1864 in Cranville, Texas, slave of Strathers and
Polly Burgess. **Will Burks Sr.** (AR). Born ca. 1862 near Columbia, Tennessee. Son
of Bill Burks and Katherine Hill; brother to four boys and three girls; slave of Frank
and Polly Burks. **Mahala Burns** (AL). Slave from Hammond, Alabama. **Annie Burton.** Born ca. 1858 near Clayton, Alabama, and raised by her mistress. She moved to
Boston in 1879, then to Georgia and Florida, where she ran a restaurant before circling back to Boston. Burton, *Memories,* pp. 35–36. **Vinnie Busby** (MS). Born ca.
1854, slave of J. D. Easterling of Hinds County, Mississippi, or William K. Easterling
of Rankin County, Mississippi. **Gabe Butler** (MS). Born March 9, ca. 1854, in Amite
County, Mississippi, son of Aaron and Letha Butler, slaves of William Butler. **Marshal Butler** (GA). Born December 25, 1849, son of John and Marilyn Butler. John
was owned by Frank Collier and Marilyn by Ben Butler, both of Washington-Wilkes,
Georgia. **Ellen Butts** (TX). Born near Centerville, Virginia. Mentions masters
named William and Conrad, and a Dr. Fatchitt, who bought a birth-defective infant
slave and pickled her in a jar. **Dave L. Byrd** (TX). Born in 1862, slave of Jack Byrd.
Sarah Byrd (GA). Born ca. 1852 in Orange County, Virginia, the youngest of three
children. Her mother and father, Judy Newman and Sam Goodan, each belonged to

a different master. The father was sold to a family in east Tennessee, and the mother and children to a Dr. Byrd of Augusta, Georgia.

C

Walter Calloway (AL). Born ca. 1848 in Richmond, Virginia. "Before I was old enough to remember much, my mammy with me and my older brother was sold to Marse John Calloway at Snowdown," ten miles south of Montgomery, Alabama. **James Cape** (TX). Born ca. 1837, slave of Bob Houston of southeastern Texas. After being wounded in the war, Cape worked for the outlaw Jesse James in Missouri, and later as a cowboy and stockyard worker. **Aron (Aaron) Carter** (MS). Born November 10, 1857, in Lincoln County, Mississippi, slave of William Gwinn. **Joseph William Carter** (GA). Born before 1836 near Gallatin, Tennessee, son of Malvina Gardner, formerly a captive of the Cherokees, and slave first of the Smith and then the Gardner family. His mistress "Puss" married a Mr. Mooney on Carthage Road in Sumner County, Tennessee. **Belle Garland Myers Caruthers** (MS). Born near Wadesboro, North Carolina, in 1847, the slave of Absalom Myers, who refugeed to Mississippi and settled near Byhalia in Marshall County. Myers served in the 30th Mississippi Infantry. **Esther King Casey** (AL). Slave of Captain Henry King of Americus, Georgia. **Abraham Chambers** (AL). Born March 25, 1854, seven miles below Salem, Alabama, son of Abraham and Violet Chambers, slaves of Abraham Chambers of Motts Mill. **Liney Chambers** (AR). Born near Memphis, Tennessee, child of John, a slave of Jim and Caroline Bledsoe, slave of Jane and Silas Wory, who also owned Liney. **Ned Chaney** (MS). Born 1857 near Butler in Choctaw County, Alabama. Son of Nat Chaney. Slave of Wiley and Virginia Coleman. **Emma Chapman** (AL). Born ca. 1852, slave of Reverend Montgomery and Ann Haynie Curry of Charleston, South Carolina. Taken at age three to Pickens County, Alabama, about five miles from Carrollton and eight miles from Pickenville. Mrs. Curry's parents, Aaron and Francis Hudson Haynie, bought Emma's grandmother Lucy Linier, who was sold to pay her master's debt, and became Ann's nurse. **Hannah Chapman** (MS). Born ca. 1861, slave of Bill K. Easterlin in Cato, Simpson County, Mississippi. **Lucy** and **Sarah Chase.** Quaker sisters who began to work among the Contrabands in 1863 on Craney Island near Norfolk, Virginia, where they set up and administered clinics and schools until the 1870s. Swift, *Dear Ones at Home*, pp. 32–33, 36, 96, 98, 123, 132, 189. **Robert J. Cheatham** (IN). His father was the slave of Robert G. Cheatham, who brought his slaves from Virginia and settled in Trigg, Kentucky; in 1860 he owned thirteen slaves. But Robert J. was apparently sold to Dr. Henry H. Farmer of Henderson County, Kentucky, who in 1860 owned five slaves. A Benjamin Vinson served in the 109th U.S. Colored Infantry, organized at Louisville, Kentucky; and a Louis Vinson served in the 13th U.S. Colored Heavy Artillery, organized at Camp Nelson, Kentucky. **Pharaoh Chesney.** Born a slave in Clarksville, Virginia, in the late 1700s, Chesney married and had four children, but around the age of sixty he was separated from his wife and children and sold to John Chesney in east Tennessee. Webster, *The Last of the Pioneers*, pp. 110, 119–20. **William Steptoe Christian** (CSA) in Alexander, "A Regular Slave Hunt," *North & South*, September 2001. **Laura Clark** (AL). Slave from western Alabama. **Hattie Clayton** in Mellon, ed.

Bullwhip Days, p. 343. Sold as a small child away from her parents to a widow named Day, who had a farm near Lafayette, Alabama. **Samuel Spottford Clement.** Born November 13, 1861, in Pittsylvania County, Virginia, slave of James Adams, then sold to Dr. Davie Ward in 1863. Clement, *Memoirs,* pp. 9–10. **Marie Sutton Clemments** (AR). Born between 1848 and 1853 in Lincoln County, Georgia, slave of a widow named Frances Sutton and her sons, Abraham and George. **Wadley Clemons** (AL). "We lived in Pine Hill, a summer resort in Jefferson County, Georgia, across the river from Louisville." **"Aunt" Clussey** (AL). Born ca. 1844 in Etowah County, Alabama. **Irene Coates** (GA). Born in Georgia in about 1859. **Pierce Cody** (GA). Born in Warren County, Georgia, the eldest son of Elbert (of Richmond, Virginia) and Dorothy Cody. Slave of Robert Cody. **Neil Coker** (FL). Born ca. 1857 in Virginia, the son of a slave mother and Senator John P. Wall, later the mayor of Tampa, Florida. **Mary "Hannah" Colbert** (GA). Born in Athens, Georgia, daughter of Polly Crawford and slave of William H. Crawford, then his son John. She was told her father was Sandy Thomas, a slave of Obadiah Thomas of Oglethorpe County. "When I found my grandma, Hannah Crawford, she was living on Major Crawford's plantation, where Crawford, Georgia, is now." **William Colbert** (AL). Born 1844 in Fort Valley, Georgia. Slave of Jim Hoddison. **John Cole** (GA). Born ca. 1852 near Athens, Georgia, son of Lucius Cole and Betsy Cole. His master hired him out to the Oglethorpe plantation. Cole was told that Robert Toombs used to boast that he "could beat the damn Yankees with corn-stalks before breakfast." **Thomas Coles** (TX). Born ca. 1845, slave of Robert T. Coles of Huntsville, but raised on his plantation in Jackson County, Alabama. **Holt Collier** (MS). Born 1846, slave of Howell Hinds on Plumridge plantation in Hinds County, Mississippi. Over the course of his life Collier was said to have killed some three thousand bears. Given his free papers, he ran away from Hinds and at the age of fifteen joined his master's son in the 9th Texas Cavalry. Acquitted of the murder of Captain James King, Collier fled to Texas and herded cattle for his former commander, future governor Sullivan Ross. He returned to Mississippi after Hinds was murdered and in 1903 gained fame as Teddy Roosevelt's hunting guide. He died in 1936. (See Howell Hinds.) **Martha Colquitt** (GA). Born the slave of Billie Glenn of Lexington, Georgia. Daughter of Anderson Mitchell of Milledgeville, who belonged to Glenn's neighbor D. Smith, and of Healon Mitchell, who was born in Virginia; she was sold as a baby with her mother to Georgia. "Grandma never did see none of her other children or her husband no more, and us never did hear nothing about them." **Jerry Cook** (MS). Born 1853 in Greene County, Alabama, between Livingston and Eutah. Son of Andrew Cook and Phyllis Smith. **Levi Jenkins Coppin.** Born Christmas Day, 1848, in Frederick Town, Maryland. Died in 1923. Coppin, *Unwritten History,* p. 80. **Tony Cox** (MS). Husband of Julia Cox, owned by Cato Miller of Mississippi. **Mary Crane** (IN). Born in 1855, slave of "Hattie Williams." There's only one outright Hattie Williams from a slaveholding state: Hattie W. Williams of Richmond, Howard County, Missouri, the seventeen-year-old wife of thirty-two-year-old John F. Williams, who owned six slaves, including a three-year-old girl. There were, however, one Texas, four Virginia, and two North Carolina Harriet Williamses who owned slaves in 1860. **Sally Crane** (AR). Born before 1847 in Hempstead County, "between Nashville and Greenville, in Arkansas, on the Military Road." **Hannah Crasson** (NC). Born March 2, ca. 1853, in Wake County, North Carolina. Son of

Frank and Flora Walton. Slave of John William and Martha Walton. "My brothers were named Johnnie and Lang; my sisters were Adeline, Violet, Mary, Sarah, Ellen." **Mary Crosby** (AR). Born ca. 1861 in Georgia, slave of Matt Fields. **Cheney Cross** (AL). Slave of Miss Mary Fields of Wilcox County, Alabama. "Then the Carters bought my daddy from Miss Mary Fields. Well, they mix up and down like that, till now my young mistress, what was to be little Frances Purifoy, married a Mr. Cunningham." **Rachel Cruze** (OH). Born March 9, 1856, slave of Major William Holden of Strawberry Plains, Knox County, Tennessee, daughter of Eliza Moley and the major's son. After her mother married a slave named John Meek, by whom she had eleven more children, Cruze was given to the major's daughter Melinda, whose new husband, "although a Southerner, hated the colored folk" and sold her to Meek's master on a neighboring plantation. Cruze observed that her kin were all light-skinned, and her grandparents had straight hair. **Albert Cumins (Commins)** (AR). A slave in Texarkana, Arkansas. **Betty Curlett** (AR). Daughter of John Johnson, slave of Daniel and Betty Johnson, who bought him and his sister Alice in North Carolina. Curlett's mother's owners were John and Molly Moore. "They come from Virginia and brought Grandma Mahaley and Grandpa Tom." **James Curry** in Blassingame, *Slave Testimony*, p. 139. Slave of Moses Chambers of Person County, North Carolina. **Letetia Custis** (AL). Slave of Thaddeus Watts of Wilcox County, Alabama.

D

Julia Frances Daniels (TX). Born in 1848 in Georgia. Slave of "Old Man Denman," then Elizabeth Denman Cramer and her husband. **Juda Dantzler** (MS). Her mother "would run the ferry when no men were at home." This was Roberts Ferry, on the Chickasawhay River in Mississippi. She was born some years before 1849, the slave of Tyra J. Roberts of Greene County, Mississippi. Though he ran away for eight days during the war, William Austin returned to hold down his master's store in Georgia. **Katie Darling** (TX). Born the slave of William McCarty, south of Marshall, Texas. **Charlie Davenport** (MS). Born ca. 1837, son of William Davenport and his wife, Lucindy, who died giving him birth. Slave of Gabriel Benoit Shields (1812–1888) of Aventine plantation, "across Second Creek" in Mississippi. "He married a Surget." **Jefferson Davis** in Botume, *First Days Among the Contrabands*, pp. 7–8. **Jefferson Franklin Davis** (GA). "I was named General Jeff Davis three weeks before I was borned. My daddy and mammy was Anne and Abraham, and they had six childrens named Henry, Alice, Monroe, Rosetta, Jacob and me. My daddy and mammy both come from Virginny to Alabama, and they lived in the quarters," slaves of Sam and Jane Nunn. **Lizzie Davis** (SC). Born the slave of Foster Brown near Centenary, South Carolina. **Minnie Davis** (GA). Born ca. 1859 in Greene County, near Penfield, Georgia, daughter of Jim Young and Aggie Crawford. Sister of Mariah, Ned, John, and Jim. Slave of the Crawford family. "Ned was a mulatto. I know who his father was, but I wouldn't want to expose my own mother or the man who was Ned's father." **Mose Davis** (GA). Born twelve miles from Perry, Georgia, son of a coachman named January and his wife, Jennie Davis, slaves of a Colonel Davis. **Rosetta Davis** (AR). Born ca. 1882 in Phillips County, Arkansas. Her parents were the slaves of Jack Spivy. **Jake Dawkins** (MS). Born 1845, son of Jim and Adeline Mays from "the Carolinas." Slave of Joe Mays of Athens, who gave him to his daughter Emily. **Fannie Dawson** ("Slave Woman's Troubles") in Johnson, *Battleground Adventures,* pp. 150–58. Identified by Jacqueline E. A. Lawson. **Mollie Dawson** (TX). Born in January 1852 in Navarro County, Texas, in the forks of Richland and Pin Oak creeks. Slave of Nathan Newman. **Sarah Debro** (NC). Born ca. 1847 in Orange County, North Carolina. Slave of Dr. and Mrs. Polly White Cain. **Hammett Dell** (AR). Born October 12, 1847, ten miles from Murfreesboro, Tennessee, slave of a Mr. White. **Edie Dennis** via Mary Gladden (GA). Mary Gladden's grandmother was born in the 1790s in Hancock County, Georgia, between Milledgeville and Sparta. Slave of Thomas Schlatter, who sold her to Judge Hines Holt of Columbus, Georgia. She died in 1901. **Katie Dillon** (AR). Born in 1855 in Rodney, Mississippi. **Mattie "Martha Ann" Dillworth** (MS). Born in the 1830s in Boyle County, Kentucky. Daughter of Clara Knox, who died when Mattie was a child "and was buried in Kentucky on the plantation with a peach tree for a head board." Slave of Betsy McClain, wife of Reuben. **Rufus Dirt** (AL). Born in Wilcox County, Alabama. **Sally Dixon** (MS). Daughter of Louise, the slave of Sally White, near Macon, Georgia. After White's death, Louise was owned by Sally's son Crawfort White near Como, Mississippi. **Tom Douglas** (AR). Born September 15, 1847, in Marion, Louisiana. **Alice Douglass** (OK). Born December 22, 1860, in Sumner County, Tennessee. Daughter of Millie Elkins and Isaac Garrett. "My sisters and brothers was Frank, Susie and Mollie." **Ambrose Douglass** (FL). Born free ca. 1845 in Detroit, enslaved in North Carolina when his parents returned south to visit relatives. **Ann Drake** (MS). Born ca. 1856 in Franklin County, Mississippi, slave of H. S. Anderson. **Kate Drumgoold.** Born ca. 1855 in Vally, present-day West Virginia, near Petersburg, she saw her mother sold away from her to raise the money to keep her master out of the war. After the war she attended school, became a teacher to freedmen in the Hinton, West Virginia, area, and became an outspoken champion of civil rights. Drumgoold, *A Slave Girl's Story,* pp. 10, 32–33. **General George Washington "Wash" Dukes** (AR). Born 1855 near Perry, in Howson County, Georgia, slave of a family named Riggins. **Simon Durr** (MS). Born ca. 1847, slave of Michael Durr in Copiah County, Mississippi.

E

George Eason (GA). Born in Forsyth, Georgia, on the plantation of Jack Ormond. **John Eaton.** He was appointed by General Grant to superintend the Contraband camps under his command. John Eaton in McPherson, *The Negro's Civil War,* p. 127. **Reverend H. H. Edmunds** (IN). Born in Lynchburg, Virginia, in 1839, slave of a man named Farmer. **Ophelia Settle Egypt** (TN). At the time she conducted her interviews, she was Ophelia Settle of Clarksville, Texas. Born in 1903, a graduate of Penn State, she was a researcher for the black sociologist Charles Johnson at Fisk University in Nashville. Over the course of her career she helped expose the infamous Tuskegee study of syphilis among black sharecroppers, and played a leading role in the "Shadow of the Plantation" study of the sharecropper system. As the Depression wore on, she left Fisk to assist with relief efforts in St. Louis. She accepted a scholarship from the National Association for the Prevention of Blindness to study medicine and sociology at Washington University in St. Louis, where she was not permitted to attend classes and had to receive her lessons from a tutor. She accepted an appointment as head of social services at a hospital in New Orleans, and five years later worked as a researcher for James Weldon Johnson. She performed social work in southeast Washington, D.C., and for eleven years was the director of its first Planned Parenthood clinic, which was named for her following her death in 1981. Taped interview with Ophelia Settle Egypt, Fisk University Special Collections. **Callie Elder** (GA). "Born in Floyd County, up nigh Rome, Georgia, on Marse Billy Neal's plantation. Ann and Washington Neal was my Mammy and Pappy." **Gabe Emanuel** (MS). "I was the house boy on old Judge [Volney] Stamps's plantation. He lived about nine miles east of Port Gibson, Mississippi." In 1860, Volney Stamps listed himself as a planter. He owned $40,000 worth of real estate and $200,000 worth of other property, mostly slaves. **Jerry Eubanks** (MS). Born ca. 1848 in Atlanta, Georgia, raised in Mississippi. Son of Jerry and Alice Hamilton. "I was brought away overnight, when I was 12 years old by a speculator, named Jack Hart. Dr. Sam Hamilton of Rome, Georgia bought me. He lived in a fine house but couldn't meet the debt, and then is when I fell into the speculator's hands and was brought to Columbus, Mississippi where I was sold to Joe Eubanks for $1100." By 1860 Joseph Eubanks was living in Carroll County, Mississippi, with his family and nine slaves. **John Eubanks** (IN). Born June 6, 1836, the slave of William G. and Susanna Everett of Barren County, Kentucky. **Millie Evans** (AR). Born in North Carolina, a young woman at the time of surrender. **Minerva Evans** (MS). Born in Covington, Louisiana, daughter of Warrington Finley and Leah McGee. Slave of Fleet McGee. Widow of Albert McGee, remarried to Andy Brown. **Mose Evans** (AR). Born in the 1850s, the slave of Thad Shackleford. "Don't remember him very well. They took me away from his place when I was little." **Lorenza Ezell** (TX). Born in 1850 on the plantation of Ned Lipscomb, in Spartanburg County, South Carolina.

F

Rachel Fairley (AR). "My father, when nine years old, was put on the speculator's block and sold at Charlottesville, North Carolina. My mother was sold on the same day to a man named Paul Barringer, who refugeed her to a place near Sardis, Mississippi. Before he was sold, my father belonged to the Greers in Charlottesville." **Lewis Favor** (GA). Born in 1855 in Meriwether County near the present location of Greenville, Georgia. "Our owner was Mrs. [Nancy?] Favors . . . My father was owned by a Mr. Darden who had a plantation in this same county." **London R. Ferebee.** Born in 1849 in Currituck County, North Carolina, the slave of Edwin Cowles. He ran to the Yankees at Shiloh, North Carolina. Reunited with his family, he went to Roanoke Island, where his father taught school. He tried his hand at politics, only to be imprisoned by a white opponent. Pardoned, he became a minister in the African Methodist Episcopal Church. Ferebee, *Brief History*, p. 6. **Frank Fikes** (AR). Born 1858, slave of a "Colonel" Williams. (See Dosia Harris and Dolly Whiteside.) **Orleans Finger** (AR). Born in Tippah County, Mississippi, raised in Arkansas, daughter of Ann Toler, who was the daughter of Captain Ellis and his wife, Minerva, apparently both slaves. She did not know who her father was. Her mother was the slave of a man named Whitely. **Elizabeth Finley** (MS). Born in Lyonsboro, Alabama, October 22, 1849. "My father's name was Dave Hearn. He belong to Dr. Joe Hearn and live on his plantation not far from where we live." **John Finnely** (TX). Born ca. 1851 in Jackson County, Alabama, slave of Martin Finnely. Escaped and joined the Union Army. Farmed from 1865 to 1917, when he moved to Fort Worth, Texas. **James Fisher.** Born in Tennessee in 1817 and interviewed in Ohio in 1843. Blassingame, *Slave Testimony*, p. 238. **Ross Fitzgerald** in Fitzgerald, *A Visit to the Cities and Camps of the Confederate States*, p. 92. **Thomas Morris Fletcher.** Born free in 1834 in Harrisburg, Pennsylvania, he became an active abolitionist and colonizationist. In 1853 he moved to Liberia, where he edited the *Star of Liberia*. In 1863 he recruited black troops, and a year later served as a correspondent for the *Philadelphia Press*, covering the Eastern Theater of the war. A fundraiser for the Freedman's Bureau, he studied law and moved to Louisiana, where he served as an educator and a brigadier general of Louisiana militia. A supporter of the Exodusters — former slaves intent on settling on homesteads in the West — he died in 1892. Blackett, ed., *Thomas Morris Chester, Black Civil War Correspondent*, pp. 296–97. **Sylvia Floyd** (male) (MS). Born ca. 1852, slave of Mrs. Polly Newson of Simpson County, Mississippi. **George Fordman** (IN). He was a full-blooded Indian whose parents migrated to Alabama, where they were enslaved by a trader named Patent George. **Thornton Forrest.** Born ca. 1845 in Shelby County, Tennessee. Served at Confederate General Forrest's headquarters with a fellow slave named Ben Davis of Fayette County, who was born March 4, 1836. Brogden, Tennessee, Colored Pension Applications for CSA Service (Tennessee State Library and Archives). **M. Fowler** (AL). Slave of William and Georgiana Shepherd in Lowndes County, Alabama. **Phillis Fox** (MS). Born in Webster County near Gasville, daughter of Mallie and Easter Parks and sister of Lucy, Ann, Mary, Catherene, and Limuel. Slave of Jessie and Darkie Hughes, parents of Sarah, Betsy, Gracie, William, and Joel. The closest to Limuel or Lemuel Fox in rolls is Lewis Fox, of Company L, 6th U.S. Colored Heavy Artillery, which was organized in Natchez, Mississippi, in September 1863 and saw light service. **Ruben Fox** (MS). Born in Washington County, Mississippi, south of Greenville, slave of June and Matilda Ward. **Robert Franklin** (MS). Born 1851 in Warren County, Mississippi, son of Watson Franklin of St. Louis, and Dellia Franklin of Vicksburg, Mississippi. Brother to six boys and two sisters, named Mandy and Martha. **Dora Franks** (MS). Born in the 1830s in Choctaw County, Mississippi. "My mammy come from Virginia. Her name was Harriet Brewer. My daddy was my young Master George Brewer." **Pet Franks** (MS). Born ca. 1845 near Bartley's Ferry on the Mississippi. First owned by Harry Allen, then, when Allen's widow remarried, by James Tatum. **Mittie Freeman** (AR). Born in Orange County, Mississippi, and taken to Camden, Arkansas, on the Ouachita before the war. Slave of a Dr. Williams.

G

Mary Gaines (AR). Born ca. 1872 in Courtland, Alabama. Her grandfather served in the war, and her mother was twelve years old at the end of the war. **Clayborn**

Gantline (FL). Born January 20, 1848, in Dawson, Terrell County, Georgia, slave of Judge Williams. **Nancy Gardner** (OK). Born in 1858 in Franklin, Tennessee. Daughter of Prophet and Callie Isaiah, sister of Prophet and Billie Isaiah. Sold at age seven by a speculator named Major Clifton. "It was thirty years before my pa knew if we was still living . . . My pa started out to see me, and on his way he was drowned in the Missouri River, and I never saw him alive after we was sold." **Elisha Doc Garey** (GA). "I was born on the upper edge of Hart County, near Shoal Crick. Sarah Anne Garey was my Ma, and I was one of them shady babies. There was plenty of that kind in them times. My own sister was Rachel, and I had a half sister named Sallie what was white as anybody. John, Lindsay, David, and Joseph was my four brothers." Slave of Joe and Julia Glover. **Angie Garrett** (AL). Born in De Kalb, Mississippi, son of Betty Scott. "I had four brothers, Ember, Johnny, Jimmie, and Henry; and three sisters, Delphie, Lizzie Sue, and Frankie, and my grandmother was Susie Scott. She lived five miles from Gainesville across Noxubee Creek and I lived with her." Her mother "lived right here in Gainesville and belonged to Mr. Sam Harwood. I belonged to the Moorings and Captain Mooring run on a boat to Mobile from Aberdeen, Mississippi." **Cicero Gaulding** (MS). Born 1847, near Senatobia, Mississippi. **Octavia George** (OK). Born in Colmesneil, Texas. Daughter of Susan and "Eleck" (Alec?), and a slave of Jack Bean. **Lizzie Gibbs** (MS). A slave of Pat Henry of Hinds County, Mississippi, she married Calvin Gibbs, a famous Vicksburg, Mississippi, carriage driver who drove visiting dignitaries, including several presidents, to and from the riverfront. **Andrew Jackson Gill** (MS). Born 1855, slave of a man named Gill. There was a farmer named Joseph Gill from Franklin County, which lies across Lincoln County's northern boundary. But in 1860 he owned no slaves and was worth only $225. **James Gill** (AR). Born the slave of Tom White and his son Jeff, who was his contemporary. Taken from Alabama to Phillips County, Arkansas, "about fifteen miles down the river from Helena." **Cora Gillam** (AR). "I lived with master and mistress in Greenville, Mississippi." She said her uncle was "Thomas P. Johnson, who was a sergeant in Company G of the 54th USCI," but Gillam or her interviewer may have conflated Johnson with her husband, Isaac Gillam, who served as a jailer and constable during Reconstruction. Gillam was a sergeant in Company I of the 54th USCI, and in the 1870 and 1880 censuses he appears as a blacksmith. **Jim Gillard** (AL). Born 1860, one of eight children belonging to James and Hannah Gillard of Spring Villa, Lee County, Alabama. **Lucy (Gillum)** in Egypt, ed., *Unwritten History of Slavery*, p. 22. **Mary Gladdy** (GA). Born ca. 1853, slave of Hines Holt in Muscogee County, near Columbus, Georgia. **Jake Goodridge** (AR). Born near Jackson, Tennessee, in Madison County, Arkansas, son of Narcissus and Jacob Goodridge, and slave of Ratford and Susan Weathers. After the war Goodridge "got hungry and naked and cold many a time. I had a good master, and I thought he always treated me heap better than that. I wanted to go back, but I had no way. I made it down to St. Charles in about a year after the surrender. I started farming. I been farming ever since. In Little Rock I found a job in a ten pin alley, picking up balls. The man paid me $12 a month, next to starvation." **Margaret Goss** (MS). Claimed to be 113 years old in 1937, born the slave of John Miller of Mississippi. **Charles Graham** (AR). Born September 27, 1859, in Clarksville, Tennessee. **Mary Ella Grandberry** (AL). Born ca. 1847 in Barton, Alabama. Daughter of Adam and Margaret Keller. "My five sisters was Martha, Sarah, Harriet, Emma and Rosanna; and my three brothers was Peter, Adam, Jr., and William." **Charles Grandy** (VA). Born February 19, 1842, in Mississippi. While still an infant, he was brought to Norfolk. "His father was arrested on some pretentious charge, and the whole family was placed in prison. After their release, they were taken to a plantation near Hickory Ground, Virginia, and sold." Grandy ran away and joined Company E of the 19th Wisconsin Regiment. **Neely Gray** (AR). "I was sold from Richmond, Virginia. Dr. Jenkins bought my mother when I was a little girl." The auctioneer "put me up on the block and sold me too. I was about three years old." **Alice Green** (GA). "Charles and Milly Green was my daddy and mammy. Daddy's overseer was a man named Green, and they said he was a powerful mean sort of man. Mammy's marster was a lawyer they called Slickhead Mitchell, and he had a plantation at Helicon Springs, Georgia." **Isaiah Green** (GA). Born in 1856 at Greensboro, Georgia, son of Bob Henderson and Cleary Marlory Willis, slave of a wealthy planter named Colonel Dick Willis and his wife, Sally, who owned three thousand acres on the Oconee River. **James Green** (TX). "Half American Indian and half Negro, he was born a slave to John Williams, of Petersburg, Va., became a 'free boy,' then was kidnapped and sold in a Virginia slave market to a Texas ranchman." **Reverend __ Green.** Green was born ca. 1845 in South Carolina, the son of a slave carpenter and a house slave, and the property of a widow. In about 1857, he was sold to a trader and bought by a man in Louisiana who enjoyed getting his slave children drunk. After the war Green's owner tried to keep him and his fellow slaves in bondage, but they ran off to a Colonel Wilson of the U.S. Army, and Green ended up a preacher in Tennessee. Johnson, ed., *God Struck Me Dead*, p. 83. **George Gregory** in Armstrong, *Old Massa's People*, p. 278. **Harriet Gresham** (FL). Born on December 6, 1838, one of many biracial slaves of Edmond Bellinger in Barnwell, South Carolina. Her interview includes an extensive genealogical account of her family. **Wheeler Gresham** (GA). Born ca. 1854, son of Franklin Gresham and Barbara Booker, slave of Jabie (J. B.?) Booker, who was killed in the war. **Annie Griegg** (AR). Born in Nashville, Tennessee, slave of "Captain Walker." One sister was named Rebecca. "I never seen her no more after I was sold. I was the youngest. Bill Steel Henderson at Columbia, Tennessee, bought us both and give my sister to his widowed sister." **Lee Guidon** (AR). Born 1848 between York and Union, Arkansas. Son of Pompey and Fannie. **Betty Guwn** (IN). Born March 25, 1832, on a tobacco plantation near Canton, Kentucky.

H

Samuel Hall. Born in 1818 in Iredell County, North Carolina. In 1830 Hugh Hall inherited him from his father. After Hugh's death, Hall was sold to a Tennessee planter named William Wallace. During the Civil War he served in the CSA, and then the Union Army after Emancipation. After the war he became a farmer in Iowa. Hall, *47 Years a Slave*, pp. 22–23. **Thomas Hall** (NC). Born February 14, 1856, in Orange County, North Carolina. Son of Daniel and Backe Hall. Slave of Jim and Polly Woods. **Milton Hammond** (GA). Born October 20, 1853, in Griffin, Georgia. Slave of Bill Freeman. **Hannah Hancock** (AR). Born in Chesterfield County, South Carolina. Her mother, Chloe, was the slave cook of the widow of Hardy Sellars, who owned a number of mature male slaves. **Julia E. Haney** (AR). Born September 18,

1859, in Gallatin, Tennessee, slave of Willard and Mary Blue. **Rachel Hankins** (AR). Born 1850 in Alabama. Sold to the "Columbus" family, though none can be found in the 1860 census for Alabama, only Mississippi. **Simon Hare** (MS). Born ca. 1849, slave of "Dick Hare" near Newman, North Carolina, who moved to Alabama when Simon was ten. John Hare (no middle initial) of Clarke County, Alabama, owned six slaves in 1860, including a thirteen-year-old male who may have been Simon, and a forty-year-old slave who may have been Uncle Robert. A John Hare served as a private in the 3rd Regiment of Alabama Reserves. I cannot find a Dick or Richard Hare in either the 1850 or 1860 slave schedules for Alabama and North Carolina, only an R. J. Hare of Butler County, who is not listed with a son named John. **George W. Harmon** (OK). Born December 25, 1854, in Lamar County, Texas. Son of Charles Harmon of Tennessee and Mary Roland of Virginia, a slave of the Roland family. **Jane Smith Hill Harmon** (GA). Born ca. 1848 on the Smith plantation near Washington-Wilkes, the tenth of fourteen children. **Eda Harper** (AR). Born 1844 in Mississippi. **Emma Harper.** (See Avalena McConico.) **Frances Ellen Watkins Harper.** Born free but impoverished in 1825 in Baltimore and orphaned as a young girl, she was raised by a black uncle who taught her to read. As a young woman she began to publish poems and essays, and moved north to teach domestic science at Union Seminary in Columbus, Ohio. After encountering runaway slaves in Ohio, she became a speaker for the Anti-Slavery Society of Maine and a friend of Mrs. John Brown. After the war Harper was active in the temperance movement. She died in 1900. Brown, *Homespun Heroines*, pp. 98–103. **Abram Harris** (AR). Born in October, ca. 1846, near Greenville, South Carolina. **Dosia Harris** (GA). Born ca. 1856. Taken to Texas by his master, a "Colonel" Williams. (See Frank Fikes and Dolly Whiteside.) **Rachel Harris** (AR). Born ca. 1847, slave of Jim and Louisa Smith of Mississippi. **Shang Harris** (female) (GA). "My master was Mr. Bob Alexander. He lived in Franklin County, Georgia, just this side of Carnesville." **Virginia Harris** (MS). Born in Louisiana, about eight miles from Vicksburg, on the other side of the river. Said she was the slave of Nat Hockett of Vicksburg, but the closest I could find in Vicksburg in the 1860 slave schedules is Thomas Hackett. **B. E. Harrison** in Jordan, *Black Confederates and Afro-Yankees*, p. 133. **Jack Harrison** (TX). Owned by "Cleave Harrison," possibly Christopher C. Harrison of Muehlenburg County, Kentucky, a slaveholder who served in the 17th Kentucky Infantry (USA). His father, Joe Grant, claimed to be an ex-slave of General Ulysses S. Grant. **Letha K. Hatcher** (TX). **Matilda Hatchett** (AR). Born ca. 1838. Slave of Jackie and Nealie George of South Carolina, but born in Arkansas. **Laura Smith Haviland.** Born a Quaker in Canada on December 20, 1808. As a child she moved to New York, and as a bride to the Michigan frontier, where she helped organize the state's first abolitionist society and played a role in the Underground Railroad. Breaking with the Quakers, she became a Methodist and established an integrated, coeducational school for orphans. Widowed at the age of thirty-six, she continued her Underground Railroad activities, venturing into Ohio, Kentucky, and Arkansas. During the war she made her way down the Mississippi, assisting with the Contrabands and the Union wounded. After the war she worked with refugees in Kansas, where the town of Haviland was named in her honor. She died in 1898. Haviland, *A Woman's Life Work*, pp. 246–47. **John G. Hawkens** (AR). Born December 9, 1866, son of Frances Hawkens, who was biracial, and a white man named Young of Lamar

County, Alabama. **Toy Hawkins** (GA). Born the slave of John Poor, four miles from Belton, Anderson County, South Carolina. **George W. Hayes.** Hayes was among those who managed to escape before Fort Donelson's surrender. He was then a twelve-year-old slave whom Secessionists had pressed into service at his master's plantation in Franklin, Kentucky. In September 1862 he ran away to Yankee-occupied Nashville, and served under Sherman on his March to the Sea. In 1901 Hayes would be elected to the Ohio legislature. **Tim Haynes** (AR). A slave in Monticello, Arkansas. **Felix Haywood** (TX). He mentions as a member of his master's family a "Colman Gudlew" of South Texas. **Robert Heard** (GA). Slave of a General Heard of Georgia, son of John and Susan, whom the general bought in Virginia and brought to Georgia. **London Law Hemmett** (OK). Born December 15, 1849, on the banks of the Flint River in Georgia, son of John Hemmett and Celia Law of North Carolina, and apparently a slave of a General Brown, one of whose fellow slaves he married. **Benjamin Henderson** (GA). Born September 8, 1858, in Monticello, Jasper County, Georgia, the youngest of three children. His parents were his master, Sam Henderson, and Sam's slave Mandy Henderson. Sam never married and operated his farm with the help of his mother, Mrs. Allie Henderson. **Mack Henderson** (MS). Born in Copiah County, Mississippi, and brought by his master to Vicksburg, Mississippi, just before the Civil War. After Grant captured Vicksburg, Henderson joined the 6th U.S. Colored Heavy Artillery as a bugler. **Nettie Henry** (MS). Born ca. 1855 on "the Chile's place" on Alamucha Creek in Livingston, Alabama. "Miss Lizzie — she was Marse Chile's girl — married Marse John C. Higgins and moved to Meridian. Me and my mammy and my two sisters, Liza and Tempe, was give to Miss Lizzie." **George H. Hepworth.** A Massachusetts chaplain who traveled from plantation to plantation during the war interviewing former slaves. McPherson, *The Negro's Civil War,* pp. 56, 164–68. **Evie Herrin** (MS). Born in Copiah County, Mississippi, slave of Winnie Evans. **Florida Hewitt** (MS). Born before 1838, the slave of Joseph E. Davis, Jefferson Davis's brother. **Lulu Heyburn (White)** (IN). **Jim Polk Hightower** (MS). Possibly born in Sardis, Mississippi. **J. H. Hill** (GA). "My parents were slaves on the plantation of [Joshua] Hill, a slave owner in Madison [Morgan County], Georgia. I was born May 21, 1855." **Laura Hill** (AL). Hill was born in north Alabama. Her mother and father were Carrie and Traylor Holloway, and her brother was Maryland. **Rebecca Brown Hill** (AR). Born October 18, 1859, in Chickasaw County, Mississippi, the slave of C. B. Baldwin. **Howell Hinds** (ca. 1809–1868) was one of Jefferson Davis's boyhood friends. He owned large holdings in Jefferson and Washington counties and served in the Mississippi state legislature. He served with Mississippi troops at Shiloh; tried and failed to raise a regiment of his own; during the war was wounded twice, captured, and paroled; and returned home, only to be killed in Greenville while intervening in a fight between two of his friends. (See Holt Collier.) **Elizabeth Hines** (AR). Born ca. 1868; her parents were slaves in Baton Rouge, Louisiana. **Lee Hobby** (TN). Born in Comblin County, Kentucky. "My pappy and mammy was slaves of a man by the name of Hobby. I think the old Master was of the Hobby that was the Governor of Texas's people." **Adeline Hodge** (AR). "The first white people I belonged to were a man named Jones, who was a colonel in the war, but I can't tell you much about them, cause I was just a little girl then." Born in Bolivar County, Mississippi, sold to Ned Collins of Shubuta, Mississippi.

Minnie Hollomon (AR). One of five children of Elsie and Manuel Jones, slaves of Oswell F. Jones of Hickory Plains. **H. B. Holloway** (AR). Apparently a slave in Atlanta, Georgia. **William Hood.** Hood was born in 1833. Armstrong, *Old Massa's People*, pp. 113, 288. **Rosa Spearman Hooper.** Josephine Hooper Armstrong, Henry Condry, Bush Hooper, Alexander Nason, R. E. Potts (chief of the criminal section, Bureau of Pensions), and Henry Weaver all gave depositions in the pension file of Thomas Hooper. Long after "all the white people [were] dead that owned said slaves, and their plantations" had been "sold and resold," Rosa Hooper died in Kansas City, Missouri, having spent the rest of her widowhood as a washerwoman. **Elijah Henry Hopkins** (AR). Born in Baker County, Georgia. His father was a slave of Tom and Phoebe Hopkins, and his mother belonged to their son Robert. Born May 15, 1856, in the Barnwell district, South Carolina, slave of Tom Willingham, who owned farms in Baker County, Georgia, and South Carolina. "Old man Willingham's wife was Phoebe Hopkins." **Molly Horn** (AR). Born ca. 1860 in North Carolina, the youngest of Sarah and Jad Nelson's six children. "When I was a baby Rubin Harriett bought me and mama. His wife was Becky Harriett. Ma was too old to sell without me. They didn't want to sell me, but they couldn't sell her without me." Horn's father, however, "didn't get to come to Arkansas. That parted them. After freedom her other children come. I heard Ma say how they kept Papa dodged round from the Yankees." **Cora L. Horton** (AR). Slave in Arkansas. **Pinkey Howard** (AR). Born ca. 1850 in Hillsboro, Tennessee, slave of the Holbrook family. ___ **Huddleston** in Egypt, ed., *Unwritten History of Slavery*, p. 34. **Carrie Hudson** (GA). Born ca. 1863, daughter of Phil and Frances Rucker, slaves of Joe Squire Rucker near Ruckersville, in Elbert County, Georgia. Her interview contains an extensive list of her kin. Married to Edwin Jones, and after his death Charlie Hudson (see following entry). **Charlie Hudson** (GA). Born March 27, 1858, in Elbert County, Georgia. "Ma lived on de Bell plantation and Marse Matt Hudson owned my Pa and kept him on de Hudson place. There was seven of us children: Will, Bynam, John and me was the boys, and the gals was Amanda, Liza Ann, and Gussie." Husband of Carrie Hudson (see previous entry). **Annie Huff** (GA). Slave of Travis Huff "on the Houston Road near Seven Bridges," Georgia. Her oldest daughter was named Mary. **Bryant Huff** (GA). "Son of Daniel and Janie Huff, who were born on neighboring plantations between Camack and Augusta. They were married while they still belonged to separate owners, but Jesse Rigerson bought Daniel so he could live with his wife and family when they moved to Warren County, where Bryant was born." **Louvenia Huff** (AR). Born ca. 1868, one of thirteen children, slave first of a Whitfield and then a Dr. Hatch of Aberdeen, Mississippi. **Louis Hughes.** Born in Virginia, bought and sold repeatedly, Hughes lived in the McGee household in Pontotoc County, Mississippi, at the time of the Civil War. After the war he became a nurse and businessman in Wisconsin. Hughes, *Thirty Years a Slave*, pp. 63, 86, 114–20, 204. **Samuel Hughes** in pension file of Charles Macklin (Koon) (NARA). **Margret Hulm** (AR). Born March 5, 1840, in Hardeman County, Tennessee, slave of James Pruitt. **Tom Hunley** (MS). Born ca. 1860, slave of Jim Baskin of Pocahontas, Mississippi. **Emma Hurley** (GA). Oldest of thirteen children of Margaret (Hurley?), on a plantation in Wilkes County, Georgia, "on the line of Oglethorpe." Owned by (Sarah A. or Sarah P. Hurley?), herself the mother of "four boys, and two girls, all grown. All four of the men went to the war and three of them died of sickness caught in the war." **Alice Hutcheson** (GA). Born ca. 1861 in Monroe County, Georgia. Daughter of William Hanson and Harriet Bell, slave of Cal Robinson.

I

Addison Ingram (or Engram) (AL). Born December 14, 1830, in Russell County, Alabama, slave of Miss Frances Ingram and then Bat Ingram. **Everett Ingram** (AL). Slave from Russell County, Alabama. Later Addison and Everett's father fled with them to the Yankees. **Squire Irvin** (MS). Born ca. 1849 near Nashville, Tennessee, son of Louis and Eveline Irvin, brother of Albert and Liza, and slave of a widow named Webster who married a Colonel Irvin. Squire was raised by his grandmother Stacey Ann. **Hannah Irwin** (AL). Born on the Bennett plantation near Louisville, Alabama, son of Sam and Hester. **Jack Island** (AR). Slave of Charles Bullock of Manchester, Dallas County, Arkansas. **Johanna Isom** (MS). Born ca. 1857 and lived during the war in Oxford, Mississippi. Slave of Jacob Thompson and servant to his daughter-in-law Mrs. Macon Thompson.

J

Dora Jackson (MS). Born ca. 1858 in Richton, Mississippi. Daughter of George and Martha Hinton, maternal granddaughter of Bud Hinton. **Easter Jackson** (GA). Born shortly before the war in Troup County, Georgia. Her mother, Frances Wilkerson, was a house slave bought by Tom Dix from a Mr. Snow of Virginia. Her father, Silas Wilkerson, was bought by the neighboring Wilkerson family. **Emma Jackson** (MS). Born July 4, 1854, four miles east of Holly Springs, Mississippi, slave of Joe Howard. **Isabella Jackson** (OK). Born in Louisiana, slave of "Dr. Joe Jackson." **Mariah Jackson** (MS). (See Violet Shaw, her niece.) **Martin Jackson** (TX). Born 1847 in Victoria County, Texas, slave of Alvy Fitzpatrick. Served in both the Civil War and World War I. "This sounds as if I liked the war racket," he said. "But, as a matter of fact, I never wore a uniform — gray coat or khaki coat — or carried a gun, unless it happened to be one worth saving after some Confederate soldier got shot." **Mattie Jackson.** Mattie (Jane) Jackson's father was a slave preacher named Westly Jackson and her mother was Ellen Turner, a slave owned by James Harris. Turner was sold to Charles Canory of St. Charles County, Missouri. In addition to Mattie, she bore Sarah Ann and Esther. Jackson and her mother then moved with their master to Bremen, Missouri, near St. Louis. Her father escaped to Chicago, where he worked as a minister. The rest of the family tried to follow him but was captured in Illinois and sold to William Lewis of St. Louis, and six years later her mother married another slave, George Brown, by whom she had two children. Jackson, *The Story of Mattie J. Jackson*, pp. 9–11, 23–24. **Snovey Jackson** (GA). Born in Clarksville, Virginia. Bought by James Jackson of Baldwin County, Georgia, who later moved to La Grange, Georgia. Returned to Baldwin County after the war. **Squires Jackson** (FL). Born September 14, 1841, in Madison, Florida, and moved to Jacksonville in 1844. **Turner Jacobs** (MS). Born July 9, 1855. Son of Jacob and Rebecca Ward. Slave of

Dr. Amos Ward, who moved from Georgia to a farm about a mile and a half east of
Gibson, Mississippi. **Thomas James.** Born a slave in 1804 in Canajoharie, New York,
owned by Asa Kimball, who sold his mother, brother, and elder sister around 1812 to
a slaveholder in Smithtown. In 1821 James was sold to Cromwell Bartlett of the same
neighborhood, who promptly traded him for a yoke of steers, a colt, and "some additional property." James, *Life*, pp. 16–17, 21–22. **Monroe Franklin Jamison.** Born
November 27, 1848, near Rome, Georgia. Son of George and Lethia Shorter, slaves
of Alford Shorter. "Mr. Shorter having moved from Georgia to Greensport, Alabama,
my mother and her two sons, Frank (the writer) and John, were sold to a Mr.
Eli Denson." Jamison became an editor, publisher, and eventually a bishop of the
conciliationist Colored African Methodist Episcopal Church in America. Jamison,
Autobiography, pp. 30–31, 34. **Lewis Jefferson** (MS). Said he was born ca. 1853 in
Pike County, Mississippi, slave of Calvin Newsome, but no Calvin Newsome appears
in Pike County censuses or schedules for 1850 and 1860, and the closest to a Calvin
Newsome in the CSA was a Caswell Newsom of the 18th Mississippi Cavalry, which
suffered enormous losses in the war. **Henry Jenkins** in Mellon, *Bullwhip Days*, p.
343. Born ca. 1850 in Sumter County, South Carolina, slave of a Mr. Reese, then sold
to Joseph and Sara Howell. Son of Emma Jenkins and a slave named Dinkins owned
by a family named Hall. **Mahala (Hailie) Jewel** (GA). Daughter of Tuggle and
Gracie Wright, probably slaves of Joseph H. McWherter, who owned thirty. Joseph
H. owned $3,000 worth of real estate and $18,750 in personal property. His father,
James H., owned $6,000 and $38,000, respectively, and named one son Hambleton,
which may have been both men's middle name, shortened to "Hamp." Jewel refers to
a Miss Mary, who was in James H.'s household. I therefore conclude that her master
was Joseph H. McWherter. **Adaline Johnson** (AR). Born on the Strickland plantation, twelve miles from the capital, Jackson, Mississippi. Her mother was born on one
of Jim Battle's plantations in Edgecombe County, North Carolina, to which her elderly master, Jim Battle, sent Adaline and her mother before the war. **Alice Johnson**
(AR). Born ca. 1860 in Crystal Springs, Mississippi, "way below Jackson." Daughter
of Diana Benson and Joe Brown, slave of a family named Ray. Moved to Arkansas in
1911. **Benjamin Johnson** (GA). Slave of Luke and Betsy Johnson of Georgia, whose
children were "named Jim, Tom, Will, and Dorn, Janie, Mary, Catherine, and Lissie."
Brandon Johnson. Born ca. 1840 in Kentucky, sold to a farmer near Vicksburg,
Mississippi. He refused to be whipped, threatening whoever tried with an ax. Fleeing
the Rebels, he joined the Union Army, and was mustered out in Mobile in 1866.
Johnson, *Battleground Adventures*, pp. 217–223. **Fanny Johnson** (AR). Born 1861
in Nashville, Tennessee, slave of Woodfork. **George Johnson** (AR). Born September 28, 1862, in Richmond, Virginia, son of Benjamin and Phoebe Johnson. Slave of a
doctor named Johnson who lived on Charleston and Morgan Street. **George Johnson** (MN). Born June 7, 1862, possibly in Missouri. **Isaac Johnson.** Born 1844 on
the banks of the Green River in Kentucky. Son of Richard and Jane Yeager. His older
brother was Louis, his younger brothers Ambrose and Eddie. "I was next to Louis in
age." Grandson of an Irishman named Griffin Yeager. Sold at Bardstown to William
"Madinglay" (Mattingly). Johnson, *Slavery Days in Old Kentucky*, p. 40. **Mag Johnson** (AR). Born ca. 1870. Her mother was a slave owned by Ed McGhee in Virginia.
Brought in a coffle to Somerville, Tennessee, and hid from Yankee cavalry in a cave
for two weeks. She was sold to Ben Trotter in Tennessee, and was "freed a long time

before she knowed of." **Mandy Johnson** (AR). "Oh my Lord, them Yankees come in just like blackbirds." Born ca. February 1839, in Bastrop, Louisiana, slave of John Lovett. **Prince Johnson** (MS). Johnson's "grandpa, Peter; grandma, Millie; my pa, John; and my ma, Frances, all come from Alabama to Yazoo County," Mississippi, with their master, D. C. Love. **Saint Johnson** (AR). "My father's name was Wiley Johnson. He was ninety years old when he died. He was born in Cave Spring, Georgia, in Floyd County. My mother was born in the same place." **Abraham Jones** (AL). Born of black and Indian lineage on August 1, 1825, in Russell County, Alabama, and taken to Blount County during the war to run a gristmill. **Cynthia Jones** (AR). Born in Drew County, Arkansas, slave of Simpson and Adeline Dabney. **Edward Jones** (MS). Born ca. 1855 in Montgomery County, Alabama. "My mother's name was Sophia Jones. The young Miss in my mother's family married Mr. Tom Dickerson and moved to his home in Hinds County, Mississippi." (See also Davis, *An Honorable Defeat,* p. 297.) **Ira Jones** (IN). Son of Ben Franklin Jones, a slave on the Tandy farm in Kentucky, almost directly across the river from the son's home. **Lidia Jones** (AR). Born ca. 1843 on the Peacock plantation in Mississippi, later moved to Arkansas. Slave of John Patterson. **Liza "Cookie" Jones** (AR). Nicknamed Cookie because "I cooked so much." Born ca. 1850 near Jackson, Tennessee, daughter of Kate and slave of "a good Christian woman." **Mandy Jones** (MS). Born ca. 1857, daughter of Wesley and Jinny, slave of Charlie and Patsy Stewart of Noxubee County, Mississippi. **Myra Jones** (MS). Born in 1849 and owned during slavery time by Robert Clark of Jackson, Mississippi. Her father lived in Rankin. **Oliver Jones** (MS). Born ca. 1858 in Amite County, Mississippi, on the Fourth of July. "Me and my mammy belonged to Marse George H. Mortimer."

K

Elizabeth Keckley. Born Elizabeth Hobbs, ca. 1819, in Hillsborough, North Carolina. Daughter of George and Agnes Hobbs. Preyed upon by her master's neighbor, she gave birth to a biracial son named George. Married James Keckley, who turned out to be a drunk. After his death, she bought her freedom and moved to Baltimore, where she opened a school of etiquette for black girls. After working as a seamstress for the Lincolns, she served as president of the first Black Contraband Relief Association and wrote her memoir, whose publisher withdrew it from publication at the insistence of the late President's son, the censorious Robert Lincoln. She died in 1907. Keckley, *Behind the Scenes,* pp. 29, 61–74, 90–95, 121, 165–66. **Tines Kendricks** (AR). Born ca. 1833 in Crawford County, Georgia; slave of Arch Kendricks and his "fractious and wicked" son, Sam. Called "Tiny" because of his short stature, he was the biracial son of an overseer and a slave. **Emmaline Kilpatrick** (GA). Slave of Judge William Moore. She was interviewed by her master's granddaughter, Sarah H. Hall, of Athens, Georgia. **Frances Kimbrough** (GA). Born in Harris County, Georgia. Said she was a slave of "Jessie Kimbrough." The only Kimbrough slaveholders in Harris County in 1860 were Henry and Raiford. **William Kinnegy.** His master's name was asterisked out in his account, but if his last name derived from his master's, he may have been the slave of the large and prominent Kincey family of Jones County, North Carolina. Colyer, *The Services of the Freed-*

People. **Nicey Kinney** (GA). Born 1851 in Jackson County, between Athens and Jefferson; daughter of Phineas (a slave of a man named Hatton) and Caroline. **Mollie Kinsey** (GA). Born and raised in Washington, Washington County, Georgia. **Mary Ann Kitchens** (MS). Born in Crystal Springs, Mississippi, ca. June 1851, daughter of Wilson and Harriet Ervin, slaves of the Ervin and Cooper families, respectively. **George L. Knox.** Born 1841 in Rutherford County, Tennessee, slave of W. C. Knox before he ran off to the Union lines. Knox, *Slave and Freeman.* **Betty Krump** (AR). Born after the war, but her parents were slaves. "Mother come to Helena, Arkansas, from Lake Charles, Louisiana. She had twelve children." Parents owned by Thomas Henry McNeil. "He treated them awful bad."

L

Barney A. Laird (AR). Born ca. 1856 in Panola County, Mississippi. **Solomon Lambert** (AR). Slave of Jordon and Judy Lambert of Arkansas. **Frank Larkin** (AR). Born ca. 1860 in Virginia, the slave of "a man named Rhodes. When I was a little fellow, me and my mother was sold separate. My mother was sent to Texas and a man named Larkin bought me." **William Lattimore** (AR). Born a slave of Absalom Myers of Canton, Mississippi, who then moved them to a large plantation "near Byhalia in Marshall County," Mississippi. **Bessie Lawson** (AR). "I was born in Georgia. My mama was brought from Virginia to one of the Carolina states, then to Georgia. She was sold twice. I don't recollect but one of her masters. I heard her speak of Master Bracknell." Her mother and father were Sallie and Matthew "Matt" Bracknell. **Joseph Lawson.** Identified by Jacqueline E. A. Lawson. He is identified as "the Colored Cooper" in Johnson, *Battleground Adventures,* pp. 143–49. **William Mack Lee.** Born 1835 in Westmoreland County, Virginia. "I was raised at Arlington Heights, in the house of General Robert E. Lee, my master." Lee, *History,* pp. 3–4, 8–9. **Adeline Rose Lennox** (IN). Born October 25, 1849, in Paris, Tennessee. **Mandy Leslie** (AL). "Then us stop and took up on a place not far from Montgomery, on Mr. Willis Biles' place. Us live there till I was grown woman, and Mr. Biles sure was a good man to live with and he treat us right every year." Slave from Alabama. **Alice Lewis** (MD). Born 1853 in Wilkes County, Georgia, slave of a family named Wakefield. **Bettie Lewis** (GA). Born May 25, 1855, near Bull Creek in Chattahoochee County, Georgia, the slave of Owen T. Thomas. (See William Lewis, her husband.) **Dellie Lewis** (AL). Born in Washington County, Alabama, slave of Winston Hunter. **George Lewis** (GA). Born December 17, 1849, in Pensacola, Florida. One of the fourteen children of Charles and Sophie Lewis, two of whom were girls. His parents belonged to different owners. However, his father's master, Jonathan Brosnahan, allowed him to visit his wife on the plantation of her owner, Mrs. Caroline Bright. A few years before the Civil War, Mrs. Bright married a Dr. Bennett Ferrel and moved to his home in Troup County, Georgia. **Talitha Island Lewis** (AR). Born 1852 in Goldsboro, Johnston County, North Carolina, slave of Maria Whitley and then her son James. **Thomas Lewis** (IN). Born 1857 in Spencer County, Kentucky. **William Lewis** (GA). William was born July 30, 1854, a slave of Alex Robertson in Muscogee County, Georgia, about seven miles south of Columbus. (See his wife, Bettie Lewis.) **Amos Lincoln** (TX). Born ca. 1852, a slave of Else

Guide on a Delta plantation about fifty miles from New Orleans. **Minerva Lofton** (AR). Born after the Civil War. Her mother was among the Parks slaves who turned back to Arkansas. **Kluie Lomack** (AR). Born ca. 1859 in Tennessee, slave of Miss Lucy Ann Dillard. Her father belonged to a family named Crowder. **Billy Abraham Longslaughter** (AL). Born near Richmond, Virginia. Gives the same last name to his master, but no Longslaughters or Slaughters turn up in 1850 or 1860 slave schedules. **Frank Loper** (CO). Loper remained with the Davis family "as a personal servant. I went with one of the daughters to Memphis Tennessee," then emigrated to Colorado, where he worked as a waiter and a doorman at the Denver Hotel. **John Love** (TX). Born ca. 1861, slave of John Smelly of Bibb County, Alabama. "Uncle Sam and Uncle John, was the oldest — and Uncle Henry," recalled Hannah Hancock. "They was the men on the farm" who "went right on with the work." (See also Hannah Hancock.) **Louis Love** (TX). Born ca. 1846, the slave of Don Caffery of St. Mary Parish, Louisiana. **Nat Love.** Born a slave in 1854 in Davidson County, Tennessee, brother of Sally and Jordan. Slave of Robert Love. After the war he went west and became "Deadwood Dick," one of the most famous cowboys and scouts of his day. When the demand for cowboys dwindled, he became a Pullman porter. He died in 1921. Love, *Life and Adventures,* p. 15. **James Lucas** (MS). An ex-slave of Jefferson Davis, sold to L. Chambers before the war. **Louis Lucas** (AR). Born in 1855 on Bayou Bartholomew near Pine Bluff, Jefferson County, Arkansas, slave of a family named Brumbaugh.

M

Chaney Mack (MS). Apparently the slave of B. W. Jernigan of Marion, South Carolina. **Dice Macy.** Macy was said to have been the slave of William Macy, the owner of Riverside plantation in Afton, Tennessee. Robinson, *Aunt Dice,* pp. 69–70, 79–80. **Primous Magee** (MS). Born May 15, 1859, slave of Dixon Magee of Lawrence County, Mississippi. **John Majors** (TX). Raised in Memphis, refugeed to Mississippi. **Jacob Manson** (NC). Born ca. 1842 in Warren County, North Carolina, slave of Colonel Bun Eden, who "liked some of the Negro womans too good." According to Manson, a woman on a neighboring plantation shot her husband, James Shaw, to death for sleeping with his slaves. **Ella Maples** (TX). **Elijah P. Marrs.** Born in 1840 near Lexington, Kentucky. After running off and joining the Union Army, he taught school in Simpsonville and New Castle, Kentucky. Ordained a Baptist minister in 1875, he established the Kentucky Normal and Theological Institute with his brother in 1879 and served as pastor until 1885. **Martin Marvel.** "A portrait of Martin Marvel, Negro Civil War hero of Washington County, will be unveiled Sunday, June 19, 1938, at 2:30 P.M., in the Martin Marvel Library for Negroes, on North Broadway." *Greenville* (MS) *Delta-Star,* June 15, 1938. **James William Massie.** Dr. Massie was a Presbyterian minister from Manchester active in Britain's antislavery movement. During the war he toured America and wrote a book intended to sway British public opinion in favor of the North. Massie, *America,* p. 343. **Susan Matthews** (GA). No names or dates given in her interview. **Ann May** (MS). Born ca. 1841, a slave of Leander Alford on a plantation between Auburn Camp Ground and

Johnston Station, Mississippi. "I was a grown woman with four children when the war broke out." **John McAdams** (TX). Born ca. 1849 in Texas, slave and possibly son of John McAdams. **Sam McAllum** (MS). Born September 2, 1842, thirteen miles north of DeKalb in Kemper County, Mississippi, slave of the Stephenson family. His father belonged to Lewis Barnes. **Tom McAlpin** (AL). Born June 1844 in Martersville, Alabama, the slave of "Dr. Augustus McAlpin." **Lucy Pulliam McBee** (MS). Born 1871. Her mother, Judie, was a slave of Robert Pulliam in Buena Vista, Mississippi. **Charlie McClendon** (AR). Born ca. 1859 in Jefferson County, Arkansas, slave of William E. Johnson. **Lizzie McCloud** (AR). Born ca. 1835 in Davidson County, Tennessee, slave of Elizabeth Williams, wife of a soldier whose pension she still collected at the age of 104. "Them Yankees wasn't playing; they was fighting. Yes, Jesus!" **Avalena McConico** (AR). Born 1888, told stories about her grandmother Emma Harper, who was born in Chesterville, Mississippi, the slave of Jim and Corrie Dozier. **Joe McCormick** (GA). Born ca. 1847. "Joe's father was born in Wilcox County and was owned by a Mr. Mitchell. The master's daughter married a man by the name of McCormick, and he was given to her. Maria Hamilton, his mother, was born in Norfolk, Virginia, and brought to Pulaski County by speculators and sold to Mr. John Harrell." **Ike McCoy** (AR). Born 1868, related the stories his slave parents told him. **Mary F. McCray.** Born on May 26, 1837, the daughter of Jonathan and Mary Taylor. Her freeborn father was born in Jefferson County, Kentucky, the son of his master. Her mother was a slave from Hamilton County, Kentucky. Her mistress died in 1859. McCray, *Life,* p. 11. **John McElroy** was a white escapee from Andersonville prison who observed that "in the presence of a white Rebel," a slave's face "took the shape of stupid, open-mouthed wonder, something akin to the look on the face of the rustic lout, gazing for the first time upon a locomotive." But out of sight of the Rebels, "the blank, vacant face lighted up with an entirely different expression." McElroy, *Andersonville,* p. 135. **Hannah McFarland** (OK). Born February 29, 1853, in Georgetown, South Carolina. Daughter of a freeman named James Gainey and a slave named Katie. "My mother was the slave of the Sampsons, some Jews. My father was the richest Negro in South Carolina during this time. He bought all three of we children for $1,000 apiece, but them Jews just wouldn't sell Mamma. They was mighty sweet to her." **Henry Lewis McGaffey** (MS). Born June 23, 1853, in Lake Charles, Louisiana, slave of Otis McGaffey, "and he was an Irishman right from Ireland. He had a brother named John, and mammy said he was my pappy." **Leah McGee.** Slave of Fleet and "Lozaine" McGee. (See Minerva Evans.) **Liza McGhee** (MS). Born near Meadville, Franklin County, Mississippi. Daughter of Pete and Lanny Jones, slave of Jim and Luella Smith. **Susan Mcintosh** (GA). Born in November 1851 in Oconee County, Georgia, slave of Judge William Stroud, daughter of Mary Jen and Christopher Harris, whom L. G. Harris bought from a man named Hudson, of Elbert County, Georgia, who turned him over to his niece, "Miss Lula Harris, when she married Marster Robert Taylor." Mcintosh's siblings were "Nanette and Ella, what was next to me; me; Isabells, Martha, Mary, Diana, Lila, William, Gus, and the twins what was born dead; and Harden. He was named for a Dr. Harden what lived here then." **Waters McIntosh** (AR). Born 1861 to fourteen-year-old Lucy Sanders and a white man named Sumter Durant, who was killed in the CSA. Slave of Dr. J. M. Sanders. Sold at age one to William Carter of

Cartersville, Georgia. **Alex McKinney** (MS). Born in Montgomery County, Mississippi. "My papa was Stephen McKinney and my mamma was Sylvia. My brothers and sisters was Myles, George, Mack, Alfred, Willis, Mary, Sarah, Emily, Susan, Anselary and me." Slave of William Kent, "and a mean old man he was. Mistus name was Ann." **Abe McKlennan** (MS). Slave of Jackson Burkett on the Pearl River in Mississippi. **Victoria McMullen** (AR). Born 1883. Her grandparents were slaves in Louisiana and Texas. **Nap McQueen** (TN). Born in Tennessee, son of Bill and Nellie McQueen, and slave of the McQueen family. **William "Shug" McWhorter** (GA). Born ca. 1858 in Greene County, Georgia. Son of Allen and Martha McWhorter; slave of Joe McWhorter. "Me and Annie, Ella, Jim, and Tom was all the children in our family." **Louis Meadows** (AL). Slave of Porter Meadows, born between Opelika and Columbus in Lee County, Georgia. **Minerva Meadows** (AL). Born ca. 1857. Slave of James and Haley Combs. In 1860 James Combs of Chamber County, Alabama, owned fourteen slaves, none of whom were Meadows's age, which may indicate that she was born later than 1857. **Frank Menefee** (AL). Born ca. 1853 in Loachapoka, Alabama, maternal grandson of Milton and Patsy Footman of Meridian, Mississippi, son of Monroe and Susan Menefee, brother of Patsy, Sally, Lula, Mary, Melvina, and Philmore. Susan Menefee came from Jefferson County and Monroe from Gold Hill, Alabama, and belonged to Willis Menefee. **Josh Miles** (TX). Born 1859 in Richmond, Virginia, slave of a man named Miles, who "owned three plantations out a few miles, and about fifteen hundred Negroes." **Annette Milledge** (GA). Born ca. 1854 in Namburg, Georgia. "Annette's master, Mr. Ransome, was not a planter. He had corn fields, but his business was general storekeeping. Her father, a free Negro who came from Virginia, did his part by his 21 children." **George Washington Miller** (MS). Born March 15, 1856, in Spartanburg, South Carolina, son of Washington Young and Emaline Hobby, brother of Walter Silas, Callie, and Florence Miller. His mother was sold to the Young family, whose daughter married Dr. Pickney Wyatt Miller and moved to Batesville in Panola County, Mississippi, before the war. **Hardy Miller** (AR). Born December 25, 1852, in Sumter County, Georgia, slave of Bright and Lizzie Harring, and refugeed to Arkansas during the war. "My father belonged to a different owner." **Joseph Miller** in Berlin et al., eds., *Free At Last*, pp. 493–95. **Matilda Miller** (AR). Born at Boone Hill, "about twelve miles north of DeWitt," Arkansas, a slave of the Boone family, whose daughter married Judge Richard Gamble and brought Miller to Crockett's Bluff. **Mintie Maria Miller** (TX). Born ca. 1862, owned by a Dr. Massie of Galveston, Texas. **Richard Miller** (IN). Born January 12, 1843, in Danville, Kentucky. His mother was a British subject, born in India, who was brought to America "by a group of people who didn't want to be under the English government." They migrated from Canada to Detroit, then moved to Danville, Kentucky, where Miller's mother married a slave and bore five children. "After slavery was abolished, they bought a little farm a few miles from Danville, Kentucky." **W. D. Miller** (AR). Born in Raleigh, North Carolina; his father's uncle John House brought about one hundred families from North Carolina to Quittenden County, Mississippi, when Miller was seven years old. **Charley Mitchell** (TX). Born 1852, slave of Nat Terry, a Lynchburg, Virginia, baker. **Alex Montgomery** (MS). Born ca. 1853 in Clyde County, Georgia, near Cary Springs, slave of William Montgomery. ___ **Moore** in Egypt, ed., *Unwritten History of Slavery*, p. 34. **A. M. "Mount" Moore** (TX). Born ca. 1846, slave of W. R. Sherrad. **John Moore**

(TX). Son of Americus Moore and grandson of his mother's white master. Slave of John and Molly Moore of Tennessee. **Patsy Moore** (AR). Mother sold to Daphney Hull in Jamestown, Virginia. Father born in Georgia, slave of the Williams family. Patsy and her mother were the slaves of William Hull, who lived "on the road to Holly Springs," Georgia. **Van Moore** (TX). Born ca. 1857 near Lynchburg, Virginia, slave of the Cunningham family. While Van was still a baby, his owner moved to a plantation near Cromby, Texas. **Ada Moorehead** (AR). Born in Huntsville, Alabama. **Mary Jane "Mattie" Mooreman** (AR). **Reverend Henry Clay Moorman** (IN). Born October 1, 1854, in slavery on the Moorman plantation in Breckinridge County, Kentucky. **Evelina Morgan** (AR). Born ca. 1855 in Wedgeboro, North Carolina, the slave of Confederate and, after the war, U.S. Congressman Thomas Samuel Ashe (1812–1887). **Charity Morris** (AR). Born near the North Carolina coast. "I was a grown woman" by the end of the war. "Ole Master Amos brought us on as far as Fordyce [Arkansas] and turned us loose." **Komma Morris** (AR). Slave of a man named McCaslin. **Tom Morris** (MS). Born ca. 1855 in Virginia, sold to Joe Bowen, who sold him to Dr. Reeber, in Rankin County, Mississippi. **George Morrison** (IN). Born ca. 1857, the slave of A. G. Ray in Union County, Kentucky. **Charlie Moses** (MS). Born 1853, slave of "mean and cruel" Jim Rankin of Marion County, Mississippi. **Claiborne Moss** (AR). Born June 18, 1857, in Washington County, Georgia, fifteen miles from Sandersville. Slave of Archie Duggins. **Mose Moss** (AR). Born in 1875 in Yell County, Arkansas. Son of Henry Moss, a Virginia slave born in 1851 who ran away and joined the Confederate Army in Tennessee. **S. O. Mullins** (AR). "I was born at Brittville, Alabama. My parents' names was George W. Mullins and Millie. They had, to my recollection, one girl and three boys." Wallace moved to Phillips County, Arkansas, before the war. **Melissa Munson** (MS). Born ca. 1835, the slave of Colonel J. R. Binford. **Henry Murray** (MS). Born September 17, 1840, in Dallas County, Alabama. Son of Joe and Malinda Murray. "My brothers and sisters was Nelson, Joe, Jeff, Liza, Ada and Martha." Slave of Charles Murray. **Robert Murray** in Armstrong, *Old Massa's People*, p. 269.

N

Wylie Nealy (AR). Born 1852 in Gordon County, South Carolina, slave of a family named Conley. **Henri Necaise** (MS). Born the oldest son of a white Frenchman, Anatole Necaise, and a slave in Harrison County, nineteen miles from Pass Christian, "along the ridge road from the swamp near Wolf River." **Henry Nelson** (AR). Born in Crittenden County, Arkansas, across the river from Memphis, Tennessee. **James Henry Nelson** (AR). Born the slave of Henry Stanley of Athens, Alabama. Moved to Pulaski, Tennessee, "and left me with young mistress to take care of things." **Lizzie Norfleet** (MS). Born the slave of Ferdinand Norfleet in Quitman County, Mississippi. Child of Jack and Sallie Flagg of Tennessee. **Solomon Northrup** in Osofsky, ed., *Puttin' On Ole Massa*, p. 253. **Hester Norton** (MS). Born before the war on Cicily Island, Louisiana. **Glascow (Glasgow) Norwood** (MS). Born ca. 1852, slave of John Norwood (whose son Donald worked as an overseer) in Simpson County, Mississippi. **General Jefferson Davis Nunn** (AL). Son of Abraham and Anne Nunn, slaves of Sam and Jane Nunn.

O

John Ogee (TX). Born ca. 1841 in Texas. Slave of Alfred Williams. **Jane Oliver** (AR). Born 1856. "Bradley County was where we lived before we went to Texas and afterward. Colonel Ed Hampton's plantation joined the Rawls plantation on the Arkansas River where it overflowed the lead." **Mark Oliver** (MS). Born 1856. Son of Jim and Fannie Oliver. Slave of (Mr.) June Ward of Washington County, Mississippi. **William O'Neal.** Born December 16, 1827, in Woodville, Mississippi, slave of Alec Gray. Became a real estate speculator and merchant. O'Neal, *Life*, p. 42. **Jane Osbrock** (AR). Born ca. 1847 within three miles of Camden, Arkansas. **George Owen** (GA). Born in Pleasant Mill District, Talbot County, Georgia, on the plantation and as the property of Jim Owen. As an old man, he observed that "white folks ain't grand and liberal like they used to be."

P

Anne Page (AR). Born ca. 1852 in Union County, Arkansas, about a mile from Bear Creek. No Jimmersons in the 1850 slave schedules, but there was a Jimmerson family in Scott County, Arkansas, in 1860, and the 1860 slave schedules show two ten-year-old girls among the fourteen slaves of Seabarn Jimmerson of Boone Township, Columbia County, Arkansas. **Jim and Martha Parke** in Armstrong, *Old Massa's People*, pp. 284, 312. **Allen Parker.** Born in Chowan, North Carolina, son of Millie Parker and Jeff "No-Eared" Ellick. Slave of Peter Parker. Parker, *Recollections*, pp. 78–79. **Ann Parker** (NC). Slave of Abner Parker of Wake County, North Carolina. **Fannie Parker** (AR). Born ca. 1861. Daughter of Edmond and Rowena Parker, slaves of a Colonel Parker of Lawrence County, Arkansas. **Anna Parkes** (GA). Her father was "Olmstead Lumpkin, and Ma was Liza Lumpkin, and us belonged to Judge Joe Henry Lumpkin. Us lived at the Lumpkin home place on Prince Avenue" in Athens, Georgia. **Richard Parrott** (IN). Son of Amos Parrott, who served as a slave in the American Revolution. Amos lived on the Kentucky plantation of his commander, Colonel Richard Parrott, but moved to Ben Smith's plantation, where Richard was born. After the war, he moved with his wife to Mitchell, Indiana, where his son became a schoolteacher. **Amy Elizabeth Patterson** (IN). Born July 12, 1850, daughter of Louisa Street and slave of a merchant named John Street, in Cadiz, Trigg County, Kentucky. **Frank A. Patterson** (AR). Born ca. 1849 in Raleigh, North Carolina, slave of Thomas Johnson Cater. **Haywood Patterson** (IN). **Sarah Jane Patterson** (AR). Born January 17, 1848, lived in Bartow County, Georgia, during the war. **Louisa Brown Pearl** in Hoobler, *Cities Under Siege*, pp. 18–19. **Cella Perkins** (AR). Born near Macon, Georgia. **Lu Perkins** (TX). Born in the early 1850s, slave of the Holmes family of Tishomingo County, Mississippi. **Dinah Perry** (AR). Born in Alabama, taken as a baby to Pine Bluff, Arkansas. **Patsy Perryman** (OK). Born ca. 1857, the slave of a Cherokee named Taylor in the Caney Creek settlement in present-day Oklahoma. **Rebecca Phillips** (MS). Born about nine miles from Vicksburg, "slave of Mr. and Mrs. [Whitaker] (Mr. Rob and Miss Fannie). Their mother, Miss

Celia, lived with them, and she was my old Miss." In Warren County there was a W. G. and Martha Whitaker with a one-year-old daughter named Fannie; an R. Whitaker with a twenty-seven-year-old wife named Cecilia and a son, John; and an Agnes C. (Celia) Whitaker, age fifty-one, in the household of an R. C. Day. **Louis Joseph Piernas** (MS). Born March 11, 1856, in Bay St. Louis, near the Cowan settlement. "I was born free, and so were all my fore parents. Some of them fought with Jackson in the Battle of New Orleans." Piernas was a political figure in Bay St. Louis during the 1880s and 1890s. **Allan Pinkerton.** Born 1819 in Glasgow, Scotland, and immigrated to the United States. Moved to Chicago and became a deputy sheriff. In 1852 he formed the Pinkerton Detective Agency. In 1861 he was given the task of guarding Abraham Lincoln, and after the war he chased Frank and Jesse James and infiltrated the Molly Maguires. He died in 1884. McPherson, *The Negro's Civil War,* p. 147. **Dempsey Pitts** (MS). Born December 10, 1837, near Charlotte, Cabarrus County, North Carolina. "My father Ned, and my mother Liza, and all their children, was born there too. I had five brothers, Jerry, Tom, Dave, Miles, and Ben, and five sisters, Lil, Haager, Judie, Rose, and Calline . . . I can remember my grandpa, Dave, and my grandma, Haager . . . They belonged to Mr. [Moses?] Pitts. That was my father's name, and for that reason, I changed my name from Avant to Pitts, after the war." The closest name to Avant in the slave schedule for 1860 is the Avent family of Wake and Chatham counties, North Carolina, fifty to eighty miles from Cabarrus County. Pitts would not reveal more: "I could tell much more about it, but I don't like to talk. I ain't never going to tell nobody all I knows about that. Will be gone pretty soon, and what I knows is going with me." **Roxy Pitts** (AL). "Pappy, he married Aunt Josie, and they had a whole passel of childrens, and they was my brothers and sisters." Raised in Limekin, Alabama. **Irene Poole** (AL). Born three miles from Uniontown, Alabama; slave of Jeff Anderson Poole. **Alec Pope** (GA). Born on the line between Clarke and Oglethorpe counties, Georgia. Son of Willis and Celia; slave of the Pope family. "My sisters was Callie, Phebie Ann, Nelia, and Millie. My brothers was Anderson, Osborn, George, Robert, Squire, Jack, and Willis." **William Porter** (AR). Born 1856 in Tennessee, slave of Tom Gray. **George Pretty** (FL). Born January 20, 1852, the freeborn son of Isaac Pretty in Altoona, Pennsylvania. His mother's last name was McCoy, and her father, Alex McCoy, like Isaac's father, was born a slave. **Allen Price** (TX). Born in 1862; owned by John Price of Texas. **Annie Price** (GA). Born in Baton Rouge, Louisiana, daughter of Willis Clapp and Sarah Mitchell, slave of Warren Offord. "And so she and her family moved away and her father began farming for himself. He was prosperous until his death." **Lafayette Price** (TX). Born ca. 1849, slave of Robert and Jim Carroll near Shreveport, Louisiana. Died in Beaumont, Texas. **Isaac Pringle** (MS). Born May 9, 1841, slave of W. S. Pringle of Mississippi. **Beverly Pullin** (male) (GA). Born the slave of C. D. or W. A. Pullen of Troup County, Georgia. **Armstrong Purdee.** Born in 1856 on the Waddell plantation in Jackson County, Florida. After the war he returned to Jackson County, where former Confederate Major Henry Milton of the 5th Florida Cavalry helped him study for the bar. He became the first black lawyer in the county. Some of the Yankees who served in the battle he witnessed were black soldiers from the 85th and 86th U.S. Colored Infantry. Purdee's account originally appeared in the *Kalendar,* the newsletter of the Men's Association of St. Luke's Episcopal Church in Marianna, dated June 1, 1931. Courtesy of Dale Cox.

Q

Doc Quinn (AR). Born March 15, 1843, in Monroe County, Mississippi, near Aberdeen, one of fifty-seven slaves owned by "Colonel" William M. Ogburn, "one of the biggest planters in the state of Mississippi."

R

Henrietta Ralls (AR). Born March 10, 1850, in Lee County, Mississippi. Moved to Pine Bluff, Arkansas, during the war. **Ella Belle Ramsey** (TX). Born ca. 1842, slave of the Goldsmith family of Atlanta. The plantation was in Cass County, which in 1861 was renamed Bartow after a Savannah attorney who was killed in the First Battle of Bull Run. **Filmore Ramsey** (MS). Daughter of Mandy, slave of Dick and Mary Stewart. She lived five miles from Baton Rouge, Louisiana. **Lee Randall** (FL). Born about 1860 in Camden, South Carolina, son of Robert and Dahlia Miller. **Emmy Randolph** (GA). Child of Daniel and Sara Moon White. She and her mother were the slaves of Robert Moon of Jackson County, Georgia. **Senia Rassberry** (AR). Born ca. 1853, slave of Jack and Priscilla Hall, on the Arkansas River in Jefferson County, Arkansas. **Jeff Rayford** (MS). Born 1840 on Ball Hill Road in Pearl River County, Mississippi. Her mother was the slave of a Mrs. Howard, but "it fell my lot to live with Mrs. Kennedy." **Andrew J. Redmon.** Identified as "the Slave Blacksmith" in Johnson, *Battleground Adventures,* pp. 54–60. Identity established by Jacqueline E. A. Lawson. **Easter Reed** (GA). Born ca. 1852 in Dodge County, Georgia, the slave of Alfred Burnham. **Rachael Santee Reed** (MS). Born ca. 1857, daughter of William and Mehalie Santee (Mehalie was born in Jackson, Tennessee), slaves of Joe McInnis of Leakesville, Mississippi. There were apparently five William Santees who served in the war, all of them white Union soldiers. **James Reeves** (AR). Born in 1870 in Ouachita County, Texas, about fourteen miles south of Camden on the way to El Dorado. **Mary Reynolds** (TX). Born in the 1830s, son of Tom Vaughn, and slave of the Kilpatrick family of Black River, Louisiana. **Susan Davis Rhodes** (MS). Born in the 1830s in Jones County, North Carolina, daughter of Lott Davis and Teeny Jones, slave of Edward and Susan Davis. **Charlie Rigger** (AR). Born "six miles from Monticello, close to the line of Morgan and Jasper County," Georgia. "Mother belong to the Smiths. Her father was part Creek. They all was sold to Floyd Malone. His wife was Betsy Malone." **Ida Rigley** (AR). Born in Richmond, Virginia, the slave of Colonel Radford and Emma Radford. "They had a older girl, Emma, and Betty and three boys. My mother was Sylvia Jones and she had five children. Bill Jones was my father. He was born a free man and a blacksmith at Lynchburg, Virginia, in slavery times." **Walter Rimm** (TX). Born 1857, the son of Robert Rimm and slave of a Captain Hatch of Corpus Christi, Texas. **Milton Ritchie** (AR). Born ca. 1859 in the Marietta Hotel, Marietta, Georgia, slave of Milton and Thursday Stevens. **Melvina Roberts** (GA). Born ca. 1857 in Macon, Georgia, slave of a man named Brewer. Her father's master was a neighbor named Mr. Scattergood. Roberts refers to the officer as "Captain Mallet," but it was common for all officers to be referred to by slaves as

"Captain" or "Colonel." There do not appear to have been any Captain Mallets in the Union Army, but there was a First Lieutenant Charles Mallet of the 51st Indiana, which fought in Georgia in the fall of 1864. (Jules Mallet, lieutenant in the 73rd and 74th, and first lieutenant in the 91st, U.S. Colored Infantry, apparently never served in Georgia.) **Cornelia Robinson** (AL). Born ca. 1860, the slave of Dr. Trammell of Chambers County, Alabama. **Ephraim Robinson** (MS). Born in Hinds County, Mississippi, on the plantation of Allen Morrison, his owner. The battles he might have witnessed in Hinds County were Raymond (May 12, 1863), Champion's Hill (May 16, 1863), and Big Black River Bridge (May 17, 1863). **Tom Robinson** (AR). Born ca. 1849 in Catawba County, North Carolina. Slave of Jacob Sigmans. **William Robinson.** Robinson was one of a slave family of twelve children born in Wilmington, North Carolina. By the time he was eleven, his father, mother, and siblings had all been sold away. Later, he too was sold, in Richmond, Virginia. In 1861 he followed his master into the war, but was captured by Union forces and thereafter fought for the North. After the war he sought out his family; performed as a singer and banjo picker; and worked as a fireman, railroad laborer, roustabout, and waiter before entering the ministry. He died in Eau Claire, Wisconsin, in 1923. Robinson, *From Log Cabin to Pulpit,* pp. 44, 49, 70, 73, 91–94, 102–5. **John Rogers** (GA). Born ca. 1830 in Upson County, Georgia, slave of Henry and Louisa Kendall Rogers. **Will Ann Rogers** (AR). Slave of a man named Hester in Henrico County, Virginia. **Joe Rollins** (MS). Slave of Joe and Beckie Malone, whose daughter Cindie married a Mr. Rollins and took Joe with her to Aberdeen, Mississippi. **Reverend William Henry Rooks** (AR). Born ca. 1853. Slave of John and Fannie Freeman, eight miles from Como, Mississippi. **Annie Row** (TX). Born ca. 1853, slave of Charles Finnely, near Rusk, Nacogdoches County, Texas. **Katie Rowe** (OK). A slave of Dr. Isaac and Betty Jones of Washington, Arkansas, close to Bois d'Arc. **Thomas Ruffin** (AR). Born ca. 1853 near Raleigh, Franklin County, North Carolina. His mother was Morina Ruffin and his father was his master, also named Thomas Ruffin, who died in the war fighting for the CSA. "He died trying to hold us." **Casper Rumple** (AR). Born ca. 1858, son of an Irish overseer named Ephraim Rumple and a slave woman owned by John Griffin of Lawrence County, South Carolina. Ephraim Rumple "went off to fight the Yankees and took Malaria fever and died on Red River." **Julia Rush** (GA). Born ca. 1828 on St. Simons Island, Georgia, slave of a Frenchman named Colonel De Binion. After the colonel's wife died, Rush was given to their daughter, "her former playmate who was at the time married and living in Carrollton, Georgia." **Rose Russell** (MS). Born ca. 1839 in Warrenton, Mississippi, the slave of a Mr. Cross. Sold ca. 1843 with her father to a merchant in Vicksburg as a future wet nurse. **Thomas Rutling.** Born in Williamson County, Tennessee, he escaped to Nashville and worked for the Yankees. He entered Fisk School and joined the Jubilee Singers as first tenor. After touring for many years, he died in England. Rutling, *Tom,* pp. 14–15.

S

Charlie Sandles (TX). Born 1857 in Jackson, Tennessee. "At the age of 8 years he was traded to Tom Lynch for 4 mules." Son of Ray and Elsie Sandles. "I have two brothers, Tom and Joe, and three sisters, Josie, Sally and Sarah." **Anna Scott** (SC). Born January 28, 1846, at Dave City, South Carolina, son "of a half-breed Cherokee-and-Negro mother and Anglo-Saxon father" who "owned the plantation adjoining that of her master." She was "a member of one of the first colonization groups that went to the West coast of Africa following the emancipation of the slaves in this country." **Lucindy Hall Shaw** (MS). Born ca. 1849. Her last owners were Reuben T. and Sarah Hall of Paris, Lafayette County, Mississippi. **Violet Shaw** (AR). Born in 1887, she told stories about her ancestors. Her aunt Mariah Jackson was freed in Dublin, Mississippi. **Will Sheets** (GA). **Cora Shepherd** (GA). Born 1858, slave of Jesse Walden of Columbia County, Georgia. **Robert Shepherd** (GA). Born ca. 1856. Son of Peyton Shepherd and Cynthia Echols, slave of Joe Echols in Oglethorpe County, Georgia, about ten miles from Lexington. **Virginia Hayes Shepherd** in Perdue et al., eds., *Weevils in the Wheat*, pp. 259–60. **William Sherman** (FL). Born June 13, 1848, slave of Jack Davis, nephew of President Jefferson Davis, at Black Swamp, about five miles from Robertsville, South Carolina. **Polly Shine** (TX). Born 1848 in Shreveport, Louisiana, daughter of Jim and Jessie Shine, slave of Joe Shine. **Mahalia Shores** (AR). Born 1860 in Greene County, Georgia, the slave of James Jackson. **Tom Siggers** (MS). Born ca. 1857, thirty-six miles from Houston, Texas. After the war his family settled in Dixon, Neshoba County, Mississippi. **Smith Simmons** (MS). Born in Montgomery County, Mississippi, about six miles from Winona. Slave of Dick and Jane Baylock. **Rosa Simons** (AR). Born ca. 1852 in Tennessee. **Millie Simpkins** (TN). Born ca. 1837 near Winchester, Tennessee, slave of Boyd and Sarah Ann Ewing Sims. After Boyd's death Sarah Ann married two more times: to Joe Carter and Judge Gork. Simpkins was sold in Nashville to a man named Simpson. **Ben Simpson** (TX). Born ca. 1847 in Norcross, Georgia, son of Roger and Betty Stielazen. "Massa Earl Stielazen captures them in Africa and brung them to Georgia. He got killed and my sister and me went to his son." The son shot Ben's mother en route to Texas. His master changed his own name to Alex Simpson, sired several slaves by Ben Simpson's sister Emma, married a Mexican woman, and began stealing horses, a crime for which he was eventually lynched. **Virginia Sims** (AR). Born ca. 1844 in Virginia, sold with his mother by Joe Poindexter and bought by Tom Murphy of (Pine Bluff?) Arkansas. **Adam Singleton** (MS). Born ca. 1850 near Newton, Alabama, slave of George Simmons. **William Henry Singleton.** Born August 10, 1835, at New Bern, North Carolina, the son of his master's brother. He claimed he was brought before Ambrose Burnside, but at the time of the expedition to capture Kinston (the town Singleton mentions as the goal of the Federal expedition), Foster was in command at New Bern, and Burnside was busy making a hash of things at Fredericksburg. Singleton, *Recollections*, pp. 8–9. **Caroline Smith** (AR). Born ca. 1855, slave of John F. Duncan, a farmer in Itawamba and later Pontotoc County, Mississippi. **Charlie Tye Smith** (GA). Born June 10, 1850, in Henry County, Georgia, near Locust Grove. Slave of Jim Smith. **Classie Blackmond Smith** (MS). Born ca. 1852, "belonging to the Blackmonds in Georgia." She mentioned a Miss Lucy, who could be twenty-one-year-old Lucy A. Blakeney, living in Smith County, Mississippi, in 1860 and born in Georgia. **E. P. Smith** in *Fisk Expositor*, Dedication of Jubilee Hall (FUA). **Eugene Wesley Smith** (GA). Born ca. 1853. "His father was a slave who belonged to Steadman Clark of Augusta, and acted as porter in Mr. Clark's jewelry store on Broad Street. His grandmother came from Pennsylvania with her white owners. In accordance with the laws of the state they had left, she was freed when she came of age, and married a man named Smith. Her name was Louisa. Eugene's mother married a slave," but because "his mother was free, her children were free." **Frank Smith** (AL). Born in Virginia, slave of "Doctor Constable." **Harry Smith.** Born in 1815 in Nelson County, Kentucky. After Emancipation he moved to Indiana and later settled in Michigan. I have transposed Smith's third-person autobiographical narrative into the first person. Smith, *Fifty Years of Slavery*, pp. 119–20, 123–24. **Henry "Hence" Smith** (TX). Born ca. 1853 in Green Parish, Louisiana, slave of Bill Smith. Died in Waco, Texas. Served as a manservant for one of his master's boys in the "Hell Roaring" 4th Texas Infantry, also known as the Lone Star Guards, whose members claimed to have introduced the Rebel yell at the Battle of Gaines' Mill, Virginia. Re Libby prisoners: In his interview, Smith conflated the identities of two of the more notable prisoners brought in from Bull Run: a Tammany Hall enforcer named Michael Corcoran, who had fought in the battle as colonel of the 69th New York Regiment; and Congressman Arthur Ely, also of New York, who had joined a number of Washingtonians, in the words of one of his captors, on "a holiday excursion in carriages to witness a battle and congratulate the Federal victors." J. L. Burrows, "Recollections of Libby Prison," *Southern Historical Society Papers* 11 (1883), pp. 83–92. **James Lindsay Smith.** "My birthplace was in Northern Neck, Northumberland County, Virginia. My mother's name was Rachel, and my father's was Charles," who were slaves of Thomas Langsdon. Smith, *Autobiography of James L. Smith,* pp. 116, 125–26. **John Smith** (AL). Born "somewhere in North Carolina." Sold to "Saddler" Smith of Selma, Alabama. Served "Saddler's" son, Confederate Jim Smith, in the Civil War. **Lou Smith** (OK). Her parents were Jackson Longacre of Mississippi and Caroline of South Carolina. Her father belonged to Uriah Longacre, her mother to a McWilliams family. Her mistress was Jo Arnold Longacre. **Malindy Smith** (MS). Born ca. 1860 in old Choctaw (now in Webster) County, Mississippi, daughter of Henry Att and Harriet Edwards. **Melvin Smith** (GA). Born 1841 in Beaufort, South Carolina, son of Henry and Nancy Smith, slave of Jim and Mary Farrell. **Nancy Smith** (GA). Born ca. 1858, daughter of Jack and Julia Carlton, slave of Joe Carlton of Athens, Georgia. **Nellie Smith** (GA). Born in 1856 in Harnett County, North Carolina, daughter of Atlas and Rosetta Williams, slave of Jack Williams. **Paul Smith** (GA). Born the slave of Jack Ellis of Oglethorpe County, Georgia. **Samuel Smith** (TX). Born February 14, 1840, slave of Jesse Sumner. **Susan Smith** (TX). Smith gives McGill's name as David. The rolls show no David McGills in the CSA, but one D. McGill, who served in the 1st Louisiana Infantry, which took part in the Battle of Mansfield and camped at New Iberia, as Smith recounts. She was the slave of Charles Weeks in Iberia, Louisiana. **James Southall** (OK). Born in Clarksville, Tennessee, son of Wesley and Hagar Southall. Slave of Dr. John Southall. **James Spikes** (AR). Born ca. 1846, location unknown. **Elmo (Elmore) Steele** (MS). Freeborn sometime between 1822 and 1827, the son of an Ohio wheat farmer. He enlisted in May 1865 in the 50th U.S. Colored Infantry. His wife's name was Manda McFarlee. **Austin Steward** in Frazier, *The Negro Family in the United States,* p. 25. **Theodore Fontaine Stewart** (AL). Born ca. late 1830s, slave of Theodore Fontaine of Georgia, who lived with his sisters Mary and Lucy. **George Stickland** (AL). Born ca. 1856 and "refugeed from Mississippi to Mobile, then to Selma, then to Montgomery and from there to Uchie [Creek], near Columbus, Georgia, where we stayed till us was freed." **Isaac Stier** (MS). Born ca. 1837 in Jefferson County, Mississippi, between Hamburg and Union Church. Slave of Jeems Stowers. Isaac either was a laborer or served under another name. No one with even a variation of his name served in a black regiment. **Miles Stone** (MS). Born in 1835, a slave of Joseph E. Davis, Jefferson Davis's older brother. **Jim Stovall** (MS). Born in Georgia. **Felix Street** (AR). Born December 28, 1864, in Dickson County, Tennessee, fifty miles north of Nashville. **Liza Strickland** (MS). Born ca. 1847, slave of Mike Strickland in Simpson County, Mississippi. **Jacob Stroyer.** Born 1846, twenty-eight miles northeast of Columbia, South Carolina, the slave of Colonel M. R. Singleton. After the war he became a minister. Stroyer, *My Life in the South,* p. 37. **Amanda Styles** (GA). Born in Georgia. Owned by Jack Lambert and born ca. 1857. **Hattie Sugg** (MS). "Born up Big Creek on the old Armstrong place here in Calhoun county [Mississippi]." **Eliza Suggs.** Her parents "were slaves. Father was born in North Carolina, August 15, 1831. He was a twin, and was sold away from his parents and twin brother, Harry, at the age of three years." His father's parents "named him James. So at this time his name was James Martin. He was sold by Mr. Martin for a hundred dollars, and taken to Mississippi. Afterward he was sold to Jack Kendrick, and again to Mr. Suggs, with whom he remained until the war broke out." Born after the war with dwarfism, unable to walk, Suggs lived in Nebraska, where she became an active evangelist. Suggs, *Shadows and Sunshine,* pp. 44–47. ___ **Sutton** in Egypt, ed., *Unwritten History of Slavery,* p. 34.

T

Baltimore and **Tishey Taylor** (MO). Baltimore was born in the late 1830s or early 1840s, son of William Waldorf(?) and Katie Cherry; slave of "Shap" Phillips, who bought his parents from Frank Parker and brought them to New Madrid County, Missouri. **Eliza Ann Taylor.** Her husband was James T. S. Taylor. Perdue et al., eds., *Weevils in the Wheat,* p. 284. **George Taylor** (AL). Born in Mobile, Alabama, carried at the age of twelve to Gosport, Alabama. Son of Gus and Sarah Taylor, slave of W. G. and "Mamie" Herrin. One of twenty-one children. "My grandfather's name was Mack Wilson and my grandmother's name was Ellen Wilson." **Susie King Taylor.** Born August 6, 1848, in Savannah, Georgia, daughter of Hagar Ann and Raymond Baker, slave of the Grest family. At the age of seven, she and her brother were sent to Savannah to live with their grandmother. Robert DeFoe served in Company G of the 33rd U.S. Colored Infantry, which had been organized from the 1st South Carolina Colored Infantry. The 33rd served in the 10th Corps, Department of the South, until April 1864. Taylor, *Reminiscences,* pp. 7–8, 28. **Amanda Tellis** (AL). Born in Grove Hill, Alabama, slave of Meredith and Fannie Pugh. "Amanda's father was a Spaniard, whose name was John Quick, and her mother's name was Sallie Pugh," who "was born a slave in Charleston South Carolina, and she and her mother were brought to Alabama and sold when Sallie was twelve years old." The mother was sold to someone in Demopolis, Alabama, and Sallie was sold to the Pugh family in Grove Hill, Alabama. **Dicey See Thomas** (AR). Born ca. 1855 in Barbour County, Alabama, daughter of Ben See. **James Thomas.** Born a slave in Nashville in

1827. His mother bought his freedom, and he became a barber in Nashville and a wealthy businessman in St. Louis, but died in poverty in 1913. Schweninger, ed., *From Tennessee Slave to St. Louis Entrepreneur,* pp. 81, 87–90, 98, 110, 158, 161, 164, 166–67, 171–72. **Omelia Thomas** (AR). Born ca. 1867 in Vidalia, Louisiana. George Grant served in a number of U.S. Colored Infantry regiments that were drawn from Corps d'Afrique regiments recruited in Louisiana: the 78th USCI (from the 6th Corps d'Afrique), the 83rd (from the 11th), and the 96th (from the 2nd). **Henry J. Thompson** in Jordan, *Black Confederates and Afro-Yankees,* p. 133. **Maria Tilden Thompson** (TX). **Tim Thornton** (GA). Born ca. 1836, the slave of Mrs. Lavinia Tinsley, whose plantation was not far from Cascade, near Danville, Virginia. **Jim Threat** (OK). Born ca. 1851. "I was one of twenty-two children. All of us lived to be grown except Tommy, Ivory and a little girl." His brother Bill Threat was a preacher in Parsons, Kansas. His mother, her brother, his grandmother, and his aunt belonged to an Indian named Johnnie Bowman. "He got in a tight fix and sold them to Russell Allen, and he made him promise not to sell them one by one but in pairs or all together. Russell sold his grandmother and aunt to Hollis Montgomery." **Lucy Thurston** (MS). Lived in Flemingsburg, Kentucky, slave of Claiborne Woods. **J. T. Tims** (AR). Born September 11, 1853, in Jefferson County, Mississippi, six miles east of Fayette. Son of Daniel and Ann Tims of Lexington, Kentucky. Slave of Blount Steward. When Daniel protested Steward's beating his wife, Steward struck him with a hammer. Daniel threatened him, then ran off with his family, up the river to Natchez. "We went there walking and wading." **Alonza Fantroy Toombs** (AL). Robert Toombs resigned to become a brigadier general, commanding the Georgia Brigade in Virginia, where he deplored the cautiousness of professional soldiers and warned that if the Confederacy died, the cause of death would be "West Point." Though he served bravely at Antietam, Richmond refused to promote him. He promptly resigned his commission, and as a civilian frequently visited an equally disillusioned Stephens and contrived to depose Davis for his handling of the conflict. Unlike Stephens, Toombs escaped capture and fled first to Cuba and then to England. In 1867 he returned to reestablish his law practice, but after his wife died a lunatic, he went blind and apparently drank himself to death. Davis, *An Honorable Defeat,* pp. 5–6; Welsh, *Medical Histories of Confederate Generals.* **Laura Towne.** Born on May 3, 1825, in Pittsburgh. A homeopathic doctor, teacher, and abolitionist, she opened the first school for freedmen during the Civil War on St. Helena Island, South Carolina. She took part in the Port Royal Experiment to benefit freedmen, and remained on the island for forty years. She died in 1901, leaving her school to the Hampton Institute. Sargent, ed., *Letters and Diary of Laura Towne,* pp. 27–30. **Phil Towns** (GA). Born 1824. Coach driver for Governor George Washington Towns, a two-term governor of Georgia who, alarmed by the growing drumbeat of abolitionism, advocated Secession. Towns retired to Macon, and died in 1854. **William Henry Towns** (AL). Born December 7, 1864, in Tuscumbia, Alabama, son of Jane Smoots of Baltimore and Joe Towns of Huntsville, Alabama. **Emmeline Trott** (MS). Born in North Carolina. As a toddler she was taken by the Thompson family to Pontotoc, Mississippi. When she was six her mistress died, willing her to a son, Turner Thompson. Her mother was sold, loaned to Mrs. Josie Pinson Wilcox, and then bought by Captain and Mrs. Sara Trott, whose slave, Alfred Trott, she married.

William B. Trotter. Sydnor, *Slavery in Mississippi,* p. 137. **Harriet Tubman.** Born Araminta Ross ca. 1820 in Dorchester County, Maryland, she married a free black named John Tubman and adopted her mother Harriet's first name. Afraid she was about to be sold, she escaped in 1849 by following the North Star into Pennsylvania. In Philadelphia she earned enough money to return to the South, once to spirit her sister to freedom, again to rescue her brother, and a third time to fetch her husband. By then he had remarried, however, which proved fortunate for the many slaves — estimates range from 70 to 300 — she would rescue, for which Southerners put a $40,000 bounty on her head. By the beginning of the war she had run nineteen missions. She died in Auburn, New York, in 1913. Radford, *Harriet, the Moses of Her People,* pp. 92–95; Bruce, *The New Man,* p. 100. **Mandy Tucker** (AR). Born ca. 1857. Her mother belonged to the Cockrills and her father to the Armstrongs of Pine Bluff, Arkansas. **Seabe Tuttle** (AR). The only Tuttle I could find in the 1860 census who served in a CSA Arkansas unit was Private George K. Tuttle of Company B, 8th Arkansas Infantry, but he does not turn up in the 1860 or 1870 census for Arkansas. Nor is there anyone with a name remotely resembling "Combinder" anywhere near any other Tuttle in Arkansas. As for "Lafe" — Lafayette? — Boone, there was an L. L. Boone listed as a twenty-six-year-old clerk in 1860 in Little Rock, and an F. L. Boone, age thirty-eight, listed as a carpenter in Jackson, Arkansas. **Mark Twain (Samuel Clemens)** in Twain, "A True Story," *Atlantic Monthly,* November 1874. The original was written in dialect, and even though Twain had a perfect ear and may have been the least bigoted white man of his time, I have given his account the same treatment as all the others. **Jane Tyler.** Her master was named after his ancestor Wat Tyler, the fourteenth-century leader of a peasant revolt. In the 1860 census, seventy-three-year-old W. H. Tyler of southeastern Hanover County, Virginia, lived with his sixty-four-year-old wife, their son J. C. (possibly John Calhoun Tyler, after his uncle's political ally), and a seven-year-old named R. Tyler. W. H. is listed as a doctor/farmer. The plantation lay near Cold Harbor. W. H. Tyler owned forty slaves, including a twenty-three-year-old and two thirty-one-year-old females. Of black women named Tyler born ca. 1843, only Jane Tyler, born ca. 1841, appears in the censuses for Hanover County from 1870 through 1900. In the 1880 census she is listed with seven children, only one of which, Laura, was old enough to have been alive during the war. This might seem to conflict with her statement that at the time of the war she had "several" children, unless some of her older children were sold off by the destitute Tyler family, otherwise separated by the war (the widow of W. H. Tyler took each slave family's oldest child with her "to town," leaving her other slaves behind), or had died before the 1880 census. In any case, it would have been unusual for a slave who would have been about twenty at the beginning of the war, and who went on to birth six children after the war, to have had only one child while in slavery.

U

Neal Upson (GA). Born ca. 1857, slave of Frank (F. L.) Upson in Oglethorpe County, near Lexington, Georgia. In 1860 Frank Upson owned nine slaves, including a three-year-old male.

V

John F. Van Hook (GA). Son of Bas and Mary Angel Van Hook, slave of George Sellars, who lived in a two-story frame house that was surrounded by an oak grove on the road leading from Franklin, North Carolina, to Clayton, Georgia. "Mother was born on Marse Dillard Love's plantation, and when his daughter, Miss Jenny, married Marse Thomas Angel's son, Marse Dillard gave Mother to Miss Jenny and when Little Miss Jenny Angel was born, Mother was her nurse. Marse Thomas and Miss Jenny Angel died, and Mother stayed right there keeping house for Little Miss Jenny and looking after her. Mother had more sense than all the rest of the slaves put together, and she even did Little Miss Jenny's shopping." Sellars "had four children, Bud, Mount, Elizabeth," and another whose name Van Hook could not recall. **Winger Van Hook** (TX). **Adelaide J. Vaughan** (AR). Born in Huntsville, Alabama. Taken to Arkansas. Her mother was a slave of a man named Hickman, but he hired her out to a family named Candle. **Archy Vaughn** was apparently one of about a dozen slaves owned by Bartlett Kyle (written as "Bartlet Ciles" in his letter) in Fayette County, Tennessee. Berlin et al., ed., *Free at Last*, pp. 112–13. **Addie Vinson (Vincent)** (GA). Born in Oconee County, Georgia, slave of Isaac S. Vincent, daughter of Peter and Minerva Vinson. "Marse Ike buyed my pappy from Marse Sam Brightwell. Me and Bill, Willis, Maze, Harrison, Easter, and Sue was all the children my Mammy and Pappy had." **Sarah Virgil** (GA). Born in Pulaski County, Georgia, slave of Nat (Madison) Snell.

W

Clara Walker (AR). Born ca. 1826 in Arkansas. **Dave** and **Edwin Walker** (MS). Dave was born in 1850, Edwin in 1849, the slaves of Richmond Walker. **Harriet Walker** (MS). Born ca. 1852, slave of George Norwood. **Sara Walker** (WA). Dr. Frank Walker of Longstreet, Pulaski (now Bleckley) County, owned Sara and her mother and father. **Ben Wall** (MS). Slave of T.H.C. Wall of Mississippi. **William Walters** (OK). Born 1852, son of Mary Ann and Jim Walters. Slave of Betsy Bradford in Bedford County, Tennessee. **Henry Walton** (MS). Born November 24, 1852. "We lived on the Widow Wagner's Place. My father was inherited by Mrs. Susan Walton who later married Mr. Wagner, and we all moved to Mr. Wagner's Place near Pontotoc," Mississippi. "Two or three years before the War, old Master Wagner died and soon after his death, the old Mistress married Mr. Hugh Miller." **Rhodus Walton** (GA). Born ca. 1852, son of Antony and Patience Walton of Lumpkin, Stewart County, Georgia. When he was three weeks old, his mother, along with the three younger children, was sold to a wealthy planter named Sam B. Walton. **George Ward** (MS). Born on the Ledbetter plantation, three miles west of Tupelo, Mississippi, son of a Negro mother and a Chickasaw father. His mother was stolen from Winchester, Tennessee, and taken to the Cotton Belt. "She was sold six times, because no man could whip her. Her name was Amy Givhan [Gibbon?]. Her first two children were girls; the oldest one, Susan, lived to be 96. My step-father helped to build Martha Washington School and Chickasaw College at Pontotoc. I was a slave of the late Dr. Edward Givhan's father, ten miles south of Pontotoc." **Sam Ward** in Mellon, ed., *Bullwhip Days,* p. 343. **William Ward** (GA). Son of Bill and Leana Ward, who were brought to this country from Jamaica, then sent back by their master, Georgia's Secessionist and populist Governor Joseph E. Brown. **Henry Warfield** (MS). Born ca. 1847 in Copiah County, Mississippi, the slave of a planter named Wilson. Sold in 1859 at Learned, Mississippi, to Matt Gray of Hinds County, not far from Cherry Grove. **Anna Washington** (AR). Daughter of Eliza Washington, who was born in Tennessee and brought to Arkansas. **Booker T. Washington.** Born in 1856, son of Jane, slave of James Burroughs of Virginia. At the age of sixteen he entered the Hampton Institute, after which he would model his own Tuskegee Institute. He became a national figure, winning over Southern whites as a proponent of bootstrap economic and moral uplift as the best means of advancing black people, against which activist intellectual blacks like W.E.B. Du Bois rebelled. He died in 1915. **Eliza Washington.** Mother of Anna Washington, she was born in Tennessee and brought to Arkansas. (See Anna Washington.) **Parrish Washington** (AR). Born ca. 1852, slave of Sam Warren of Jefferson County, Arkansas. **Hillary Watson.** Born ca. 1832 near Calamus Run, Maryland, the slave of David F. Otto, who took Watson to his farm on the outskirts of Sharpsburg when he was ten months old. Both Watson and the slave cook were interviewed in 1913, almost half a century after the war. I have been unable to determine the cook's identity. Hillary Watson ("the Slave Foreman") in Johnson, *Battleground Adventures,* pp. 105–8. **Mollie Watson** (OK). Born 1854 in Centerville, Leon County, Texas. Daughter of Wesley and Patience Garner. Slave of Squire Garner and Sebastian Stroud. **Samuel Watson** (IN). Born February 14, 1862, slave of Thomas Watson in Webster County, Kentucky, a half mile from Clay, Kentucky, on Crab Orchard Creek. **William W. Watson** (OK). Son of Baker Watson, slave of Henry Watson; and Eliza Davis, slave of Tom Davis of Tennessee. Grew up on Davis's plantation "in the deep country," ten miles south of Pulaski, Tennessee. **Dave Weathersby** (MS). Born 1851 near Monticello, Lawrence County, Mississippi, slave of William Weathersby. **Jennie Webb** (MS). Born 1846, one of twenty-six slaves of Fredman H. C. Dent of Rankin County, Mississippi. **William Webb.** Born 1836 in Georgia, moved with his master to Italia in central Mississippi. After escaping from his master, he became a major figure in the Underground Railroad. Webb, *History,* pp. 13–16, 30, 33, 36. **John Wells** (AR). Slave from Edmondson, Arkansas, refugeed to Texas. **James West** (TX). Born ca. 1853, one of six slaves of William West in Tippah County, near Ripley, Mississippi. **Maggie Wesmoland (Westmoreland?)** (AR). Born ca. 1858 (according to slave schedule for 1860), the daughter of Simon and Caroline Wright, slaves of Benjamin P. (or S.) and June C. Cuney of Sicily Island, Catahoula Parish, Louisiana. **Eliza White** (AL). Born in Alabama. **Julia White** (AR). Born ca. 1857. Daughter of James Page Jackson, who was born on the Jackson plantation in Lancaster County, Virginia. "A man named Galloway bought my father and brought him to Little Rock, Arkansas. There were fourteen of us, but only ten lived to grow up." **Mingo White** (AL). Born in Chester, South Carolina, raised in Alabama. "When I was about four or five years old, I was loaded in a wagon with a lot more people in it" and sold. "Whatever become of my mammy and pappy I don't know for a long time." During the auction, "us had to tell them all sorts of lies for our Master or else take a beating." **Dolly Whiteside** (AR). Born 1856 in Pine Bluff, Arkansas, slave of a "Colonel" Williams, who took his slaves to Texas. (See Frank Fikes and Dosia Harris.) **Adelia Wicker** ("the Mulatto Girl") in Johnson, *Battleground Adventures,* pp. 289–96. Her identity was determined by Jacqueline E. A. Lawson from the 1860 census, which shows only one black farmer named Amos in Hamilton County, Tennessee, who had two girls in his household: Winnie, age thirteen, and Adelia, age five. (The baby sister Wicker mentions would have been born after 1860.) She described her other sister as "larger," and herself as a "mere stripling of a girl," which indicates that Adelia was the younger of the two and would have been about eight when Chattanooga was captured by the Yankees in 1863. **Alice Wilkins** (TX). Born 1855, in Springfield, near Grosbeck, Texas, in Limestone County. She was a slave of a man named Peoples, who sold her to Mrs. Aline Oliver in Grosbeck. **Allen Williams** (TX). Born 1846, slave of Senator John Alexander Greer of Texas. **Charley Williams** (LA). Born 1856, the slave of Reed Williams of New London, Oklahoma. **Ed Williams** (MS). Son of Bonney and Liddy, slaves of Jim Quin, who lived eight miles north of Holmesville, Mississippi, on the Bogue Chitto River. **Gus Williams** (AR). **Hulda Williams** (OK). Born July 18, 1857, in Jefferson County, Arkansas. Daughter of a white overseer named Kelly and Emmaline, a slave of a family named Burns. Hulda was the wife of a Bond slave, George Washington Bond. **Isaac D. Williams.** Born ca. 1821 in King George County, Virginia, slave of John O. Washington. Williams, *Sunshine and Shadows,* p. 89. **Mollie Williams** (MS). Born September 15, 1853, about three miles from Utica, Mississippi, slave of George Newsome. "Pappy was name Martin Newsome," and "Mammy was a Missourian name Marylin Napier Davenport. She was big and strengthy," and Newsome "wanted her powerful bad," so his wealthy uncle, John Davenport, bought her and loaned her to him, on condition that each receive every other child she bore. **Olin Williams** (GA). Born around 1854, slave of John Whitlow of Clarke County, Georgia. **William Ball "Soldier" Williams III** (AR). Born in Greensburg, Arkansas. Not listed under this name in Union Army rolls. In his quote regarding black troops being employed as shields, I have changed "they" to "us" for clarity's sake. **Anna Williamson** (AR). Born and raised in Somerville, Tennessee. **Callie Halsey Williamson** (AR). Daughter of her Alabama master and his slave. **Aaron Willis** (MS). Born December 25, 1858, in Columbus, Mississippi, son of Ben and Octave, slave of Ed Moore. "He bought them from a man name Willis and that is where they got there name." **Adeline Willis** (GA). Her mother, Marina, was born on the Ragan plantation on Little River in Greene County, Georgia. After the Ragans' daughter married Moses C. B. Wright, she took Marina to her husband's plantation in neighboring Oglethorpe County, where Adeline was born. **Charles Willis** (OK). Born ca. 1830 in Lawrence County, Mississippi, slave of John and Sang Sharp. **Frances Willis** (MS). Born ca. 1847 in Choctaw County, Mississippi. Daughter of Andy and Adeline Shaw, sister of Mandy, who died soon after the war. Slave of John and Betsy Ingraham Shaw, whose children were "James, John, Roena, Fannie, Buck, Hugh, Mae, and Charlie." After her master was killed by a falling tree, "I was the children's property, and they hired me out from one to another" as a nurse. "Jesse Shaw, the father of John, was my guardian." **Claude Augusta Wilson** (FL). Born 1857, slave of a Unionist named Tom Dexter and his Secessionist wife, Mary Ann, of Lake City, Columbia County, Florida. **Jake Wilson** (TX). Born ca. 1855, slave of

         A Directory of Witnesses

John and Mary Etta Wilson of Georgia, who refugeed to Waco, Texas, during the war. **Lulu Wilson** (TX). "We went to a place called Wadefield, in Texas, and settled for some short passing of time." Born ca. 1841, slave of Wash Hodges of Texas. **Robert Wilson** (TX). Born in 1861, owned by Henry Byas, who was also his father. **Sarah Wilson** (OK). "I was born in 1850 along the Arkansas river, about halfway between Fort Smith and old Fort Coffee and the Skullyville boat landing on the river. The farm place was on the north side of the river on the old wagon road what run from Fort Smith out to Fort Gibson. I was a Cherokee slave, and now I am a Cherokee freedwoman; and besides that, I am a quarter Cherokee my own self." **Temple Wilson** (MS). Born ca. 1857, slave of Jim Percow in Madison County, Mississippi. **Willis Winn** (TX). Claimed to have been born ca. 1832 when interviewed in 1938. Owned by Bob Winn of Louisiana. **Rube Witt** (TX). Born ca. 1850, slave of Jess Witt of Texas. **George Womble** (GA). His master was Robert Ridley of Clinton, Georgia. **Anna Woods** (AR). Lived near Natchez, Mississippi. **Samuel M. Woods** in Jordan, *Black Confederates and Afro-Yankees,* p. 128. **Ike Woodward** (MS). Born July 4, 1855, at Pittsboro, Calhoun County, Mississippi. "My papa was Nelson Woodward who was born in Richmond, Virginia, and my mama was Dolly Pruitt from Alabama. My brothers was Jeff, Sam, Ben, and Jim and my sisters was Tilla, Lena and Rosetta. My job during the war was to lead [blind] Bob Conner all through the war. You know, Master Conner was the papa of Mr. Fox Conner who is now such a big man in the army." **Sam Word** (AR). Born February 14, 1859, in Arkansas County, the slave of Bill Word. **Ellaine Wright** (TX). Born March 1, 1840, just outside Springfield, Missouri; slave of Tom Evanson. Married Pete Wright in 1866. **Henry Wright** (GA). Born the slave of a family named House. His master "was not present, for when he heard of the approach of Sherman he took his family, a few valuables and some slaves and fled to Augusta." **John Wright** in Armstrong, *Old Massa's People,* pp. 276–77.

Y

William A. Yancey. Born a slave in Caswell County, North Carolina, in March 1850. His mother was a slave cook and wet nurse. His father's master was William Waddleton of Guilford County, North Carolina. His mother's and Yancey's master was W. W. Williamson. In November 1859, his master moved with about forty slaves to Arkansas. Yancey returned to North Carolina in 1861 and was hired out until the end of the war. William A. Yancey Collection, Schomburg Library, MG194, Box 1, "Biographical Sketch," pp. 15–17. **Annie Young** (OK). Born ca. 1861. Slave of Sam Knox, presumably of Greenville, Clark County, Arkansas. **George Young** (AL). Born August 10, 1846, five miles east of Livingston, Alabama. "My name was George Chapman, and I had five brothers: Anderson, Harrison, William, Henry and Sam; and three sisters: Phoebe, Frances and Amelia. My mother's name was Mary Ann Chapman and my father's name was Sam Young. Us all belonged to Governor Reuben Chapman of Alabama." Governor Chapman was born ca. 1800 in Caroline County, Virginia, and served as Alabama's thirteenth governor from 1847 to 1849. A Huntsville lawyer, he served in Congress from 1835 to 1847. Chapman tried to make peace between the Northern and Southern Democrats, but after Secession he served as an elector for Jefferson Davis. His house was burned during the war, and Chapman was imprisoned. He died in Huntsville in 1882. **Litt Young** (TX). Slave of a Dr. Gibbs in Vicksburg, Mississippi, and refugeed to Texas after Vicksburg's surrender. **Robert Young** (MS). Born May 15, 1844, about twelve miles east of Crystal Springs, Mississippi. Son of Emily Watkins and Prince Watkins, slave of Gus Watkins and Margaret Watkins and their son Henry, who disemboweled his own father during a fight over a slave. "After that Miss Margaret married Freeman Young and that's how come we come by name of Young."

ACKNOWLEDGMENTS

SINCE MUCH OF THIS material was gathered while I was researching my two previous books, readers will find a nearly comprehensive list of those who have assisted me along the way in *Dark Midnight When I Rise: The Story of the Fisk Jubilee Singers* and *River Run Red: The Fort Pillow Massacres in the American Civil War.* But I want to thank particularly those who were directly involved in this project: my researcher, Nate Weston, for his resourcefulness, diligence, and insights, not to mention his formal education in American history, which helped to keep a sometimes befuddled high school graduate from straying too far from the straight and narrow; Jacqueline E. A. Lawson of Diversitudes and the Black Genealogy Research Group of Seattle for her role in identifying the freedmen and anonymous former slaves who testified in Clifton Johnson's *Battleground Adventures;* and Ameya Krishnan for her careful transcriptions of testimony from many disparate sources.

I thank Professor Quintard Taylor, the Scott and Dorothy Bullitt Professor of American History at the University of Washington, for his friendship and helpful suggestions; Jeff Coopersmith, for sharing his extraordinary collection of material relating to American slavery; my brother Geoffrey C. Ward; and my one-time elementary school classmate Kathleen Cleaver, senior lecturer at the Yale and Emory University law schools, for her encouragement and advice.

I also want to acknowledge the help of Reggie Washington, the resident authority on African-American records at the National Archives and Records Administration, and its retired Civil War expert Michael Musick. I am indebted to the many archivists who assisted me, especially the staff of the Schomburg Library in New York.

Thanks also, in alphabetical order, to Ted Alexander, senior staff historian at Antietam National Battlefield; Myers Brown of the Alabama Historical Commission and curator of Pond Spring; the novelist John F. Burgwyn; Dan Cashin of the Fort Delaware Society; Mark Christ of Arkansas Heritage; Dale Cox, for Armstrong Purdee's account of the Battle of Mansfield; Steve Davis of *Blue & Grey* magazine; Fritz Jacobs; Kay Jorgensen of *Civil War News;* Ned Leigh of McBride Creative; Ken McCother, president of the New Bern Historical Society; Marsha Mullins, curator of The Hermitage; James H. Ogden III, historian at the Chickamauga and Chattanooga National Military Park; Ken Rice; Brian Roberson of the Butler Center in Little Rock, Arkansas; Sister Carol Scott-Sciotto; Kim Stepno; Julie Udani; and Laura Wahl, program coordinator at the Belle Grove plantation in Middletown, Virginia.

Thanks also to the officers and members of the Civil War Roundtables who assisted me: Bettie Enloe (Indianapolis), Daniel Giallombardo (McHenry County, Illinois), Anna Howland (Orange County, California), Richard R. Reed (Lakewood County, Colorado), Liz Stringer (Abraham Lincoln Civil War Roundtable), and Janet Whalley (San Gabriel Valley, California).

Many thanks to my agent, Ellen Levine of Trident Media, for championing this project from the start; my editor at Houghton Mifflin, Webster Younce, for his unflagging support and uncanny understanding of the book I envisioned, and Larry Cooper for making me appear far smarter than I am. Finally I want to thank my wife, Debbie, for her shrewd reading of this manuscript and her patient support of a project that too often took me away from her. This book is dedicated with love to our son, Jake, and his wife, Julie Tinker; and our daughter, Casey, and her husband, Pablo Federico.

SOURCES

——◆——

SOME OF THE TITLES on this list were found on the University of North Carolina at Chapel Hill's pioneering website Documenting the American South (UNCCH/DAS), where there are searchable texts of scores of otherwise unavailable and obscure biographies and memoirs of former slaves. I wish to thank the University of North Carolina at Chapel Hill for allowing me to use these transcriptions. Lest I be accused of bibliography-creep, though much of the material cited below contains testimony directly quoted in this book, I cite others for the contextual information they provided. Some of the books that seem merely to contain more of the same WPA interviews archived at the Library of Congress actually feature material from state archives that was not collected in Rawick's multivolume compilation *The American Slave,* and also sometimes provide more thorough and accurate transcriptions, while others feature additional biographical information developed by their editors.

For background on the war itself, I leaned hard on the field's great reference works, especially Boatner's *Civil War Dictionary;* Davis, Kirkley, and Perry's *Official Military Atlas of the Civil War;* Denney's *Civil War Prisons & Escapes;* Garrison's *Encyclopedia of Civil War Usage; The Collected Works of Abraham Lincoln;* E. B. Long and Barbara Long's *The Civil War Day by Day;* MacMillan's encyclopedic *The Confederacy;* Miller's *Uniforms, Weapons and Equipment of the Civil War;* Neely's *Abraham Lincoln Encyclopedia;* Sifakis's *Who Was Who in the Civil War;* and Welsh's *Medical Histories of Confederate Generals* and its Union companion volume.

I also frequently turned to the following websites: the National Park Service's Soldiers and Sailors System; Rootsweb, Genweb, Ancestry; and the Library of Congress's Making of America. I also made use of *The Civil War*

CD-Rom: The Official Records of the War of the Rebellion, containing the complete text of the compiled official records of the Union and Confederate armies.

ABBREVIATIONS

CV *Confederate Veteran*
CWH *Civil War History*
THQ *Tennessee Historical Quarterly*
TSLA Tennessee State Library and Archives
SHC/UNCCH Southern History Collection, University of North Carolina at
   Chapel Hill
WTHSP West Tennessee Historical Society Papers

Adams, Virginia M., editor. *On the Altar of Freedom: A Black Soldier's Civil War Letters from the Front: Corporal James Henry Gooding.* New York, 1991.
Adler, Mortimer J., Charles Van Doren, and George Ducas, editors. *The Negro in American History.* 3 volumes. Chicago, 1969.
Agnew, Samuel A. "Battle of Tishomingo Creek." *CV.* September 1900.
Agnew, Samuel. Diary. SHC/UNCCH.
Albert, Mrs. Octavia V. Rogers. *The House of Bondage; or, Charlotte Brooks and Other Slaves.* New York, 1890.
Aleckson, Sam. *Before the War, and After the Union; an Autobiography.* Boston, 1929.
Alexander, Ted. "'A Regular Slave Hunt': The Army of Northern Virginia and Black Civilians in the Gettysburg Campaign." *North & South* 4, no. 7 (September 2001): 82–89.
Alston, Primus P. "Up from Slavery." *Spirit of Missions* (No. 72). UNCCH/DAS.
American Missionary Association Papers (microfilm).
American Missionary Association. *History of the American Missionary Association: Its Churches and Educational Institutions Among the Freedmen, Indians, and Chinese, with Illustrative Facts and Anecdotes.* New York, 1874.
———. *Twenty-fifth Annual Report of the American Missionary Association.* New York, 1871.
Ames, Mary. *A New England Woman's Diary in Dixie in 1865.* Springfield, 1906.
Anders, Leslie. "Confederate Dead at Lone Jack." *The Prairie Gleaner.* December 1989.
Anderson, Charles W. "Col. Wiley M. Reed." *CV.* March 1897.
Anderson, Major Charles W. "The True Story of Fort Pillow." *CV.* September 1886.
Anderson, Robert. *The Life of Rev. Robert Anderson. Born the 22d Day of February, in the Year of Our Lord 1819, and Joined the Methodist Episcopal Church in 1839. This Book Shall Be Called the Young Men's Guide, or, the Brother in White.* Macon, 1892.
Andrews, William L., editor. *From Fugitive Slave to Free Man: The Autobiographies of William Wells Brown.* New York, 1993.

Anglo African, April 23 and May 7, 1864.

Anonymous. *Old Times in West Tennessee.* Memphis, 1873.

Aptheker, Herbert. *American Negro Slave Revolts.* New York, 1968.

———. *The Negro in the Civil War.* New York, 1940.

———. *To Be Free.* New York, 1991.

Armstrong, Mrs. Mary Francis, and Helen Ludlow. *Hampton and Its Students. By Two of Its Teachers, Mrs. M. F. Armstrong and Helen W. Ludlow. With Fifty Cabin and Plantation Songs, Arranged by Thomas P. Fenner.* New York, 1874.

Armstrong, Orland Kay. *Old Massa's People: The Old Slaves Tell Their Story.* Indianapolis, 1931.

Army of the Cumberland. Philadelphia, 1863.

Avary, Myrta Lockett, editor. *Recollections of Alexander H. Stephens: His Diary: Kept When a Prisoner at Fort Warren, Boston Harbour, 1865; Giving Incidents and Reflections of His Prison Life and Some Letters and Reminiscences.* New York, 1920.

Bailey Casson Family Reunion. *Genealogy and History of Stephen Bailey, Descendant of Isaac Bailey, Free Man, and Betsy Bailey, His Wife, Slave, 1720–1982.* Philadelphia, 1983. UNCCH/DAS.

Bailey, David T. "A Divided Prism: Two Sources of Black Testimony on Slavery." *Journal of Southern History* 46, no. 3 (August 1980): 381–404.

Bailey, Fred Arthur. *Class and Tennessee's Confederate Generation.* Chapel Hill, 1987.

Baker, Ronald L. *Homeless, Friendless, and Penniless: The WPA Interviews with Former Slaves Living in Indiana.* Bloomington, 2000.

Baker, T. Lindsay, and Julie P. Baker, editors. *The WPA Oklahoma Slave Narratives.* Norman, 1996.

Ballard, Michael B. *A Long Shadow: Jefferson Davis and the Final Days of the Confederacy.* Jackson, 1986.

Bancroft, Frederic. Papers, Box 11, Special Collections, Columbia University.

———. *Slave Trading in the Old South.* Reprint of 1931 edition. New York, 1959.

Baptist, Edward E., and Stephanie M. H. Camp, editors. *New Studies in the History of American Slavery.* Athens, 2006.

Basler, Roy P., editor. *The Collected Works of Abraham Lincoln.* 8 volumes. New Brunswick, 1953–1955.

Beard, Augustus Field. *A Crusade of Brotherhood: A History of the American Missionary Association.* Boston, 1909.

Berlin, Ira. *Slaves Without Masters: The Free Negro in the Antebellum South.* New York, 1974.

Berlin, Ira, et al., editors. *Free At Last: A Documentary History of Slavery, Freedom, and the Civil War.* New York, 1992.

———. *Freedom: A Documentary History of Emancipation, 1861–1867.* New York, 1985.

———. *The Wartime Genesis of Free Labor: The Upper South.* Series I, Volume II of *Freedom: A Documentary History of Emancipation, 1861–1867. Selected from the Holdings of the National Archives of the United States.* Cambridge, 1993.

Berwanger, Eugene. *As They Saw Slavery.* Minneapolis, 1973.

Billings, John D. *Hardtack & Coffee: The Unwritten Story of Army Life.* Reprint of 1887 edition. Lincoln, 1993.

Black, Hugh. Letters. Robert Manning Strozier Library, Florida State University.

Blackett, R.J.M., editor. *Thomas Morris Chester, Black Civil War Correspondent: His Dispatches from the Virginia Front.* Baton Rouge, 1989.

Blassingame, John W. *Slave Testimony: Two Centuries of Letters, Speeches, Interviews and Autobiographies.* Baton Rouge, 1977.

Blight, David W. *Race and Reunion: The Civil War in American Memory.* Cambridge, 2001.

Blockson, Charles L. *Black Genealogy.* Baltimore, 1991.

Bodnia, George, editor. "Fort Pillow 'Massacre': Observations of a Minnesotan." *Minnesota History* (Spring 1873).

Boime, Albert. *The Art of Exclusion: Representing Blacks in the Nineteenth Century.* London, 1990.

Boles, John B. *Masters and Slaves in the House of the Lord: Race and Religion in the American South, 1740–1870.* Lexington, 1988.

Botkin, B. A., editor. *Lay My Burden Down: A Folk History of Slavery.* Chicago, 1969.

Bradford, Sarah H. *Harriet, the Moses of Her People.* New York, 1886.

Bragg, George F. *Men of Maryland.* Baltimore, 1914.

Branch, Mary Polk. *Memoirs of a Southern Woman "Within the Lines" and a Genealogical Record.* Chicago, 1912. SHC/UNCCH.

Brandt, Nat. *The Town That Started the Civil War.* Syracuse, 1990.

Branham, Levi. *My Life and Travels.* Dalton, 1929.

Bratton, Mary J., editor. "Fields' Observations: The Slave Narrative of a Nineteenth-Century Virginian." *Virginia Magazine of History and Biography* 88, no. 1 (January 1980): 75–93.

Britton, Wiley. *The Aftermath of the Civil War Based on Investigation of War Claims.* Kansas City, 1924.

Brockett, L. P., and Mary C. Vaughan. *Woman's Work in the Civil War: A Record of Heroism, Patriotism and Patience.* Boston, 1867.

Brown, Hallie Q. *Tales My Father Told, and Other Stories.* Wilberforce, 1925.

Brown, Sterling Nelson. *My Own Life Story.* Washington, 1924.

Brown, Virginia Pounds, and Laurella Owens. *Toting the Lead Row: Ruby Pickens Tartt, Alabama Folklorist.* Tuscaloosa, 1981.

Brown, William Wells. *My Southern Home; or, The South and Its People.* Boston, 1880.

———. *The Negro in the American Rebellion — His Heroism and His Fidelity.* Boston, 1867.

———. See Andrews.

Browne, Francis Fisher. *The Everyday Life of Abraham Lincoln.* N.p., n.d.

Browne, Frederick W. *My Service in the U.S. Colored Cavalry: A Paper Read Before the Ohio Commandery of the Loyal Legion, March 4, 1908.* Cincinnati, 1908.

Brownlee, Frederick Leslie. *New Day Ascending.* Boston, 1946.

Bruce, Henry Clay. *The New Man: Twenty-Nine Years a Slave. Twenty-Nine Years a Free Man.* York, 1895.

Bruner, Peter. *A Slave's Adventures Toward Freedom. Not Fiction, but the True Story of a Struggle.* Oxford, 1918.

The History of Buchanan County, Missouri, Containing a History of the County, its cities, towns, etc. Cape Girardeau, 1881.

Buckley, Gail. *American Patriots: The Story of Blacks in the Military from the Revolution to Desert Storm.* New York, 2001.

Burton, Annie L. *Memories of Childhood's Slavery Days.* Boston, 1909.

Burton, Thomas William. *What Experience Has Taught Me.* Cincinnati, 1910.

Butchart, Ronald E. *Northern Schools, Southern Blacks, and Reconstruction: Freedmen's Education, 1862–1875.* Westport, 1980.

Byrd, S. Clifton. *Transplant: The Biography of 135-Year-Old Charlie Smith, a Former Slave.* Hicksville, 1978.

Cain, Alfred E., editor. *The Winding Road to Freedom: A Documentary Survey of Negro Experiences in America.* Yonkers, 1965.

Caldwell, Merrill S. "A Brief History of Slavery in Boone County, Kentucky." Unpublished paper delivered to the Boone County Historical Society at Florence, Kentucky, June 21, 1957.

California Department of Insurance. Slavery-Era Insurance Registry by Name of Slaveholder.

Capeheart, L. C. *Reminiscences of Issac and Sukey, Slaves of B. F. Moore, of Raleigh, N.C.* Raleigh, 1907. UNCCH/DAS.

Casstevens, Francis H. *Edward A. Wild and the African Brigade in the Civil War.* Jefferson, 2003.

Chapman, Abraham, editor. *Steal Away: Slaves Tell Their Own Stories.* London, 1973.

Chesney, Pharaoh Jackson, and J. C. Webster. *The Last of the Pioneers: Old Times in East Tennessee; Being the Life and Reminiscences of Pharaoh Jackson Chesney (Aged 120 Years).* Knoxville, 1902.

Christian Reconstruction: The American Missionary Association and Southern Blacks, 1861–1890. Athens, 1986.

Christian Recorder, January 9, April 30, May 7, 14, 21, 28, June 11, September 3, November 26, and December 11, 1864; January 7, April 29, June 24, July 1, 22, September 23, and November 11, 18, 1865; June 9, July 9, and December 15, 1866.

Cimprich, John. *Slavery's End in Tennessee, 1861–1865.* Tuscaloosa, 1985.

Cimprich, John, and Robert C. Mainfort, Jr. "Dr. Fitch's Report on the Fort Pillow Massacre." *THQ* 44, no. 1 (Spring 1985): 27–39.

———. "The Fort Pillow Massacre: A Statistical Note." *Journal of American History* 76, no. 3 (1989): 830–37.

———. "Fort Pillow Revisited: New Evidence About an Old Controversy." *CWH* 28, no. 4 (1982): 293–306.

Clark, Lewis Garrard. *Narratives of the Sufferings of Lewis and Milton Clark, sons of a soldier of the Revolution, during a Captivity of more than Twenty Years among the Slaveholders of Kentucky, one of the So Called Christian States of North America.* Boston, 1846.

Clayton, Ronnie W., editor. *Mother Wit: The Ex-Slave Narratives of the Louisiana Writers' Project.* New York, 1990.

Clement, Samuel Spottford. *Memoirs of Samuel Spottford Clement Relating Interesting Experiences in Days of Slavery and Freedom.* Steubenville, 1908.

Colyer, Vincent. *The Services of the Freed-People to the Union Army in North Carolina in the spring of 1862, after the battle of New Bern.* New York, 1864.

Connecticut Historical Society. African American Collection. MS 90111.

Coombe, Jack D. *Thunder Along the Mississippi: The River Battles That Split the Confederacy.* New York, 1998.

Copley, John M. "A Sketch of the Battle of Franklin, Tenn.; with Reminiscences of Camp Douglas." UNCCH/DAS.

Coppin, Levi Jenkins. *Unwritten History.* Philadelphia, 1919.

Cornelius, Janet Duitsman. *"When I Can Read My Title Clear": Literacy, Slavery, and Religion in the Antebellum South.* Columbia, 1991.

Cornish, Dudley Taylor. *The Sable Arm: Negro Troops in the Union Army, 1861–1865.* New York, 1966.

Cupples, Douglas W. "Rebel to the Core: Memphis' Confederate Civil War Refugees." *WTHSP* 51 (1997): 64–73.

Curry, Richard O., editor. *The Abolitionist.* New York, 1965.

Davis, Carrie E. *What Experience Has Taught Me.* Cincinnati, 1910. UNCCH/DAS.

Davis, William C. *The Cause Lost: Myths and Realities of the Confederacy.* Lawrence, 1996.

———, editor. *The Confederate General.* Volume I. Washington, 1991.

Delaney, Lucy A. Berry. *From Darkness Cometh the Light; or, Struggles for Freedom.* St. Louis, 1891. UNCCH/DAS.

Dew, Charles B. *Apostles of Disunion: Southern Secession Commissioners and the Causes of the Civil War.* Charlottesville, 2001.

Dobak, William A., editor. "Civil War on the Kansas-Missouri Border: The Narrative of Former Slave Andrew Williams." *Kansas History* 6, no. 4 (1983–1984): 237–42.

Donald, David Herbert. *Lincoln.* New York, 1995.

Donhardt, Gary L. "On the Road to Memphis with General Ulysses S. Grant." *WTHSP* 53 (1999): 1–15.

Douglass, Frederick. *Life and Times of Frederick Douglass. His Early Life as a Slave, His Escape from Bondage, and His Complete History.* Reprint of 1892 edition. New York, 1993.

———. *Narrative of the Life of Frederick Douglass, An American Slave. Written by Himself.* Reprint of 1845 edition. New York, 1968.

———. "Address at Twelfth Baptist Church, New York City." *The Liberator,* April 29, 1864.

Drew, Benjamin. *The Narratives of Fugitive Slaves.* Toronto, 2000.

Drumgoold, Kate. *A Slave Girl's Story. Being an Autobiography of Kate Drumgoold.* Brooklyn, 1898.

Duberman, Martin, editor. *The Antislavery Vanguard: New Essays on the Abolitionists.* Princeton, 1965.

Du Bois, W.E.B. *Black Reconstruction in America, 1860–1880.* New York, 1935.

Early, Sarah J. W. *Life and Labors of Rev. Jordan W. Early: One of the Pioneers of African Methodism in the West and South.* Nashville, 1894.

Eden, Horatio. Memoir. TSLA.

Egypt, Ophelia Settle, editor. *Unwritten History of Slavery: Autobiographical Accounts of Negro Ex-Slaves.* Nashville, 1945.

Eisenschiml, Otto, and Ralph Newman, editors. *Eyewitness: The Civil War as We Lived It: The American Iliad.* New York, 1956.

Eliot, William. *The Story of Archer Alexander: From Slavery to Freedom, March 30, 1863.* Boston, 1885.

Elizabeth: A Colored Minister of the Gospel Born in Slavery. Philadelphia, 1889. UNCCH/DAS.

Elkins, Stanley M. *Slavery: A Problem in American Institutional and Intellectual Life.* Chicago, 1967.

Emancipation League of Boston, compilers. *Facts Concerning the Freedmen: Their Capacity and Their Destiny.* Boston, 1863.

Escott, Paul D. *Slavery Remembered: A Record of Twentieth-Century Slave Narratives.* Chapel Hill, 1979.

Everly, Elaine C. "Marriage Registers of Freedmen." *Prologue: The Journal of the National Archives* 5, no. 3 (1973): 150–54.

Faulk, W. L. Diary. Vicksburg National Military Park.

Faust, Drew Gilpin, editor. *The Ideology of Slavery: Proslavery Thought in the Antebellum South, 1830–1860.* Baton Rouge, 1981.

———. *Mothers of Invention: Women of the Slaveholding South in the American Civil War.* New York, 1996.

Federal Writers' Project. *American Life Histories: Manuscripts from the Federal Writers' Project, 1936–1940.* Library of Congress website.

Fedric, Francis. *Slave Life in Virginia and Kentucky; or, Fifty Years of Slavery in the Southern States of America.* London, 1863. UNCCH/DAS.

Fehrenbacher, Don E. *The Slaveholding Republic: An Account of the United States Government's Relations to Slavery.* New York, 2001.

Ferebee, London R. *A Brief History of the Slave Life of Rev. L. R. Ferebee, and the Battles of Life, and Four Years of His Ministerial Life. Written from Memory. To 1882.* Raleigh, 1882.

Fields, Barbara Jean. *Slavery and Freedom on the Middle Ground.* New Haven, 1985.

Filler, Louis. *The Crusade Against Slavery, 1830–1860.* New York, 1960.

Fitzgerald, Ross. *A Visit to the Cities and Camps of the Confederate States.* London, 1865.

Fleming, Walter L. *Civil War and Reconstruction in Alabama.* New York, 1905.

Fletcher, Robert Samuel. *A History of Oberlin College: From Its Foundation Through the Civil War.* Volume I. New York, 1971.

Foner, Eric. *Reconstruction: America's Unfinished Revolution, 1863–1877.* New York, 1988.

Foster, Francis Smith. *Witnessing Slavery: The Development of Ante-Bellum Slave Narratives.* Madison, 1979.

Francis, Edward. See Meyers and Propes.

Frankel, Noralee. "From Slave Women to Free Women: The National Archives and Black Women's History in the Civil War Era." *Prologue: The Journal of the National Archives* 29, no. 2 (1997): 100–104.

Franklin, John Hope, editor. *The Diary of James T. Ayers, Civil War Recruiter.* Springfield, 1947.

Frazier, E. Franklin. *The Negro Family in the United States.* New York, 1951.

Freehling, William W. *The South vs. the South: How Anti-Confederate Southerners Shaped the Course of the Civil War.* New York, 2001.

Freehling, William W. and Craig M. Simpson, editors. *Secession Debated: Georgia's Showdown in 1860.* New York, 1992.

Frisby, Derek. "'Remember me to everybody': The Civil War Letters of Samuel Henry Eells, Twelfth Michigan Infantry." Unpublished manuscript. Courtesy of the author.

Frost, Griffin. *Prison Journal. Embracing Scenes in Camp, on the March, and in Prisons: Springfield, Gratiot Street, St. Louis, and Macon City, Mo., Fort Delaware. Alton and Camp Douglas, Ill. Camp Morton, Ind., and Camp Chase, Ohio. Also, Scenes and Incidents during a Trip for Exchange, from St. Louis, Mo., via. Philadelphia, Pa., to City Point, Va.* Quincy, 1867.

Furman, Jan, editor. *Slavery in the Clover Bottoms: John McCline's Narrative of His Life During Slavery and the Civil War.* Knoxville, 1998.

Gallagher, Gary W., and Alan T. Nolan, editors. *The Myth of the Lost Cause and Civil War History.* Bloomington, 2000.

Garrison, Webb. *Civil War Curiosities: Strange Stories, Oddities, Events, and Coincidences.* Nashville, 1994.

Gates, Henry Louis, Jr., editor. *The Classic Slave Narratives.* New York, 1987.

Gaudet, Frances Joseph. *"He Leadeth Me."* New Orleans, 1913. UNCCH/DAS.

Genovese, Eugene D. *The Political Economy of Slavery: Studies in the Economy and Society of the Slave South.* New York, 1967.

———. *Roll, Jordan, Roll: The World the Slaves Made.* New York, 1976.

Gibson, J. W., and W. H. Crogman. *The Colored American: From Slavery to Honorable Citizenship.* Cincinnati, 1902.

Gillette, William. *Retreat from Reconstruction, 1869–1879.* Baton Rouge, 1979.

Gladstone, William A. *United States Colored Troops, 1863–1867.* Gettysburg, 1990.

Glatthaar, Joseph T. *Forged in Battle: The Civil War Alliance of Black Soldiers and White Officers.* New York, 1990.

———. *The March to the Sea and Beyond.* Baton Rouge, 1995.

Goldhurst, Richard. *Many Are the Hearts: The Agony and Triumph of Ulysses S. Grant.* New York, 1975.

Goodstein, Anita Shafer. *Nashville, 1780–1860: From Frontier to City.* Gainesville, 1989.

Grant, Joel. Letters. American Missionary Association. TSLA.

Green, Elisha Winfield. *Life of the Rev. Elisha W. Green.* Maysville, 1888. UNCCH/DAS.

Green, Nathaniel E. *The Silent Believers.* Louisville, 1972.

Greene, Lorenzo, Gary R. Kremer, and Antonio F. Holland. *Missouri's Black Heritage.* Columbia, 1993.

Griest, Elwood. *John and Mary; or, the Fugitive Slaves: A Tale of South-Eastern Pennsylvania.* Lancaster, 1873.

Grigsby, Melvin. *The Smoked Yank.* Sioux Falls, 1888.

Grimes, William. See Venture Smith.

Grimsley, Mark. *The Hard Hand of War: Union Military Policy Toward Southern Civilians, 1861–1865.* New York, 1995.

Guthrie, J. Letter. Hyacinth Laselle Papers, Indiana State Library.

Gutman, Herbert G. *The Black Family in Slavery and Freedom, 1750–1925.* New York, 1977.

Hall, Samuel. *Samuel Hall, 47 Years a Slave: A Brief History of His Life Before and After Freedom Came to Him.* Washington, 1912.

Harley, Sharon. *The Timetables of African-American History: A Chronology of the Most Important People and Events in African-American History.* New York, 1995.

Harris, Elizabeth Johnson. "Elizabeth Johnson Harris, Life Story." The Digital Scriptorium, Special Collections Library, Duke University.

Harrison, Samuel. *Rev. Samuel Harrison: His Life Story as Told by Himself.* Pittsfield, 1899. UNCCH/DAS.

Harvey, Meriwether. *Slavery in Auburn, Alabama.* Auburn, 1907.

Heard, William Henry (Harrison). *From Slavery to the Bishopric of the A.M.E. Church: An Autobiography.* Philadelphia, 1924. UNCCH/DAS.

Henry, George. *Life of George Henry: Together with a Brief History of the Colored People in America.* Providence, 1894. UNCCH/DAS.

Henry, Thomas W. *From Slavery to Salvation: The Autobiography of Rev. Thomas W. Henry.* Baltimore, 1872.

Henson, Josiah. *"Uncle Tom's Story of His Life." An Autobiography of the Rev. Josiah Henson (Mrs. Harriet Beecher Stowe's "Uncle Tom"). From 1789 to 1876. With a Preface by Mrs. Harriet Beecher Stowe, and an Introductory Note by George Sturge, and S. Morley, Esq., M.P.* London, 1876. UNCCH/DAS.

Hepworth, George H. *The Whip, Hoe and Sword.* Freeport, 1971.

Hermann, Janet Sharp. *The Pursuit of a Dream.* Jackson, 1999.

Higginson, Thomas Wentworth. *Army Life in a Black Regiment.* Boston, 1870. Also see Looby.

Hill, I. J. *A Sketch of the 29th Regiment of Connecticut Colored Troops.* Hartford, 1867.

Hinton, Thomas C. Letter. *The Christian Recorder,* May 21, 1864.

Hirshson, Stanley P. *Farewell to the Bloody Shirt: Northern Republicans and the Southern Negro, 1877–1893.* Chicago, 1968.

Historical Atlas of Cooper County, Missouri. Boonesville, 1897.

History of Rush County, Indiana. Reprint of 1888 edition. Knightstown, 1966.

History of Tennessee: From the Earliest Time to the Present; Together With an Historical and a Biographical Sketch of Lauderdale, Tipton, Haywood, and Crockett Counties; Besides a Valuable Fund of Notes, Reminiscences, Etc., Etc. Reprint of 1886 edition. Greenville, 1997.

Hopping, James Mason. *Life of Andrew Hull Foote, Rear Admiral, United States Navy.* New York, 1874.

Howard, Goldena Roland. *Ralls County.* New London, 1980.

Howard, James H. W. *Bond and Free: A True Tale of Slave Times.* Harrisburg, 1886.

Howe, S. G. *Report to the Freedmen's Inquiry Commission, 1864: The Refugees from Slavery in Canada West.* Reprint of 1864 edition. New York, 1964.

Hughes, Louis. *Thirty Years a Slave. From Bondage to Freedom. The Institution of Slavery as Seen on the Plantation and in the Home of the Planter.* Reprint of 1897 edition. Miami, 1969.

Hurmence, Belinda. *We Lived in a Little Cabin in the Yard.* Winston-Salem, 1994.

————, editor. *Before Freedom, When I Just Can Remember.* Winston-Salem, 1989.

————. *My Folks Don't Want Me to Talk About Slavery.* Winston-Salem, 1993.

————. "'It Is Good to Be Religious': A Loyal Slave on God, Masters, and the Civil War." *North Carolina Historical Review* 54, no. 1 (1977): 66–71.

Jackson, George. *A Brief History of the Life and Works of G. W. Jackson, Forty-five Years Principal of the G. W. Jackson High School, Corsicana, Texas.* Corsicana, 1938. UNCCH/DAS.

Jackson, Mattie J. *The Story of Mattie J. Jackson; Her — Experience of Eighteen Years in Slavery — Incidents During the War — Her Escape from Slavery. A True Story.* Lawrence, 1866.

Jacobs, Harriet A. *Incidents in the Life of a Slave Girl.* Cambridge, 1987.

James, Thomas. *The Life of Rev. Thomas James, by Himself.* Rochester, 1886.

Jamison, Monroe Franklin. *Autobiography and Work of Bishop M. F. Jamison, D.D. ("Uncle Joe"), Editor, Publisher, and Church Extension Secretary. A Narration of His Whole Career from the Cradle to the Bishopric of the Colored M. E. Church in America.* Nashville, 1912.

Jasper, John. See Edwin Randolph.

Johnson, Clifton, editor. *Battleground Adventures. The Stories of Dwellers on the Scenes of Conflict in Some of the Most Notable Battles of the Civil War, Collected in Personal Interviews.* Boston, 1915.

Johnson, Clifton H., editor. *God Struck Me Dead: Religious Conversion Experiences and Autobiographies of Ex-Slaves.* Philadelphia, 1969.

————. *God Struck Me Dead: Voices of Ex-Slaves.* Cleveland, 1969.

Johnson, Isaac. *Slavery Days in Old Kentucky.* Reprint of 1901 edition. Canton, 1994.

Johnson, James Weldon. *The Autobiography of an Ex-Colored Man.* New York, 1995.

Jones, J. Ralph. See Landess and Jones.

Jones, Jacqueline. *Labor of Love, Labor of Sorrow: Black Women, Work and the Family, from Slavery to the Present.* New York, 1986.

Jordan, Ervin L., Jr. *Black Confederates and Afro-Yankees in Civil War Virginia.* Charlottesville, 1995.

Jordan, Lewis Garnett. *On Two Hemispheres: Bits from the Life Story of Lewis G. Jordan, as Told by Himself.* N.p., ca. 1935.

Jordan, Winthrop D. *Tumult and Silence at Second Creek: An Inquiry into a Civil War Slave Conspiracy.* Baton Rouge, 1995.

Katz, William Loren, compiler. *Flight from the Devil: Six Slave Narratives.* Trenton, 1996.

Keckley, Elizabeth. *Behind the Scenes; or, Thirty Years a Slave, and Four Years in the White House.* New York, 1868.

Keifer, Joseph Warren. *Slavery and Four Years of War: A Political History of Slavery in the United States.* New York, 1900.

Kelley, William Darrah. *Replies of the Hon. William D. Kelley to George Northrop, esq., in the joint debate in the Fourth congressional district.* Philadelphia, 1864.

Kendrick, Albert S. *The Waukesha Freedman.* Waukesha, 1864. Courtesy of Kent A. Peterson at www.28thwisconsin.com.

Khan, Lurey. *One Day, Levin . . . He Be Free: William Still and the Underground Railroad.* New York, 1972.

Killion, Ronald, and Charles Waller, editors. *Slavery Time When I Was Chillun Down on Marster's Plantation: Interviews with Georgia Slaves.* Savannah, 1973.

Kimbrough, Robert. See Landess and Jones.

Kirke, Edmund. *Down in Tennessee.* Reprint of 1864 edition. Westport, 1970.

Kirkland, Frazar. *The Pictorial Book of Anecdotes and Incidents of the War of the Rebellion, Civil, Military, Naval and Domestic: Embracing the Most Brilliant and Remarkable Anecdotal Events of the Great Conflict in the United States.* Hartford, 1866.

Kittredge, Frank Edward. *The Man with the Branded Hand: An Authentic Sketch of the Life and Services of Capt. Jonathan Walker, with Portraits and Illustrations.* Rochester, 1899.

Knox, George L. *Slave and Freeman: The Autobiography of George L. Knox.* Edited by Willard B. Gatewood, Jr. Lexington, 1979.

Lamon, Lester C. *Blacks in Tennessee, 1791–1970.* Knoxville, 1993.

Landess, Tom, and J. Ralph Jones, editors. "Portraits of Georgia Slaves." *Georgia Review* 21, no. 1 (1967): 126–32; no. 2 (1967): 268–73; no. 3 (1967): 407–11; no. 4 (1967): 521–25; *Georgia Review* 22, no. 1 (1968): 125–27; no. 2 (1968): 254–57.

Lane, Isaac. *Autobiography of Bishop Isaac Lane, LL.D., with a Short History of the C.M.E. Church in America and of Methodism.* Nashville, 1916. UNCCH/DAS.

Langston, John Mercer. *From the Virginia Plantation to the National Capital; or, the First and Only Negro Representative in Congress from the Old Dominion.* Hartford, 1894. UNCCH/DAS.

Larison, C. W. *Sylvia Dubois (Now 116 Years old): A Biografy of the Slav Who whipt her Mistres and Gand her Freedom.* Ringoes, 1883.

Latta, Morgan London. *The History of My Life and Work: Autobiography.* Raleigh, 1903.

Lee, George R. *Slavery North of St. Louis.* Canton, 1999.

Lee, William Mack. *History of the Life of Rev. Wm. Mack Lee: Body Servant of General Robert E. Lee Through the Civil War: Cook from 1861 to 1865.* Norfolk, 1918.

Lester, Julius. *To Be a Slave.* New York, 1968.

Lewis, J. Vance. "Out of the Ditch: A True Story of an Ex-Slave." Mildred Stock Research Collection, Schomburg Library.

Library of Congress. Recording of Slave Narratives and Related Materials in the Archive of Folk Song: Reference Tapes. Washington, 1981.

Lincoln, Abraham. See Basler.

Litwack, Leon F. *Been in the Storm So Long: The Aftermath of Slavery.* New York, 1980.

———. *North of Slavery.* Chicago, 1961.

Looby, Christopher, editor. *The Complete Civil War Journal and Selected Letters of Thomas Wentworth Higginson.* Chicago, 2000.

Love, Nat. *The Life and Adventures of Nat Love, Better Known in the Cattle Country as "Deadwood Dick," by Himself; a True Story of Slavery Days, Life on the Great Cattle Ranges and on the Plains of the "Wild and Woolly" West, Based on Facts, and Personal Experiences of the Author.* Los Angeles, 1907. UNCCH/DAS.

Lovett, Bobby L. "The West Tennessee Colored Troops in Civil War Combat." *WTHSP* 34 (1980): 53–70.

————, editor. *The Afro-American History of Nashville, Tennessee, 1870–1930.* Nashville, 1981.

Lovett, Bobby L. and Linda T. Wynn, editors. *Profiles of African Americans in Tennessee.* Nashville, 1996.

Lowery, Irvin E. *Life on the Old Plantation in Ante-Bellum Days; or, A Story Based on Facts.* Columbia, 1911.

Lowry, Thomas P. *The Story the Soldiers Wouldn't Tell: Sex in the Civil War.* Mechanicsburg, 1994.

————. "The Sperryville Outrage." *Civil War Times Illustrated* 38, no. 1 (1998/1999): 24–29.

————, compiler. *Index to Civil War Courtmartial Records at the National Archives and Records Administration.*

Lynch, John Roy. *Reminiscences of an Active Life: The Autobiography of John Roy Lynch.* Chicago, 1970. UNCCH/DAS.

Main, Ed. M. *The Story of the Marches, Battles and Incidents of the Third United States Colored Cavalry: A Fighting Regiment in the War of the Rebellion, 1861–65.* New Orleans, 1908.

Marrs, Elijah P. *Life and History of the Rev. Elijah P. Marrs, First Pastor of Beargrass Baptist Church, and Author.* Louisville, 1885.

Mars, James. See Venture Smith.

Marsh, J.B.T. *The Story of the Jubilee Singers; with their Songs.* Boston, 1881.

Marvel, William. *Andersonville: The Last Depot.* Chapel Hill, 1994.

Maslowski, Peter. *Treason Must Be Made Odious: Military Occupation and Wartime Reconstruction in Nashville, Tennessee, 1862–65.* Millwood, 1978.

Massie, James William. *America: Her Prospect for the Slave, and Her Claim for Anti-Slavery Sympathy.* London, 1864.

McCarthy, Agnes, and Lawrence Reddick. *Worth Fighting For: A History of the Negro in the United States During the Civil War and Reconstruction.* Garden City, 1965.

McConnell, Roland C. *Negro Troops of Antebellum Louisiana: A History of the Battalion of Free Men of Color.* Baton Rouge, 1968.

McCray, Mary F. *Life of Mary F. McCray: Born and Raised a Slave in the State of Kentucky.* Lima, 1898.

McDougle, Ivan E. *Slavery in Kentucky, 1792–1865.* Lancaster, 1918.

McElroy, John. *Andersonville: A Story of Rebel Military Prisons.* Toledo, 1879.

McFeely, William S. *Frederick Douglass.* New York, 1991.

McKay, John. "Final Report of the American Freedman's Inquiry Commission: June 22, 1864." Records of the U.S. Senate, 38th Congress, National Archives and Records Administration.

McKivigan, John R., editor. *The Roving Editor; or, Talks with Slaves in the Southern States, by James Redpath.* Reprint of 1859 edition. University Park, 1996.

McPherson, James M. *Battle Cry of Freedom: The Civil War Era.* New York, 1988.

————. *The Negro's Civil War: How American Negroes Felt and Acted During the War for the Union.* New York, 1965.

Melden, Charles M. *From Slave to Citizen.* Cincinnati, 1921.

Mellon, James, editor. *Bullwhip Days: The Slaves Remember (An Oral History).* New York, 1988.

Merritt, Raleigh H. *From Captivity to Fame; or, The Life of George Washington Carver.* Boston, 1929.

Meyers, Marshall, and Chris Propes, editors. "'I Don't Fear Nothing in the Shape of Man': The Civil War and Texas Border Letters of Edward Francis, United States Colored Troops." *Register of the Kentucky Historical Society* 101, no. 4 (2003): 457–78.

Miles, Jim. *A River Unvexed: A History and Tour Guide of the Campaign for the Mississippi River.* Nashville, 1994.

———. "Letters from Nashville, 1862. II. 'Dear Master.'" *THQ* 33, no. 1 (1974): 85–92.

Miller, Randall M. *"Dear Master": Letters of a Slave Family.* Ithaca, 1878.

Mitchell, Cora. *Reminiscences of the Civil War.* Providence, 1916.

Mohr, Clarence L. *On the Threshold of Freedom: Masters and Slaves in Civil War Georgia.* Athens, 1986.

Montgomery, Isaiah. "Isaiah Montgomery" at pbs.org/wnet/jimcrow.

Montgomery, Michael. "The Linguistic Value of the Ex-Slave Recordings." In Guy Bailey, Natalie Maynor, and Patricia Cukor-Avila, editors. *The Emergence of Black English: Text and Commentary.* Philadelphia, 1991.

Moore, Frank. *Anecdotes, poetry, and incidents of the war: North and South. 1860–1865: Collected and arranged by Frank Moore.* New York, 1867.

———. *Women of the war; their heroism and self-sacrifice.* Chicago, 1866.

———, editor. *The Rebellion Record: A Diary of American Events with Documents, Narratives, Illustrative Incidents, Poetry, Etc.* Volume 8. New York, 1865.

Morgan, Mrs. Irby. *How It Was; Four Years Among The Rebels.* Nashville, 1892. UNCCH/DAS.

Nall, Jasper Rastus. *Freeborn Slave: Diary of a Black Man in the South.* Birmingham, 1996.

Naval Official Records and Army Official Records Covering Mississippi, Tennessee, and Gulf Coast Operations. H-Bar Enterprises.

Nevin, David. *Sherman's March: Atlanta to the Sea.* New York, 1986.

Newton, A. H. *Out of the Briars: An Autobiography. Sketch of the Twenty-ninth Regiment Connecticut Volunteers.* Miami, 1969.

Nicholson, Alfred W. *Brief Sketch of the Life and Labors of Rev. Alexander Bettis. Also an account of the Founding and Development of the Bettis Academy.* Trenton, 1913.

Nicolay, John G., and John Hay. *Abraham Lincoln: A History.* 10 volumes. New York, 1890.

Nieman, Donald G., editor. *The Day of the Jubilee: The Civil War Experience of Black Southerners.* New York, 1994.

Nolen, Claude H. *African American Southerners in Slavery, Civil War and Reconstruction.* Jefferson, 2001.

Nordhoff, Charles. *The Freedmen of South-Carolina: Some Account of their Appearance, Character, Condition, and Peculiar Customs.* New York, 1863.

Northcross, Rev. W. E. *Autobiography.* Tuscumbia, 1937.

Oates, Stephen B. *The Fires of Jubilee: Nat Turner's Fierce Rebellion.* New York, 1975.

O'Connor, (Mrs.) T. P. *My Beloved South.* New York, 1914. UNCCH/DAS.

Offley, G. W. See Venture Smith.

Olmsted, Frederick Law. *The Slave States.* New York, 1959.

O'Neal, William. *Life and History of William O'Neal; or, The Man who Sold his Wife.* St. Louis, 1896.

Osofsky, Gilbert, editor. *Puttin' On Ole Massa: The Slavery Narratives of Henry Bibb, William Wells Brown, and Solomon Northrup.* New York, 1969.

Painter, Nell Irvin. *Exodusters: Black Migration to Kansas After Reconstruction.* New York, 1992.

Parker, Allen. *Recollections of Slavery Times.* Worcester, 1895.

Patterson, Caleb Perry. *The Negro in Tennessee, 1790–1865.* Reprint of 1941 edition. Spartanburg, 1974.

Perdue, Charles L., Thomas E. Barden, and Robert K. Phillips, editors. *Weevils in the Wheat: Interviews with Virginia Ex-Slaves.* Charlottesville, 1976.

Phillips, Charles Henry. *From the Farm to the Bishopric: An Autobiography.* Nashville, 1932.

Phillips, Margaret I. *The Governors of Tennessee.* Gretna, 1998.

Pickens, William. *Bursting Bonds: The Heir of Slaves.* Boston, 1923.

Pike, [Gustavus Dorman]. *The Jubilee Singers, and their Campaign for Twenty thousand Dollars.* Boston, 1873.

Pipkin, J. J. *The Negro in Revelation, in History, and in Citizenship: What the Race Has Done and is Doing: in Arms, Arts, Letters, the Pulpit, the Forum, the School, the Marts of Trade: and with those Mighty Weapons in the Battle of Life the Shovel and the Hoe: A Message to all Men that He is in the Way to Solve the Race Problem for Himself.* St. Louis, 1902.

Powers, Auburn. "Juno, aka 'Pinch': Henderson County, Tennessee." Parker's Crossroads Battlefield Association (Tennessee), 1930.

Pratt, Fletcher. *The Civil War on Western Waters.* New York, 1956.

Proctor, Henry Hugh. *Between Black and White.* Boston, 1925.

Puckett, Newbell Niles. *Black Names in America.* Boston, 1975.

Quarles, Benjamin. *The Negro in the Civil War.* New York, 1989.

Raboteau, Albert J. *Slave Religion: The "Invisible Institution" in the Antebellum South.* Oxford, 1978.

Randolph, Edwin Archer. *The Life of Rev. John Jasper, Pastor of Sixth Mt. Zion Baptist Church, Richmond, Va. from His Birth to the Present Time, with His Theory on the Rotation of the Sun.* Richmond, 1884.

Randolph, Peter. *From Slave Cabin to the Pulpit. The Autobiography of Rev. Peter Randolph: The Southern Question Illustrated and Sketches of Slave Life.* Boston, 1893.

Ransom, John. *John Ransom's Andersonville Diary.* New York, 1988.

Rawick, George P., editor. *The American Slave: A Composite Autobiography.* 41 volumes. Westport, 1972–1979.

Ray, Emma J. Smith. *Twice Sold, Twice Ransomed: Autobiography of Mr. and Mrs. L. P. Ray.* Freeport, 1926. UNCCH/DAS.

"Rebel Atrocities." *Harper's Weekly.* May 21, 1864.

Redford, Dorothy Spruill, and Michael D'Orso. *Somerset Homecoming: Recovering a Lost Heritage.* New York, 1988.

Redpath, James. See McKivigan.

Reed, John C. *The Brothers' War.* Boston, 1904.

"Request for Information." *CV.* July 1909.

Ripley, C. Peter. *Slaves and Freedmen in Civil War Louisiana.* Baton Rouge, 1976.

Robbins, Faye Wellborn. *World-Within-a-World: Black Nashville, 1880–1915.* Ann Arbor, 1980.

Robinson, Armstead L. *Bitter Fruits of Bondage: The Demise of Slavery and the Collapse of the Confederacy, 1861–1865.* Charlottesville, 2005.

Robinson, Nina Hill. *Aunt Dice: The Story of a Faithful Slave.* Nashville, 1897.

Robinson, W. H. *From Log Cabin to the Pulpit; or, Fifteen Years of Slavery.* Eau Claire, 1913.

Rollins, Richard, editor. *Black Southerners in Gray: Essays on Afro-Americans in Confederate Armies.* Murfreesboro, 1994.

Ronnick, Michele Valerie, editor. *The Autobiography of William Sanders Scarborough: An American Journey from Slavery to Scholarship.* Detroit, 2005.

Rose, Peter I., editor. *Old Memories, New Moods: Americans from Africa.* New York, 1970.

Rudd, Daniel A., and Theodore Bond. *From Slavery to Wealth: The Life of Scott Bond.* Madison, 1917.

Rutling, Thomas. *"Tom": An Autobiography with Revised Negro Melodies by Thomas Rutling, Late Member of the Celebrated Fisk University Choir (Jubilee Singers).* Torrington, 1909.

Scarborough, Dorothy. *On the Trail of Negro Folk-Songs.* Hatboro, 1963.

Schwalm, Leslie A. *A Hard Fight for We: Women's Transition from Slavery to Freedom in South Carolina.* Chicago, 1997.

Schweninger, Loren. *James T. Rapier and Reconstruction.* Chicago, 1978.

———, editor. *From Tennessee Slave to St. Louis Entrepreneur: The Autobiography of James Thomas.* Columbia, 1984.

Sellers, James Benson. *Slavery in Alabama.* Montgomery, 1964.

Sifakis, Stewart. *Compendium of the Confederate Armies: Kentucky, Maryland, Missouri, the Confederate Units and the Indian Units.* New York, 1995.

Silver, James W., editor. *Mississippi in the Confederacy as Seen in Retrospect.* Baton Rouge, 1961.

Singleton, William Henry. *Recollections of My Slavery Days.* Peekskill, 1922.

Sink, Elijah. *Memoirs.* Indiana State Library.

Smalls, Robert. *From Slavery to Public Service: Robert Smalls, 1839–1915.* New York, 1971.

Smith, Harry. *Fifty Years of Slavery in the United States of America.* Grand Rapids, 1891.

Smith, James L. *Autobiography of James L. Smith, Including, also, Reminiscences of Slave Life, Recollections of the War, Education of Freedmen, Causes of the Exodus, Etc.* Norwich, 1881.

Smith, Venture, et al. *Five Black Lives: The Autobiography of Venture Smith, James Mars, William Grimes, the Rev. G. W. Offley, James L. Smith.* Middletown, 1971.

Stafford, A. O. "The Mind of the African Negro as Reflected in His Proverbs." *Journal of Negro History* 1, no. 1 (January 1916): 42–48.

Starling, Marion Wilson. *The Slave Narrative: Its Place in American History.* Washington, 1988.

Starobin, Robert S., editor. *Blacks in Bondage: Letters of American Slaves.* New York, 1974.

Stearns, Charles. *The Black Man of the South, and the Rebels.* Reprint of 1872 edition. New York, 1969.

Stroyer, Jacob. *My Life in the South.* Salem, 1885.

Sullivan, Marge Nichols, editor. *My Folks and the Civil War.* Topeka, 1994.

Tadman, Michael. *Speculators and Slaves: Masters, Traders, and Slaves in the Old South.* Madison, 1996.

Tap, Bruce. *Over Lincoln's Shoulder: The Committee on the Conduct of the War.* Lawrence, 1998.

———. "'These Devils Are Not Fit to Live on God's Earth': War Crimes and the Committee on the Conduct of the War." *CWH* 42, no. 2 (1996): 116–32.

Taylor, Alrutheus Ambush. *The Negro in Tennessee, 1865–1880.* Washington, 1941.

———. "Fisk University and the Nashville Community, 1866–1900." *The Journal of Negro History* 39, no. 2 (April 1954): 111–26.

Taylor, Richard. *Destruction and Reconstruction: Personal Experiences of the Late War.* New York, 1879.

Taylor, Susie King. *A Black Woman's Civil War Memoirs.* Princeton, 1988.

———. *Reminiscences of My Life in Camp with the 33d United States Colored Troops, Late 1st S.C. Volunteers.* Boston, 1902.

Thomas, Hugh. *The Slave Trade.* New York, 1998.

Thompson, Charles. *Biography of a Slave; Being the Experiences of Rev. Charles Thompson, a Preacher of the United Brethren Church, While a Slave in the South. Together with Startling Occurrences Incidental to Slave Life.* Dayton, 1875.

Tilly, Belle Baird. *Aspects of Social and Economic Life in West Tennessee Before the Civil War.* Ph.D. dissertation, Memphis State University, 1974.

———. "The Spirit of Improvement: Reformism and Slavery in West Tennessee." *WTHSP* 28 (1974): 25–42.

Toombs, Robert. Letters. dlg.galileo.usg.edu/hargrett/toombs/rato16.php.

Troutman, Richard L., editor. *The Heavens Are Weeping: The Diaries of George Richard Browder, 1852–1886.* Grand Rapids, 1987.

Trowbridge, J. T. *A Picture of the Desolated States; and the Work of Restoration, 1865–1868.* Hartford, 1868.

———. *The South: A Tour of its Battle-fields and Ruined Cities, a Journey through the Desolated States, and Talks with the People: Being a Description of the Present State of the Country — its Agriculture — Railroads — Business and Finances.* Ann Arbor, 1866.

Trudeau, Noah Andre. *Like Men of War: Black Troops in the Civil War, 1862–1865.* Boston, 1998.

Tucker, Phillip Thomas. *Cathy Williams: From Slave to Female Buffalo Soldier.* Mechanicsburg, 2002.

Twain, Mark. "A True Story, Repeated Word for Word as I Heard It." *Atlantic Monthly,* November 1874.

Tyler, Ronnie C., and Lawrence R. Murphy, editors. *The Slave Narratives of Texas.* Austin, 1974.

United Daughters of the Confederacy. *Reminiscences of the Women of Missouri During the Sixties, Gathered, Compiled and Published by Missouri Division, United Daughters of the Confederacy.* Jefferson City, 1913.

United States. Office of the American Freedmen's Inquiry Commission. *Final Report of the American Freedmen's Inquiry Commission to the Secretary of War, May 15, 1864,* at civilwarhome.com/commissionreport.htm.

United States. Records of the Southern Claims Commission. National Archives and Records Administration.

United States. Testimony Before the Hunter Commission, May 9 to June 30, 1865, Washington, D.C., at www.surratt.org/documents.

United States Army. *Proceedings of a Military Commission Convened at St. Louis, Mo. [October 16, 1864], by virtue of [Special Orders 287].* Special Collections Division, University of Arkansas Libraries.

United States Army. *Report of the Board of Education for Freedmen, Department of the Gulf, for the year 1864.*

United States Army. *Report of the General Superintendent of Freedmen, Department of the Tennessee and State of Arkansas, for 1864.*

United States Census. 1850 to 1930.

United States Congress. *Journal of the House of Representatives of the United States of America, 1789–1873.* Washington, 1873.

United States Congress. *Journal of the Senate of the United States of America, 1789–1873.* Washington, 1873.

United States Congress. *Ku Klux Conspiracy: Report of the Joint Select Committee to Inquire into the Condition of Affairs in the Late Insurrectionary States.* Washington, 1872.

United States Congress. *Report of the Joint Select Committee on the Condition of Affairs in the Late Insurrectionary States. Made to the two Houses of Congress, February 19, 1872.*

United States Congress. *Report of the Joint Committee on the Conduct of the War at the Second Session, Thirty-eighth Congress.* Washington, 1865.

United States Congress. Speech of Hon. Wm. D. Kelley of Pa. on Freedmen's Affairs: Delivered in the House of Representatives, February 23, 1864.

United States Fish and Wildlife Service. "Holt Collier: The Man." fws.gov/holtcollier/.

United States Western Sanitary Commission. *A Report on the Condition of the Freedmen of the Mississippi: Presented to the Western Sanitary Commission (1864).*

Vansina, Jan. *Oral Tradition: A Study in Historical Methodology.* Translated by H. M. Wright. Chicago, 1965.

Wagandt, Charles Lewis. *The Mighty Revolution: Negro Emancipation in Maryland, 1862–1864.* Baltimore, 1964.

Walker, Thomas Calhoun. *The Honey-Pod Tree: The Life Story of Thomas Calhoun Walker.* New York, 1958.

Wallace, Frances. "A Trip to Dixie: Diary, March 19–August 25, 1864." UNCCH/DAS.

Walters, Alexander. *My Life and Work*. New York, 1917.

Walthall, George. Letters. Lionel Baxter Collection, University of Mississippi.

Walvin, James. *Questioning Slavery*. London, 1996.

Ward, Geoffrey C., Ric Burns, and Ken Burns. *The Civil War: An Illustrated History*. New York, 1990.

Warner, Ezra J. *Generals in Blue: Lives of the Union Commanders*. New Orleans, 1964.

Washington, Booker T. *An Autobiography: The Story of My Life*. Naperville, 1901.

———. *Up from Slavery: An Autobiography*. New York, 1901.

Weatherred, John. "Wartime Diary of John Weatherred." jackmasters.net.

Webb, William. *The History Of William Webb, Composed By Himself*. Detroit, 1873.

Wells, Ida Barnett. *Crusade for Justice: The Autobiography of Ida B. Wells*. Chicago, 1970.

Wesley, Charles H., and Patricia W. Romero. *Negro Americans in the Civil War: From Slavery to Citizenship*. New York, 1967.

West, Carroll Van, editor. *Trial and Triumph: Essays in Tennessee's African American History*. Knoxville, 2002.

Wharton, Vernon Lane. *The Negro in Mississippi, 1865–1890*. New York, 1965.

Wiefering, Edna. *Tennessee's Confederate Widows and Their Families*. Edited by Charles A. Sherrill. Cleveland, 1992.

Wiley, Bell Irvin. *The Plain People of the Confederacy*. Chicago, 1963.

———. *Southern Negroes, 1861–1865*. Reprint of 1938 edition. New Haven, 1965.

Williams, Andrew. See Dobak.

Williams, Edward F., III. "Memphis Early Triumph over Its River Rivals." *WTHSP* 22 (1968): 5–27.

Williams, Eric. *Capitalism and Slavery*. Reprint of 1944 edition. Chapel Hill, 1994.

Williams, George W. *A History of the Negro Troops in the War of the Rebellion, 1861–1865, preceded by a Review of the Military Services of Negroes in Ancient and Modern Times*. New York, 1888.

Williams, Isaac D. (as told to William Ferguson Goldie). *Sunshine and Shadow of Slave Life. Reminiscences as Told by Isaac D. Williams to "Tege."* East Saginaw, 1885.

Williams, James. *Life and Adventures of James Williams, a fugitive slave*. San Francisco, 1873.

Williams, Sally. *Aunt Sally; or, The Cross The way of Freedom. A Narrative of the Slave-life and Purchase of the Mother of Rev. Isaac Williams of Detroit, Michigan*. Cincinnati, 1858.

Williams, Walter, editor. *A History of Northeast Missouri*. Chicago, 1913.

Wilson, Joseph T. *The Black Phalanx*. Hartford, 1888.

Wilson, L. W., editor. "Reminiscences of Jim Tomm." *Chronicles of Oklahoma* 44, no. 3 (1966): 290–306.

Wilson, (Mrs.) Robert H. Letter. *The Liberator*, June 10, 1864.

Winn, Ralph B., editor. *A Concise Lincoln Dictionary: Thoughts and Statements*. New York, 1959.

Wish, Harvey, editor. *Slavery in the South*. New York, 1964.

Wood, Betty. *The Origins of American Slavery: Freedom and Bondage in the English Colonies*. New York, 1997.

Woodson, Carter G., editor. *Free Negro Owners of Slaves in the United States in 1830 Together with Absentee Ownership of Slaves in the United States in 1830.* Reprint of 1924 edition. New York, 1968.

Woodward, C. Vann. *The Burden of Southern History.* New York, 1968.

Wright, Louise Wigfall. *A Southern Girl in '61: The War-Time Memories of a Confederate Senator's Daughter.* New York, 1905 edition. UNCCH/DAS.

Yancey, William A. Miscellaneous manuscripts. MG194. Schomburg Library.

Young, Amy L., and Milburn J. Crowe. "Descendant Community Involvement in African-American Archaeology in Mississippi: Digging for the Dream in Mound Bayou." Paper presented at the First Annual South Central Historical Archeology Conference, Jackson, Mississippi, 1998.

Zack, Naomi. *Race and Mixed Race.* Philadelphia, 1993.

INDEX